2010

by
Jack Gillis

with
Amy Curran
and
Julia Redmon
and
Brian Gillis

D1160090

Foreword by
Clarence Ditlow
Center for Auto Safety

A Center for Auto Safety Publication

ACKNOWLEDGMENTS

This 30th edition of *The Car Book* is the result of the hard work of Amy Curran and Julia Redmon. For over nineteen years, Amy has been keeping this complex project on track as well as expertly preparing all the graphics necessary to present the data. In her second year as lead co-author, Julia managed the complex database programs that enable you to have access to the information you need to make a truly informed vehicle purchase. Thanks to Amy and Julia, the multi-faceted process of compiling the information you need to make a smart, sensible new car choice was expertly accomplished. This year's edition would not have been possible without the excellent research and data input of Brian Gillis and essential contributions from Clarence Ditlow and the staff of the Center for Auto Safety, including Michael Brooks.

During the 30 years that *The Car Book* has been published, it has been accompanied by a variety of auto-related consumer guides including *The Used Car Book* 1998-2002; *The Truck Van and 4x4 Book* 1991-1999; *The Value and Luxury Car Books* 2000; *How to Make Your Car Last Forever* 1987; *The Armchair Mechanic* 1988; and, *The Car Repair Book* 1991. In all, we've produced 60 auto-related books. In recognition of 30 years of publications, I want to honor and thank the legions of people who have helped make these books possible. The number of books each person worked on follows their name.

Coauthors:
Ailis Aaron 14, Deirdre Aaron 2, Ivy Baer 1, Scott Beatty 12, Ashley Cheng 11, Amy Curran 42, Dabney Edwards 2, Jay Einhorn 6, Alisa Feingold 16, Karen Fierst 34, Brian Gillis 1, John Gillis Jr. 1, Katie Gillis 2, Daniel Gustafson 4, Ben Hardaway 3, David Iberkleid 3, Tom Kelly 2, Nicole Klein 3, Seth Krevat 3, Julia Redmon 3, Jerilyn Saxon 7, Evan Shurak 2, Andrew Siegel 1, Julie Beth Wright 4.

Contributors:
Stephanie Ackerman 7, Jim Armstrong 1, Stu Armstrong 1, Anu Ashutosh 2, Chris Atkinson 1, Judith Bailey 3, Jessica Baldwin 1, Debra Barclay 11, Jennifer Barrett 3, Ben Becker 2, Carol Berger 1, Nancy Berk 2, Kristin Beyard 1, Debbie Bindeman 15, David Biss 4, Michael Brooks 6, Elizabeth Brown 2, Joe Bruha 1, Kevin Busen 1, Martha Casey 9, Andrew Chap 1, Jeff Clark 1, David Cokely 1, Susan Cole 24, Jennifer Cook Mirabito 1, Alan Coombs 1, Ben Crenshaw 1, Caroline Cruz 1, Jim Cullum 5, Brad Daniels 1, Jennifer Davidson 2, John DeCicco 2, Joe DeGrande 1, Cheryl Denenberg 7, Pat Donlon 6, Rosemary Dunlap 3, Bill Earp 1, Marshall Einhorn 2, Morshed El Hag 6, Mari Beth Emigh 1, Jerret Engle 3, Meaghan Farrell 1, Barry Fierst 9, Eyal Fierst 4, Matthew Figueroa 1, Anne Fleming 1, Nicole Freydberg 1, Edna Friedberg 3, Grant Gasson 1, Sherrie Good 4, Christy Goodrich 1, Carolyn Gorman 12, Nancy Green 7, Sharon Guttman 2, John Guyton 1, Kim Hazelbaker 11, Karen Heckler 5, Vico Henriques 6, Maggie Herman 3, Kaz Hickok 4, Ann Himmelberg 1, Neene Hirata 2, Susan Hoffmann 1, Bill Hogan 1, Bryan Hoopman 1, Dan Howell 1, Mizuho Ikeuchi 1, Mark Jacobson 1, Richard Jester 1, Alisa Joaquin 3, Evan Johnson 7, Steve Julius 3, Irvine Kaplan 2, George Kaveney 1, Al Kettler 1, Mike Kido 4, Lisa Kitei 3, Michael Kott 3, Stuart Krichevsky 45, Bill Kumbar 3, Sonia Kundert 1, Christopher Lank 1, Ann Lavie 10, Elaine Lawless 1, Ed Lewis 3, David Lewkowict 3, Shelley Liebman 3, Mary Kay Linge 1, Faith Little 5, Lou Lombardo 3, Ann Lyons 1, Roger MacBride Allen 2, Joel Makower 3, James Marshall 4, Patricia McCullen-Noettl 1, Kathy Melborn 2, Cristina Mendoza 6, John Michel 9, Cynthia Miller 1, Trina Mohrbacher 1, Rick Morgan 2, Stephanie Narva 6, Debra Anne Naylor 1, David Noettl 3, John Noettl 24, Karen Noettl 5, Steven Noettl 7, Bill North-Rudin 6, Phil Nowicki 15, Ted Orme 1, Stephanie Ortbals 3, George Ottoson 1, Pete Packer 15, Wendy Pellow 2, Mary Penrose 1, Elisa Petrini 1, Fran Pflieger 1, Torryn Phelps 2, Sarah Phillips 3, Laura Polachek 3, Carol Pollack 1, Wayne Powell 3, Bryan Pratt 2, Stephen Quine 1, Toufic Rahman 6, Tammy Rhodes 1, Jennifer Rieder 2, Sara Roberts 2, Sara Roschwalb 3, Jill Rosensweig 2, Harriet Rubin 4, Beth Schelske 1, Susan Schneider 3, Roger Scholl 1, Lois Sharon 1, Jerry Sheehan 1, Anne Marie Shelness 1, Russell Shew 16, Amy Shock 4, David Smith 1, Malcolm Smith 2, Steve Smith 4, Sherri Soderberg Pittman 4, Beverly Southerland 1, Tanny Southerland 1, Erika Sova 3, Karen Steinke 2, Martin Thomas 2, Susan Tiffany 1, Stephanie Tombrello 2, Barbara Tracey 2, Keren Trost 1, Buddy Vagoni 1, Jon Vernick 1, Darlene Watson 1, Elaine Weinstein 2, Ray Weiss 11, Clay White 1, Donna Whitlow 1, Teresa Wooten-Talley 8, Ken Wright 2, Susan Beth Wright 1, Peter Zetlin 1.

As always, the most important factor in being able to bring this information to the American car buyer for 30 years is the encouragement, support, and love from my brilliant and beautiful wife, Marilyn Mohrman-Gillis. For her and four terrific children–Katie, John, Brian and Brennan–I am eternally grateful.
—J.G.

Dedicated to Joan Claybrook and Clarence Ditlow
Mentors, visionaries, and true advocates
With deep appreciation for 30 years of undying support and encouragement

BY CLARENCE DITLOW

Who would have thought the Center for Auto Safety (CAS) would outlive General Motors–but that, and a whole lot more, happened in 2009. CAS wants to make 2010 the year of safety to mark our 40th Anniversary of consumer advocacy watching the auto industry to safeguard your health and pocketbook from unsafe cars and consumer ripoffs. Over the years, CAS has gotten lemon laws in every state, airbags in every car, and more recalls than you can count from the Ford Pinto to Firestone tires in 1978 and 2000–some companies never learn. Plus we rescued *The Car Book* in 1981 when the auto companies got the government to kill it making this the 30th year we have brought consumers life saving information and advice in *The Car Book*.

In 2009 CAS exposed the hazards of cell phone use while driving by using a Freedom of Information Act lawsuit to reveal a six year coverup by the National Highway Traffic Safety Administration (NHTSA) of the dangers of talking and driving. The day after CAS acted, the US Department of Transportation announced a national summit to toughen cell phone laws. Now states across the country are banning texting and driving which is worse than drinking and driving.

In 2009 CAS did the first dynamic roof crush tests showing which new models had strong roofs that could save your life in a rollover. (See page 31.)

Prodded by our testing, NHTSA under the direction of Transportation Secretary Ray LaHood issued a new roof crush standard that was more than twice as stringent as the old standard issued in 1971 when there were no rollover prone SUV's on the road. Even Oklahoma got into the act in 2009 by passing an improved lemon law pushed by lemon owner and citizen activist, Angie Gallant of Broken Arrow.

When GM and Chrysler filed for bankruptcy, they asked the court to void consumer lemon law rights and throw out liability suits for deadly defects that maim and kill consumers. CAS stood up for consumer rights in the courts and Congress forcing the companies to honor the lemon laws and take responsibility for deadly defects in crashes after the bankruptcy like the GM pickups with side saddle gas tanks and Jeep Grand Cherokee with exposed rear gas tanks that continue to claim victims in fire crashes every year.

The biggest safety news in 2009 was the continued drop in vehicle fatalities to below 37,000 for the first time since 1961 when vehicle travel less than one-fourth today's levels and the death rate per mile traveled was four times higher. This is not good enough for the Center and it's not good enough for you. Think of how many lives are shattered by 37,000 deaths and 250,000 serious injuries in vehicle crashes each year.

The Center has a vision–we want to reduce traffic deaths to less than 34,000 in 2010 for our fortieth anniversary. And for our fiftieth anniversary in 2020, we want to be well on our well to our Vision of Zero Traffic Deaths. There is no reason why we should not treat traffic deaths like the terrible disease it is. There's a Race for the Cure in breast cancer. We should have a Drive for the Cure in traffic deaths. Every consumer should have the right to buy a vehicle whose occupants survive 50-mph front, rear and side impact crashes–goals which were set by NHTSA in 1970 but which were derailed by industry lobbyists and bureaucratic inertia. No one should be killed in a rollover and pedestrians should have the rights to safe streets. Our mission is to dream the impossible and achieve it.

By using *The Car Book* to buy a safer car at the price you can afford, you have taken an important first step toward your personal vehicle safety and CAS' goal of eliminating traffic deaths. The next step is to support the Center for Auto Safety which works every day on your behalf to ensure that all Americans ride in safe and reliable vehicles. Go to our Website, www.autosafety.org, and find out how you can help CAS help you.

BY JACK GILLIS

The 30th anniversary edition of *The Car Book* comes following a year that totally transformed the auto industry leaving some carmakers in bankruptcy and others making huge positive jumps in sales rankings.

Because of the uncertain economy, those of us buying a new vehicle this year desperately need unbiased, comparative information to make the best car buying decision possible. As it has for 30 years, let *The Car Book* be your guide to the best for 2010.

Amazingly, it was 30 years ago when *The Car Book* began as a government publication and the first published guide to the safety and performance of cars. As its primary author, my goal was to sift through the myriad of government data on cars and present it so consumers could actually use it. For the first time, *The Car Book* gave consumers the ability to make an informed choice on one of the most important and complex items that they will ever purchase.

After becoming one of the government's most requested publications, the U.S. Department of Transportation caved to intense car company pressure and halted its publication. At the time, the car companies were the main source of auto information and wanted to keep it that way.

Thanks to the Center for Auto Safety, in 1982 *The Car Book* continued as an independent publication. Since then, working closely with the Center's Clarence Ditlow and his staff, our goal has been to give you the information you need to make a smart, sensible and safe choice among today's new cars. We reasoned that if you knew that one car was safer than another you'd buy the safer car and your action would put enormous pressure on the auto makers to improve safety. It worked and cars today are safer than ever before!

The Car Book set out to change the way people buy their cars and, more importantly, the way car companies make them. Because *The Car Book* kept crash test information flowing to the public in the 80's and 90's, consumers were able to vote for safer cars with their pocketbooks. The result, car companies were forced to build safer cars. After spending millions of dollars trying to kill the crash test program, nary an ad today doesn't tout a good crash test rating.

In keeping with *The Car Book*'s philosophy of making it as easy as possible to identify the truly good performances in the government crash tests, we provide a unique Car Book Combined Crash Test Rating which combines the results of the front and side tests.

Another unique and important feature of *The Car Book* is that we compare the crash tests on a relative basis among the 2010 cars. In looking at the government ratings you will notice that nearly every car gets a 4 or 5 star rating. As a result, it's impossible to distinguish the best from the worst. So we've analyzed the crash tests using *The Car Book*'s unique Crash Test Index described in the Safety Chapter and rated the 2010 vehicles from best to worst. Now, you will be able to make a much more informed choice based on comparative crash test results and the car makers have a new basis on which to compete.

Before *The Car Book*, consumers had no idea which warranties were better, what you could expect to pay for typical repairs, which cars cost the most and least to insure, and how they stacked up in government complaints. Now you have this information all in one place.

Our exclusive car-by-car ratings at the end of the book provide an overview of all the criteria you need to make a good choice. Here, you'll be able to quickly assess key features and see how the car you're interested in stacks up against its competition so you can make sure your selection is the best car for you.

Even though the choices get better each year and safety is improved, it's still a challenge to separate the lemons from the peaches. There are notable differences in how cars protect you in a crash, how much they cost to maintain, the benefits of their warranties, and how far they'll go on a gallon of expensive gasoline. Nevertheless, if you use the information in *The Car Book*, there is no reason why your next car should not last at least 150,000 miles.

Buying a car means you have to stay on your toes and not be "schnookered" in the showroom. *The Car Book* will help you do just that. It's not easy matching wits with a seasoned salesperson, but our "Showroom Strategies" section will give you the keys to getting the best deal. In spite of all the new car technology and the Internet, the fundamentals of buying a good, safe, reliable car remain the same: do your homework; shop around; and remember that car dealers need you more than you need them!

The information in The Car Book is based on data collected and developed by our staff, the U.S. Department of Transportation, and the Center for Auto Safety. With all of this information in hand, you'll find some great choices for 2010.

-J.A.G.

USING THE BUYING GUIDE

The "Buying Guide" provides a quick comparison of the 2010 cars in terms of their safety, warranty, fuel economy, complaint rating, and price range—arranged by size class. To fully understand the information in the charts, it is important to read the related section in the book.

Overall Rating: This shows how well this car stacks up on a scale of 1 to 10 when compared to all others on the market. Because safety is the most important component of our ratings, cars with no crash test results at printing are not given an overall rating.

Combined Crash Test Rating: This indicates how well the car performed in the government's frontal and side crash test programs compared to this year's vehicles tested to date.

Warranty Rating: This is an overall comparative assessment of the car's warranty.

Fuel Economy: This is the EPA city/highway mpg for, what is expected to be, the most popular model.

Complaint Rating: This is based on complaints received by the U.S. Department of Transportation. If not rated, the vehicle is too new to have a complaint rating.

Price Range: This will give you a general idea of the "sticker," or suggested retail price.

(car) Indicates a *Car Book* Best Bet. See page 13.

Vehicle	Page #	Overall Rating	Combined Crash Test Rating	Warranty Rating	Fuel Economy	Complaint Rating	Price Range
Subcompact							
Chevrolet Aveo	106	3	Worst	Average	25/34	Poor	$11-$14,000
(car) Honda Fit	150	8	Above Avg.	Very Poor	27/33	Good	$14-$19,000 (car)
Honda Insight	151	4	Worst	Very Poor	40/43		$19-$23,000
(car) Hyundai Accent	156	8	Average	Very Good	27/36	Very Good	$9-$14,000 (car)
Kia Rio	177	5	Worst	Good	27/36	Good	$11-$16,000
Kia Soul	181	6	Average	Good	24/30		$13-$17,000
Mazda MX-5 Miata	201			Very Poor	21/28	Very Good	$22-$27,000
Mini Cooper	212	6	Worst	Very Good	25/33	Very Poor	$18-$34,000
Nissan 370Z	216			Very Poor	18/25		$36-$41,000
Nissan Cube	220	5	Below Avg.	Very Poor	28/30		$13-$19,000
Nissan Versa	228	5	Worst	Very Poor	28/34	Good	$9-$16,000
Scion xB	233	1	Worst	Very Poor	22/28	Very Poor	$15-$16,000
Scion xD	234	4	Worst	Very Poor	27/33	Very Good	$14-$15,000

Vehicle	Page #	Overall Rating	Combined Crash Test Rating	Warranty Rating	Fuel Economy	Complaint Rating	Price Range
Subcompact (cont.)							
Smart ForTwo	235	1	Worst	Very Poor	33/41	Very Poor	$11-$16,000
Suzuki SX4	242	2	Worst	Average	23/30	Average	$13-$19,000
Toyota Yaris	257	4	Worst	Very Poor	29/35	Very Good	$12-$13,000
Volkswagen Beetle	258	5	Worst	Very Good	20/29	Poor	$18-$26,000
Compact							
Audi A4	86	10	Best	Very Good	23/30	Average	$31-$35,000
BMW 1 Series	91			Very Good	18/28	Poor	$29-$40,000
BMW 3 Series	92	7	Below Avg.	Very Good	18/28	Average	$32-$50,000
Chevrolet Cobalt	108	4	Below Avg.	Average	24/33	Very Poor	$14-$24,000
Chrysler PT Cruiser	120	2	Worst	Poor	19/24	Poor	$18-$18,000
Dodge Caliber	124	7	Average	Poor	23/27	Average	$16-$25,000
Ford Focus	138	6	Worst	Poor	24/34	Very Good	$15-$18,000
Ford Mustang	140	7	Best	Poor	16/24	Average	$20-$51,000
Honda Civic	146	8	Average	Very Poor	25/36	Poor	$15-$27,000
Honda Civic Coupe	147	8	Above Avg.	Very Poor	25/36	Poor	$15-$24,000
Hyundai Elantra	157	8	Average	Very Good	26/34	Average	$14-$17,000
Kia Forte	175	7	Below Avg.	Good	25/34		$13-$18,000
Mazda 3	196	6	Average	Very Poor	24/33	Good	$15-$23,000
Mercedes Benz C-Class	203			Poor	17/25	Average	$33-$57,000
Mitsubishi Lancer	214	5	Average	Very Good	17/25	Very Poor	$14-$26,000
Nissan Altima Coupe	218	6	Below Avg.	Very Poor	23/32	Very Good	$22-$29,000
Nissan Sentra	226	7	Average	Very Poor	26/34	Good	$15-$20,000
Saab 9-3	231	6	Worst	Good	19/28	Very Poor	$30-$51,000
Scion tC	232	3	Below Avg.	Very Poor	21/29	Poor	$17-$17,000
Subaru Impreza	237	4	Below Avg.	Poor	20/26	Very Poor	$17-$38,000
Suzuki Kizashi	241			Average	23/31		$18-$24,000
Toyota Corolla	246	5	Below Avg.	Very Poor	26/34	Good	$15-$20,000
Toyota Matrix	249	5	Average	Very Poor	25/31	Average	$16-$21,000
Toyota Prius	250	5	Below Avg.	Very Poor	51/48		$22-$27,000
Volkswagen Eos	259			Very Good	22/29	Very Poor	$31-$35,000
Volkswagen Golf	261	6	Below Avg.	Very Good	23/30		$18-$23,000
Volkswagen Jetta	262	7	Below Avg.	Very Good	23/30	Very Poor	$17-$25,000

Vehicle	Page #	Overall Rating	Combined Crash Test Rating	Warranty Rating	Fuel Economy	Complaint Rating	Price Range
Compact (cont.)							
Volvo S40	266	9	Below Avg.	Very Good	20/31	Good	$26-$31,000
Intermediate							
Acura TL	83	9	Average	Average	18/26	Very Good	$35-$43,000
Acura TSX	84	10	Best	Average	21/30	Very Poor	$29-$37,000
Audi A5	87			Very Good	23/30	Very Good	$36-$53,000
BMW 5 Series	93	7	Below Avg.	Very Good	18/27	Average	$45-$60,000
Buick LaCrosse	98	10	Best	Good	17/26		$27-$33,000
Cadillac CTS	100	7	Above Avg.	Good	18/27	Poor	$36-$60,000
Chevrolet Camaro	107	6	Below Avg.	Average	18/29		$22-$30,000
Chevrolet Corvette	110			Average	15/25	Very Poor	$48-$106,000
Chevrolet Impala	113	9	Best	Average	18/29	Average	$23-$29,000
Chevrolet Malibu	114	9	Above Avg.	Average	22/30	Good	$21-$26,000
Chrysler Sebring	121	9	Above Avg.	Poor	21/30	Good	$20-$34,000
Dodge Avenger	123	6	Average	Poor	21/30	Very Poor	$20-$21,000
Ford Fusion	139	9	Above Avg.	Poor	22/31	Very Good	$19-$27,000
Honda Accord	144	8	Average	Very Poor	21/31	Very Poor	$21-$31,000
Honda Accord Coupe	145	8	Above Avg.	Very Poor	21/31	Very Poor	$22-$31,000
Hyundai Genesis	158	9	Above Avg.	Very Good	18/27	Average	$22-$31,000
Hyundai Sonata	160	7	Average	Very Good	22/32	Poor	$18-$26,000
Infiniti EX	163	7	Below Avg.	Good	16/23	Very Good	$33-$37,000
Infiniti G	165	7	Average	Good	19/27	Good	$33-$40,000
Kia Optima	176	8	Above Avg.	Good	22/32	Good	$17-$22,000
Lexus ES	184	6	Average	Good	19/27	Poor	$35-$35,000
Lexus GS	185			Good	19/26	Good	$45-$57,000
Lexus HS	187	10	Best	Good	35/34		$34-$36,000
Lexus IS	188	5	Below Avg.	Good	21/29	Very Good	$32-$58,000
Lincoln MKZ	194	8	Above Avg.	Average	18/27	Very Good	$34-$36,000
Mazda 6	198	8	Above Avg.	Very Poor	21/30	Poor	$19-$26,000
Mercedes Benz E-Class	204	7	Average	Poor	18/26		$48-$58,000
Mercury Milan	211	9	Above Avg.	Poor	22/31	Very Good	$21-$27,000
Mitsubishi Galant	213	9	Average	Very Good	21/30	Very Good	$21-$23,000
Nissan Altima	217	9	Above Avg.	Very Poor	23/32	Very Good	$19-$24,000
Nissan Maxima	222	7	Above Avg.	Very Poor	19/26	Poor	$30-$33,000
Subaru Outback, Legacy	238	7	Best	Poor	22/29		$22-$30,000
Toyota Avalon	244	6	Best	Very Poor	19/28	Poor	$27-$35,000
Toyota Camry	245	7	Average	Very Poor	22/32	Average	$19-$29,000
Volkswagen CC	260	6	Worst	Very Good	22/31	Good	$27-$40,000
Volkswagen Passat	263	6	Worst	Very Good	22/31	Very Poor	$26-$28,000

Vehicle	Page #	Overall Rating	Combined Crash Test Rating	Warranty Rating	Fuel Economy	Complaint Rating	Price Range
Intermediate (cont.)							
Volvo V70	268			Very Good	18/27	Very Good	$33-$38,000
Large							
Audi A6	88			Very Good	18/26	Good	$45-$76,000
BMW 7 Series	94			Very Good	14/21		$80-$136,000
Buick Lucerne	99	9	Average	Good	17/26	Average	$29-$39,000
Cadillac DTS	101	6	Worst	Good	15/23	Good	$46-$60,000
Cadillac STS	104	5	Worst	Good	18/27	Average	$46-$56,000
Chrysler 300	119	8	Best	Poor	18/26	Average	$26-$48,000
Dodge Challenger	125	4	Above Avg.	Poor	17/25	Very Poor	$22-$41,000
Dodge Charger	126	8	Best	Poor	18/26	Average	$24-$38,000
Ford Taurus	142	8	Best	Poor	18/28	Poor	$25-$37,000
Infiniti M	166			Good	17/25	Poor	$45-$54,000
Jaguar XF	167			Poor	16/25	Very Poor	$51-$79,000
Lexus LS	189			Good	16/24	Very Good	$64-$73,000
Lincoln MKS	191	6	Above Avg.	Average	17/24	Very Poor	$40-$47,000
Lincoln Town Car	195	7	Above Avg.	Average	16/24	Good	$45-$52,000
Mercedes Benz S-Class	208			Poor	15/23	Very Good	$87-$201,000
Mercury Grand Marquis	209	6	Above Avg.	Poor	14/19	Good	$29-$29,000
Volvo S80	267			Very Good	18/27	Very Good	$39-$50,000
Minivan							
Chrysler Town and Country	122	8	Above Avg.	Poor	17/24	Average	$25-$35,000
Dodge Grand Caravan	128	7	Above Avg.	Poor	17/24	Average	$21-$26,000
Honda Odyssey	152	6	Average	Very Poor	16/23	Poor	$26-$40,000
Kia Rondo	178	5	Below Avg.	Good	20/27	Very Poor	
Kia Sedona	179	5	Above Avg.	Good	17/23	Poor	$22-$28,000
Mazda 5	197	4	Below Avg.	Very Poor	21/27	Poor	$17-$19,000
Toyota Sienna	253	1	Below Avg.	Very Poor	17/23	Poor	$24-$37,000
Volkswagen Routan	264	5	Above Avg.	Very Good	16/23	Very Poor	$25-$42,000
Small SUV							
Acura RDX	82	8	Average	Average	19/24	Very Good	$32-$37,000
Chevrolet HHR	112	7	Average	Average	22/30	Poor	$18-$26,000
Ford Escape	133	6	Below Avg.	Poor	21/28	Average	$20-$34,000
Honda CR-V	148	10	Above Avg.	Very Poor	21/27	Very Good	$21-$29,000
Honda Element	149	7	Average	Very Poor	20/25	Poor	$20-$25,000
Hyundai Tucson	161			Very Good	23/31		$18-$18,000
Jeep Compass	169	5	Worst	Poor	21/24	Good	$18-$25,000
Jeep Liberty	171	7	Above Avg.	Poor	15/21	Good	$23-$28,000
Jeep Patriot	172	6	Below Avg.	Poor	21/24	Average	$17-$24,000

Vehicle	Page #	Overall Rating	Combined Crash Test Rating	Warranty Rating	Fuel Economy	Complaint Rating	Price Range
Small SUV (cont.)							
Jeep Wrangler	173			Poor	15/19	Very Poor	$21-$32,000
Kia Sportage	182	5	Below Avg.	Good	20/25	Good	$16-$23,000
Mazda Tribute	202	5	Below Avg.	Very Poor	21/28	Very Poor	$20-$28,000
Mercury Mariner	210	6	Below Avg.	Poor	20/26	Very Good	$23-$31,000
Mitsubishi Outlander	215	6	Average	Very Good	19/25	Poor	$20-$29,000
Subaru Forester	236	6	Above Avg.	Poor	20/26	Very Poor	$20-$28,000
Suzuki Grand Vitara	240	1	Worst	Average	19/25	Poor	$18-$26,000
Toyota RAV4	251	4	Worst	Very Poor	21/27	Good	$21-$27,000
Volkswagen Tiguan	265	6	Average	Very Good	18/24	Very Poor	$23-$33,000
Mid-Size SUV							
Acura MDX	81			Average	16/21	Very Good	$40-$48,000
Acura ZDX	85			Average	16/22		$45-$56,000
Audi Q5	89	7	Average	Very Good	18/23	Very Good	$37-$51,000
BMW X3	95			Very Good	17/24	Good	$38-$38,000
BMW X5	96	8	Average	Very Good	15/21	Very Good	$47-$56,000
Buick Enclave	97	7	Above Avg.	Good	17/24	Poor	$35-$38,000
Cadillac SRX	103	5	Below Avg.	Good	18/25		$33-$47,000
Chevrolet Equinox	111	6	Below Avg.	Average	22/32	Poor	$22-$29,000
Dodge Journey	129	7	Average	Poor	19/25	Very Poor	$20-$28,000
Dodge Nitro	130	6	Above Avg.	Poor	16/22	Poor	$21-$24,000
Ford Edge	132	4	Worst	Poor	18/25	Good	$26-$35,000
Ford Explorer	135	5	Average	Poor	13/19	Average	$28-$41,000
GMC Terrain	111	6	Below Avg.	Average	22/32		$24-$29,000
Honda Pilot	153	7	Above Avg.	Very Poor	16/22	Very Good	$27-$40,000
Hummer H3	155	6	Above Avg.	Good	14/18	Average	$33-$43,000
Hyundai Santa Fe	159			Very Good	22/27	Poor	$21-$30,000
Hyundai Veracruz	162	4	Below Avg.	Very Good	17/23	Very Poor	$28-$35,000
Infiniti FX	164			Good	16/23		$42-$58,000
Kia Borrego	174	8	Best	Good	16/21	Good	$26-$32,000
Kia Sorento (2011)	180			Good	21/28		$28-$28,000
Lexus GX	186			Good	15/20	Very Good	$52-$57,000
Lexus RX	190	6	Average	Good	18/24		$36-$43,000
Lincoln MKX	193	5	Worst	Average	17/23	Very Good	$38-$40,000
Mazda CX-7	199	6	Average	Very Poor	20/28	Very Poor	$21-$32,000
Mazda CX-9	200	6	Above Avg.	Very Poor	16/22	Very Good	$28-$30,000
Mercedes Benz GLK-Class	206			Poor	16/22		$33-$35,000
Mercedes Benz M-Class	207	6	Above Avg.	Poor	15/20	Good	$45-$91,000

Vehicle	Page #	Overall Rating	Combined Crash Test Rating	Warranty Rating	Fuel Economy	Complaint Rating	Price Range
Mid-Size SUV (cont.)							
Mercury Mountaineer	135	5	Average	Poor	13/19	Average	$29-$36,000
Nissan Murano	223	2	Worst	Very Poor	18/23	Very Poor	$28-$38,000
Nissan Pathfinder	224			Very Poor	15/22	Average	$27-$42,000
Nissan Rogue	225	5	Below Avg.	Very Poor	22/27	Average	$20-$23,000
Nissan Xterra	229	3	Average	Very Poor	15/20	Poor	$22-$30,000
Porsche Cayenne	230			Poor	14/20	Very Poor	$48-$126,000
Subaru Tribeca	239	5	Average	Poor	16/21	Poor	$30-$35,000
Toyota 4Runner	243			Very Poor	17/22	Very Good	$27-$39,000
Toyota Highlander	248	4	Average	Very Poor	17/23	Very Good	$25-$41,000
Toyota Venza	256	6	Average	Very Poor	21/29	Good	$26-$29,000
Volkswagen Touareg	230	5	Below Avg.	Very Good	14/19	Very Poor	$40-$43,000
Volvo XC60	269			Very Good	16/21		$32-$37,000
Volvo XC90	270	10	Best	Very Good	15/22	Poor	$37-$47,000
Large SUV							
Audi Q7	90	7	Average	Very Good	14/19	Good	$46-$61,000
Cadillac Escalade	102	6	Best	Good	13/20	Average	$62-$87,000
Cadillac Escalade ESV	116	7	Best	Good	12/16	Good	$65-$86,000
Chevrolet Suburban	116	7	Best	Average	15/21	Average	$40-$55,000
Chevrolet Tahoe	117	8	Best	Average	15/21	Good	$37-$53,000
Chevrolet Traverse	118	9	Above Avg.	Average	17/24	Very Good	$29-$39,000
Ford Expedition	134	6	Best	Poor	12/17	Average	$32-$48,000
Ford Flex	137	6	Above Avg.	Poor	17/24		$28-$42,000
GMC Acadia	143	8	Above Avg.	Average	17/24	Poor	$31-$40,000
GMC Yukon	117	7	Best	Average	15/21	Average	$38-$61,000
GMC Yukon XL	116	8	Best	Average	12/18	Good	$41-$58,000
Infiniti QX56	219			Good	12/18	Average	$56-$59,000
Jeep Commander	168			Poor	14/19	Very Poor	$31-$42,000
Jeep Grand Cherokee	170	5	Above Avg.	Poor	15/20	Average	$30-$43,000
Land Rover Range Rover	183			Poor	12/18	Poor	$78-$94,000
Lincoln MKT	192			Average	17/23		$44-$49,000
Lincoln Navigator	134	6	Best	Average	14/20	Average	$54-$59,000
Mercedes Benz GL-Class	205			Poor	13/17	Poor	$60-$82,000
Nissan Armada	219			Very Poor	12/18	Poor	$37-$52,000
Toyota FJ Cruiser	247	1	Average	Very Poor	17/21	Very Poor	$23-$25,000
Toyota Sequoia	252			Very Poor	14/19	Good	$38-$58,000
Compact Pickup							
Chevrolet Colorado	109	3	Worst	Average	17/23	Very Good	$16-$28,000

Vehicle	Page #	Overall Rating	Combined Crash Test Rating	Warranty Rating	Fuel Economy	Complaint Rating	Price Range
Compact Pickup (cont.)							
Dodge Dakota	127	7	Best	Poor	15/20	Average	$22-$33,000
Ford Ranger	141	3	Below Avg.	Poor	16/21	Good	$17-$25,000
GMC Canyon	109	2	Worst	Average	17/23	Average	$16-$31,000
Nissan Frontier	221	4	Below Avg.	Very Poor	14/19	Good	$17-$29,000
Toyota Tacoma	254	2	Above Avg.	Very Poor	17/21	Very Poor	$15-$25,000
Standard Pickup							
Cadillac Escalade EXT	105	7	Best	Good	12/16	Very Good	$61-$69,000
Chevrolet Avalanche	105	7	Best	Average	15/21	Poor	$35-$48,000
Chevrolet Silverado	115	8	Best	Average	15/21	Good	$20-$41,000
Dodge Ram Pickup	131			Poor	14/20	Very Good	$20-$42,000
Ford F-150	136	9	Best	Poor	15/21	Very Good	$21-$45,000
GMC Sierra	115	8	Best	Average	14/19	Good	$20-$46,000
Honda Ridgeline	154	7	Above Avg.	Very Poor	15/20	Average	$28-$36,000
Nissan Titan	227			Very Poor	13/18	Very Poor	$26-$39,000
Toyota Tundra	255			Very Poor	15/20	Good	$23-$42,000

BEST BETS

T he following is our list of the highest rated vehicles in each size category. The ratings are based on expected performance in nine important categories–Combined Crash Rating, Safety Features, Rollover, Preventive Maintenance, Repair Costs, Warranty, Fuel Economy, Complaints, and Insurance Costs–with the heaviest emphasis placed on safety.

It is important to consult the specific chapters to learn more about how the ratings are developed and to look on the car pages, beginning on page 81, for more details on these vehicles. In order to be considered as a "Best Bet" the vehicle must have a crash test rating as safety is a critical factor in gaining that recognition. Because most people are considering vehicles in the same size category, the "Best Bets" are by size—indicating how these vehicles compared against others in the same size class.

HONDA FIT

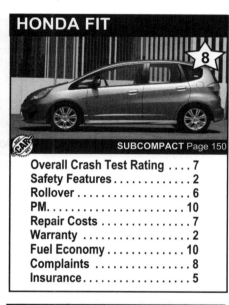

SUBCOMPACT Page 150

Overall Crash Test Rating	7
Safety Features	2
Rollover	6
PM	10
Repair Costs	7
Warranty	2
Fuel Economy	10
Complaints	8
Insurance	5

HYUNDAI ACCENT

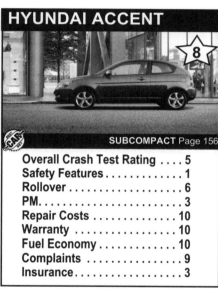

SUBCOMPACT Page 156

Overall Crash Test Rating	5
Safety Features	1
Rollover	6
PM	3
Repair Costs	10
Warranty	10
Fuel Economy	10
Complaints	9
Insurance	3

AUDI A4

COMPACT Page 86

Overall Crash Test Rating	10
Safety Features	9
Rollover	8
PM	5
Repair Costs	4
Warranty	9
Fuel Economy	8
Complaints	6
Insurance	3

HONDA CIVIC

COMPACT Page 146

Overall Crash Test Rating	6
Safety Features	4
Rollover	8
PM	10
Repair Costs	9
Warranty	2
Fuel Economy	10
Complaints	4
Insurance	5

HONDA CIVIC COUPE

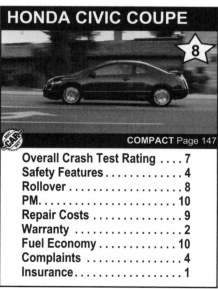

COMPACT Page 147

Overall Crash Test Rating	7
Safety Features	4
Rollover	8
PM	10
Repair Costs	9
Warranty	2
Fuel Economy	10
Complaints	4
Insurance	1

HYUNDAI ELANTRA

COMPACT Page 157

Overall Crash Test Rating	5
Safety Features	2
Rollover	8
PM	3
Repair Costs	10
Warranty	10
Fuel Economy	10
Complaints	5
Insurance	3

VOLVO S40

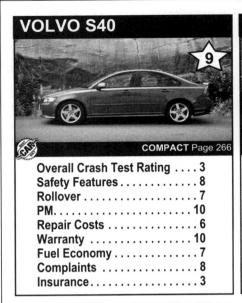

9

COMPACT Page 266

Overall Crash Test Rating 3
Safety Features 8
Rollover 7
PM. 10
Repair Costs 6
Warranty 10
Fuel Economy 7
Complaints 8
Insurance 3

ACURA TL

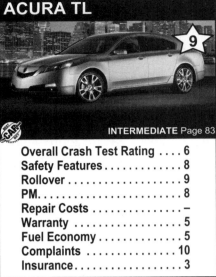

9

INTERMEDIATE Page 83

Overall Crash Test Rating 6
Safety Features 8
Rollover 9
PM. 8
Repair Costs . . . . –
Warranty 5
Fuel Economy 5
Complaints 10
Insurance 3

ACURA TSX

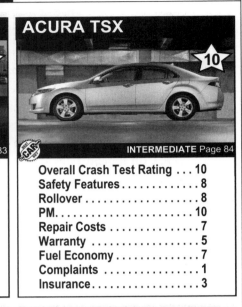

10

INTERMEDIATE Page 84

Overall Crash Test Rating . . . 10
Safety Features 8
Rollover 8
PM. 10
Repair Costs 7
Warranty 5
Fuel Economy 7
Complaints 1
Insurance 3

BUICK LACROSSE

10

INTERMEDIATE Page 98

Overall Crash Test Rating . . . 10
Safety Features 10
Rollover 6
PM. 9
Repair Costs 4
Warranty 7
Fuel Economy 4
Complaints . . . . –
Insurance 8

CHEVROLET IMPALA

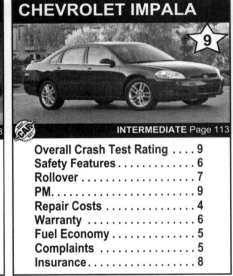

9

INTERMEDIATE Page 113

Overall Crash Test Rating 9
Safety Features 6
Rollover 7
PM. 9
Repair Costs 4
Warranty 6
Fuel Economy 5
Complaints 5
Insurance 8

CHEVROLET MALIBU

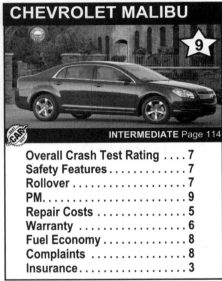

9

INTERMEDIATE Page 114

Overall Crash Test Rating 7
Safety Features 7
Rollover 7
PM. 9
Repair Costs 5
Warranty 6
Fuel Economy 8
Complaints 8
Insurance 3

CHRYSLER SEBRING

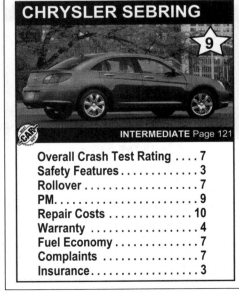

9

INTERMEDIATE Page 121

Overall Crash Test Rating 7
Safety Features 3
Rollover 7
PM. 9
Repair Costs 10
Warranty 4
Fuel Economy 7
Complaints 7
Insurance 3

FORD FUSION

9

INTERMEDIATE Page 139

Overall Crash Test Rating 7
Safety Features 5
Rollover 8
PM. 6
Repair Costs 9
Warranty 3
Fuel Economy 8
Complaints 10
Insurance 3

HYUNDAI GENESIS

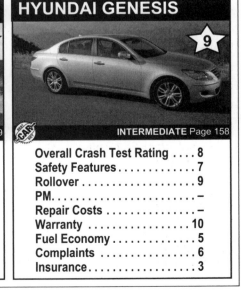

9

INTERMEDIATE Page 158

Overall Crash Test Rating 8
Safety Features 7
Rollover 9
PM. . . . . –
Repair Costs . . . . –
Warranty 10
Fuel Economy 5
Complaints 6
Insurance 3

LEXUS HS

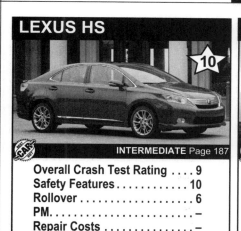

INTERMEDIATE Page 187

Overall Crash Test Rating 9
Safety Features 10
Rollover 6
PM. . . . . –
Repair Costs . . . . –
Warranty 7
Fuel Economy 10
Complaints . . . . –
Insurance 3

MERCURY MILAN

INTERMEDIATE Page 211

Overall Crash Test Rating 7
Safety Features 4
Rollover 8
PM. 6
Repair Costs 9
Warranty 3
Fuel Economy 8
Complaints 10
Insurance 5

MITSUBISHI GALANT

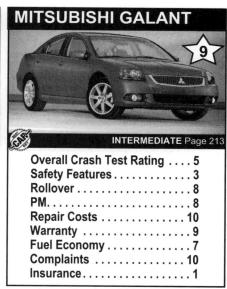

INTERMEDIATE Page 213

Overall Crash Test Rating 5
Safety Features 3
Rollover 8
PM. 8
Repair Costs 10
Warranty 9
Fuel Economy 7
Complaints 10
Insurance 1

NISSAN ALTIMA

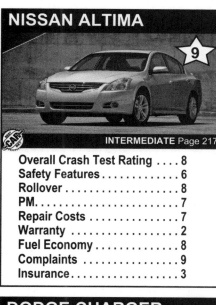

INTERMEDIATE Page 217

Overall Crash Test Rating 8
Safety Features 6
Rollover 8
PM. 7
Repair Costs 7
Warranty 2
Fuel Economy 8
Complaints 9
Insurance 3

BUICK LUCERNE

LARGE Page 99

Overall Crash Test Rating 6
Safety Features 7
Rollover 8
PM. 9
Repair Costs 7
Warranty 7
Fuel Economy 4
Complaints 5
Insurance 8

CHRYSLER 300

LARGE Page 119

Overall Crash Test Rating . . . 10
Safety Features 1
Rollover 7
PM. 8
Repair Costs 8
Warranty 4
Fuel Economy 5
Complaints 5
Insurance 5

DODGE CHARGER

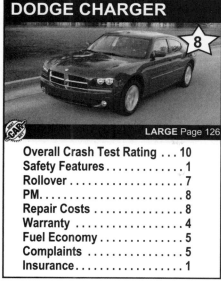

LARGE Page 126

Overall Crash Test Rating . . . 10
Safety Features 1
Rollover 7
PM. 8
Repair Costs 8
Warranty 4
Fuel Economy 5
Complaints 5
Insurance 1

FORD TAURUS

LARGE Page 142

Overall Crash Test Rating 9
Safety Features 9
Rollover 7
PM. 10
Repair Costs 3
Warranty 3
Fuel Economy 5
Complaints 3
Insurance 8

CHRYSLER T & C

MINIVAN Page 122

Overall Crash Test Rating 7
Safety Features 6
Rollover 4
PM. 8
Repair Costs 10
Warranty 4
Fuel Economy 4
Complaints 5
Insurance 10

DODGE GR. CARAVAN

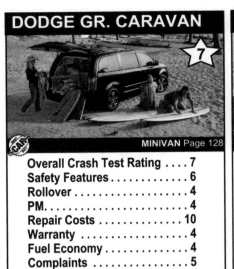

7

MINIVAN Page 128

Overall Crash Test Rating 7
Safety Features 6
Rollover 4
PM. 4
Repair Costs 10
Warranty 4
Fuel Economy 4
Complaints 5
Insurance. 10

ACURA RDX

8

SMALL SUV Page 82

Overall Crash Test Rating 5
Safety Features 9
Rollover 4
PM. 8
Repair Costs 6
Warranty 5
Fuel Economy 5
Complaints 10
Insurance. 8

HONDA CR-V

10

SMALL SUV Page 148

Overall Crash Test Rating 7
Safety Features 9
Rollover 3
PM. 10
Repair Costs 7
Warranty 2
Fuel Economy 7
Complaints 10
Insurance. 10

BMW X5

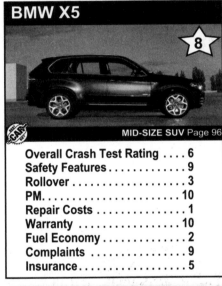

8

MID-SIZE SUV Page 96

Overall Crash Test Rating 6
Safety Features 9
Rollover 3
PM. 10
Repair Costs 1
Warranty 10
Fuel Economy 2
Complaints 9
Insurance. 5

KIA BORREGO

8

MID-SIZE SUV Page 174

Overall Crash Test Rating 9
Safety Features 8
Rollover 2
PM. –
Repair Costs . . . . –
Warranty 8
Fuel Economy 3
Complaints 8
Insurance. 5

VOLVO XC90

10

MID-SIZE SUV Page 270

Overall Crash Test Rating . . . 10
Safety Features 10
Rollover 3
PM. 10
Repair Costs 3
Warranty 10
Fuel Economy 2
Complaints 4
Insurance. 10

AUDI Q7

7

LARGE SUV Page 90

Overall Crash Test Rating 6
Safety Features 10
Rollover 3
PM. 9
Repair Costs 2
Warranty 9
Fuel Economy 2
Complaints 7
Insurance. 3

CAD. ESCALADE ESV

7

LARGE SUV Page 116

Overall Crash Test Rating . . . 10
Safety Features 10
Rollover 1
PM. 6
Repair Costs 2
Warranty 7
Fuel Economy 1
Complaints 8
Insurance. 1

CHEV. SUBURBAN

7

LARGE SUV Page 116

Overall Crash Test Rating . . . 10
Safety Features 9
Rollover 1
PM. 7
Repair Costs 4
Warranty 6
Fuel Economy 2
Complaints 5
Insurance. 8

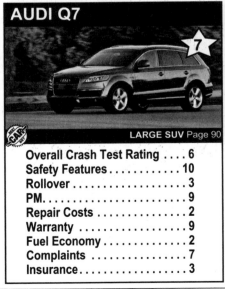

CHEVROLET TAHOE

⭐ 8

LARGE SUV Page 117

Overall Crash Test Rating	10
Safety Features	9
Rollover	1
PM	7
Repair Costs	4
Warranty	6
Fuel Economy	2
Complaints	7
Insurance	8

CHEV. TRAVERSE

⭐ 9

LARGE SUV Page 118

Overall Crash Test Rating	7
Safety Features	10
Rollover	4
PM	8
Repair Costs	4
Warranty	6
Fuel Economy	4
Complaints	10
Insurance	8

GMC ACADIA

⭐ 8

LARGE SUV Page 143

Overall Crash Test Rating	7
Safety Features	10
Rollover	4
PM	9
Repair Costs	4
Warranty	6
Fuel Economy	4
Complaints	4
Insurance	8

GMC YUKON

⭐ 7

LARGE SUV Page 117

Overall Crash Test Rating	10
Safety Features	9
Rollover	1
PM	7
Repair Costs	3
Warranty	6
Fuel Economy	2
Complaints	5
Insurance	8

GMC YUKON XL

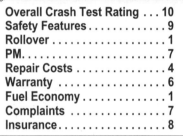

⭐ 8

LARGE SUV Page 116

Overall Crash Test Rating	10
Safety Features	9
Rollover	1
PM	7
Repair Costs	4
Warranty	6
Fuel Economy	1
Complaints	7
Insurance	8

DODGE DAKOTA

⭐ 7

COMPACT PICKUP Page 127

Overall Crash Test Rating	9
Safety Features	1
Rollover	3
PM	8
Repair Costs	9
Warranty	4
Fuel Economy	2
Complaints	6
Insurance	8

CHEV. SILVERADO

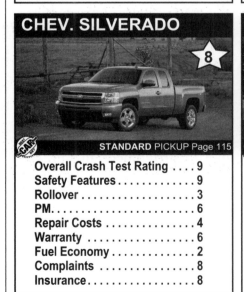

⭐ 8

STANDARD PICKUP Page 115

Overall Crash Test Rating	9
Safety Features	9
Rollover	3
PM	6
Repair Costs	4
Warranty	6
Fuel Economy	2
Complaints	8
Insurance	8

FORD F-150

⭐ 9

STANDARD PICKUP Page 136

Overall Crash Test Rating	10
Safety Features	7
Rollover	2
PM	8
Repair Costs	8
Warranty	3
Fuel Economy	2
Complaints	10
Insurance	8

GMC SIERRA

⭐ 8

STANDARD PICKUP Page 115

Overall Crash Test Rating	9
Safety Features	9
Rollover	3
PM	6
Repair Costs	5
Warranty	6
Fuel Economy	2
Complaints	7
Insurance	5

CRASH TESTS

Safety is likely the most important factor that most of us consider when choosing a new car. In the past, evaluating safety was difficult. Now, thanks to the information in *The Car Book*, it's much easier to pick a safe vehicle. We begin with our unique presentation of the government crash test results.

Crash Test Program:

A key factor in occupant protection is how well the car protects you in a crash. This depends on the car's ability to *absorb* the force of an impact rather than transfer it to the occupant. In the government's frontal crash test program, a vehicle is sent into a concrete barrier at 35 mph, causing an impact similar to two identical cars crashing head-on at 35 mph. The car contains electronically monitored dummies in the driver and passenger seats which measure the impact of such a collision on the head, chest, and legs of the occupants.

For the side crash tests, a moving barrier is smashed into the side of the vehicle at 38.5 mph. This simulates a typical intersection collision between two vehicles. The dummies in the side crash tests measure the impact on the pelvis and chest of front and back seat passengers.

In both crash tests the dummies are securely belted. Therefore, these test results do not apply to unbelted occupants. *The Car Book Crash Text Index* (CTI) combines the results of both passengers. In the case of side tests, when there is no back seat, then the *Index* is based on a single occupant.

It is best to compare the results within the same weight class, such as compacts to compacts. Do not compare cars with differing weights. For example, a subcompact that is rated "Best" may not be as safe as a large car with the same rating.

How the Cars are Rated:

The tables on the following pages indicate how this year's cars can be expected to perform in crash tests when compared on a relative basis among all the 2010 cars.

The government ratings have nearly every car getting a 4 or 5 star rating. On one hand, that means today's vehicles have improved. This makes it impossible to distinguish the best from the worst. For example a vehicle may have done well according to government injury ratings, but still be one of the worst performers among this year's models.

The first column provides *The Car Book*'s <u>Combined Crash Test Rating</u>. This number combines both the front and side tests, weighted 60% for front tests and 40% for side tests, and compares the result among all of the 2010 vehicles with crash tests to date. The cars are rated from 10 best to 1 worst.

Next you can see how the vehicles did in the front and side tests.

Again, relative to all other 2010 vehicles, we indicate if the vehicle was rated *Best, Above Average, Average, Below Average or Worst*. For side tests, the cars are rated separately from the trucks. Meaning a car rated *Good* should not be compared to a truck with the same rating. Again, these ratings provide a *relative* comparison of this year's cars or trucks.

The next four columns indicate the likelihood of each occupant sustaining a life-threatening injury, based on the front test head and chest scores and the side test chest scores. Lower percentages mean a lower likelihood of being seriously injured. This information is taken directly from the government's analysis of the crash test results.

In addition to head and chest measurements, the government tests the crash forces on the occupant's femurs (in the front test) and pelvis (in the side tests). This year an asterisk indicates that the femur or pelvis scores for the particular vehicle was moderate, no poor scores exist for 2010 vehicles. Otherwise the femur/pelvis scores were good or very good. The leg or pelvic injury ratings are included in the Crash Test Index but are not weighted as heavily as the head and chest in determining overall CTI performance.

Crash test results may vary due to differences in the way cars are manufactured, in how models are equipped, and in test conditions. There is no absolute guarantee that a car which passed the test will adequately protect you in an accident.

Crash Test Performance	Combined Car Book Crash Test Rating	Test Type	Car Book Crash Test Rating - Index (Lower numbers are better)	Front Crash Test		Side Crash Test	
				Driver	Pass.	Front Occup.	Rear Occup.
Subcompact							
Chevrolet Aveo	2	Front	Poor - 2033	10%	11%		
		Side	Very Poor - 1830			7%	13%
Hatchback	3	Front*	Poor - 1886	10%	8%		
		Side*	Very Poor - 1811			10%	9%
Honda Fit	7	Front	Very Good - 1406	7%	7%		
		Side	Poor - 1033			4%	7%
Honda Insight	2	Front	Poor - 2123	9%	14%		
		Side	Very Poor - 1354			5%	9%
Hyundai Accent	5	Front	Good - 1510	9%	7%		
		Side	Very Poor - 2281			6%	19%
Kia Rio	2	Front	Poor - 1999	11%	10%		
		Side	Very Poor - 1775			8%	12%
Hatchback	2	Front	Poor - 1999	11%	10%		
		Side	Very Poor - 1775			8%	12%
Kia Soul	5	Front	Good - 1603	7%	8%		
		Side	Poor - 1123			3%	9%
Mazda RX-8	3	Front	Poor - 2011	12%	9%		
		Side	Very Poor - 1277			6%	8%
Mini Cooper, S, John Cooper Works	1	Front	Very Poor - 2344	12%	14%		
		Side	Very Poor - 1365			4%	10%
Nissan Cube	3	Front	Very Poor - 3194	18%	18%		
		Side	Good - 835			3%	6%
Nissan Versa	1	Front	Very Poor - 2351	11%	14%		
		Side	Very Poor - 1376			8%	7%
Scion xB	3	Front	Very Poor - 2332	12%	13%		
		Side	Average - 1012			5%	5%
Scion xD	2	Front*	Very Poor - 3046	13%	20%		
		Side	Average - 983			4%	6%
Smart Fortwo	1^^	Front	Very Poor - 3675	18%	24%		
		Side^	Poor - 1094			6%	
Suzuki SX-4	3	Front	Very Poor - 2821	19%	13%		
		Side	Average - 936			3%	7%
Wagon	3	Front	Very Poor - 2821	19%	13%		
		Side	Average - 936			3%	7%
Toyota Yaris & Liftback 4-dr.	2	Front	Poor - 2178	11%	13%		
		Side	Very Poor - 1627			8%	9%
Liftback 2-dr.	2	Front	Poor - 2033	9%	11%		
		Side	Very Poor - 1689			4%	14%
Volkswagen New Beetle	1	Front	Very Poor - 2249	11%	12%		
		Side	Very Poor - 1800			5%	15%
Convertible		Front	Very Poor - 2249	11%	12%		
Compact							
Audi A4	10	Front	Very Good - 1372	7%	8%		
		Side	Very Good - 642			2%	4%

*Additional Injury Potential: In addition to head and chest measurements, the government tests measure the crash forces on the occupant's femurs (in the front test) and pelvis (in the side tests). Generally, if the scores were Good or Very Good, injury to these areas will be minimal. An asterisk indicates that the femur/pelvis scores for this particular vehicle were moderate, otherwise the scores were good or very good. ^Vehicle has no back seat, so the index is based on a single front occupant. **Vehicle to be tested in 2010. Results expected to be the same or better. ***During the side impact test, the head of the left rear passenger dummy struck the convertible roof linkage resulting in a higher likelihood of serious head injury. ^^During the side impact test, the driver door unlatched and opened. A door opening during a side impact crash increases the likelihood of occupant ejection.

Crash Test Performance	Combined Car Book Crash Test Rating	Test Type	Car Book Crash Test Rating - Index (Lower numbers are better)	Likelihood of Life Threatening Injury			
				Front Crash Test		Side Crash Test	
				Driver	Pass.	Front Occup.	Rear Occup.
Audi S4	10	Front	Very Good - 1372	7%	8%		
		Side	Very Good - 642			2%	4%
BMW 3 Series, Wagon	3	Front	Very Poor - 3024	16%	20%		
		Side	Good - 825			5%	4%
2 dr.	3	Front	Very Poor - 2248	16%	20%		
		Side	Good - 658			5%	4%
Chevrolet Cobalt 4-dr.	3	Front	Average - 1789	11%	8%		
		Side	Very Poor - 1934			16%	5%
2-dr.	3	Front	Average - 1789	11%	8%		
		Side	Very Poor - 1339			8%	6%
Chrysler PT Cruiser	1	Front*	Very Poor - 2958	19%	11%		
		Side	Very Poor - 1289			8%	6%
Dodge Caliber	7	Front	Average - 1692	8%	9%		
		Side	Good - 836			3%	6%
Ford Focus 4-dr.	2	Front	Very Poor - 2259	12%	11%		
		Side	Poor - 1075			4%	7%
2-dr. Hatchback	2	Front*	Average - 1859	10%	8%		
		Side	Very Poor - 2949			17%	18%
Ford Mustang	9	Front	Very Good - 1421	7%	8%		
		Side	Good - 763			3%	5%
Convertible	9***	Front	Good - 1496	8%	8%		
		Side	Good - 847			4%	5%
Honda Civic	6	Front	Good - 1598	9%	8%		
		Side	Average - 993			6%	4%
Honda Civic Coupe	7	Front	Very Good - 1393	8%	7%		
		Side	Poor - 1061			7%	4%
Hybrid	6	Front	Good - 1598	9%	8%		
		Side	Average - 993			6%	4%
Hyundai Elantra	5	Front	Good - 1629	7%	8%		
		Side	Poor - 1175			6%	6%
Wagon	5	Front	Good - 1629	7%	8%		
		Side	Poor - 1175			6%	6%
Kia Forte 4-dr.	4	Front	Average - 1714	10%	8%		
		Side	Very Poor - 1509			4%	12%
Mazda 3	6	Front	Good - 1590	9%	8%		
		Side	Average - 972			3%	8%
Hatchback	6	Front	Good - 1590	9%	8%		
		Side	Average - 972			3%	8%
Mitsubishi Lancer	6	Front	Good - 1637	6%	11%		
		Side	Average - 942			2%	8%
Nissan Altima Coupe	3	Front	Very Poor - 2798	15%	18%		
		Side	Good - 874			5%	4%
Nissan Sentra	5	Front	Good - 1598	9%	8%		
		Side	Very Poor - 1274			6%	8%
Pontiac Vibe	5	Front	Poor - 1895	10%	10%		
		Side	Good - 869			3%	6%
Saab 9-3	1	Front	Very Poor - 2343	12%	15%		
		Side	Very Poor - 1306			5%	8%
Scion tC	4	Front	Poor - 1959	8%	13%		
		Side	Average - 992			6%	5%

Crash Test Performance	Combined Car Book Crash Test Rating	Test Type	Car Book Crash Test Rating - Index (Lower numbers are better)	Likelihood of Life Threatening Injury			
				Front Crash Test		Side Crash Test	
				Driver	Pass.	Front Occup.	Rear Occup.
Subaru Impreza	4	Front	Average - 1678	9%	9%		
		Side	Very Poor - 1353			4%	10%
Wagon	4	Front	Average - 1678	9%	9%		
		Side	Very Poor - 1353			4%	10%
Toyota Corolla	3	Front	Poor - 2119	13%	11%		
		Side	Poor - 1067			2%	9%
Toyota Matrix	5	Front	Poor - 1895	10%	10%		
		Side	Good - 869			3%	6%
Toyota Prius	4	Front	Poor - 2094	11%	11%		
		Side	Average - 934			2%	8%
Volkswagen Golf, GTI	4	Front	Very Poor - 3178	18%	18%		
		Side	Very Good - 733			3%	4%
Volkswagen Jetta	4	Front	Very Poor - 3178	18%	18%		
		Side	Very Good - 733			3%	4%
Volvo S40	4	Front	Poor - 1939	11%	9%		
		Side	Average - 1007			5%	6%
Intermediate							
Acura TL	6	Front	Average - 1679	8%	9%		
		Side	Average - 932			5%	4%
Acura TSX	10	Front	Very Good - 1205	6%	7%		
		Side	Very Good - 684			4%	3%
BMW 5 Series	3	Front	Very Poor - 2907	23%	9%		
		Side	Good - 826			5%	3%
Wagon	3	Front	Very Poor - 2907	23%	9%		
		Side	Good - 826			5%	3%
Buick Lacrosse	10	Front	Very Good - 1239	8%	6%		
		Side	Very Good - 645			2%	4%
Cadillac CTS	8	Front	Average - 1670	11%	7%		
		Side	Very Good - 574			3%	3%
CTS V	8	Front	Poor - 2116	12%	13%		
		Side	Very Good - 574			3%	3%
Wagon	8	Front	Average - 1670	11%	7%		
		Side	Very Good - 574			3%	3%
Chevrolet Camaro	4	Front	Very Poor - 2966	19%	15%		
		Side^	Very Good - 545			3%	
Chevrolet Impala	9	Front	Very Good - 1306	6%	7%		
		Side	Average - 888			3%	6%
Chevrolet Malibu	7	Front	Good - 1624	9%	9%		
		Side	Good - 872			5%	4%
Chrysler Sebring	8	Front	Very Good - 1228	6%	6%		
		Side	Poor - 1122			3%	9%
Convertible	8	Front	Poor - 1889	12%	9%		
		Side	Average - 949			5%	5%
Dodge Avenger	6	Front	Average - 1706	8%	10%		
		Side	Average - 907			3%	7%
Ford Fusion	7	Front	Very Good - 1323	7%	6%		
		Side	Poor - 1023			4%	6%
Hybrid	7	Front	Average - 1801	10%	8%		
		Side	Poor - 1023			4%	6%

*Additional Injury Potential: In addition to head and chest measurements, the government tests measure the crash forces on the occupant's femurs (in the front test) and pelvis (in the side tests). Generally, if the scores were Good or Very Good, injury to these areas will be minimal. An asterisk indicates that the femur/pelvis scores for this particular vehicle were moderate, otherwise the scores were good or very good. ^Vehicle has no back seat, so the index is based on a single front occupant. **Vehicle to be tested in 2010. Results expected to be the same or better. ***During the side impact test, the head of the left rear passenger dummy struck the convertible roof linkage resulting in a higher likelihood of serious head injury. ^^During the side impact test, the driver door unlatched and opened. A door opening during a side impact crash increases the likelihood of occupant ejection.

Crash Test Performance	Combined Car Book Crash Test Rating	Test Type	Car Book Crash Test Rating - Index (Lower numbers are better)	Likelihood of Life Threatening Injury			
				Front Crash Test		Side Crash Test	
				Driver	Pass.	Front Occup.	Rear Occup.
Honda Accord	7	Front	Very Good - 1062	5%	6%		
		Side	Very Poor - 1621			4%	13%
Honda Accord Coupe	8	Front	Very Good - 1444	8%	7%		
		Side	Average - 953			6%	4%
Hyundai Genesis	8	Front	Average - 1718	8%	8%		
		Side	Very Good - 565			3%	2%
Coupe	8	Front	Poor - 1994	10%	12%		
		Side^	Average - 970			5%	
Hyundai Sonata	5	Front	Average - 1852	9%	10%		
		Side	Average - 931			5%	4%
Infiniti EX35	5	Front	Very Poor - 2444	12%	14%		
		Side	Very Good - 678			2%	5%
Infiniti G37	5	Front	Very Poor - 2510	10%	18%		
		Side	Very Good - 534			2%	3%
Kia Optima	8	Front	Good - 1550	7%	8%		
		Side	Average - 899			4%	5%
Lexus ES350	6	Front	Good - 1585	8%	8%		
		Side	Average - 985			3%	7%
Lexus HS	9	Front	Good - 1522	9%	7%		
		Side	Very Good - 636			2%	4%
Lexus IS250/350	3	Front	Poor - 2125	12%	12%		
		Side	Poor - 1081			2%	9%
Lincoln MKZ	7	Front	Very Good - 1323	7%	6%		
		Side	Poor - 1023			4%	6%
Mazda 6	9	Front	Good - 1550	7%	9%		
		Side	Good - 815			4%	4%
Mercedes Benz E-Class	5	Front	Very Poor - 2594	13%	15%		
		Side	Very Good - 536			2%	3%
Mercury Milan	7	Front	Very Good - 1323	7%	6%		
		Side	Poor - 1023			4%	6%
Hybrid	7	Front	Average - 1801	10%	8%		
		Side	Poor - 1023			4%	6%
Mitsubishi Galant	6	Front	Poor - 1901	11%	9%		
		Side	Very Good - 697			3%	4%
Nissan Altima, Hybrid	8	Front	Good - 1538	8%	8%		
		Side	Good - 982			3%	5%
Nissan Maxima	9	Front	Good - 1582	9%	8%		
		Side	Very Good - 649			3%	3%
Pontiac G6	4	Front	Poor - 2175	10%	14%		
		Side	Average - 965			5%	5%
Saturn Aura	6	Front	Average - 1842	9%	10%		
		Side	Good - 860			4%	4%
Subaru Legacy	8	Front	Good - 1585	10%	7%		
		Side	Very Good - 676			2%	4%
Subaru Outback	10	Front	Very Good - 1311	7%	7%		
		Side	Very Good - 468			2%	3%
Toyota Avalon	9	Front	Very Good - 1408	6%	9%		
		Side	Good - 784			2%	5%

Crash Test Performance	Combined Car Book Crash Test Rating	Test Type	Car Book Crash Test Rating - Index (Lower numbers are better)	Likelihood of Life Threatening Injury			
				Front Crash Test		Side Crash Test	
				Driver	Pass.	Front Occup.	Rear Occup.
Toyota Camry	6	Front	Average - 1845	10%	10%		
		Side	Good - 816			3%	5%
Hybrid	6	Front	Average - 1845	10%	10%		
		Side	Good - 816			3%	5%
Volkswagen CC	2	Front	Very Poor - 2320	14%	12%		
		Side	Poor - 1111			3%	8%
Volkswagen Passat	2	Front	Very Poor - 2320	14%	12%		
		Side	Poor - 1111			3%	8%
Wagon	2	Front	Very Poor - 2320	14%	12%		
		Side	Poor - 1111			3%	8%
Large							
Acura RL	9	Front	Good - 1510	7%	9%		
		Side	Good - 791			4%	4%
Buick Lucerne	6	Front	Very Good - 1454	5%	10%		
		Side	Very Poor - 1509			8%	9%
Cadillac DTS	2	Front	Poor - 2027	8%	13%		
		Side	Very Poor - 1342			7%	8%
Cadillac STS	2	Front	Very Poor - 2505	11%	17%		
		Side	Poor - 1122			8%	4%
Chrysler 300	10	Front	Very Good - 1348	6%	7%		
		Side	Very Good - 595			3%	3%
Dodge Challenger	8	Front	Good - 1531	6%	9%		
		Side	Average - 889			4%	5%
Dodge Charger	10	Front	Very Good - 1348	6%	7%		
		Side	Very Good - 595			3%	3%
Ford Crown Victoria	7	Front	Good - 1606	10%	7%		
		Side	Good - 870			6%	3%
Ford Taurus	9	Front	Good - 1530	7%	7%		
		Side	Very Good - 643			4%	5%
Lincoln MKS	8	Front	Average - 1682	8%	10%		
		Side	Very Good - 683			1%	6%
Lincoln Town Car	7	Front	Good - 1606	10%	7%		
		Side	Good - 870			6%	3%
Mercury Grand Marquis	7	Front	Good - 1606	10%	7%		
		Side	Good - 870			6%	3%
Minivan							
Chrysler Town & Country	7	Front	Good - 1571	8%	8%		
		Side	Very Good - 539			2%	3%
Dodge Grand Caravan	7	Front	Good - 1571	8%	8%		
		Side	Very Good - 539			2%	3%
Honda Odyssey	6	Front	Very Good - 1392	6%	8%		
		Side	Very Good - 670			3%	3%
Kia Rondo	4	Front	Good - 1640	9%	7%		
		Side	Poor - 1016			3%	8%
Kia Sedona	8	Front	Good - 1536	8%	7%		
		Side	Very Good - 475			2%	2%
Mazda 5	4	Front	Average - 1693	8%	9%		
		Side*	Average - 1005			3%	7%

*Additional Injury Potential: In addition to head and chest measurements, the government tests measure the crash forces on the occupant's femurs (in the front test) and pelvis (in the side tests). Generally, if the scores were Good or Very Good, injury to these areas will be minimal. An asterisk indicates that the femur/pelvis scores for this particular vehicle were moderate, otherwise the scores were good or very good. ^Vehicle has no back seat, so the index is based on a single front occupant. **Vehicle to be tested in 2010. Results expected to be the same or better. ***During the side impact test, the head of the left rear passenger dummy struck the convertible roof linkage resulting in a higher likelihood of serious head injury. ^^During the side impact test, the driver door unlatched and opened. A door opening during a side impact crash increases the likelihood of occupant ejection.

Crash Test Performance	Combined Car Book Crash Test Rating	Test Type	Car Book Crash Test Rating - Index (Lower numbers are better)	Front Crash Test		Side Crash Test	
				Driver	Pass.	Front Occup.	Rear Occup.
Toyota Sienna	4	Front	Average - 1838	11%	8%		
		Side	Very Good - 580			2%	3%
Volkswagen Routan	7	Front	Good - 1571	8%	8%		
		Side	Very Good - 539			2%	3%
Small SUV							
Acura RDX	6	Front	Good - 1480	7%	8%		
		Side	Very Poor - 695			4%	3%
Chevrolet HHR	5	Front	Good - 1486	8%	7%		
		Side	Very Poor - 848			5%	3%
Panel Truck	5	Front	Good - 1486	8%	7%		
		Side^	Very Poor - 1057			5%	
Ford Escape	4	Front	Average - 1833	9%	10%		
		Side	Poor - 563			2%	3%
Hybrid	4	Front	Average - 1833	9%	10%		
		Side	Poor - 563			2%	3%
Honda CR-V	8	Front	Good - 1475	7%	7%		
		Side	Poor - 544			3%	3%
Honda Element	6	Front	Good - 1535	7%	8%		
		Side	Poor - 608			2%	4%
Jeep Compass	1	Front	Very Poor - 2944	13%	19%		
		Side	Poor - 585			3%	3%
Jeep Liberty	9	Front	Very Good - 1313	7%	6%		
		Side	Average - 513			2%	3%
Jeep Patriot	4	Front	Average - 1840	11%	8%		
		Side	Poor - 585			3%	3%
Jeep Wrangler w/o SAB		Front	Poor - 1958	10%	10%		
Kia Sportage	2	Front*	Poor - 2021	9%	10%		
		Side	Very Poor - 687			2%	5%
Mazda Tribute	4	Front	Average - 1833	9%	10%		
		Side	Poor - 563			2%	3%
Hybrid	4	Front	Average - 1833	9%	10%		
		Side	Poor - 563			2%	3%
Mercury Mariner	4	Front	Average - 1833	9%	10%		
		Side	Poor - 563			2%	3%
Hybrid	4	Front	Average - 1833	9%	10%		
		Side	Poor - 563			2%	3%
Mitsubishi Outlander	7	Front	Average - 1684	10%	8%		
		Side**	Good - 433			2%	2%
Saturn Vue	7	Front	Poor - 1995	10%	10%		
		Side	Poor - 543			2%	3%
Subaru Forester	8	Front	Very Good - 1451	7%	8%		
		Side	Average - 499			2%	3%
Suzuki Grand Vitara	2	Front	Very Poor - 2479	13%	15%		
		Side	Poor - 580			3%	3%
Toyota RAV4	2	Front	Poor - 2028	9%	13%		
		Side	Very Poor - 908			4%	5%
Volkswagen Tiguan	5	Front	Poor - 1941	11%	9%		
		Side	Average - 442			2%	3%
Mid-Size SUV							
Acura MDX		Front	Average - 1758	9%	10%		

24

Crash Test Performance	Combined Car Book Crash Test Rating	Test Type	Car Book Crash Test Rating - Index (Lower numbers are better)	Likelihood of Life Threatening Injury			
				Front Crash Test		Side Crash Test	
				Driver	Pass.	Front Occup.	Rear Occup.
Audi Q5	6	Front	Poor - 1896	10%	10%		
		Side	Good - 353			1%	2%
BMW X5	6	Front	Poor - 2109	9%	14%		
		Side	Very Good - 268			1%	1%
Buick Enclave	7	Front	Average - 1775	10%	8%		
		Side	Very Good - 342			2%	2%
Chevrolet Equinox	4	Front	Average - 1749	10%	8%		
		Side	Poor - 622			4%	3%
Dodge Journey	7	Front	Average - 1681	8%	8%		
		Side	Good - 414			1%	3%
Dodge Nitro	7	Front	Good - 1567	8%	7%		
		Side	Average - 521			3%	2%
Ford Edge	2	Front	Very Poor - 2680	10%	20%		
		Side	Poor - 591			2%	4%
Ford Explorer	6	Front	Average - 1791	10%	9%		
		Side	Good - 407			2%	2%
GMC Terrain	4	Front	Average - 1749	10%	8%		
		Side	Poor - 622			4%	3%
Honda Pilot	7	Front	Average - 1701	8%	10%		
		Side	Good - 390			2%	2%
Hummer H3	7	Front	Average - 1878	9%	11%		
		Side	Very Good - 301			1%	2%
Hyundai Santa Fe		Front	Average - 1758	8%	9%		
Hyundai Veracruz	5	Front	Poor - 1910	10%	9%		
		Side	Average - 451			1%	3%
Kia Borrego	8	Front	Very Good - 1421	7%	7%		
		Side	Average - 436			2%	2%
Lexus RX350	6	Front	Average - 1791	9%	11%		
		Side	Good - 398			1%	2%
Lincoln MKX	2	Front	Very Poor - 2680	10%	20%		
		Side	Poor - 591			2%	4%
Mazda CX-7	6	Front	Good - 1509	8%	8%		
		Side	Poor - 573			2%	3%
Mazda CX-9	8	Front	Good - 1508	7%	7%		
		Side	Average - 463			2%	2%
Mercedes-Benz ML-Class	7	Front	Average - 1761	10%	8%		
		Side	Very Good - 283			1%	1%
Hybrid	7	Front	Average - 1761	10%	8%		
		Side	Very Good - 283			1%	1%
Mercury Mountaineer	6	Front	Average - 1791	10%	9%		
		Side	Good - 407			2%	2%
Nissan Murano	2	Front	Very Poor - 3006	20%	15%		
		Side	Poor - 558			2%	4%
Nissan Pathfinder		Front	Very Poor - 2754	17%	14%		
Nissan Rogue	3	Front	Very Poor - 2342	11%	15%		
		Side	Poor - 538			3%	2%
Nissan Xterra	5	Front*	Very Poor - 2685	16%	13%		
		Side	Very Good - 247			1%	1%

*Additional Injury Potential: In addition to head and chest measurements, the government tests measure the crash forces on the occupant's femurs (in the front test) and pelvis (in the side tests). Generally, if the scores were Good or Very Good, injury to these areas will be minimal. An asterisk indicates that the femur/pelvis scores for this particular vehicle were moderate, otherwise the scores were good or very good. ^Vehicle has no back seat, so the index is based on a single front occupant. **Vehicle to be tested in 2010. Results expected to be the same or better. ***During the side impact test, the head of the left rear passenger dummy struck the convertible roof linkage resulting in a higher likelihood of serious head injury. ^^During the side impact test, the driver door unlatched and opened. A door opening during a side impact crash increases the likelihood of occupant ejection.

| Crash Test Performance | Combined Car Book Crash Test Rating | Test Type | Car Book Crash Test Rating - Index (Lower numbers are better) | Likelihood of Life Threatening Injury | | | |
| | | | | Front Crash Test | | Side Crash Test | |
				Driver	Pass.	Front Occup.	Rear Occup.
Subaru Tribeca	6	Front	Good - 1610	9%	9%		
		Side	Average - 532			2%	3%
Toyota Highlander	4	Front	Average - 1811	8%	12%		
		Side	Poor - 540			2%	3%
Hybrid	4	Front	Average - 1811	8%	12%		
		Side	Poor - 540			2%	3%
Toyota Venza	6	Front	Very Good - 1323	7%	7%		
		Side	Very Poor - 708			2%	5%
Volkswagen Touareg	5	Front	Poor - 1934	9%	10%		
		Side	Average - 452			2%	2%
Volvo XC90	9	Front	Good - 1479	8%	6%		
		Side	Good - 351			1%	2%
Large SUV							
Audi Q7	7	Front	Poor - 1934	9%	10%		
		Side	Very Good - 288			1%	2%
Cadillac Escalade	10	Front	Very Good - 1174	6%	6%		
		Side**	Very Good - 299			2%	1%
ESV	10	Front	Very Good - 1101	5%	6%		
		Side**	Very Good - 309			2%	1%
Chevrolet Suburban 1500	10	Front	Very Good - 1101	5%	6%		
		Side**	Very Good - 309			2%	1%
Chevrolet Tahoe	10	Front	Very Good - 1174	6%	6%		
		Side**	Very Good - 299			2%	1%
Chevrolet Traverse	7	Front	Average - 1775	10%	8%		
		Side	Very Good - 342			2%	2%
Ford Expedition	8	Front	Average - 1661	8%	10%		
		Side	Very Good - 239			1%	1%
Extended	8	Front	Average - 1661	8%	10%		
		Side	Very Good - 239			1%	1%
Ford Flex	7	Front	Good - 1617	10%	6%		
		Side	Good - 412			2%	2%
GMC Acadia	7	Front	Average - 1775	10%	8%		
		Side	Very Good - 342			2%	2%
GMC Yukon	10	Front	Very Good - 1174	6%	6%		
		Side	Very Good - 299			2%	1%
XL 1500	10	Front	Very Good - 1101	5%	6%		
		Side**	Very Good - 309			2%	1%
Infiniti QX56		Front	Poor - 2139	9%	14%		
Jeep Commander		Front	Very Good - 1291	6%	7%		
Jeep Grand Cherokee		Front**	Very Good - 1283	6%	6%		
Lincoln Navigator	8	Front	Average - 1661	8%	10%		
		Side	Very Good - 239			1%	1%
Nissan Armada		Front	Poor - 2139	9%	14%		
Saturn Outlook	7	Front	Average - 1775	10%	8%		
		Side	Very Good - 342			2%	2%
Toyota FJ Cruiser	6	Front	Poor - 1914	9%	12%		
		Side	Good - 400			2%	2%

*Additional Injury Potential: In addition to head and chest measurements, the government tests measure the crash forces on the occupant's femurs (in the front test) and pelvis (in the side tests). Generally, if the scores were Good or Very Good, injury to these areas will be minimal. An asterisk indicates that the femur/pelvis scores for this particular vehicle were moderate, otherwise the scores were good or very good. ^Vehicle has no back seat, so the index is based on a single front occupant. **Vehicle to be tested in 2010. Results expected to be the same or better. ***During the side impact test, the head of the left rear passenger dummy struck the convertible roof linkage resulting in a higher likelihood of serious head injury. ^^During the side impact test, the driver door unlatched and opened. A door opening during a side impact crash increases the likelihood of occupant ejection.

Crash Test Performance	Combined Car Book Crash Test Rating	Test Type	Car Book Crash Test Rating - Index (Lower numbers are better)	Likelihood of Life Threatening Injury			
				Front Crash Test		Side Crash Test	
				Driver	Pass.	Front Occup.	Rear Occup.
Compact Pickup							
Chevrolet Colorado Crew	1	Front*	Poor - 2087	10%	10%		
		Side*	Very Poor - 1452			11%	4%
Regular, Extended Cab	1	Front	Very Poor - 2290	11%	14%		
		Side@	Very Poor - 2055			11%	
Dodge Dakota Crew w/o SAB	9	Front	Very Good - 1229	5%	6%		
		Side	Good - 430			2%	3%
Extended Cab w/o SAB	9	Front	Good - 1558	6%	10%		
		Side^	Good - 413			2%	
Ford Ranger	3	Front	Poor - 1981	9%	12%		
		Side	Very Poor - 860			4%	
GMC Canyon Crew	1	Front*	Poor - 2087	10%	10%		
		Side*	Very Poor - 1452			11%	4%
Regular, Extended Cab	1	Front	Very Poor - 2290	11%	14%		
		Side@	Very Poor - 2055			11%	
Nissan Frontier King Cab	4	Front	Very Poor - 2303	16%	9%		
		Side^	Good - 359			2%	
4-dr.	4	Front	Very Poor - 2851	15%	17%		
		Side	Average - 454			2%	2%
Toyota Tacoma 4-dr.	7	Front	Good - 1602	7%	10%		
		Side	Average - 478			2%	2%
Regular, Extended Cab	7	Front	Good - 1511	7%	9%		
		Side^	Poor - 623			3%	
Standard Pickup							
Cadillac Escalade EXT	10	Front	Very Good - 1165	5%	7%		
		Side**	Very Good - 327			2%	1%
Chevrolet Avalanche	10	Front	Very Good - 1165	5%	7%		
		Side**	Very Good - 327			2%	1%
Chevrolet Silverado 1500 4-dr.	9	Front	Very Good - 1451	7%	9%		
		Side**	Good - 407			2%	2%
1500 Regular, Extended Cab		Front	Good - 1628	7%	9%		
Dodge Ram 1500 Crew Cab		Front	Average - 1778	9%	9%		
1500 Regular, Quad Cab		Front	Good - 1567	7%	9%		
Ford F-150 Regular Cab	10	Front	Very Good - 1375	8%	7%		
		Side^	Very Good - 289			1%	
Super Cab Cab	10	Front	Very Good - 1375	8%	7%		
		Side	Very Good - 277			1%	1%
Super Crew	10	Front	Good - 1471	8%	8%		
		Side	Very Good - 261			1%	1%
GMC Sierra 1500 4-dr.	9	Front	Very Good - 1451	7%	9%		
		Side**	Good - 407			2%	2%
1500 Regular, Extended Cab		Front	Good - 1628	7%	9%		
Honda Ridgeline	8	Front	Very Good - 1204	5%	6%		
		Side	Poor - 588			3%	2%
Nissan Titan 4-dr.		Front	Poor - 1977	10%	11%		
Extended Cab		Front	Poor - 2132	9%	13%		
Toyota Tundra Crew Cab		Front	Poor - 1913	10%	10%		
Double Cab		Front	Good - 1461	7%	8%		
Regular Cab		Front	Poor - 1924	11%	10%		

@Additional Injury Potential: Poor pelvis scores in side crash test, risk of serious injury high.

AUTOMATIC CRASH PROTECTION

The concept of automatic safety protection is not new. Automatic fire sprinklers in public buildings, oxygen masks in airplanes, purification of drinking water, and pasteurization of milk are all commonly accepted forms of automatic safety protection. Airbags provide automatic crash protection in cars.

Automatic crash protection protects people from what is called the "second collision," when the occupant collides with the interior of the vehicle. Because the "second collision" occurs within milliseconds, providing automatic rather than manual protection dramatically improves the chances of escaping injury.

Automatic crash protection comes in two basic forms, airbags and automatic control of safety features.

Since airbags were introduced over 30 years ago, they have been so successful in saving lives that car makers now include a variety of types which deploy from 4 to 8 different points.

The automatic control of safety features was first introduced with anti-lock brakes. Today, Electronic Stability Control (ESC) and other automatic functions are improving the safety of new cars.

Electronic Stability Control (ESC) takes advantage of anti-lock brake technology and helps minimize the loss of control. Each car maker will have its own name for this feature, but they all work in a similar fashion.

For ESC, anti-lock brakes work by using speed sensors on each wheel to determine if one or more of the wheels is locking up or skidding. ESC then uses these speed sensors and a unit that determines the steering angle to monitor what's happening with the vehicle. A special control device measures the steering and rotation of the tires in order to detect when a vehicle is about to go in a direction different from the one indicated by the steering wheel–or out of control! This will typically occur during a hard turn or on slippery surfaces. The control unit will sense whether the car is over-steering (turning sharper than you intended resulting in the back wheels slipping sideways) or under-steering (continuing to move forward despite your intended turn).

When either of these events occur, the control unit will automatically apply the brakes to the appropriate wheels to correct the situation and, in some cases, automatically slow down the engine.

As amazing as this device is, it will not keep the vehicle under control in severely out of control situations. Nevertheless, according to the IIHS, ESC can reduce the chance of a single vehicle crash by over 50%. Its benefit is that it will prevent more typical losses of control from escalating into a crash. It is an extremely important and recommended safety feature.

⚠ TELEMATICS ⚠

Telematic systems are subscription-based services ($200-$300 per year) that use a combination of cellular technology and global positioning systems to provide a variety of safety and convenience features. The main safety feature is automatic crash notification (ACN) which connects the vehicle's occupants to a private call center that directs emergency medical teams to the car. This system can be activated by pressing a button on the dash or rear view mirror or it is automatically activated if the airbag deploys. Once the system is activated, the call center receives the exact location of your vehicle and notifies the local emergency response team. This can potentially reduce the time it takes for an emergency team to reach your vehicle. Other safety features can include roadside assistance, remote door unlocking, stolen vehicle tracking, and driving directions.

Caution! Some manufacturers are adding cell phone capability to the ACN system which increases the risk of a crash 4-fold when talking on the ACN cell phone. This is about the same effect as drinking and driving. Don't drink and drive or telephone and drive!

CHILD SAFETY

Seat Belts for Kids: How long should children use car seats? For school-age children, a car seat is twice as effective in preventing injury as an adult lap and shoulder harness—use a booster as long as possible. Most children can start using seat belts at 4'9" and when tall enough for the shoulder belt to cross the chest, not the neck. The lap section of the belt should be snug and as low on the hips as possible. If the shoulder belt does cross the face or neck, use a booster seat.

Never:

☒ Use the same belt on two children.

☒ Move a shoulder belt behind a child's back or under an arm.

☒ Buckle in a pet or any large toys with the child.

☒ Recline a seat with a belted child.

☒ Use a twisted seat belt. The belt must be straight and flat.

☒ Use pillows or cushions to boost your child.

☒ Place a belt around you with a child in your lap. In an accident or sudden stop, your child would absorb most of the crash force.

Incorrect Installation: Surveys show up to 85 percent of parents do not install their child seats properly. Incorrect installation of a child safety seat can deny the child lifesaving protection and may even contribute to further injuring the child. Read the installation instructions carefully. If you have any questions about the correct installation in your particular car, contact the National Highway Traffic Safety Administration's website at www.nhtsa.gov. They can direct you to the nearest child seat inspection station that will check to see if you have installed your child seat correctly and instruct you on the proper way to install the seat if you have any questions. There is no charge for this service.

Following are some common mistakes parents make when installing a child safety seat.

☒ Infant is in safety seat facing forward, rather than to the rear.

☒ Child safety seat in front with an airbag.

☒ Child is not secured by safety seat harness and is sitting loose in safety seat.

☒ Booster seat used without a shield or a shoulder belt.

☒ Safety belt is fastened to or around wrong part of safety seat.

☒ Tether strap is not used, missing, or at wrong angle of attachment, when required.

☒ Use of incompatible safety belts.

☒ Safety belt is not used to secure safety seat in vehicle. The safety seat is loose on vehicle seat.

☒ Harness strap adjustment slides are not securely locked, permitting straps to release in a crash.

Warning: After an accident, rescue experts suggest that the entire seat be removed from the car, rather than unbuckling the child first.

! CHILD SAFETY SEAT RECALLS !

Manufacturers are required to put address cards in child seat packages. Mail the registration card as soon as you open the box! This is the only way you will receive notification of a seat recall. Keep a copy of the manufacturer's address and contact the manufacturer if you move. To find out if the seat you are using has ever been recalled go to http://www-odi.nhtsa.dot.gov/cars/problems/recalls/childseat.cfm. You can also contact the Auto Safety Hotline at 800-424-9393, (D.C. call 202-366-0123.)

ROLLOVER

The risk of rollover is a significant safety issue, especially with sport utility vehicles. Because of their relatively high center of gravity, they don't hug the road like smaller, lower automobiles and trucks. As a result, they are more likely to turn over on sharp turns or corners. Not only does a rollover increase the likelihood of injuries, but it also increases the risk of the occupant being thrown from the vehicle. In fact, the danger of rollover with sport utilities is so severe that manufacturers are now required to place a sticker where it can be seen by the driver every time the vehicle is used. Each year, approximately 10,000 people die in rollover-related accidents.

To understand the concept behind these vehicles' propensity to roll over, consider this: place a section of 2x4 lumber on its 2-inch side. It is easily tipped over by a force pushing against the side. But if you place it on its 4-inch side, the same force will cause it to slide rather than tip over. Similarly, in a moving vehicle, the forces generated by a turn can cause a narrow, tall vehicle to roll over. This is why SUVs are more susceptible to rolling over.

This year in the safety checklist we include a feature called roll-sensing side airbags. Roll-sensing side airbags are a special side airbag system which keeps the side airbags inflated longer in the event of a rollover. This feature is found in many SUVs and can reduce the likelihood of injury when a vehicle flips. See the car pages (81-270) for which 2010 models have this feature.

Congress required the U.S. Department of Transportation to develop a dynamic (moving) rating system to accompany the static (stationary) rating system. To date, this complex test has resulted in a simple "tip" or "no-tip" rating. Consumers are never told the speed of the tip and certain vehicles are not tested, just listed as "no tip."

Following are rollover ratings for many 2010 vehicles. We have been publishing these ratings for a number of years and recently, the National Highway Traffic Safety Administration adopted this rating system.

The rollover rating is based on the Static Stability Factor (SSF) and consists of a formula that uses the track width of the vehicle (tire to tire) and height to determine which vehicles are more or less likely to roll over when compared to each other. You can't use this information to exactly predict rollovers. However, all things being equal, if two vehicles are in the same situation where a rollover could occur, the one with a high SSF is less likely to roll over than one with a lower SSF. Because this formula doesn't consider such things as driver behavior and the weight of the vehicle, among other factors, some experts do not believe it tells the whole story. We agree, and urged the government to provide an even better rollover rating system.

In the meantime, knowing how the vehicles rate using the SSF can be a key consideration in your evaluation of the vehicle.

! ROOF CRUSH !

The government standard for roof crush (the ability of the roof to keep from collapsing in a rollover) is woefully inadequate. Roofs often crush in rollover accidents and seriously injure seat-belted occupants. Rollovers and roof crush break windshields and windows creating portals for occupants to be ejected from the vehicle. See next page for more details.

! GOVERNMENT WARNING !

To alert consumers to rollover, the following warning is required on certain vehicles:

This is a multipurpose passenger vehicle which will handle and maneuver differently from an ordinary passenger car, in driving conditions which may occur on streets and highways and off road. As with other vehicles of this type, if you make sharp turns or abrupt manuevers, the vehicle may roll over or may go out of control and crash. You should read driving guielines and instructions in the Owner's Manual, and wear your seat belt at all times.

ROOF CRUSH

Since 1970, the auto industry has fought efforts by the National Highway Traffic Safety Administration to issue a dynamic roof crush standard to protect occupants in rollover crashes. From 1970 to 2007, the number of deaths to occupants in rollover crashes climbed from 1,400 to over 10,000 each year while annual occupant fatalities declined from 43,200 to 28,900. NHTSA has stuck with the outdated, static roof crush standard issued in 1971 even though it was to have been phased out by 1977 for a dynamic standard. On the other hand, NHTSA has issued effective dynamic front and side crash test standards that have significantly reduced death and serious injury.

The current standard calls for roofs to withstand 1.5 times the weight of the vehicle, applied to one side of the roof, for vehicles up to 6,000 pounds. Vehicles weighing more need not meet any standard. A new standard will be phased in for 2013 to 2017 models which will double the roof strength requirement for vehicles weighing up to 6,000 pounds. Both the driver and passenger sides of the roof will have to withstand a force equal to three times the weight of the vehicle. While an improvement, the new standard falls short of requiring a dynamic crash test that better replicates what happens in real world crashes.

Today, some vehicles have strong roofs but all too many have weak roofs. In a rollover crash, the first side of a vehicle that hits the ground generally does not crush but the second, or trailing side, that hits the ground often does crush. This failure will either break the windows and allow the occupants to eject or crush the occupants that stay in the vehicle. To identify which vehicles today have strong roofs, the Center for Auto Safety (CAS) had the Center for Injury Research (CfIR) conduct dynamic rollover roof crush tests using the Jordan Rollover System (JRS).

The table below shows the results of the CAS testing. The cumulative crush is how much the roof will crush inward after two full rolls. More than 5 inches of roof crush is unacceptable because an occupant's head is likely to be hit. The Strength to Weight Ratio (SWR) is how much weight the roof on one side will support before crushing inward 5 inches when tested in a static fashion as the government does.

The dynamic rollover test shows that good roof design can result in a vehicle with a lower static SWR outperforming a vehicle with a higher static SWR in limiting roof intrusion in a rollover, demonstrating the problem with the static government test. CAS has developed a comparative rating for the roof strength that ranges from Very Good to Very Poor.

Dynamic tests, such as the JRS, show how vehicle geometry effects safety. Vehicles with the very square roofs such as the Ridgeline are more vulnerable to roof crush. A vehicle with a more rounded roof, such as the XC90, will roll more like a barrel with less force on the corners of the roof.

The design of the roof in unison with the body of the vehicle is critical to its ability to protect occupants. If any of the critical roof structural elements buckles the roof will collapse and injure belted occupants who are seated underneath.

Good design will also keep windows in place to prevent occupants from being ejected in rollovers. Only a dynamic test can demonstrate whether seat belts, pre-tensioners and side curtains function together to protect occupants from ejection and injury in rollovers.

Center for Auto Safety Roof Crush Test Results

Vehicle*	Cumulative Crush (in.)	Dynamic SWR	Static SWR	Rating
Volvo XC90 2005-09	1.8	5.2	4.6	Very Good
VW Jetta 2007-09	3.4	4.4	5.1	Good
Honda CR-V 2007-10	3.6	4.3	2.6	Good
Toyota Camry 2007-09	4.3	4.0	4.3	Good
Subaru Forester 2003-08	4.6	3.9	4.3	Moderate
Hyundai Sonata 2006-09	4.6	3.9	3.2	Moderate
Pontiac G6 2006-09	7.0	2.8	2.3	Poor
Chrysler 300 2006-09	7.4	2.6	2.5	Poor
Jeep Gr. Cherokee 2007-10	9.1	1.8	2.2	Very Poor
Chevy Tahoe 2007-09	10.9	1.0	2.1	Very Poor
Honda Ridgeline 2006-09	10.9	1.0	2.4	Very Poor

*Year tested is first model year listed with later models having similar roof strength and design.

This work was funded by the Santos Family Foundation on eleven vehicles donated by the State Farm Insurance Company.

STATIC STABILITY FACTOR

Vehicle	SSF (High=Better)	Chance of Rollover	Vehicle	SSF (High=Better)	Chance of Rollover	Vehicle	SSF (High=Better)	Chance of Rollover
Acura MDX	1.30	Moderate	GMC Yukon	1.12	Very High	Merc-Benz S-Class	1.45*	Low
Acura RDX	1.26	High	GMC Yukon XL	1.13	Very High	Mercury Grand Marquis	1.51	Very Low
Acura TL	1.49	Very Low	Honda Accord	1.48	Very Low	Mercury Mariner	1.13	Very High
Acura TSX	1.46	Low	Honda Accord Coupe	1.47	Very Low	Mercury Milan	1.43	Low
Acura ZDX	1.40*	Low	Honda Civic	1.43	Low	Mercury Mountaineer	1.13	Very High
Audi A4	1.46	Low	Honda Civic Coupe	1.44	Low	Mini Cooper	1.45	Low
Audi A5	1.54*	Very Low	Honda CR-V	1.22	High	Mitsubishi Galant	1.42	Low
Audi A6	1.48*	Very Low	Honda Element	1.15	Very High	Mitsubishi Lancer	1.36	Moderate
Audi Q5	1.27	High	Honda Fit	1.35	Moderate	Mitsubishi Outlander	1.19	High
Audi Q7	1.20	High	Honda Insight	1.39	Low	Nissan 370Z	1.58*	Very Low
BMW 1 Series	1.40	Low	Honda Odyssey	1.30	Moderate	Nissan Altima	1.43	Low
BMW 3 Series	1.44	Low	Honda Pilot	1.22	High	Nissan Altima Coupe	1.49	Very Low
BMW 5 Series	1.43	Low	Honda Ridgeline	1.29	Moderate	Nissan Armada	1.16	Very High
BMW 7 Series	1.47*	Very Low	Hummer H3	1.12	Very High	Nissan Cube	1.22	High
BMW X3	1.19*	High	Hyundai Accent	1.35	Moderate	Nissan Frontier	1.16	Very High
BMW X5	1.22	High	Hyundai Elantra	1.42	Low	Nissan Maxima	1.45	Low
Buick Enclave	1.23	High	Hyundai Genesis	1.48	Very Low	Nissan Murano	1.21	High
Buick LaCrosse	1.37	Moderate	Hyundai Santa Fe	1.22	High	Nissan Pathfinder	1.13	Very High
Buick Lucerne	1.45	Low	Hyundai Sonata	1.44	Low	Nissan Rogue	1.18	Very High
Cadillac CTS	1.44	Low	Hyundai Tucson	1.24*	High	Nissan Sentra	1.38	Low
Cadillac DTS	1.40	Low	Hyundai Veracruz	1.23	High	Nissan Titan	1.19	High
Cadillac Escalade	1.12	Very High	Infiniti EX	1.33	Moderate	Nissan Versa	1.30	Moderate
Cadillac Escalade ESV	1.13	Very High	Infiniti FX	1.27*	High	Nissan Xterra	1.12	Very High
Cadillac Escalade EXT	1.16	Very High	Infiniti G	1.45	Low	Porsche Cayenne	1.27*	High
Cadillac SRX	1.21	High	Infiniti M	1.36*	Moderate	Saab 9-3	1.36	Moderate
Cadillac STS	1.45	Low	Infiniti QX56	1.16	Very High	Scion tC	1.38	Low
Chevrolet Avalanche	1.14	Very High	Jaguar XF	1.44*	Low	Scion xB	1.30	Moderate
Chevrolet Aveo	1.32	Moderate	Jeep Commander	1.09	Very High	Scion xD	1.27	High
Chevrolet Camaro	1.53	Very Low	Jeep Compass	1.20	High	Smart ForTwo	1.16	Very High
Chevrolet Cobalt	1.40	Low	Jeep Grand Cherokee	1.17	Very High	Subaru Forester	1.21	High
Chevrolet Colorado	1.20	High	Jeep Liberty	1.11	Very High	Subaru Impreza	1.44	Low
Chevrolet Corvette	1.67*	Very Low	Jeep Patriot	1.20	High	Subaru Outback	1.22	High
Chevrolet Equinox	1.22*	High	Jeep Wrangler	1.18	Very High	Subaru Tribeca	1.24	High
Chevrolet HHR	1.29	Moderate	Kia Borrego	1.18	Very High	Suzuki Grand Vitara	1.19	High
Chevrolet Impala	1.39	Low	Kia Forte	1.44	Low	Suzuki Kizashi	1.41*	Low
Chevrolet Malibu	1.41	Low	Kia Optima	1.40	Low	Suzuki SX4	1.32	Moderate
Chevrolet Silverado	1.19	High	Kia Rio	1.37	Moderate	Toyota 4Runner	1.17*	Very High
Chevrolet Suburban	1.13	Very High	Kia Rondo	1.32	Moderate	Toyota Avalon	1.40	Low
Chevrolet Tahoe	1.12	Very High	Kia Sedona	1.31	Moderate	Toyota Camry	1.42	Low
Chevrolet Traverse	1.23	High	Kia Sorento	1.23*	High	Toyota Corolla	1.36	Moderate
Chrysler 300	1.41	Low	Kia Soul	1.27	High	Toyota FJ Cruiser	1.11	Very High
Chrysler PT Cruiser	1.31	Moderate	Kia Sportage	1.17	Very High	Toyota Highlander	1.18	Very High
Chrysler Sebring	1.39	Low	Land Rover Range Rvr	1.13*	Very High	Toyota Matrix	1.31	Moderate
Chrysler Town & Cntry	1.24	High	Lexus ES	1.41	Low	Toyota Prius	1.36	Moderate
Dodge Avenger	1.37	Moderate	Lexus GS	1.44*	Low	Toyota RAV4	1.20	High
Dodge Caliber	1.26	High	Lexus GX	1.12*	Very High	Toyota Sequoia	1.20	High
Dodge Challenger	1.40	Low	Lexus HS	1.33	Moderate	Toyota Sienna	1.25	High
Dodge Charger	1.41	Low	Lexus IS	1.45	Low	Toyota Tacoma	1.28	Moderate
Dodge Dakota	1.19	High	Lexus LS	1.46*	Low	Toyota Tundra	1.17	Very High
Dodge Grand Caravan	1.24	High	Lexus RX	1.21	High	Toyota Venza	1.26	High
Dodge Journey	1.20	High	Lincoln MKS	1.37	Moderate	Toyota Yaris	1.33	Moderate
Dodge Nitro	1.14	Very High	Lincoln MKT	1.27	High	Volkswagen Beetle	1.39	Low
Dodge Ram Pickup	1.18	Very High	Lincoln MKX	1.25	High	Volkswagen CC	1.37	Moderate
Ford Edge	1.25	High	Lincoln MKZ	1.43	Low	Volkswagen Eos	1.43*	Low
Ford Escape	1.13	Very High	Lincoln Navigator	1.16	Very High	Volkswagen Golf	1.36	Moderate
Ford Expedition	1.16	Very High	Lincoln Town Car	1.48	Very Low	Volkswagen Jetta	1.36	Moderate
Ford Explorer	1.13	Very High	Mazda 3	1.41	Low	Volkswagen Passat	1.37	Moderate
Ford F-150	1.18	Very High	Mazda 5	1.30	Moderate	Volkswagen Routan	1.24	High
Ford Flex	1.24	High	Mazda 6	1.49	Very Low	Volkswagen Tiguan	1.20	High
Ford Focus	1.33	Moderate	Mazda CX-7	1.28	Moderate	Volkswagen Touareg	1.23	High
Ford Fusion	1.43	Low	Mazda CX-9	1.27	High	Volvo S40	1.40	Low
Ford Mustang	1.53	Very Low	Mazda MX-5 Miata	1.60*	Very Low	Volvo S80	1.41*	Low
Ford Ranger	1.15	Very High	Mazda Tribute	1.13	Very High	Volvo V70	1.37*	Moderate
Ford Taurus	1.39	Low	Merc-Benz C-Class	1.43	Low	Volvo XC60	1.22*	High
GMC Acadia	1.23	High	Merc-Benz E-Class	1.46	Low	Volvo XC90	1.19	High
GMC Canyon	1.20	High	Merc-Benz GL-Class	1.17*	Very High			
GMC Sierra	1.19	High	Merc-Benz GLK-Class	1.21*	High	*Calculated		
GMC Terrain	1.22*	High	Merc-Benz M-Class	1.22	High			

FUEL ECONOMY

While gas prices have subsided, driving driving still takes a big bite out of our pocketbooks. The good news is that higher fuel efficiency standards are forcing car companies to provide more fuel efficient vehicles. Buying right and practicing more fuel efficient driving will make a huge difference in your vehicle's operating costs.

Using the EPA ratings is the best way to incorporate fuel efficiency in selecting a new car. By comparing these ratings, even among cars of the same size, you'll find that fuel efficiency varies greatly. One compact car might get 36 miles per gallon (mpg) while another compact gets only 22 mpg. If you drive 15,000 miles a year and you pay $2.70 per gallon for fuel, the 36 mpg car will save you $715 *a year* over the "gas guzzler."

In 2008, the EPA changed the way it estimates miles per gallon to better represent today's driving conditions. Their new method adjusts for aggressive driving (high speeds and faster acceleration), air conditioning use, and cold temperature operation.

Octane Ratings: Once you've purchased your car, you'll be faced with choosing the right gasoline. Oil companies spend millions of dollars trying to get you to buy so-called higher performance or high octane fuels. Using high octane fuel can add considerably to your gas bill, and the vast majority of vehicles do not need it. Check your owner's manual and only use what's recommended, which is usually 87. Very few vehicles require "premium" gasoline.

The octane rating of a gasoline is not a measure of power or quality. It is simply a measure of the gas' resistance to engine knock, which is the pinging sound you hear when the air and fuel mixture in your engine ignites prematurely during acceleration.

Your engine may knock when accelerating a heavily loaded car uphill or when the humidity is low. This is normal and does not call for a higher-octane gasoline.

FIVE FACTORS AFFECTING FUEL ECONOMY

1. Engine Size: The smaller the engine the better your fuel efficiency. A 10% increase in the size of your engine can increase your fuel consumption rate by 6%. Smaller engines can be cheaper to maintain as well.

2. Transmission: If used properly, manual transmissions are generally more fuel-efficient than automatics. In fact, a 5-speed manual can add up to 6.5 mpg over a 4-speed automatic transmission. Getting an automatic with an overdrive gear can improve your fuel economy by up to 9 percent.

3. Cruise Control: Using cruise control can save fuel because driving at a constant speed uses less fuel than changing speeds frequently.

4. Trim Packages and Power Options: Upgrading a car's trim level and adding options such as power steering, brakes, windows, or a sunroof can increase the weight of your car. Every 200 pounds of weight shaves off about 1 mile per gallon off your mileage. The weight of the average car in 1981 was 3,202 pounds, today its around 4,000 pounds.

5. Hybrids: Some manufacturers offer hybrid vehicles that have both gasoline and electric engines. Hybrids offer 30% better fuel economy and lower emissions. Beware, until they are more readily available, you'll still have to pay considerably more to buy them.

TWELVE WAYS TO SAVE MONEY AT THE PUMP

Here are a few simple things you can do that will save you a lot of money. Note: Savings are based on gas at $2.70.

1. Make Sure Your Tires are Inflated Properly: 27% of vehicles have tires that are under-inflated. Properly inflated tires can improve mileage by 3%, which is like getting 8 cents off a gallon of gas. Check the label on your door or glove box to find out what the pressure range should be for your tires. Don't use the "max pressure" written on your tire. Electronic gauges are fast, easy to use and accurate. Don't rely on the numbers on the air pump.

2. Check Your Air Filter: A dirty air filter by itself can rob a car by as much as 10% percent of its mileage. If an engine doesn't get enough air, it will burn too much gasoline. Replacing a dirty filter can knock 27 cents off a gallon of gas.

3. Get Your Alignment Checked: Not only does poor alignment cause your tires to wear out faster and cause poor handling, but it can cause your engine to work harder and reduce your fuel efficiency by 10%.

4. Don't Use High Octane Gasoline: Check your owner's manual. Very, very few cars actually need high-octane gas. Using 87-octane gas will save you over 10 cents per gallon over mid-grade and 20 cents over premium.

5. Get a Tune Up: A properly tuned engine is a fuel saver. Have a trusted mechanic tune your engine to exact factory specifications and save up to 11 cents a gallon.

6. Check Your Gas Cap: It is estimated that nearly 17 % of the cars on the road have broken or missing gasoline caps. This hurts your mileage and can harm the environment by allowing your gasoline to evaporate.

7. Don't Speed: A car moving at 55 mph gets better fuel economy than the same car at 65 mph. For every 5 mph you reduce your highway speed, you can reduce fuel consumption by 7% which is like getting 19 cents off a gallon of gas.

8. Avoid Excess Idling: An idling car gets 0 mpg. Cars with larger engines typically waste more gas at idle than cars with smaller engines.

9. Drive Smoother: The smoother your accelerations and decelerations, the better your mileage. A smooth foot can save 48 cents a gallon.

10. Combine Trips: Short trips can be expensive because they usually involve a "cold" vehicle. For the first mile or two before the engine gets warmed up, a cold vehicle only gets 30 to 40% of the mileage it gets at full efficiency.

11. Empty your Roof Rack and Trunk: 50% of engine power, traveling at highway speed, is used in overcoming aerodynamic drag or wind resistance. Any protrusion on a vehicle's roof can reduce gas mileage, typical roof racks reduce fuel economy by about 6 mpg. 100 lbs. of extra weight will reduce your mileage by .5 mpg.

12. Choose Your Gas Miser: If you own more than one vehicle, choosing to drive the one with better gas mileage will save you money. If you drive 15,000 miles per year, half in a vehicle with 20 mpg and half with a 30 mpg vehicle and switch to driving 75% of your trips in the 30 mpg vehicle, you will save $168.75 annually with gas at $2.70.

TIP

FUEL ECONOMY

Get up-to-date information about fuel economy at www.fueleconomy.gov, a joint website created by the U.S. Department of Energy and the EPA. There you'll find the EPA's Fuel Economy Guide, allowing you to compare fuel economy estimates for 2010 models back to 1985 models. You'll also find out about the latest technological advances pertaining to fuel efficiency. The site is extremely useful and easy to navigate. We've added fuel economy ratings and a Fuel Factor section to the At-a-glance box on our car rating pages.

FUEL ECONOMY MISERS AND GUZZLERS

Because the success of the EPA program depends on consumers' ability to compare the fuel economy ratings easily, we have included key mileage figures on our ratings pages. Listed below are the best and worst of this year's ratings according to annual fuel cost. The complete EPA fuel economy guide is available at www.fueleconomy.gov.

FUEL ECONOMY MISERS AND GUZZLERS

Vehicle	Specifications	MPG (city/hwy)	Annual Fuel Cost
THE BEST			
Toyota Prius	1.8L, 4cyl., Continuously Variable, FWD	51/48	$810
Honda Civic Hybrid	1.3L, 4cyl., Continuously Variable, FWD	40/45	$964
Honda Insight	1.3L, 4cyl., Continuously Variable, FWD	40/43	$988
Ford Fusion Hybrid	2.5L, 4cyl., Continuously Variable, FWD	41/36	$1,038
Mercury Milan Hybrid	2.5L, 4cyl., Continuously Variable, FWD	41/36	$1,038
Smart Fortwo (Cabr. & Coupe)	1L, 3cyl., 5-sp. Automated Manual, RWD	33/41	$1,125
Lexus HS 250H	2.4L, 4cyl., Continuously Variable, FWD	35/34	$1,157
Nissan Altima Hybrid	2.5L, 4cyl., Continuously Variable, FWD	35/33	$1,191
Toyota Camry Hybrid	2.4L, 4cyl., Continuously Variable, FWD	33/34	$1,191
Audi A3	2L, 4cyl., 6-sp. Semi-Automatic, FWD	30/42	$1235^
Volkswagen Golf	2L, 4cyl., 6-sp. Semi-Automatic, FWD	30/42	$1235^
Volkswagen Golf	2L, 4cyl., 6-sp. Manual, FWD	30/42	$1235^
Volkswagen Jetta	2L, 4cyl., 6-sp. Semi-Automatic, FWD	30/41	$1235^
Volkswagen Jetta	2L, 4cyl., 6-sp. Manual, FWD	30/41	$1235^
Volkswagen Jetta Sportwagen	2L, 4cyl., 6-sp. Semi-Automatic, FWD	30/42	$1235^
Volkswagen Jetta Sportwagen	2L, 4cyl., 6-sp. Manual, FWD	30/41	$1235^
Ford Escape Hybrid	2.5L, 4cyl., Continuously Variable, FWD	34/31	$1,266
Mercury Mariner Hybrid	2.5L, 4cyl., Continuously Variable, FWD	34/31	$1,266
Mini Cooper	1.6L, 4cyl., 6-sp. Manual, FWD	28/37	$1,266
Mazda Tribute Hybrid	2.5L, 4cyl., Continuously Variable, FWD	34/31	$1,266
Toyota Yaris	1.5L, 4cyl., 5-sp. Manual, FWD	29/36	$1,266
THE WORST			
Bugatti Veyron	8L, 16cyl., 7-sp. Semi-Automatic, 4WD	8/14	$4,350*
Lamborghini Murcielago & Roadster	6.5L, 12cyl., 6-sp. Manual, AWD	8/13	$4,050
Ferrari 612 Scaglietti	5.7L, 12cyl., 6-sp. Automated Manual, RWD	9/16	$3,955*
Bentley Azure	6.8L, 8cyl., 6-sp. Semi-Automatic, RWD	9/15	$3,682
Bentley Brooklands	6.8L, 8cyl., 6-sp. Semi-Automatic, RWD	9/15	$3,682
Lamborghini Murcielago & Reventon Roadster	6.5L, 12cyl., 6-sp. Automated Manual, AWD	9/14	$3,682
Ferrari 599 GTB Fiorano	5.7L, 12cyl., 6-sp. Auto Man./Manual, RWD	11/15	$3,625*
Ferrari 612 Scaglietti	5.7L, 12cyl., 6-sp. Manual, RWD	10/15	$3,625*
Mercedes-Benz Maybach 57	5.5L, 12cyl., 5-sp. Automatic, RWD	10/16	$3,625*
Mercedes-Benz Maybach 57 S	6L, 12cyl., 5-sp. Automatic, RWD	10/16	$3,625*
Mercedes-Benz ML 63 AMG	6.3L, 8cyl., 7-sp. Automatic, 4WD	11/15	$3,625*
Bentley Continental Flying Spur & GTC	6L, 12cyl., 6-sp. Semi-Automatic, AWD	10/17	$3,375
Mercedes-Benz CL 65 AMG	6L, 12cyl., 5-sp. Automatic, RWD	11/17	$3,346*
Mercedes-Benz G 550	5.5L, 8cyl., 7-sp. Automatic, 4WD	11/15	$3,346*
Jeep Grand Cherokee SRT8 AWD	6.1L, 8cyl., 5-sp. Automatic, 4WD	12/16	$3,346*
Mercedes-Benz S 600	5.5L, 12cyl., 5-sp. Automatic, RWD	11/17	$3,346*
Mercedes-Benz S 65 AMG	6L, 12cyl., 5-sp. Automatic, RWD	11/17	$3,346*
Porsche Cayenne GTS & TransSiberia	4.8L, 8cyl., 6-sp. Manual, AWD	11/17	$3,115
Bentley Continental GT	6L, 12cyl., 6-sp. Semi-Automatic, AWD	10/17	$3,115
Aston Martin DB9 & DBS	5.9L, 12cyl., 6-sp. Manual, RWD	11/17	$3,115
BMW M5 & M6/Convertible	5L, 10cyl., 7-sp. Semi-Automatic, RWD	11/17	$3,115
BMW M5 & M6/Convertible	5L, 10cyl., 6-sp. Manual, RWD	11/17	$3,115

Note: 2010 annual fuel cost is based on driving 15,000 miles per year and a projected regular gas price at $2.70.
^diesel required at $2.80   *premium required at $2.90

COMPARING WARRANTIES

After buying your car, maintenance will be a significant portion of your operating costs. The strength of your warranty and the cost of repairs after the warranty expires will determine these costs. Comparing warranties and repair costs, before you buy, can save you thousands of dollars down the road.

Along with your new car comes a warranty which is a promise from the manufacturer that the car will perform as it should. Most of us never read the warranty until it is too late. In fact, because warranties are often difficult to read and understand, most of us don't really know what our warranty offers.

To keep your warranty in effect, you must operate and maintain your car according to the instructions in your owner's manual. It is important to keep a record of all maintenance performed on your car.

Be careful not to confuse a warranty with a service contract. A service contract must be purchased separately while a warranty is yours at no extra cost when you buy the car.

Warranties are difficult to compare because they contain fine print and confusing language. The following table will help you compare this year's new car warranties. Because the table does not contain all the details about each warranty, review the actual warranty to understand its fine points. You have the right to inspect a warranty before you buy—it's the law.

The table provides information on four critical items in a warranty:

The Basic Warranty covers most parts against manufacturer's defects. Tires, batteries, and items you add to the car are covered under separate warranties. The table describes coverage in terms of months and miles. For example, 48/50 means the warranty is good for 48 months or 50,000 miles, whichever comes first. This is the most important part of your warranty.

The Power Train Warranty usually lasts longer than the basic warranty. Because each manufacturer's definition of the power train is different, it is important to find out exactly what your warranty will cover. Power train coverage should include parts of the engine, transmission, and drive train. The warranty on some luxury cars will often cover some additional systems such as steering, suspension, and electrical systems.

The Corrosion Warranty usually applies only to actual holes due to rust. Read this section carefully because many corrosion warranties do not apply to what the manufacturer may describe as cosmetic rust or bad paint.

The Roadside Assistance column indicates whether or not the warranty includes a program for helping with problems on the road. In addition to mechanical failures, these programs cover such things as lockouts, jump starts, flat tires, running out of gas, and towing. Most are offered for the length of the basic warranty. Some have special limitations or added features, some of which we point out. Because each one is different, check yours carefully. If it is an option that you have to pay extra for, we don't list it.

The last column, the **Warranty Rating Index**, provides an overall assessment of this year's warranties. **The higher the Index number, the better the warranty.** The Index number incorporates the important features of each warranty. In developing the Index, we gave the most weight to the basic and power train components of the warranties. The corrosion warranty was weighted somewhat less, and roadside assistance received the least weight. We also considered special features such as the manufacturer offering free scheduled maintenance or if rental cars were offered when warranty repairs were being done.

The best ratings are in *BOLD*.

WARRANTY OFFERS THAT CAN SAVE YOU HUNDREDS

This year a few manufacturers are offering free maintainance and free wear and tear part replacement for the first three, four and even five years. These programs will save you hundreds of dollars in ownership costs.

WARRANTY COMPARISON

Manufacturer	Basic Warranty	Power Train Warranty	Corrosion Warranty	Roadside Assistance	Index	Warranty Rating
Acura	48/50	72/70	60/Unlimited	48/50	1295	Average
Audi	**48/50**	**48/50**	**144/Unlimited**	**48/Unlimited**	**1676**	**Very Good**
BMW	**48/50[2]**	**48/50**	**144/Unlimited**	**48/Unlimited**	**1772**	**Very Good**
Buick	48/50	60/100	72/100	60/100	1456	Good
Cadillac	48/50	60/100	72/100	60/100	1456	Good
Chevrolet	36/36	60/100	72/100	60/100	1352	Average
Chrysler	36/36	60/100	60/100	36/36[7]	1220	Poor
Dodge	36/36	60/100	60/100	36/36[7]	1220	Poor
Ford	36/36	60/60	60/Unlimited	60/60	1158	Poor
GMC	36/36	60/100	72/100	60/100	1352	Average
Honda	36/36	60/60	60/Unlimited	Optional	978	Very Poor
Hummer	48/50	60/100	72/100	60/100	1456	Good
Hyundai[8]	**60/60**	**120/100[11]**	**84/Unlimited**	**60/Unlimited**	**1802**	**Very Good**
Infiniti	48/60	72/70	84/Unlimited	48/Unlimited	1518	Good
Jaguar	48/50	48/50	72/Unlimited	48/50	1229	Poor
Jeep	36/36	60/100	60/100	36/36[7]	1220	Poor
Kia	60/60	120/100[11]	60/100	60/60	1580	Good
Land Rover	48/50	48/50	72/Unlimited	48/50	1229	Poor
Lexus	48/50	72/70	72/Unlimited	48/Unlimited	1412	Good
Lincoln	48/50	72/70	60/Unlimited	72/70	1361	Average
Mazda	36/36	60/60	60/Unlimited	36/36	1086	Very Poor
Mercedes-Benz	48/50	48/50	48/50	Unlimited	1191	Poor
Mercury	36/36	60/60	60/Unlimited	60/60	1158	Poor
Mini[5]	**48/50[4]**	**48/50**	**144/Unlimited**	**48/50**	**1769**	**Very Good**
Mitsubishi	**60/60[10]**	**120/100[12]**	**84/100**	**60/Unlimited**	**1662**	**Very Good**
Nissan	36/36	60/60	60/Unlimited	36/36	1086	Very Poor
Porsche	48/50	48/50	96/80	48/50	1185	Poor
Saab	48/50	60/100	72/100[6]	60/100	1516	Good
Scion	36/36[9]	60/60	60/Unlimited	Optional	990	Very Poor
Smart	24/24	24/24	48/50	24/Unlimited	631	Very Poor
Subaru[5]	36/36	60/60	60/Unlimited	36/36	1158	Poor
Suzuki	36/36	84/100	60/Unlimited	36/36	1278	Average
Toyota	36/36	60/60	60/Unlimited	Optional	978	Very Poor
Volkswagen	**36/36[4]**	**60/60**	**144/Unlimited**	**36/36**	**1608**	**Very Good**
Volvo[3]	**48/50[1]**	**48/50**	**144/Unlimited**	**48/Unlimited**	**1880**	**Very Good**

Factors Improving Warranty*
[1] Free scheduled maintenance up to 60,000 miles
[2] Free scheduled maintenance 48/50
[3] Wear Items 60/60
[4] Free schedule maintenance 36/36
[5] Wear Items 36/36
[6] 9-3 model 120/Unlimited
[7] Roadside assistance for parts covered under powertrain warranty 50/100
[8] Wear Items 12/12
[9] First two scheduled maintenance free

Factors Reducing Warranty
[10] Lancer Ralliart 36/36
[11] Subsequent owners 60/60
[12] Subsequent owners 60/60, Ralliart 60/60 non-transferable

*In descending order of improvement value.

SECRET WARRANTIES

If dealers report a number of complaints about a certain part and the manufacturer determines that the problem is due to faulty design or assembly, the manufacturer may permit dealers to repair the problem at no charge to the customer even though the warranty is expired. In the past, this practice was often reserved for customers who made a big fuss. The availability of the free repair was never publicized, which is why we call these "secret warranties."

Manufacturers deny the existence of secret warranties. They call these free repairs "policy adjustments" or "goodwill service." Whatever they are called, most consumers never hear about them.

Many secret warranties are disclosed in service bulletins that the manufacturers send to dealers. These bulletins outline free repair or reimbursement programs, as well as other problems and their possible causes and solutions.

Service bulletins from many manufacturers may be on file at the National Highway Traffic Safety Administration. You can visit www.nhtsa.gov to access NHTSA's Service Bulletin database.

If you find that a secret warranty is in effect and repairs are being made at no charge after the warranty has expired, contact the Center for Auto Safety, 1825 Connecticut Ave. NW, #330, Washington, DC 20009. They will publish the information so others can benefit.

Disclosure Laws: Spurred by the proliferation of secret warranties and the failure of the FTC to take action, California, Connecticut, Virginia, Wisconsin, and Maryland have passed legislation that requires consumers to be notified of secret warranties on their cars. Several other states have introduced similar warranty bills.

Typically, the laws require the following: direct notice to consumers within a specified time after the adoption of a warranty adjustment policy; notice of the disclosure law to new car buyers; reimbursement within a number of years after payment to owners who paid for covered repairs before they learned of the extended warranty service; and dealers must inform consumers who complain about a covered defect that it is eligible for repair under warranty.

If you live in a state with a secret warranty law already in effect, write your state attorney general's office (in care of your state capital) for information. To encourage passage of such a bill, contact your state representative (in care of your state capital).

Some state lemon laws require dealers and manufacturers to give you copies of Technical Service Bulletins on problems affecting your vehicle. These bulletins may alert you to a secret warranty on your vehicle or help you make the case for a free repair if there isn't a secret warranty. See page 59 for an overview of your state's lemon law. If you would like to see the complete law, go to www.autosafety.org to view your state's lemon laws.

LITTLE SECRETS OF THE AUTO INDUSTRY

TIP

Every auto company makes mistakes building cars. When they do, they often issue technical service bulletins telling dealers how to fix the problem. Rarely do they publicize these fixes, many of which are offered for free, called secret warranties. The Center for Auto Safety has published a book called *Little Secrets of the Auto Industry*, a consumer guide to secret warranties. This book explains how to find out about secret warranties, offers tips for going to small claims court and getting federal and state assistance, and lists information on state secret warranty laws. To order a copy, send $17.50 to: Center for Auto Safety, Pub. Dept. CB, 1825 Connecticut Ave. NW, Suite 330, Washington, DC 20009.

KEEPING IT GOING

Comparing maintenance costs before you buy can help decide which car to purchase. These costs include preventive maintenance servicing—such as changing the oil and filters—as well as the cost of repairs after your warranty expires. Following, we enable you to compare the costs of preventive maintenance and nine likely repairs for the 2010 models.

Preventive Maintenance: The first column in the table is the periodic servicing, specified by the manufacturer, that keeps your car running properly. For example, regularly changing the oil and oil filter. Every owner's manual specifies a schedule of recommended servicing for at least the first 60,000 miles and many now go to 100,000 miles. The tables on the following pages estimate the labor cost of following this preventive maintenance schedule for 60,000 miles, the length of a typical warranty. Service parts are not included in this total.

Repairs Costs: The tables also list the costs for nine repairs that typically occur during the first 100,000 miles. There is no precise way to predict exactly when a repair will be needed. But if you keep a car for 75,000 to 100,000 miles, it is likely that you will experience most of these repairs at least once. The last column provides a relative indication of how expensive these nine repairs are for many cars. Repair cost is rated as Very Good if the total for nine repairs is in the lower fifth of all the cars rated, and Very Poor if the total is in the highest fifth.

Most repair shops use "flat-rate manuals" to estimate repair costs. These manuals list the approximate time required for repairing many items. Each automobile manufacturer publishes its own manual and there are several independent manuals as well. For many repairs, the time varies from one manual to another. Some repair shops even use different manuals for different repairs. To determine a repair

bill, a shop multiplies the time listed in its manual by its hourly labor rate and then adds the cost of parts.

Some dealers and repair shops create their own maintenance schedules which call for more frequent (and thus more expensive) servicing than the manufacturer's recommendations. If the servicing recommended by your dealer or repair shop don't match what the manufacturer recommends, make sure you understand and agree to the extra items. Our cost estimates are based on published repair times multiplied by a nationwide average labor rate of $60 per hour and include the cost of replaced parts and related adjustments.

Prices in the following tables may not predict the exact costs of these repairs. For example, labor rates for your area may be more or less than the national average. However, the prices will provide you with a relative comparison of costs for various automobiles.

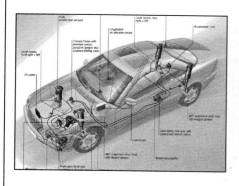

	PM Costs to 60,000 Miles	REPAIR COSTS									
		Front Brake Pads	Starter	Fuel Injector	Fuel Pump	Struts/ Shocks	Timing Belt/Chain	Water Pump	Muffler	Headlamps	Relative Repair Cost*
Subcompact											
Chevrolet Aveo	1,074	134	397	155	491	444	217	374	480	315	Good
Honda Fit	192	117	614	220	364	434	404	203	229	331	Good
Hyundai Accent	1,176	122	247	112	228	350	235	297	346	266	Vry. Gd.
Kia Rio	1,422	122	310	166	279	362	255	295	351	281	Vry. Gd.
Mazda MX-5 Miata	762	145	233	188	210	263	361	185	614	556	Good
Mini Cooper	624	149	339	155	341	421	635	442	453	351	Average
Nissan Versa	714	142	324	240	392	410	313	207	374	364	Good
Scion xB	1,206	121	364	225	377	470	563	248	217	368	Good
Scion xD	1,158	103	431	215	380	507	787	246	239	220	Average
Suzuki SX4	1,428	195	578	202	732	565	614	374	358	344	Poor
Toyota Yaris	1,122	103	371	210	382	485	401	203	210	254	Vry. Gd.
Volkswagen Beetle	504	158	637	266	485	224	387	316	238	472	Average
Compact											
Audi A4	804	170	506	251	316	488	962	319	318	406	Poor
BMW 1 Series	90	191	445	403	316	467	635	697	727	458	Vry. Pr.
BMW 3 Series	90	219	451	182	353	775	665	644	691	1,089	Vry. Pr.
Chevrolet Cobalt	468	182	332	133	430	390	564	509	613	227	Average
Chrysler PT Cruiser	696	240	202	106	317	344	436	487	275	266	Vry. Gd.
Dodge Caliber	552	197	172	99	249	406	323	156	401	240	Vry. Gd.
Ford Focus	900	177	297	88	536	258	362	180	314	320	Vry. Gd.
Ford Mustang	960	170	257	112	350	153	470	280	382	247	Vry. Gd.
Honda Civic	192	117	310	200	536	329	429	212	222	321	Vry. Gd.
Honda Civic Coupe	192	117	310	200	536	329	429	212	222	317	Vry. Gd.
Hyundai Elantra	1,194	116	295	107	228	322	206	250	261	254	Vry. Gd.
Mazda 3	732	136	259	117	581	423	355	227	716	493	Average
Mercedes-Benz C-Class	984	149	728	197	339	687	659	504	709	514	Vry. Pr.
Mitsubishi Lancer	762	154	249	274	573	580	400	428	383	420	Average
Nissan Altima Coupe	678	142	286	271	387	507	725	179	217	364	Good
Nissan Sentra	702	142	266	264	380	447	277	183	451	364	Good
Saab 9-3	288	165	368	119	474	364	246	386	336	383	Good
Scion tC	1,296	111	352	216	369	411	548	259	365	238	Good
Subaru Impreza	822	155	486	322	372	528	258	310	330	484	Average
Toyota Corolla	1,206	117	299	223	376	446	425	202	330	316	Vry. Gd.
Toyota Matrix	1,170	117	299	223	382	446	425	160	402	334	Good
Volkswagen Eos	504	146	491	312	345	448	387	485	354	354	Average
Volkswagen Jetta	426	146	484	254	269	587	398	329	481	324	Average
Volvo S40	0	167	377	236	611	530	330	329	295	374	Average
Intermediate											
Acura TSX	192	132	661	203	341	418	351	248	260	465	Good
Audi A5	648	165	556	320	402	435	1,325	265	397	337	Poor
BMW 5 Series	90	236	379	164	461	777	1,067	656	707	670	Vry. Pr.
Buick LaCrosse	474	188	352	148	588	352	523	327	982	341	Poor
Cadillac CTS	948	193	307	183	640	350	541	369	1,604	482	Vry. Pr.
Chevrolet Corvette	102	308	589	149	1,131	213	774	477	843	1,106	Vry. Pr.
Chevrolet Impala	462	185	535	234	618	455	500	369	673	308	Poor
AVERAGE OF ALL VEHICLES	**$765**	**$166**	**$388**	**$217**	**$442**	**$464**	**$571**	**$361**	**$527**	**$445**	

*A comparison of the 9 listed repair items.

	PM Costs to 60,000 Miles	REPAIR COSTS									
		Front Brake Pads	Starter	Fuel Injector	Fuel Pump	Struts/ Shocks	Timing Belt/Chain	Water Pump	Muffler	Headlamps	Relative Repair Cost*
Chevrolet Malibu	540	162	332	122	714	466	443	335	396	404	Average
Chrysler Sebring	492	151	130	96	418	262	323	267	438	255	Vry. Gd.
Dodge Avenger	468	221	130	96	418	340	323	267	463	311	Vry. Gd.
Ford Fusion	732	161	265	132	405	265	402	204	518	304	Vry. Gd.
Honda Accord	174	120	336	110	365	375	332	219	450	353	Vry. Gd.
Honda Accord Coupe	174	120	336	110	365	375	332	219	450	353	Vry. Gd.
Hyundai Sonata	1,074	128	295	133	261	395	430	215	432	299	Vry. Gd.
Infiniti EX	804	141	370	282	401	509	470	566	575	437	Poor
Infiniti G	684	141	385	265	393	555	613	441	453	963	Vry. Pr.
Kia Optima	1,164	139	309	199	303	443	453	317	449	380	Good
Lexus ES	1,380	114	379	315	387	506	1,408	1,266	431	500	Vry. Pr.
Lexus GS	1,692	119	519	284	458	569	1,795	357	761	1,224	Vry. Pr.
Lexus IS	1,476	119	537	584	439	583	1,684	357	788	496	Vry. Pr.
Lincoln MKZ	732	161	235	174	330	260	775	870	894	442	Poor
Mazda 6	738	135	363	188	345	322	327	202	336	660	Good
Mercury Milan	732	161	265	132	330	260	402	204	518	424	Vry. Gd.
Mitsubishi Galant	594	128	283	211	282	279	206	313	323	355	Vry. Gd.
Nissan Altima	678	142	286	271	387	507	725	179	217	364	Good
Nissan Maxima	714	142	298	284	399	522	649	285	243	413	Average
Toyota Avalon	1,200	136	355	307	394	434	1,164	304	310	373	Poor
Toyota Camry	1,260	113	340	235	399	446	500	266	347	338	Good
Volkswagen CC	732	142	635	385	340	584	230	554	354	673	Poor
Volkswagen Passat	498	130	635	385	402	584	195	531	373	353	Average
Volvo V70	0	162	358	281	629	596	380	291	471	481	Average
Large											
BMW 7 Series	90	224	715	216	353	994	1,631	390	978	1,375	Vry. Pr.
Buick Lucerne	510	195	466	148	455	254	401	272	521	344	Good
Cadillac DTS	552	174	475	114	506	450	303	549	936	892	Vry. Pr.
Cadillac STS	756	252	361	352	705	447	649	357	1,652	656	Vry. Pr.
Chrysler 300	606	206	179	127	210	316	374	362	822	249	Good
Dodge Challenger	816	181	166	138	250	450	377	369	1,109	241	Average
Dodge Charger	564	217	179	127	210	205	380	362	884	300	Good
Ford Taurus	432	149	295	162	327	372	775	882	611	396	Poor
Infiniti M	792	153	385	236	429	592	716	658	560	1,288	Vry. Pr.
Jaguar XF	594	173	763	124	840	437	1,524	236	339	520	Vry. Pr.
Lexus LS	1,788	141	934	406	495	626	901	319	514	768	Vry. Pr.
Lincoln MKS	732	184	289	165	269	336	706	830	940	950	Vry. Pr.
Lincoln Town Car	792	184	354	202	589	414	535	190	410	401	Average
Mercedes-Benz S-Class	792	158	730	226	524	3,091	722	549	813	1,340	Vry. Pr.
Mercury Grand Marquis	864	184	354	202	589	414	625	220	284	143	Good
Volvo S80	0	162	379	370	629	567	467	325	471	481	Poor
Minivan											
Chrysler Town and Country	612	155	148	148	197	359	322	432	457	272	Vry. Gd.
Dodge Grand Caravan	936	155	148	148	209	353	322	432	457	131	Vry. Gd.
Honda Odyssey	534	132	762	140	400	512	325	395	534	329	Average
Kia Rondo	948	191	309	181	273	451	423	317	432	345	Good
AVERAGE OF ALL VEHICLES	**$765**	**$166**	**$388**	**$217**	**$442**	**$464**	**$571**	**$361**	**$527**	**$445**	

*A comparison of the 9 listed repair items.

	PM Costs to 60,000 Miles	REPAIR COSTS									
		Front Brake Pads	Starter	Fuel Injector	Fuel Pump	Struts/ Shocks	Timing Belt/Chain	Water Pump	Muffler	Headlamps	Relative Repair Cost*
Kia Sedona	1,212	140	395	170	336	509	1,048	265	500	313	Average
Mazda 5	798	136	259	160	303	352	333	163	380	693	Good
Toyota Sienna	1,230	132	421	306	718	486	1,156	837	317	309	Vry. Pr.
Small SUV											
Acura RDX	552	132	433	116	408	368	338	238	357	860	Average
Chevrolet HHR	528	222	332	125	494	430	414	509	583	318	Average
Ford Escape	930	143	285	120	385	237	342	180	271	284	Vry. Gd.
Honda CR-V	180	132	855	110	347	394	402	236	342	290	Good
Honda Element	168	121	429	110	366	368	330	290	413	270	Vry. Gd.
Hyundai Tucson	648	118	403	107	327	422	220	262	588	252	Vry. Gd.
Jeep Compass	744	149	148	102	305	385	323	181	376	275	Vry. Gd.
Jeep Liberty	762	185	180	133	502	229	662	205	389	150	Vry. Gd.
Jeep Patriot	816	149	148	102	305	385	323	181	376	246	Vry. Gd.
Jeep Wrangler	552	185	140	166	261	294	292	153	273	162	Vry. Gd.
Kia Sportage	990	134	210	231	281	431	303	372	364	224	Vry. Gd.
Mazda Tribute	786	142	309	106	470	191	345	175	303	308	Vry. Gd.
Mercury Mariner	942	193	309	144	385	237	342	180	276	302	Vry. Gd.
Mitsubishi Outlander	720	152	228	260	720	513	265	452	339	524	Average
Subaru Forester	1,014	138	492	172	378	468	222	310	350	356	Good
Suzuki Grand Vitara	1,110	154	472	309	707	455	806	815	463	338	Vry. Pr.
Toyota RAV4	1,194	121	364	210	479	428	494	256	222	246	Good
Mid-Size SUV											
Acura MDX	552	132	377	290	388	402	283	359	295	793	Average
BMW X3	90	223	463	193	443	823	545	650	957	611	Vry. Pr.
BMW X5	90	254	421	182	347	1,123	578	692	807	1,545	Vry. Pr.
Buick Enclave	570	207	384	438	523	401	628	334	467	390	Poor
Cadillac SRX	606	182	307	243	797	338	529	282	1,712	718	Vry. Pr.
Chevrolet Equinox	558	159	427	468	703	761	470	430	975	510	Vry. Pr.
Dodge Journey	456	129	148	120	410	310	356	156	552	272	Vry. Gd.
Dodge Nitro	660	227	180	139	481	230	662	235	431	240	Good
Ford Edge	852	177	289	192	416	327	583	870	798	275	Poor
Ford Explorer	912	156	337	202	473	452	569	274	350	260	Good
GMC Terrain	558	158	427	463	703	769	470	322	970	463	Vry. Pr.
Honda Pilot	588	132	548	170	410	492	295	395	630	482	Average
Hummer H3	618	228	573	244	495	292	700	292	564	320	Average
Hyundai Santa Fe	1,068	110	412	227	313	394	358	329	530	497	Average
Hyundai Veracruz	1,032	135	345	217	232	403	1,071	199	432	333	Average
Infiniti FX	750	121	388	227	386	587	514	201	298	1,194	Poor
Lexus GX	1,560	117	493	279	395	473	256	365	396	353	Average
Lincoln MKX	828	177	289	192	417	367	583	870	798	392	Poor
Mazda CX-7	714	164	277	438	219	365	442	151	823	682	Average
Mazda CX-9	798	164	386	182	196	393	650	693	463	893	Poor
Mercury Mountaineer	828	156	337	202	461	454	569	274	350	309	Good
Nissan Pathfinder	666	142	395	259	459	299	538	255	321	378	Good
Nissan Rogue	684	142	268	259	314	385	859	200	603	317	Average
Nissan Xterra	822	142	344	295	364	265	559	256	321	344	Good
AVERAGE OF ALL VEHICLES	**$765**	**$166**	**$388**	**$217**	**$442**	**$464**	**$571**	**$361**	**$527**	**$445**	

*A comparison of the 9 listed repair items.

	PM Costs to 60,000 Miles	REPAIR COSTS									
		Front Brake Pads	Starter	Fuel Injector	Fuel Pump	Struts/ Shocks	Timing Belt/Chain	Water Pump	Muffler	Headlamps	Relative Repair Cost*
Porsche Cayenne	750	257	432	223	366	1,058	1,095	275	1,020	440	Vry. Pr.
Subaru Tribeca	1,170	151	354	187	348	516	302	442	330	443	Good
Toyota 4Runner	1,230	123	407	309	383	484	898	334	219	393	Average
Toyota Highlander	1,314	115	400	357	491	501	1,648	1,251	1,080	360	Vry. Pr.
Volkswagen Touareg	510	230	412	314	253	768	435	374	809	475	Poor
Volvo XC90	0	178	361	296	617	598	461	301	612	486	Poor
Large SUV											
Audi Q7	510	234	624	279	377	1,026	940	429	673	363	Vry. Pr.
Cadillac Escalade	720	225	529	215	534	410	582	414	705	924	Vry. Pr.
Cadillac Escalade ESV	720	225	529	215	594	370	582	414	1,038	924	Vry. Pr.
Chevrolet Suburban	690	225	488	215	594	379	498	414	736	322	Poor
Chevrolet Tahoe	696	225	488	215	594	309	582	414	699	323	Poor
Chevrolet Traverse	558	208	387	438	538	401	691	322	467	390	Poor
Ford Expedition	912	202	254	125	473	482	724	240	527	333	Average
Ford Flex	732	184	289	165	320	357	625	830	657	469	Poor
GMC Acadia	534	204	381	173	565	407	565	357	811	390	Poor
GMC Yukon	690	225	488	215	594	388	582	414	699	345	Poor
GMC Yukon XL	702	225	488	215	594	345	582	414	736	287	Poor
Infiniti QX56	762	142	443	217	447	315	919	219	475	853	Poor
Jeep Commander	660	229	113	133	365	265	662	235	505	310	Good
Jeep Grand Cherokee	1,224	191	159	120	453	358	675	231	472	185	Good
Land Rover Range Rover	1,030	302	624	356	505	2,007	587	347	348	848	Vry. Pr.
Lincoln Navigator	888	202	254	125	473	492	724	240	527	1,093	Poor
Mercedes-Benz GL-Class	930	228	760	178	331	2,095	626	588	630	538	Vry. Pr.
Nissan Armada	912	190	443	217	447	315	1,009	219	475	433	Poor
Toyota FJ Cruiser	1,554	136	371	295	477	432	1,218	357	308	308	Poor
Toyota Sequoia	1,266	135	523	285	740	390	340	453	360	353	Average
Compact Pickup											
Chevrolet Colorado	534	229	699	360	559	293	904	311	637	209	Poor
Dodge Dakota	636	123	138	121	635	270	662	217	277	230	Vry. Gd.
Ford Ranger	888	163	223	180	469	191	368	192	373	123	Vry. Gd.
GMC Canyon	540	229	699	360	559	243	1,012	311	637	209	Vry. Pr.
Nissan Frontier	714	142	280	271	459	255	455	197	433	370	Good
Toyota Tacoma	1,566	115	407	276	707	340	1,111	301	413	341	Poor
Standard Pickup											
Cadillac Escalade EXT	756	234	529	227	594	712	582	414	1,038	924	Vry. Pr.
Chevrolet Avalanche	756	224	488	215	594	317	498	414	1,051	322	Poor
Chevrolet Silverado	762	224	466	264	585	379	443	380	658	344	Poor
Dodge Ram Pickup	792	201	141	121	373	304	662	217	351	260	Vry. Gd.
Ford F-150	552	175	245	202	381	152	661	255	419	260	Good
GMC Sierra	744	224	466	264	591	379	443	380	607	344	Average
Honda Ridgeline	636	132	530	140	452	403	325	419	402	284	Good
Nissan Titan	912	142	443	217	483	272	919	219	429	433	Average
Toyota Tundra	1,626	135	571	321	740	423	469	351	478	302	Poor
AVERAGE OF ALL VEHICLES	$765	$166	$388	$217	$442	$464	$571	$361	$527	$445	

*A comparison of the 9 listed repair items.

SERVICE CONTRACTS

Service contracts are one of the most expensive options you can buy. In fact, service contracts are a major profit source for many dealers.

A service contract is not a warranty. It is more like an insurance plan that, in theory, covers repairs that are not covered by your warranty or that occur after the warranty runs out. They are often inaccurately referred to as "extended warranties."

Service contracts are generally a poor value. The companies who sell contracts are very sure that, on average, your repairs will cost considerably less that what you pay for the contract—if not, they wouldn't be in business.

Here are some important questions to ask before buying a service contract:

How reputable is the company responsible for the contract? If the company offering the contract goes out of business, you will be out of luck. The company may be required to be insured but they may not. Find out if they are insured and by whom. Check with your Better Business Bureau or office of consumer affairs if you are not sure of a company's reputation. Service contracts from car and insurance companies are more likely to remain in effect than those from independent companies.

Exactly what does the contract cover and for how long? Service contracts vary considerably—different items are covered and different time limits are offered. This is true even among service contracts offered by the same company. For example, one company has plans that range from 4 years/36,000 miles maximum coverage to 6 years/100,000 miles maximum coverage, with other options for only power train coverage. Make sure you know what components are covered because if a breakdown occurs on a part that is not covered, you are responsible for the repairs.

If you plan to resell your car in a few years, you won't want to purchase a long-running service contract. Some service contracts automatically cancel when you resell the car, while others require a hefty transfer fee before extending privileges to the new owner.

Some automakers offer a "menu" format, which lets you pick the items you want covered in your service contract. Find out if the contract pays for preventive maintenance, towing, and rental car expenses. If not written into the contract, assume they are not covered.

Make sure the contract clearly specifies how you can reach the company. Knowing this before you purchase a service contract can save you time and aggravation in the future.

How will the repair bills be paid? It is best to have the service contractor pay bills directly. Some contracts require you to pay the repair bill, and reimburse you later.

Where can the car be serviced? Can you take the car to any mechanic if you have trouble on the road? What if you move?

What other costs can be expected? Most service contracts will have a deductible expense. Compare deductibles on various plans. Also, some companies charge the deductible for each individual repair while other companies pay per visit, regardless of the number of repairs being made.

What are your responsibilities? Make sure you know what you have to do to uphold the contract. For example if you have to follow the manufacturer's recommended maintenance, keep detailed records or the contract could void. You will find your specific responsibilities in the contact. Be sure to have the seller point them out.

One alternative to buying a service contract is to deposit the cost of the contract into a savings account. If the car needs a major repair not covered by your warranty, the money in your account will cover the cost. Most likely, you'll be building up your down payment for your next car!

TIPS FOR DEALING WITH A MECHANIC

Call around. Don't choose a shop simply because it's nearby. Calling a few shops may turn up estimates cheaper by half.

Don't necessarily go for the lowest price. A good rule is to eliminate the highest and lowest estimates; the mechanic with the highest estimate is probably charging too much, and the lowest may be cutting too many corners.

Check the shop's reputation. Call your local consumer affairs agency and the Better Business Bureau. They don't have records on every shop, but unfavorable reports on a shop should disqualify it.

Look for certification. Mechanics can be certified by the National Institute for Automotive Service Excellence, an industry-wide yardstick for competence. Certification is offered in eight areas of repair and shops with certified mechanics are allowed to advertise this fact. However, make sure the mechanic working on your car is certified for the repair you need.

Take a look around. A well-kept shop reflects pride in workmanship. A skilled and efficient mechanic would probably not work in a messy shop.

Don't sign a blank check. The service order you sign should have specific instructions or describe your vehicle's symptoms. Avoid signing a vague work order. Be sure you are called for final approval before the shop does extra work. Many states require a written estimate signed by you and require that the shop get your permission for repairs that exceed the estimate by 10%.

Show interest. Ask about the repair. But don't act like an expert if you don't really understand what's wrong. Express your satisfaction. If you're happy with the work, compliment the mechanic and ask for him or her the next time you come in. You will get to know each other and the mechanic will get to know your vehicle.

Take a test-drive. Before you pay for a major repair, you should take the car for a test-drive. The few extra minutes you spend checking out the repair could save you a trip back to the mechanic. If you find that the problem still exists, there will be no question that the repair wasn't properly completed.

REPAIR PROTECTION BY CREDIT CARD

Paying your auto repair bills by credit card can provide a much needed recourse if you are having problems with an auto mechanic. According to federal law, you have the right to withhold payment for sloppy or incorrect repairs. Of course, you may withhold no more than the amount of the repair in dispute.

In order to use this right, you must first try to work out the problem with the mechanic. Also, unless the credit card company owns the repair shop (this might be the case with gasoline credit cards used at gas stations), two other conditions must be met. First, the repair shop must be in your home state (or within 100 miles of your current address), and second, the cost of repairs must be over $50. Until the problem is settled or resolved in court, the credit card company cannot charge you interest or penalties on the amount in dispute.

If you decide to take action, send a letter to the credit card company and a copy to the repair shop, explaining the details of the problem and what you want as settlement. Send the letter by certified mail with a return receipt requested.

Sometimes the credit card company or repair shop will attempt to put a "bad mark" on your credit record if you use this tactic. Legally, you can't be reported as delinquent if you've given the credit card company notice of your dispute, but a creditor can report that you are disputing your bill, which goes in your record. However, you have the right to challenge any incorrect information and add your side of the story to your file.

For more information, write to the Federal Trade Commission, Credit Practices Division, 601 Pennsylvania Avenue, NW, Washington, DC 20580.

TIRE RATINGS

Buying tires has become an infrequent task because today's radial tires last much longer than the tires of the past. Surprisingly, a tire has to perform more functions simultaneously than any other part of the car (steering, bearing the load, cushioning the ride, and stopping).

Because comparing tires is difficult, many consumers mistakenly use price and brand name to determine quality. Because there are hundreds of tire lines to choose from, and only a few tire manufacturers, the difference in many tires may only be the brand name.

But there is help. The U.S. government requires tires to be rated according to their safety and expected mileage.

Treadwear, traction, and heat resistance grades are printed on the sidewall and are attached to the tire on a paper label. Ask the dealer for the grades of the tires they sell. Using this rating system, a sampling of top rated tires follows on page 48.

Treadwear: The treadwear grade gives you an idea of the mileage you can expect from a tire. It is shown in numbers–720, 700, 680, 660, and so forth. Higher numbers mean longer tire life. A tire with a grade of 600 should give you twice as much mileage as one rated 300. Use the treadwear grade as a relative basis of comparison.

Traction: Traction grades of AA, A, B, and C describe the tire's ability to stop on wet surfaces. Tires graded AA will stop on a wet road in a shorter distance than tires graded B or C. Tires rated C have poor traction.

Heat Resistance: Heat resistance is graded A, B, and C. An A rating means the tire will run cooler than one rated B or C and be less likely to fail if driven over long distances at highway speeds. Tires that run cooler tend to be more fuel-efficient. Hot-running tires can result in blowouts or tread separation.

TIRE CARE

Pump 'em Up: An estimated one-third of us are driving on underinflated tires. Because even good tires lose air, it is important to check your tire pressure monthly. Underinflated tires can be dangerous, use more fuel and cause premature tire failure. When checking your tires, be sure to use an accurate gauge and inflate to the pressure indicated in your owner's manual, not the maximum pressure printed on your tire.

When to Replace: If any part of Lincoln's head is visible when you insert the top of a penny into a tread groove, it's time to replace the tire. While this old rule of thumb is still valid, today's tires also have a built-in wear indicator. A series of horizontal bars appear across the surface when the tread depth reaches the danger zone.

GETTING THE BEST PRICE

The price of the same tire can vary depending on where you shop so shopping around is vital to finding a good buy. Most tire ads appear in the sports section of your Wednesday and Saturday daily newspaper. You are most likely to find the best prices at independent tire dealers who carry a variety of tire brands.

The price of a tire is based on its size, and tires come in as many as nine sizes. For example, the list price of the same tire can range from $74.20 to $134.35, depending on its size.

To get the best buy:

1. Check to see which manufacturer makes the least expensive "off brand." Only a few manufacturers produce the over 1,800 types of tires sold in the U.S.

2. Don't forget to compare balancing and mounting costs. These extra charges can add up to more than $25 or be offered at no cost.

3. Never pay list price for a tire. A good rule of thumb is to pay at least 30-40 percent off the suggested list price.

4. Use the treadwear grade the same way you would the "unit price" in a supermarket. The tire with the lowest cost per grade point is the best value. For example, if tire A costs $100 and has a treadwear grade of 600, and tire B costs $80 and has a treadwear grade of 300, tire A is the better buy, even though its initial cost is more.

Tire A: $100÷600=$0.17 per point
Tire B: $80÷300=$0.27 per point

Where you live is a key factor in how long your tires will last. In addition to construction and design, tire wear is affected by the level of abrasive material in the road surface. Generally, the road surfaces of the West Coast, Great Lakes region, and northern New England are easiest on tires. The Appalachian and Rocky Mountain areas are usually hardest on tires.

HOW TO READ A TIRE

Tire Type and Size: The most important information on a tire are the letters and the numbers indicating its type and size.

1. Tire Type: The P at the beginning of the tire size indicates that the tire is a passenger vehicle tire. LT indicates light truck tire, and T indicates a temporary or spare tire.

2. Tire Width is the first part of the number and is measured in millimeters, from sidewall to sidewall.

3. Tire Height is the next number and tells you the height of the tire from the bead to the tread. This is described as a percentage of the tire width. In our example, the tire's height is 65 percent of its width. The smaller the aspect ratio, the wider the tire in relation to its height.

4. Tire Construction designates how the tire was made. R indicates radial construction which is the most common type. Older tires were made using diagonal bias D or bias belted B construction, but these tire types are no longer used on passenger vehicles.

5. Wheel Diameter identifies the wheel rim diameter (in inches-15) needed for this tire.

6. Load Index: The load rating indicates the maximum load for that tire. A higher number indicates a higher load capacity. The rating 95, for example, corresponds to a load capacity of 1521 pounds. Larger vehicles, SUVs and pickups need tires with a higher load capacity.

Labels: 1. Tire Type, 2. Width, 3. Height, 4. Construction, 5. Wheel Diameter, 6. Load Index, 7. Speed Rating, 9. U.S. DOT Tire Identification Number, 10. Tire ply composition and material, 11. Treadwear, traction, and temperature grades, 12. Max. Load, 13. Max. Pressure. Tire reads: P215/65R15 95H

7. Speed Rating indicates the maximum speed that the tire can sustain a ten minute endurance test without being in danger. All passenger car tires are rated at least S and pass the test at speeds up to 112 mph. Other ratings are as follows: T up to 118 mph, H up to 130 mph, V up to 149 mph and Z 150 mph or higher. Other types of tires, temporary spares and snow tires are lower on the rating scale.

8. Severe Conditions: M+S indicates the tire meets the Rubber Manu. Association's definition of a mud and snow tire. There are no performance tests for this standard. If the tire has an M+S and a "mountain and snowflake" symbol then the traction is at least 10% bestter than the regular version of the tire. These symbols are not in the above example.

9. Tire Identification Number
Example: DOT NJ HR 2AF 5203
The letters DOT certify compliance with all applicable safety standards established by the U.S. Department of Transportation. The next four characters is a code where the first two characters indicate the manufacturer and the second two characters indicate the plant where the tire was made.

Next you may see an optional string of three to four characters. Most manufacturers use these to record company specific information they use to identify their products or that can be used to identify tires in the market for recall purposes.

The last four digits determine the week and year the tire was made. The digits 5203 would signify that the tire was made during the 52nd week of 2003. Don't buy tires more than two years old. Tires naturally degrade with age, so you want the newest possible tires for the longest life (and safe operation.)

10. Tire Ply Composition and Material indicates the type of cord (polyester or steel) and number of plies in the tire, 4-ply, 6-ply, 8-ply, for both the tread and the sidewall.

11. Treadwear, Traction and Temperature Grades are three performance grades assigned to the tire are are the best way to truly evaluate the tires expected performance in these three critical areas. See page 46 for more information.

12. Max Load Limit tells you the cold inflation load limit in lbs. (pounds) and in kg (kilograms). The number corresponds to the load index.

13. Max Pressure is the maximum recommended pressure in psi (pounds per square inch) and in kPa (kilopascals). However, this is not the tire pressure for your car. You must check your owner's manual for the proper tire pressure for the tires on your car.

A Sampling of Top Rated Tires

Brand Name	Model	Description	Traction	Heat	Treadwear
Michelin	Hydroedge	ALL	A	B	800
Pirelli	P4 Four Seasons	ALL	A	B	760
Goodyear	Assurance Tripletred	ALL	A	B	740
Michelin	Harmony	ALL	A	B	740
Michelin	X Radial	ALL	A	B	740
Michelin	Destiny	ALL	A	B	740
Michelin	Agility	ALL	A	B	740
Big-O	Legacy Tour Plus (S & T Rated)	ALL	A	B	720
Vogue	Wide Trac Touring II	S-RATED	A	B	720
Big-O	Legacy Tour Plus	P185,195,205 & 215/70R14 T	A	B	700
Big-O	Legacy Tour Plus	P205,215/65R15 T	A	B	700
Big-O	Legacy Tour Plus	P205,215,225 & 235/70R15 T	A	B	700
Big-O	Legacy Tour Plus	P255 & 215/60R16 T	A	B	700
Big-O	Legacy Tour Plus	P215/65R16 T	A	B	700
Big-O	Legacy Tour Plus	P195/65R14 T	A	B	700
Big-O	Legacy Tour Plus	P195/65R15 T	A	B	700
Big-O	Dueler H/L Alenza "T"	ALL	A	B	700
Big-O	Turanza Ls "T"	ALL	A	B	700
Co-Op	Goldenmark Luxury Touring (T)	ALL	A	B	700
Cooper	Lifeliner STE	ALL	A	B	700
Cordovan	Century	ALL	A	B	700
Cordovan	Grand Spirit Touring LS	ALL	A	B	700
Delta	Esteem XLE	P235/75R15	A	B	700
Goodyear	Assurance Comfortred	ALL	A	B	700
Hankook	Optimo H727	ALL	A	B	700
Kelly	Navigator Platinum TE	ALL EXCEPT	A	B	700
Laramie	Grandeur Touring Gt 60/65/70 Ser.	14 -16	A	B	700
Lee	Ultra Tour LS	ALL	A	B	700
Mastercraft	Touring LX	ALL	A	B	700
Mentor	Vantage Touring LE	ALL	A	B	700
Michelin	Cross Terrain Suv S-Rated	ALL	A	B	700
Monarch	Ultra Tour LS	ALL	A	B	700
Multi-Mile	Excel	ALL	A	B	700
National	Ovation	P235/75R15	A	B	700
Neutral	Touring LST	ALL OTHERS	A	B	700
Republic	Ultra Tour LS	ALL	A	B	700
Spartan	Avista (S & T)	ALL EXCEPT	A	B	700
Spartan	Avista	P205/65R16 94T	A	B	700
Spartan	Avista	P225/60R16 97S	A	B	700
Toyo	800 Ultra	ALL	A	B	700
Yokohama	Avid TRZ	P185/60R14	A	B	700
Yokohama	Avid TRZ	P185/60R15	A	B	700
Yokohama	Avid TRZ	P185/65R14	A	B	700
Yokohama	Avid TRZ	P195/60R15	A	B	700
Yokohama	Avid TRZ	P195/65R15	A	B	700
Yokohama	Avid TRZ	P195/70R14	A	B	700
Yokohama	Avid TRZ	P205/55R16	A	B	700
Yokohama	Avid TRZ	P205/60R15	A	B	700
Yokohama	Avid TRZ	P205/60R16	A	B	700
Yokohama	Avid TRZ	P205/65R15	A	B	700
Yokohama	Avid TRZ	P205/65R16	A	B	700
Yokohama	Avid TRZ	P205/70R15	A	B	700
Yokohama	Avid TRZ	P215/55R16	A	B	700
Yokohama	Avid TRZ	P215/60R15	A	B	700
Yokohama	Avid TRZ	P215/60R16	A	B	700
Yokohama	Avid TRZ	P215/65R15	A	B	700

For a complete listing of all the tires on the market, you can call the Auto Safety Hot Line toll free, at 888-327-4236 or 800-424-9153 (TTY). Or, go to www.safercar.gov

! WARNING !

As tires age, they naturally dry out and can become potentially dangerous. Some experts recommend getting rid of a six-year-old tire no matter what condition it is in. Recently, a national news organization went undercover and found 12 year old tires for sale, so be sure to check your tire date before purchasing. Ask for tires that are less than one year old.

*I*nsurance is a big part of ownership expenses, yet it's often forgotten in the show-room. As you shop, remember that the car's design and accident history may affect your insurance rates. Some cars cost less to insure because experience has shown that they are damaged less, less expensive to fix after a collision, or stolen less.

Shop Around: You can save hundreds of dollars by shopping around for insurance.

There are a number of factors that determine what coverage will cost you. A car's design can affect both the chances and severity of an accident. For example, a well-designed bumper may escape damage in a low-speed crash. Some cars are easier to repair than others or may have less expensive parts. Cars with four doors tend to be damaged less than cars with two doors.

Other factors that effect your insurance costs include:

Your Annual Mileage: The more you drive, the more your vehicle will be "exposed" to a potential accident. Driving less than 7,500 miles per year often gets a discount. Ask your insurer if they offer this option.

Where You Drive: If you regularly drive and park in the city, you will most likely pay more than if you drive in rural areas.

Youthful Drivers: Usually the highest premiums are paid by male drivers under the age of 25. Whether or not the under-25-year-old male is married also affects insurance rates. (Married males pay less.) As the driver gets older, rates are lowered.

Insurance discounts and surcharges depend upon the way a vehicle is traditionally driven. Sports cars, for example, are usually surcharged due, in part, to the typical driving habits of their owners. Four-door sedans and station wagons generally merit discounts.

Not all companies offer discounts or surcharges, and many cars receive neither. Some companies offer a discount or impose a surcharge on collision premiums only. Others apply discounts and surcharges on both collision and comprehensive coverage. Discounts and surcharges usually range from 10–30 percent. Remember that one company may offer a discount on a particular car while another may not.

TIP

TYPES OF COVERAGE

Collision Insurance: This pays for the damage to your car after an accident.

Comprehensive Physical Damage Insurance: This pays for damages when your car is stolen or damaged by fire, flood, or other perils.

Property Damage Liability: This pays claims and defense costs if your car damages someone else's property.

Medical Payments Insurance: This pays for your car's occupants' medical expenses resulting from an accident.

Bodily Injury Liability: This provides money to pay claims against you and to pay for the cost of your legal defense if your car injures or kills someone.

Uninsured Motorists Protection: This pays for injuries caused by an uninsured or a hit-and-run driver.

REDUCING INSURANCE COSTS

Get Your Discounts: After you have shopped around and found the best deal by comparing the costs of different coverages, be sure you get all the discounts you are entitled to.

Most insurance companies offer discounts of 5 to 30 percent on various parts of your insurance bill. Ask your insurance company for a complete list of the discounts that it offers. These can vary by company and from state to state.

Here are some of the most common insurance discounts:

Driver Education/Defensive Driving Courses: Discounts for completing a state-approved driver education course can mean a $40 reduction in the cost of coverage. Discounts of 5–15 percent are available in some states to those who complete a defensive driving course.

Good Student Discounts of up to 25 percent for full-time high school or college students who are in the upper 20 percent of their class, on the dean's list, or have a B or better grade point average.

Good Driver Discounts are available to drivers with an accident and violation-free record, (or no incidents in 3 years).

Mature Driver Credit: Drivers ages 50 and older may qualify for up to a 10 percent discount or a lower price bracket.

Sole Female Driver: Some companies offer discounts of 10 percent for females, ages 30 to 64, who are the only driver in a household.

Non-Drinkers and Non-Smokers: A limited number of companies offer incentives ranging from 10–25 percent to those who abstain.

Farmer Discounts: Many companies offer farmers either a discount of 10–30 percent or a lower price bracket.

Car Pooling: Commuters sharing driving may qualify for discounts of 5–25 percent or a lower price bracket.

Children away at school don't drive the family car very often, so if they're on your policy and they're at school, let your company know. If you insure them separately, discounts of 10–40 percent or a lower price bracket are available.

Desirable Cars: Premiums are usually much higher for cars with high collision rates or that are the favorite target of thieves.

Anti-Theft Device Credits: Discounts of 5 to 15 percent are offered in some states for cars equipped with a hood lock and an alarm or a disabling device (active or passive) that prevents the car from being started.

Multipolicy and Multicar Policy Discount: Some companies offer discounts of up to 10–20 percent for insuring your home and auto with the same company, or more than one car.

First Accident Allowance: Some insurers offer a "first accident allowance," which guarantees that if a customer achieves five accident-free years, his or her rates won't go up after the first at-fault accident.

Deductibles: Opting for the largest reasonable deductible is the obvious first step in reducing premiums. Increasing your deductible to $500 from $200 could cut your collision premium

---

! DON'T SPEED !

Besides endangering the lives of your passengers and other drivers, speeding tickets will increase your insurance premium. It only takes one speeding ticket to lose your "preferred" or "good driver" discount, which requires a clean driving record. Two or more speeding tickets or accidents can increase your premium by 40% to 200%. Some insurers may simply drop your coverage. According to the Insurance Institute for Highway Safety (IIHS), you are 17% more likely to be in an accident if you have just one speeding ticket. Insurance companies know this and will charge you for it.

about 20 percent. Raising the deductible to $1,000 from $200 could lower your premium about 45 percent. The discounts may vary by company.

Collision Coverage: The older the car, the less the need for collision insurance. Consider dropping collision insurance entirely on an older car. Regardless of how much coverage you carry, the insurance company will only pay up to the car's "book value." For example, if your car requires $1,000 in repairs, but its "book value" is only $500, the insurance company is required to pay only $500.

Organizations: If you are a member of AARP, AAA, the military, a union, a professional group, an alumni association, or similar organization, you may be able to get a discount. Often insurance companies will enter joint ventures with organizations.

YOUNG DRIVERS

Each year, teenagers account for about 15 percent of highway deaths. According to the Insurance Institute for Highway Safety (IIHS), the highest driver death rate per 100,000 people is among 18-year-olds. Parents need to make sure their children are fully prepared to be competent, safe drivers before letting them out on the road. All states issue learner's permits. However, only 35 states and the District of Columbia require permits before getting a driver's license. It isn't difficult for teenagers to get a license and only 14 states prohibit teenagers from driving during night and early morning. Call your state's MVA for young driver laws.

AUTO THEFT

The Highway Loss Data Institute (HLDI) regularly compiles statistics on motor vehicle thefts. Using the frequency of theft claims per 1,000 insured vehicle, the HLDI lists the following as the most and least stolen vehicles among the 2006-2008 models.

Most Stolen	Claim Frequency*
Cadillac Escalade EXT 4dr 4WD	13.2
Cadillac Escalade 4dr & ESV 4dr 4WD	12.9
Dodge Magnum	12.8
Dodge Charger	11.2
Cadillac Escalade 4dr 4WD	11.0
Ford F-250 supercrew 4WD	10.8
Dodge Magnum HEMI	10.2
Infiniti G37 2dr	10.1
Honda S2000 convertible	8.7

Least Stolen	
Acura 3.5 RL 4dr 4wd	0.6
Subaru Forester 4dr 4WD	0.7
Saturn Vue 4dr	0.7
Volkswagen New Beetle	0.7
Toyota Sienna 4WD	0.7
Toyota Prius Hybrid	0.8
BMW 5 series 4dr 4WD	0.8
Mercedes E class 4dr 4WD	0.8
Dodge Grand Caravan	0.8
Pontiac Vibe	0.8
Average All Passenger Vehicles	**2.41**

*Claim Frequency means the number of vehicles stolen per 1000 insured vehicles, for example on average 13 Cadillac Escalade EXT 4dr 4WD are stolen or broken into for every 1,000 insured.
Source: Highway Loss Data Institute (www.iihs.org)

BUMPERS

The main purpose of the bumper is to protect your car in low-speed collisions. Despite this intention, many of us have been victims of a $500-$2500 repair bill resulting from a seemingly minor impact. The federal government used to require that automakers equip cars with bumpers capable of withstanding up to 5 mph crashes with no damage. Unfortunately, in the early eighties, under pressure from car companies, the government rolled back this requirement. Now, the federal law only requires car companies to build bumpers to protect only cars in 2.5 mph collisions—about the speed at which we walk. This rollback has cost consumers millions of dollars in increased insurance premiums and repair costs.

The good news is that Canada has a 5 mph (8k) standard and many car companies use the same designs in models sold in the U.S. In addition, the state of California requires that companies disclose which bumpers meet the old 5 mph standard which has motivated some companies to build better bumper systems.

In order to see how well bumpers actually protect our vehicles, the Insurance Institute for Highway Safety conducts four types of bumper tests: front and rear straight-on at 6 mph and front and rear corner impacts at 3 mph.

These results are rather startling when you consider that the sole purpose of a bumper is to protect a car from damage in low-speed collisions. As the Institute's tests show, there is no correlation between the price of the car and how well the bumper worked.

Unfortunately, we can't simply look at a bumper and determine how good it will be at doing its job—protecting a car from inevitable bumps. The solution to this problem is quite simple—require carmakers to tell the consumer the highest speed at which their car could be crashed with no damage.

Following are the repair costs for recent models tested in IIHS three and six miles per hour bumper crash tests. This gives you an indication of the huge differences in repair costs from the exact same accident. For more results, visit the Insurance Institute for Highway Safety at www.iihs.org.

REPAIR COSTS FOR RECENT MODELS IN LOW SPEED CRASHES
(Most to least expensive repairs)

Source: IIHS	Front Full 6 mph	Front Corner 3 mph	Rear Full 6 mph	Rear Corner 3 mph	Total Damage
Kia Rio	$3,701	$1,758	$3,148	$773	**$9,380**
Chevrolet Malibu	$2,092	$1,685	$3,494	$1,116	**$8,387**
Ford Fusion	$2,529	$1,889	$2,610	$1,073	**$8,101**
Hyundai Accent	$3,476	$839	$2,057	$831	**$7,203**
Honda Fit	$1,124	$1,216	$3,648	$999	**$6,987**
Toyota Yaris	$1,688	$1,167	$3,345	$474	**$6,674**
Nissan Maxima	$997	$1,787	$2,494	$1,352	**$6,630**
Mini Cooper	$2,291	$2,637	$929	$743	**$6,600**
Honda Accord	$941	$1,461	$974	$1,507	**$4,883**
Hyundai Sonata	$1,791	$1,019	$1,131	$729	**$4,670**
Chevrolet Aveo	$1,071	$1,437	$1,370	$612	**$4,490**
Mazda 6	$742	$1,437	$768	$767	**$3,714**
Subaru Legacy	$847	$850	$903	$778	**$3,378**
Smart Fortwo	$1,480	$663	$631	$507	**$3,281**

*A*mericans spend billions of dollars on vehicle repairs every year. While many of those repairs are satisfactory, there are times when getting your vehicle fixed can be a very difficult process. In fact, vehicle defects and repairs are the number one cause of consumer complaints, according to the Federal Trade Commission. This chapter is designed to help you resolve your complaint, whether it's for a new vehicle still under warranty or for one you've had for years. In addition, we offer a guide to arbitration, the names and addresses of consumer groups, federal agencies, and the manufacturers themselves. Finally, we tell you how to take the important step of registering your complaint with the U.S. Department of Transportation.

No matter what your complaint, keep accurate records. Copies of the following items are indispensable in helping to resolve your problems:

☑ your service invoices

☑ bills you have paid

☑ letters you have written to the manufacturer or the repair facility owner

☑ written repair estimates from your independent mechanic.

☑ notes on discussion with company representatives including names and dates.

RESOLVING COMPLAINTS

Here are some basic steps to help you resolve your problem:

1 First, return your vehicle to the repair facility that did the work. Bring a written list of the problems and make sure that you keep a copy of the list. Give the repair facility a reasonable opportunity to examine your vehicle and attempt to fix it. Speak directly to the service manager (not to the service writer who wrote up your repair order), and ask him or her to test drive the vehicle with you so that you can point out the problem.

2 If that doesn't resolve the problem, take the vehicle to a diagnostic center for an independent examination. This may cost $45 to $60. Get a written statement defining the problem and outlining how it may be fixed. Give your repair shop a copy. If your vehicle is under warranty, do not allow any warranty repair by an independent mechanic; you may not be reimbursed by the manufacturer.

3 If your repair shop does not respond to the independent assessment, present your problem to a mediation panel. These panels hear both sides of the story and try to come to a resolution.

If the problem is with a new vehicle dealer, or if you feel that the manufacturer is responsible, you may be able to use one of the manufacturer's mediation programs.

If the problem is solely with an independent dealer, a local Better Business Bureau (BBB) may be able to mediate your complaint. It may also offer an arbitration hearing. In any case, the BBB should enter your complaint into its files on that establishment.

When contacting any mediation program, determine how long the process takes, who makes the final decision, whether you are bound by that decision, and whether the program handles all problems or only warranty complaints.

4 If there are no mediation programs in your area, contact private consumer groups, local government agencies, or your local "action line" newspaper columnist, newspaper editor, or radio or TV broadcaster. A phone call or letter from them may persuade a repair facility to take action. Send a copy of your letter to the repair shop.

5 One of your last resorts is to bring a lawsuit against the dealer, manufacturer, or repair facility in small claims court. The fee for filing such an action is usually small, and you generally act as your own attorney, saving attorney's fees. There is a monetary limit on the amount you can claim, which varies from state to state. Your local consumer affairs office, state attorney general's office, or the clerk of the court can tell you how to file such a suit.

6 Finally, talk with an attorney. It's best to select an attorney who is familiar with handling automotive problems. Call the lawyer referral service listed in the telephone directory and ask for the names of attorneys who deal with

automobile problems. If you can't afford an attorney, contact the Legal Aid Society.

WARRANTY COMPLAINTS
If your vehicle is under warranty or you are having problems with a factory-authorized dealership, here are some special guidelines:

1 Have the warranty available to show the dealer. Make sure you call the problem to the dealer's attention before the end of the warranty period.

2 If you are still dissatisfied after giving the dealer a reasonable opportunity to fix your vehicle, contact the manufacturer's representative (also called the zone representative) in your area. This person can authorize the dealer to make repairs or take other steps to resolve the dispute. Your dealer will have your zone representative's name and telephone number. Explain the problem and ask for a meeting and a personal inspection of your vehicle.

3 If you can't get satisfaction from the zone representative, call or write the manufacturer's owner relations department. Your owner's manual contains this phone number and address. In each case, as you move up the chain, indicate the steps you have already taken and keep careful records of your efforts.

4 Your next option is to present your problem to a complaint handling panel or to the arbitration program in which the manufacturer of your vehicle participates.

If you complain of a problem during the warranty period, you have a right to have the problem fixed even after the warranty runs out. If your warranty has not been honored, you may be able to "revoke acceptance," which means that you return the vehicle to the dealer. If you are successful, you may be entitled to a replacement vehicle or to a full refund of the purchase price and reimbursement of legal fees under the Magnuson-Moss Warranty Act. Or, if you are covered by one of the state lemon laws, you may be able to return the vehicle and receive a refund or replacement from the manufacturer.

NEED HELP?

If you need legal assistance with your repair problem, the Center for Auto Safety has a list of lawyers who specialize in helping consumers with auto repair problems. For the names of attorneys in your area, send a stamped, self-addressed envelope to: Center for Auto Safety, 1825 Connecticut Ave. NW, Suite 330, Washington, DC 20009. Check their website at www.autosafety.org for a shorter list of lemon law attorneys.

In addition, the Center has published *The Lemon Book*, a detailed 368-page guide to resolving automobile complaints. The book is available for $17.50 directly from the Center.

Attorneys Take Note: For information on litigation assistance provided by the Center for Auto Safety, including *The Lemon Law Litigation Manual*, please contact the Center for Auto Safety at the above address.

AUTO SAFETY HOT LINE
800-424-9393
IN WASHINGTON, DC: 202-366-0123
TTY FOR HEARING IMPAIRED:
800-424-9153 OR DC: 202-366-7800

The toll-free Auto Safety Hot Line can provide information on recalls, record information about safety problems, and refer you to the appropriate government experts on other vehicle related problems. You can even have recall information mailed to you within 24 hours of your call at no charge. Most importantly, you can call the hot line to report safety problems which will become part of the National Highway Traffic Safety Administration's complaint database.

COMPLAINT INDEX

Thanks to the efforts of the Center for Auto Safety, we are able to provide you with the vehicle complaints on file with the National Highway Traffic Safety Administration (NHTSA). Each year, thousands of Americans file online or call the government in order to register complaints about their vehicles. The federal government collects this information but has never released it to the public.

The complaint index is the result of our analysis of these complaints. It is based on a ratio of the number of complaints for each vehicle to the sales of that vehicle. In order to predict the expected complaint performance of the 2010 models, we have examined the complaint history of that car's series. The term series refers to the fact that when a manufacturer introduces a new model, that vehicle remains essentially unchanged, on average, for four to six years. For example, the Chrysler PT Cruiser was redesigned in 2000 and remains essentially the same car for 2010. As such, we have compiled the complaint experience for that series in order to give you some information to use in deciding which car to buy. For vehicles introduced or significantly changed in 2010, we do not yet have enough data to develop a complaint index.

The following table presents the projected best and worst complaint ratings for the 2010 models for which we can develop ratings. Higher index numbers mean the vehicle generated a greater number of complaints. Lower numbers indicate fewer complaints.

2010 PROJECTED COMPLAINT INDEX

THE BEST	INDEX*
Audi A5	0
Infiniti EX	0
Scion xD	151
Acura TL	362
Lincoln MKZ	391
Lexus LS	414
Ford F-150	522
Lexus GX	542
Acura MDX	570
Honda Pilot	603
Mercury Milan	636
Cadillac Escalade EXT	686
Honda CR-V	692
Dodge Ram Pickup	727
Acura RDX	733
Ford Fusion	801
Lexus IS	814
Chevrolet Traverse	821
Mazda MX-5 Miata	833
Mitsubishi Galant	864

THE WORST	INDEX*
Volkswagen Jetta	4405
Lincoln MKS	4418
Mazda Tribute	4463
Hyundai Veracruz	4559
Honda Accord	4577
Toyota FJ Cruiser	4730
Nissan Murano	4768
Nissan Titan	5278
Scion xB	5447
Chevrolet Cobalt	5682
Volkswagen Tiguan	5707
Jeep Wrangler	5840
Toyota Tacoma	6080
Toyota Prius	6471
Volkswagen Routan	6952
Mitsubishi Lancer	7258
Volkswagen Eos	7574
Jaguar XF	7907
Acura TSX	8277
Dodge Journey	10152

*IMPORTANT NOTE: The numbers represent relative index scores, not the number of complaints received. The complaint index score considers sales volume and years on the road. Lower index numbers are better.

CENTER FOR AUTO SAFETY

Every year automobile manufacturers spend millions of dollars making their voices heard in government decision making. For example, General Motors and Ford have large staffs in Detroit and Washington that work solely to influence government activity. But who looks out for the consumer?

For over 30 years, the non-profit Center for Auto Safety (CAS) has told the consumer's story to government agencies, to Congress, and to the courts. Its efforts focus on all consumers rather than only those with individual complaints.

CAS was established in 1970 by Ralph Nader and Consumers Union. As consumer concerns about auto safety issues expanded, so did the work of CAS. It became independent of its founders in 1972. CAS' activities include:

Initiating Safety Recalls: CAS analyzes over 50,000 consumer complaints each year. By following problems as they develop, CAS requests government investigations and recalls of defective vehicles. CAS was responsible for the Ford Pinto faulty gas tank recall, the Firestone 500 steel-belted radial tire recall, and the record recall of over three million Evenflo One Step child seats.

Representing the Consumer in Washington: CAS follows the activities of federal agencies and Congress to ensure that they carry out their responsibilities to the American taxpayer. CAS brings a consumer's point of view to vehicle safety policies and rule-making. Since 1970, CAS has submitted more than 500 petitions and comments on federal safety standards.

One major effort on safety standards has been the successful fight to get airbags in every car. After opposing airbags for decades, the auto industry now can't get enough lifesaving airbags in cars with some models having eight airbags. With airbags to protect consumers in front and side crashes, CAS is now working to strengthen weak roofs that cannot support a vehicle's own weight and crush in rollovers that result in 27,000 deaths and serious injuries each year.

In 1992, CAS uncovered a fire defect that dwarfed the highly publicized flammability of the Ford Pinto. It had to do with the side saddle gas tanks on full size 1973–87 GM pickups and 1988–90 crew cabs that can explode on impact. Over 2,000 people have been killed in fire crashes involving these trucks. After mounting a national campaign to warn consumers to steer clear of these GM fire hazards, the U.S. Department of Transportation granted CAS' petition and conducted one of its biggest defect investigations in history. The result—GM was asked to recall its pickups. GM, sadly, denied this request.

Exposing Secret Warranties: CAS played a prominent role in the disclosure of secret warranties, "policy adjustments," as they are called by manufacturers. These occur when an automaker agrees to pay for repair of certain defects beyond the warranty period but refuses to notify consumers.

Lemon Laws: CAS' work on Lemon Laws aided in the enactment of state laws which make it easier to return a defective new automobile and get money back.

Tire Ratings: After a suspension between 1982 and 1984, consumers have reliable tread-wear ratings to help them get the most miles for their dollar. CAS's lawsuit overturned DOT's revocation of this valuable tire information program.

Initiating Legal Action: When CAS has exhausted other means of obtaining relief for consumer problems, it will initiate legal action. For example, in 1978 when the Department of Energy attempted to raise the price of unleaded gasoline four

TIP

CENTER FOR AUTO SAFETY ONLINE

The Center for Auto Safety has a website at www.autosafety.org to provide information to consumers and to organize consumer campaigns against auto companies on safety defects. Detailed packages of information and advice on defects in specific makes and models are on CAS's website. Consumers with lemons and safety defects can file electronic complaints with CAS and get referred to lemon lawyers.

www.autosafety.org

cents per gallon without notice or comment, CAS succeeded in stopping this illegal move through a lawsuit, thus saving consumers $2 billion for the 3-year period that the decision was in effect.

A 1985 CAS lawsuit against the Environmental Protection Agency (EPA) forced the EPA to recall polluting cars, rather than let companies promise to make cleaner cars in the future. As part of the settlement, GM (which was responsible for the polluting cars) funded a $7 million methanol bus demonstration program in New York City.

CAS' latest legal victory came in 2003 when it overturned a Department of Transportation (DOT) rule that allowed auto makers to install indirect tire pressure monitors in cars that were accurate half the time. Instead, DOT will have to require auto makers to use more accurate direct tire pressure monitors that identify, on the dash, when a particular tire has low pressure.

Help CAS help you: CAS depends on public support. Annual consumer membership is $20. All contributions to this nonprofit organization are tax-deductible. To join, send a check to:

Center for Auto Safety
1825 Connecticut Ave. NW, #330
Washington, DC
20009-5708

Consumer Groups and Government

Below are the names of additional consumer groups you may find helpful:

Advocates for Highway and Auto Safety
750 First St., NE, Suite 901
Washington, DC 20002
(202) 408-1711/408-1699 fax
www.saferoads.org
An alliance of consumer, health and safety groups and insurance companies.

Consumer Action
P.O. Box 70037
Washington, DC 20024
(202) 544-3088
(415) 777-9635 (Complaint Hotline)
www.consumer-action.org
Complaint handling and advocacy related to consumer rights.

**Consumers for Auto
Reliability and Safety**
1303 J St., Suite 270
Sacramento, CA 95814
(530) 759-9440/www.carconsumers.com
Auto safety, airbags, and lemon laws.

KIDS AND CARS
2913 West 113th St.
Leawood, KS 66211
(913) 327-0013/327-0014 fax
www.kidsandcars.org
Safety and advocacy related to protecting children in and around motor vehicles.

**Public Health Advocacy Institute
Motor Vehicle Hazard Archives Project**
www.AutoHazardInfo.org
mvhap_phai@yahoo.com
The Project's mission is to preserve and broaden access to historical and current information about motor vehicle hazards and injury control. The website offers free information about vehicle safety and motor vehicle hazard control.

SafetyBelt Safe, U.S.A.
P.O. Box 553
Altadena, CA 91003
(800) 745-SAFE, stombrella@carseat.org
www.carseat.org
Excellent information and training on child safety seats and safety belt usage.

S.A.N.E., Inc.
2490 N. Park Road, #114 North
Hollywood, CA 33021
(954) 989-1251/www.saferautos.org
Advocates and distributes information for better driving behavior and vehicle safety.

Several federal agencies conduct automobile- related programs. Following is each agency with a description of the type of work it performs and how to contact them.

National Highway Traffic Safety Administration
1200 New Jersey Ave., SE, West Bldg.
Washington, DC 20590
(888) DASH-2-DOT/www.nhtsa.dot.gov
www.safercar.gov
NHTSA issues safety and fuel economy standards for new motor vehicles; investigates safety defects and enforces recall of defective vehicles and equipment; conducts research and demonstration programs on vehicle safety, fuel economy, driver safety, and automobile inspection and repair; provides grants for state highway safety programs in areas such as police traffic services, driver education and licensing, emergency medical services, pedestrian safety, and alcohol abuse.

Environmental Protection Agency
1200 Pennsylvania Ave., NW
Washington, DC 20460
(202) 272-0167/www.epa.gov
www.fueleconomy.gov
EPA's responsibilities include setting and enforcing air and noise emission standards for motor vehicles and measuring fuel economy in new vehicles (EPA Fuel Economy Guide).

Federal Trade Commission
600 Pennsylvania Ave., NW
Washington, DC 20580
(877) FTC-HELP/www.ftc.gov
The FTC regulates advertising, credit practices, marketing abuses, and professional services and ensures that products are properly labeled (as in fuel economy ratings). The commission covers unfair or deceptive trade practices in motor vehicle sales and repairs, as well as non-safety defects.

U.S. Department of Justice
Office of Consumer Litigation
950 Pennsylvania Ave., NW
Washington, DC 20503
(800) 869-4499 or 202-514-2000
www.justice.gov
The DOJ enforces federal law that requires manufacturers to label new automobiles and forbids removal or alteration of labels before delivery to consumers. Labels must contain make, model, vehicle identification number, dealer's name, suggested base price, manufacturer option costs, and manufacturer's suggested retail price.

AUTOMOBILE MANUFACTURERS

Acura (Division of Honda)
See Honda for address and executive
Customer Relations: 800-382-2238

Audi (See Volkswagen for address)
Johan de Nysschen, Executive VP
Customer Relations: 800-822-2834
E-mail: auditalk@audi.com

BMW
Jim O'Donnell, Chairman and CEO
300 Chestnut Ridge Road
Woodcliff Lake, NJ 07677-7731
Customer Relations: 800-831-1117
Fax: 201-930-8362

Buick (Division of General Motors)
PO Box 33136
Detroit, MI 48232-5136
Customer Relations: 800-521-7300

Cadillac (Division of General Motors)
PO Box 33169
Detroit, MI 48232-5169
Customer Relations: 800-458-8006

Chevrolet (Division of General Motors)
PO Box 33170
Detroit, MI 48232-5170
Customer Relations: 800-222-1020
Fax: 313-556-5108

Chrysler (Chrysler, Dodge, Jeep)
Sergio Marchionne, CEO
1000 Chrysler Drive
Auburn Hills, MI 48321-8004
Customer Relations: 800-992-1997

Dodge (See Chrysler)

Ford (Ford, Lincoln, Mercury)
Alan Mulally, President and CEO
The American Road
Dearborn, MI 48126
Customer Relations: 800-392-3673

General Motors
(Buick, Cadillac, Chev., GMC)
Ed Whitacre, Chairman and CEO
300 Renaissance Center
Detroit, MI 48243

GMC (Division of General Motors)
PO Box 33172
Detroit, MI 48232
Customer Relations: 800-462-8782

Honda (Honda, Acura)
Tetsuo Iwamura, President and CEO
1919 Torrance Blvd.
Torrance, CA 90501
Customer Relations: 800-999-1009

Hyundai
John Krafcik, President and CEO
PO Box 20850
Fountain Valley, CA 92728-0850
Customer Relations: 800-633-5151
E-mail: consumeraffairs@hmausa.com

Infiniti (Division of Nissan)
See Nissan for address and executive
Customer Relations: 800-662-6200

Jaguar, Land Rover
Gary Temple, President
555 MacArthur Blvd.
Mahwah, NJ 07430
Jag Customer Relations: 800-452-4827

Jeep (See Chrysler)

Kia
Byung Mo Ahn, President and CEO
PO Box 52410
Irvine, CA 92619-2410
Customer Relations: 800-333-4542

Land Rover (See Jaguar)
Customer Relations: 800-637-6837
Fax: 201-760-8514

Lexus (Division of Toyota)
Mark Templin, VP and General Mgr.
PO Box 2991, Mail Drop L201
Torrance, CA 90501-2732
Customer Relations: 800-255-3987

Lincoln (Division of Ford)
PO Box 6128
Dearborn, MI 48121
Customer Relations: 800-521-4140

Mazda
Jim O' Sullivan, President and CEO
PO Box 19734
Irvine, CA 92623-9734
Customer Relations: 800-222-5500

Mercedes-Benz
Ernst Lieb, President and CEO
Three Mercedes Dr.
Montvale, NJ 07645
Customer Relations: 800-367-6372

Mercury (Division of Ford)
PO Box 6128
Dearborn, MI 48121
Customer Relations: 800-521-4140

Mini (Division of BMW)
Jim McDowell, Vice President
PO Box 1227
Westwood, NJ 07675-1227
Customer Relations: 866-275-6464

Mitsubishi
Shinichi Kurihara, President and CEO
PO Box 6014, Cypress, CA 90630-0014
Customer Relations: 888-648-7820

Nissan
Carlos Ghosn, President and CEO
PO Box 685003
Franklin, TN 37068-5003
Customer Relations: 800-647-7261

Porsche
Detlev von Platen, President & CEO
980 Hammond Dr., Suite 1000
Atlanta, GA 30328
Customer Relations: 800-767-7243

Saab
Steve Shannon, Interim General Manager
PO Box 33166, Detroit, MI 48232-5166
Customer Relations: 800-955-9007

Scion (Division of Toyota)
Jack Hollis, Vice President
D102 PO Box 2742
Torrence, CA 90509-2742
Customer Relations: 866-707-2466

Smart
David Schembri, President
2555 Telegraph Rd.
Bloomfield Hills, MI 48302
Customer Relations: 800-762-7887

Subaru
Yoshio Hasunuma, Chairman and CEO
Subaru Plaza, P.O. Box 6000
Cherry Hill, NJ 08034-6000
Customer Relations: 800-782-2783

Suzuki
Kevin Saito, President
PO Box 1100, Brea, CA 92822-1100
Customer Relations: 800-934-0934

Toyota (Toyota, Lexus, Scion)
Jim Lentz, President and COO
19001 S. Western Ave.
Torrance, CA 90501
Customer Relations: 800-331-4331

Volkswagen
Stefan Jacoby, President and CEO
2200 Ferdinand Porsche Drive
Herndon, VA 20171
Customer Relations: 800-822-8987

Volvo
Doug Speck, President and CEO
One Volvo Dr., PO Box 914
Rockleigh, NJ 07647
Customer Relations: 800-458-1552

LEMON LAWS

Sometimes, despite our best efforts, we buy a vehicle that just doesn't work right. There may be little problem after little problem, or perhaps one big problem that never seems to be fixed. Because of the "sour" taste that such vehicles leave in the mouths of consumers who buy them, these vehicles are known as "lemons."

In the past, it's been difficult to obtain a refund or replacement if a vehicle was a lemon. The burden of proof was left to the consumer. Because it is hard to define exactly what constitutes a lemon, many lemon owners were unable to win a case against a manufacturer. And when they won, consumers had to pay for their attorneys giving them less than if they had traded in their lemon.

Thanks to "Lemon Laws" passed by all states, lemon-aide is available when consumers get stuck with a lemon. Although there are some important state-to-state variations, all of the laws have similarities: They establish a period of coverage, usually two years from delivery or the written warranty period, whichever is shorter; they may require some form of noncourt arbitration; and most importantly they define a lemon. In most states a new car, truck, or van is "presume" to be a lemon when it has been taken back to the shop 3 to 4 times for the same problem or is out of service for a total of 30 days during the covered period. This time does not mean consecutive days and can be for different problems. 15 states have safety lemon provisions which presume a vehicle is a lemon after only 1 to 2 repairs of a defect likely to cause death or serious injury. Be sure to keep careful records of your repairs since some states now require only one of the repairs to be within the specified time period. 33 states provide for the award of attorney fees with the other 17 relying on the Federal lemon law for fees. A vehicle may be covered by the lemon law even though it doesn't meet the "presumption."

Specific information about your state's law can be obtained from your state attorney general's office or at the Center for Auto Safety's website. The following table offers a general description of the Lemon Law in your state and what you need to do to set it in motion (Notification/Trigger). We indicate where state-run arbitration programs are available. State-run programs are the best type of arbitration. Be aware a few state lemon laws are so bad consumers should only rely on the Federal lemon law and state contract law. We have marked these bad laws with a ☒ while the best laws have a ☑.

> ☑ **The Best Lemon Laws**
> ☒ **The Worst Lemon Laws**

Alabama	Qualification: 3 unsuccessful repairs or 30 calendar days within shorter of 24 months or 24,000 miles, provided 1 repair attempt or 1 day out of service is within shorter of 1 year or 12,000 miles. Notice/Trigger: Certified mail to manufacturer + opportunity for final repair attempt within 14 calendar days.
Alaska	Qualification: 3 unsuccessful repairs or 30 business days out of service within shorter of 1 year or warranty. Notice/Trigger: Certified mail to manufacturer + dealer (or repair agent) that problem has not been corrected in reasonable number of attempts + refund or replacement demanded within 60 days. Manufacturer has 30 calendar days for final repair attempt.
Arizona	Qualification: 4 unsuccessful repairs or 30 calendar days out of service within warranty period or shorter of 2 years or 24,000 miles. Notice/Trigger: Written notice + opportunity to repair to manufacturer.
Arkansas ☑ BEST	Qualification: 3 unsuccessful repairs, 5 total repairs of any nonconformity, or 1 unsuccessful repair of problem likely to cause death or serious bodily injury within longer of 24 months or 24,000 miles. Notice/Trigger: Certified or registered mail to manufacturer who has 10 days to notify consumer of repair facility. Facility has 10 days to repair.

L—Law specifically applies to leased vehicles; S-C—State has certified guidelines for arbitration; S-R—State-run arbitration mechanism available

California ☑ BEST	Qualification: 4 repair attempts or 30 calendar days out of service or 2 repair attempts for defect likely to cause death or serious bodily injury within shorter of 18 months or 18,000 miles, or "reasonable" number of attempts during entire express warranty period. Notice/Trigger: Direct written notice to manufacturer at address clearly specified in owner's manual. Covers small businesses with up to 5 vehicles under 10,000 pounds GVWR.
Colorado ☒ WORST	Qualification: 4 unsuccessful repairs or 30 business days out of service within shorter of 1 year or warranty. Notice/Trigger: Prior certified mail notice + opportunity to repair for manufacturer.
Connecticut	Qualification: 4 unsuccessful repairs or 30 calendar days out of service within shorter of 2 years or 24,000 miles, or 2 unsuccessful repairs of problem likely to cause death or serious bodily injury within warranty period or 1 year. Notice/Trigger: Report to manufacturer, agent, or dealer. Written notice to manufacturer only if required in owner's manual or warranty. S-R
Delaware	Qualification: 4 unsuccessful repairs or 30 calendar days out of service within shorter of 1 year or warranty. Notice/Trigger: Written notice + opportunity to repair to manufacturer.
D.C.	Qualification: 4 unsuccessful repairs or 30 calendar days out of service or 1 unsuccessful repair of safety-related defect, within shorter of 2 years or 18,000 miles. Notice/Trigger: Report to manufacturer, agent, or dealer.
Florida	Qualification: 3 unsuccessful repairs or 15 calendar days within 24 months from delivery. Notice/Trigger: Certified or express mail notice to manufacturer who has 10 days to notify consumer of repair facility plus 10 more calendar days for final repair attempt after delivery to designated dealer. S-R
Georgia	Qualification: 3 unsuccessful repair attempts, 30 days out of service, or 1 unsuccessful repair of serious safety defect that impedes the consumers ability to control or operate the vehicle or creates a risk of fire or explosion, within shorter of any 24,000 miles or 24 months from delivery. Notice/Trigger: Certified mail return receipt requested. Manufacturer has 7 days to notify consumer of repair facility which has 14 calendar days to repair. S-R Note: Proceeding under lemon law may cause consumer to lose rights under other laws.
Hawaii	Qualification: 3 unsuccessful repair attempts, or 1 unsuccessful repair attempt of defect likely to cause death or serious bodily injury, or out of service for total of 30 days within shorter of 2 years or 24,000 miles. Notice/Trigger: Written notice + opportunity to repair to manufacturer. S-R
Idaho	Qualification: 4 repair attempts or 30 business days out of service within shorter of 2 years or 24,000 miles, or 1 repair of complete failure of braking or steering likely to cause death or serious bodily injury. Notice/Trigger: Written notice to manufacturer or dealer + one opportunity to repair to manufacturer. S-R.
Illinois	Qualification: 4 unsuccessful repairs or 30 business days out of service within shorter of 1 year or 12,000 miles. Notice/Trigger: Written notice + opportunity to repair to manufacturer.
Indiana ☒ WORST	Qualification: 4 unsuccessful repairs or 30 business days out of service within shorter of 18 months or 18,000 miles. Notice/Trigger: Written notice to manufacturer only if required in the warranty.

L—Law specifically applies to leased vehicles; S-C—State has certified guidelines for arbitration; S-R—State-run arbitration mechanism available

Iowa	Qualification: 3 unsuccessful repairs, or 1 unsuccessful repair of nonconformity likely to cause death or serious bodily injury, or 30 calendar days out of service within shorter of 2 years or 24,000 miles. Notice/Trigger: Certified registered mail + final opportunity to repair within 10 calendar days of receipt of notice to manufacturer.
Kansas	Qualification: 4 unsuccessful repairs or 30 calendar days out of service or 10 total repairs within shorter of 1 year or warranty. Notice/Trigger: Actual notice to manufacturer.
Kentucky	Qualification: 4 unsuccessful repairs or 30 calendar days out of service within shorter of 1 year or 12,000 miles. Notice/Trigger: Written notice to manufacturer.
Louisiana	Qualification: 4 unsuccessful repairs or 90 calendar days out of service within shorter of 1 year or warranty. Notice/Trigger: Report to manufacturer or dealer.
Maine	Qualification: 3 unsuccessful repairs (or 1 unsuccessful repair of serious failure of brakes or steering) or 15 business days out of service within shorter of warranty or 3 years or 18,000 miles. Applies to vehicles within first 18,000 miles or 3 years regardless of whether claimant is original owner. Notice/Trigger: Written notice to manufacturer or dealer. Manufacturer has 7 business days after receipt for final repair attempt. S-R
Maryland	Qualification: 4 unsuccessful repairs, 30 calendar days out of service or 1 unsuccessful repair of braking or steering system within shorter of 15 months or 15,000 miles. Notice/Trigger: Certified mail return receipt requested + opportunity to repair within 30 calendar days of receipt of notice to manufacturer or factory branch.
Massachusetts	Qualification: 3 unsuccessful repairs or 10 business days out of service within shorter of 1 year or 15,000 miles. Notice/Trigger: Notice to manufacturer or dealer who has 7 business days to attempt final repair. S-R
Michigan	Qualification: 4 unsuccessful repairs within 2 years from date of first unsuccessful repair or 30 calendar days within shorter of 1 year or warranty. Notice/Trigger: Certified mail return receipt requested to manufacturer who has 5 business days to repair after delivery. Consumer may notify manufacturer after third repair attempt.
Minnesota	Qualification: 4 unsuccessful repairs or 30 business days or 1 unsuccessful repair of total braking or steering loss likely to cause death or serious bodily injury within shorter of 2 years or warranty. Notice/Trigger: Written notice + opportunity to repair to manufacturer, agent, or dealer.
Mississippi	Qualification: 3 unsuccessful repairs or 15 business days out of service within shorter of 1 year or warranty. Notice/Trigger: Written notice to manufacturer who has 10 business days to repair after delivery to designated dealer.
Missouri	Qualification: 4 unsuccessful repairs or 30 business days out of service within shorter of 1 year or warranty. Notice/Trigger: Written notice to manufacturer who has 10 calendar days to repair after delivery to designated dealer.
Montana	Qualification: 4 unsuccessful repairs or 30 business days out of service after notice within shorter of 2 years or 18,000 miles. Notice/Trigger: Written notice + opportunity to repair to manufacturer. S-R
Nebraska	Qualification: 4 unsuccessful repairs or 40 calendar days out of service within shorter of 1 year or warranty. Notice/Trigger: Certified mail + opportunity to repair to manufacturer.

L—Law specifically applies to leased vehicles; S-C—State has certified guidelines for arbitration; S-R—State-run arbitration mechanism available

Nevada	Qualification: 4 unsuccessful repairs or 30 calendar days out of service within shorter of 1 year or warranty. Notice/Trigger: Written notice to manufacturer.
New Hampshire	Qualification: 3 unsuccessful repairs by same dealer or 30 business days out of service within warranty. Notice/Trigger: Report to manufacturer, distributor, agent, or dealer (on forms provided by manufacturer) + final opportunity to repair before arbitration. S-R
New Jersey ☑ BEST	Qualification: 3 unsuccessful repairs or 20 calendar days out of service within shorter of 2 years or 18,000 miles. Notice/Trigger: Certified mail notice, return receipt requested to manufacturer who has 10 days to repair. Consumer may notify manufacturer any time after the second repair attempt.
New Mexico ☒ WORST	Qualification: 4 unsuccessful repairs or 30 business days out of service within shorter of 1 year or warranty. Notice/Trigger: Written notice + opportunity to repair to manufacturer, agent, or dealer.
New York	Qualification: 4 unsuccessful repairs or 30 calendar days out of service within shorter of 2 years or 18,000 miles. Notice/Trigger: Notice to manufacturer, agent, or dealer.
North Carolina	Qualification: 4 unsuccessful repairs within shorter of 24 months, 24,000 miles or warranty or 20 business days out of service during any 12 month period of warranty. Notice/Trigger: Written notice to manufacturer + opportunity to repair within 15 calendar days of receipt only if required in warranty or owner's manual.
North Dakota ☒ WORST	Qualification: 3 unsuccessful repairs or 30 business days out of service within shorter of 1 year or warranty. Notice/Trigger: Direct written notice + opportunity to repair to manufacturer. (Manufacturer's informal arbitration process serves as prerequisite to consumer refund or replacement.)
Ohio ☑ BEST	Qualification: 3 unsuccessful repairs of same nonconformity, 30 calendar days out of service, 8 total repairs of any nonconformity, or 1 unsuccessful repair of problem likely to cause death or serious bodily injury within shorter of 1 year or 18,000 miles. Notice/Trigger: Report to manufacturer, its agent, or dealer.
Oklahoma	Qualification: 4 unsuccessful repairs or 30 calendar days out of service within shorter of 1 year or warranty. Notice/Trigger: Written notice + opportunity to repair to manufacturer.
Oregon	Qualification: 4 unsuccessful repairs or 30 business days within shorter of 1 year or 12,000 miles. Notice/Trigger: Direct written notice + opportunity to repair to manufacturer.
Pennsylvania	Qualification: 3 unsuccessful repairs or 30 calendar days within shorter of 1 year, 12,000 miles, or warranty. Notice/Trigger: Delivery to authorized service + repair facility. If delivery impossible, written notice to manufacturer or its repair facility obligates them to pay for delivery.
Rhode Island	Qualification: 4 unsuccessful repairs or 30 calendar days out of service within shorter of 1 year or 15,000 miles. Notice/Trigger: Report to dealer or manufacturer who has 7 days for final repair opportunity.
South Carolina	Qualification: 3 unsuccessful repairs or 30 calendar days out of service within shorter of 1 year or 12,000 miles. Notice/Trigger: Certified mail + opportunity to repair (not more than 10 business days) to manufacturer only if manufacturer informed consumer of such at time of sale.

L—Law specifically applies to leased vehicles; S-C—State has certified guidelines for arbitration; S-R—State-run arbitration mechanism available

South Dakota	Qualification: 4 unsuccessful repairs, 1 of which occurred during shorter of 1 year or 12,000 miles, or 30 calendar days out of service during shorter of 24 months or 24,000 miles. Notice/Trigger: Certified mail to manufacturer + final opportunity to repair + 7 calendar days to notify consumer of repair facility.
Tennessee	Qualification: 4 unsuccessful repairs or 30 calendar days out of service within shorter of 1 year or warranty. Notice/Trigger: Certified mail notice to manufacturer + final opportunity to repair within 10 calendar days.
Texas	Qualification: 4 unsuccessful repairs when 2 occurred within shorter of 1 year or 12,000 miles, + other 2 occur within shorter of 1 year or 12,000 miles immediately following second repair attempt; or 2 unsuccessful repairs of serious safety defect when 1 occurred within shorter of 1 year or 12,000 miles + other occurred within shorter of 1 year or 12,000 miles immediately following first repair; or 30 calendar days out of service within shorter of 2 years or 24,000 miles + at least 2 attempts were made within shorter of 1 year or 12,000 miles. Notice/Trigger: Written notice to manufacturer. S-R
Utah	Qualification: 4 unsuccessful repairs or 30 business days out of service within shorter of 1 year or warranty. Notice/Trigger: Report to manufacturer, agent, or dealer.
Vermont	Qualification: 3 unsuccessful repairs when at least first repair was within warranty, or 30 calendar days out of service within warranty. Notice/Trigger: Written notice to manufacturer (on provided forms) after third repair attempt, or 30 days. Arbitration must be held within 45 days after notice, during which time manufacturer has 1 final repair. S-R Note: Repairs must been done by same authorized agent or dealer, unless consumer shows good cause for taking vehicle to different agent or dealer.
Virginia	Qualification: 3 unsuccessful repairs, or 1 repair attempt of serious safety defect, or 30 calendar days out of service within 18 months. Notice/Trigger: Written notice to manufacturer. If 3 unsuccessful repairs or 30 days already exhausted before notice, manufacturer has 1 more repair attempt not to exceed 15 days.
Washington	Qualification: 4 unsuccessful repairs, 30 calendar days out of service (15 during warranty period), or 2 repairs of serious safety defect, first reported within shorter of warranty or 24 months or 24,000 miles. One repair attempt + 15 of 30 days must fall within manufacturer's express warranty of at least 1 year of 12,000 miles. Notice/Trigger: Written notice to manufacturer. S-R Note: Consumer should receive replacement or refund within 40 calendar days of request.
West Virginia ☑BEST	Qualification: 3 unsuccessful repairs or 30 calendar days out of service or 1 unsuccessful repair of problem likely to cause death or serious bodily injury within shorter of 1 year or warranty. Notice/Trigger: Written notice + opportunity to repair to manufacturer.
Wisconsin	Qualification: 4 unsuccessful repairs or 30 calendar days out of service within shorter of 1 year or warranty. Notice/Trigger: Report to manufacturer or dealer. Note: Consumer should receive replacement or refund within 30 calendar days after offer to return title.
Wyoming	Qualification: 3 unsuccessful repairs or 30 business days out of service within 1 year. Notice/Trigger: Direct written notice + opportunity to repair to manufacturer. S-R State-run arbitration mechanism available.

L—Law specifically applies to leased vehicles; S-C—State has certified guidelines for arbitration; S-R—State-run arbitration mechanism available

5 BASIC STEPS TO CAR BUYING

Buying a car means matching wits with a seasoned professional. But if you know what to expect, you'll have a much better chance of getting a really good deal!

There's no question that buying a car can be an intimidating experience. But it doesn't have to be. First of all, you have in your hands all of the information you need to make an informed choice. Secondly, if you approach the purchase logically, you'll always maintain control of the decision. Start with the following basic steps:

1 Narrow your choice down to a particular class of car—sports, station wagon, minivan, sedan, large luxury, or economy car. These are general classifications and some cars may fit into more than one category. In most cases, *The Car Book* presents the vehicles by size class.

2 Determine what features are really important to you. Most buyers consider safety on the top of their list, which is why the "Safety" chapter is right up front in *The Car Book*. Airbags, power options, ABS, and the number of passengers, as well as "hidden" elements such as maintenance and insurance costs, should be considered at this stage in your selection process.

3 Find three or four cars that meet the needs you outlined above and your pocketbook. It's important not to narrow your choice down to one car because then you lose all your bargaining power in the showroom. (Why? Because you might lose the psychological ability to walk away from a bad deal!) In fact, because cars today are more similar than dissimilar, it's not hard to keep three or four choices in mind. In the car rating pages in the back of the book, we suggest some competitive choices for your consideration. For example, if you are interested in the Honda Accord, you should also consider the Toyota Camry and Ford Fusion.

4 Make sure you take a good, long test drive. The biggest car buying mistake most of us make is to overlook those nagging problems that seem to surface only after we've brought the car home. Spend at least an hour driving the car without a salesperson preferably. If a dealership won't allow you to test-drive a car without a salesperson, go somewhere else. The test-drive should include time on the highway, parking, taking the car in and out of your driveway or garage, sitting in the back seat, and using the trunk or storage area.

TIP: Whatever you do, don't talk price until you're ready to buy!

5 This is the stage most of us dread—negotiating the price. While price negotiation is a car buying tradition, a few carmakers and dealers are trying to break tradition by offering so-called "no-haggle pricing." Since they're still in the minority and because it's very hard for an individual to establish true competition between dealers, we offer a great means to avoid negotiating altogether by using the non-profit CarBargains pricing service described on page 68.

THE 180-DEGREE TURN

TIP

When buying a car, remember that you have the most important weapon in the bargaining process: the 180-degree turn. Be prepared to walk away from a deal, even at the risk of losing the "very best deal" your salesperson has ever offered, and you will be in the best position to get a real "best deal." Remember: Dealerships need you, the buyer, to survive.

IN THE SHOWROOM

Being prepared is the best way to turn a potentially intimidating showroom experience into a profitable one. Here's some advice on handling what you'll find in the showroom.

Beware of silence. Silence is often used to intimidate, so be prepared for long periods of time when the salesperson is "talking with the manager." This tactic is designed to make you want to "just get the negotiation over with." Instead of becoming a victim, do something that indicates you are serious about looking elsewhere. Bring the classified section of the newspaper and begin circling other cars or review brochures from other manufacturers. By sending the message that you have other options, you increase your bargaining power and speed up the process.

Don't fall in love with a car. Never look too interested in any particular car. Advise family members who go with you against being too enthusiastic about any one car. Tip: Beat the dealers at their own game— bring along a friend who tells you that the price is "too much compared to the other deal."

Keep your wallet in your pocket. Don't leave a deposit, even if it's refundable. You'll feel pressure to rush your shopping, and you'll have to return and face the salesperson again before you are ready.

Shop at the end of the month. Salespeople anxious to meet sales goals are more willing to negotiate a lower price at this time.

Buy last year's model. The majority of new cars are the same as the previous year, with minor cosmetic changes. You can save considerably by buying in early fall when dealers are clearing space for "new" models. The important trade-off you make using this technique is that the carmaker may have added a new safety feature to an otherwise unchanged vehicle.

Buying from stock. You can often get a better deal on a car that the dealer has on the lot. However, these cars often have expensive options you may not want or need. Do not hesitate to ask the dealer to remove an option (and its accompanying charge) or sell you the car without charging for the option. The longer the car sits there, the more interest the dealer pays on the car, which increases the dealer's incentive to sell.

Ordering a car. Cars can be ordered from the manufacturer with exactly the options you want. Simply offering a fixed amount over invoice may be attractive because it's a sure sale and the dealership has not invested in the car. All the salesperson has to do is take your order.

If you do order a car, make sure when it arrives that it includes only the options you requested. Don't fall for the trick where the dealer offers you unordered options at a "special price," because it was their mistake. If you didn't order an option, don't pay for it.

⚠ BEWARE OF MANDATORY ARBITRATION AGREEMENTS ⚠

More and more dealers are adding mandatory binding arbitration agreements, which they often call "dispute resolution mechanisms," to your purchase contract. What this means is that you wave the right to sue or appeal any problem you have with the vehicle. Before you start negotiating the price, ask if the dealer requires Mandatory Binding Arbitration. If so, and they won't remove that requirement, you should buy elsewhere. Many dealers do not have this requirement.

GETTING THE BEST PRICE

One of the most difficult aspects of buying a new car is getting the best price. Most of us are at a disadvantage negotiating because we don't know how much the car actually cost the dealer. The difference between what the dealer paid and the sticker price represents the negotiable amount.

Beware, now that most savvy consumers know to check the so-called "dealer invoice," the industry has camouflaged this number. Special incentives, rebates, and kickbacks can account for $500 to $2,000 worth of extra profit to a dealer selling a car at "dealer invoice." The non-profit Center for the Study of Services recently discovered that in 37 percent of cases when dealers are forced to bid against each other for the sale, they offered the buyer a price below the "dealer invoice"—an unlikely event if the dealer was actually losing money. The bottom line is that "dealer invoice" doesn't really mean dealer cost.

You can't really negotiate with only one dealer, you need to get two or three bidding against each other. Introducing competition is the best way to get the lowest price on a new car. To do this you have to convince two or three dealers that you are, in fact, prepared to buy a car; that you have decided on the make, model, and features; and that your decision now rests solely on which dealer will give you the best price. You can try to do this by phone, but often dealers will not give you the best price, or will quote you a price over the phone that they will not honor later. Instead, you should try to do this in person. As anyone knows who has ventured into an auto showroom simply to get the best price, the process can be lengthy as well as terribly arduous. Nevertheless, if you can convince the dealer that you are serious and are willing to take the time to go to a number of dealers, it will pay off. Otherwise, we suggest you use the CarBargains service described on page 68.

Here are some other showroom strategies:

Shop away from home. If you find a big savings at a dealership far from your home or on the Internet, call a local dealer with the price. They may very well match it. If not, pick up the car from the distant dealer, knowing your trip has saved you hundreds of dollars. You can still bring it to your local dealer for warranty work and repairs.

Beware of misleading advertising. New car ads are meant to get you into the showroom. They usually promise low prices, big rebates, high trade-in, and spotless integrity—don't be deceived. Advertised prices are rarely the true selling price. They usually exclude transportation charges, service fees, or document fees. And always look out for the asterisk, both in advertisements and on invoices. It can be a signal that the advertiser has something to hide.

Don't talk price until you're ready to buy. On your first few trips to the showroom, simply look over the cars, decide what options you want, and do your test-driving.

Shop the corporate twins. Page 75 contains a list of corporate twins—nearly identical cars that carry different name plates. Check the price and options of the twins of the car you like. A higher-priced twin may have more options, so it may be a better deal than the lower-priced car without the options you want.

Watch out for dealer preparation overcharges. Before paying the dealer to clean your car, make sure that preparation is not included in the basic price. The price sticker will state: "Manufacturer's suggested retail price of this model includes dealer preparation."

If you must negotiate . . . negotiate up from the "invoice" price rather than down from the sticker price. Simply make an offer close to or at the "invoice" price. If the salesperson says that your offer is too low to make a profit, ask to see the factory invoice.

Don't trade in. Although it is more work, you can usually do better by selling your old car yourself than by trading it in. To determine what you'll gain by selling the car yourself, check the NADA Official Used Car Guide at your credit union or library. On the web, the Kelly Blue Book website at kbb.com is a good source for invoice pricing. The difference between the trade-in price (what the dealer will give you) and the retail price (what you typically can sell it for) is your extra payment for selling the car yourself.

If you do decide to trade your car in at the dealership, keep the buying and selling separate. First, negotiate the best price for your new car, then find out how much the dealer will give you for your old car. Keeping the two deals separate ensures that you know what you're paying for your new car and simplifies the entire transaction.

Question everything the dealer writes down. Nothing is etched in stone. Because things are written down, we tend not to question them. This is wrong—always assume that anything written down is negotiable.

BUYING FOR SAFETY

So how do you buy for safety? Many consumers mistakenly believe that handling and performance are the key elements in the safety of a car. While an extremely unresponsive car could cause an accident, most new cars meet basic handling requirements. In fact, many people actually feel uncomfortable driving high performance cars because the highly responsive steering, acceleration, and suspension systems can be difficult to get used to. But the main reason handling is overrated as a safety measure is that automobile collisions are, by nature, accidents. Once they've begun, they are beyond human capacity to prevent, no matter how well your car handles. So the key to protecting yourself is to purchase a car that offers a high degree of crash protection.

! AVOIDING LEMONS !

One way to avoid the sour taste of a lemon after you've bought your car is to protect yourself before you sign on the dotted line. These tips will help you avoid problems down the road.

1 **Avoid new models.** Any new car in its very first year of production often turns out to have a lot of defects. Sometimes the manufacturer isn't able to remedy the defects until the second, third, or even fourth year of production. If the manufacturer has not worked out problems by the third model year, the car will likely be a lemon forever.

2 **Avoid the first cars off the line.** Most companies close down their assembly lines every year to make annual changes. In addition to adding hundreds of dollars to the price of a new car, these changes can introduce new defects. It can take a few months to iron out these bugs. Ask the dealer when the vehicle you are interested in was manufactured, or look on the metal tag found on the inside of the driver-side door frame to find the date of manufacture.

3 **Avoid delicate options.** Delicate options have the highest frequency-of-repair records. Power seats, power windows, power antennas, and special roofs are nice conveniences—until they break down. Of all the items on the vehicles, they tend to be the most expensive to repair.

4 **Inspect the dealer's checklist.** Request a copy of the dealer's pre-delivery service and adjustment checklist (also called a "make-ready list") at the time your new vehicle is delivered. Write the request directly on the new vehicle order. This request informs the dealer that you are aware of the dealer's responsibility to check your new car for defects.

5 **Examine the car on delivery.** Most of us are very excited when it comes time to take the vehicle home. A few minutes of careful inspection can save hours of misery later. Look over the body for any damage; check for the spare tire and jack equipment; make sure all electrical items work, and all the hubcaps and body molding are on. You may want to take a short test-drive. Finally, make sure you have the owner's manual, warranty forms, and all the legal documents.

CarBargains' Best Price Service

Even with the information that we provide you in this chapter of *The Car Book*, many of us still will not be comfortable negotiating for a fair price. In fact, as we indicated on the previous page, we believe it's really very difficult to negotiate the best price with a single dealer. The key to getting the best price is to get dealers to compete with each other.

CarBargains is a service of the non-profit Center for the Study of Services, a Washington, DC, consumer group, set up to provide comparative price information for many products and services.

CarBargains will "shop" the dealerships in your area and obtain at least five price quotes for the make and model of the car that you want to buy. The dealers who submit quotes know that they are competing with other area dealerships and have agreed to honor the prices that they submit. It is important to note that CarBargains is not an auto broker or "car buying" service; they have no affiliation with dealers.

Here's how the service works:

1. You provide CarBargains with the make, model, and style of car you wish to buy (Toyota Camry XLE, for example) by phone or mail.

2. Within two weeks, CarBargains will send you dealer quote sheets from at least five local dealers who have bid against one another to sell you that car. Each dealer's offer is actually a commitment to a dollar amount above (or below) "factory invoice cost" for that model. You get the name and phone number of the manager responsible for handling the quote.

You will also receive a printout that enables you to figure the exact cost for each available option you might want on the vehicle.

3. Determine which dealer offers the best price using the dealer quote sheets. Add up the cost including the specific options you want. Contact the sales manager of that dealership and arrange to purchase the car.

If a car with the options you want is not available on the dealer's lot, you can, in many cases, have the dealer order the car from the factory or from another dealer at the agreed price.

When you receive your quotes, you will also get some suggestions on low-cost sources of financing and a valuation of your used car (trade-in).

The price for this service ($200) may seem expensive, but when you consider the savings that will result by having dealers bid against each other, as well as the time and effort of trying to get these bids yourself, we believe it's a great value. The dealers know they have a bona fide buyer (you've paid for the service); they know they are bidding against five to seven of their competitors; and, you have CarBargains' experts on your side.

To obtain CarBargains' competitive price quotes, call them at 800-475-7283 or visit their website at www.carbargains.org. Or, you can send a check for $200 to CarBargains, 1625 K St., NW, 8th Floor, Washington, DC 20006. Be sure to include your complete mailing address, phone number (in case of questions), and the exact make, model, style, and year of the car you want to buy. You should receive your bids within two to three weeks.

! AUTO BROKERS !

While CarBargains is a non-profit organization created to help you find the best price for the car you want to purchase, auto brokers are typically in the business to make money. As such, whatever price you end up paying for the car will include additional profit for the broker. There have been cases where the auto broker makes certain promises, takes your money, and you never hear from him or her again. While many brokers are legitimately trying to get their customers the best price, others have developed special relationships with certain dealers and may not do much shopping for you. As a consumer, it is difficult to tell which are which. This is why we recommend CarBargains. If CarBargains is not for you, then we suggest you consider using a buying service associated with your credit union or auto club, which can arrange for the purchase of a car at some fixed price over "dealer invoice."

FINANCING

You've done your test-drive, researched prices, studied crash tests, determined the options you want, and haggled to get the best price. Now you have to decide how to pay for the car.

If you have the cash, pay for the car right away. You avoid finance charges, you won't have a large debt haunting you, and the full value of the car is yours. You can then make the monthly payments to yourself to save up for your next car.

However, most of us cannot afford to pay cash for a car, which leaves two options: financing or leasing. While leasing may seem more affordable, financing will actually cost you less. When you finance a car, you own it after you finish your payments. At the end of a lease, you have nothing. We don't recommend leasing, but if you want more information, see page 71.

Here are some tips when financing your car:

Shop around for interest rates. Most banks and credit unions will knock off at least a quarter of a percent for their customers. Have these quotes handy when you talk financing with the dealer.

The higher your down payment, the less you'll have to finance. This will not only reduce your overall interest charges, but often qualifies you for a lower interest rate. Down payments are typically 10–20 percent of the final price.

Avoid long car loans. The monthly payments are lower, but you'll pay far more in overall interest charges. For example, a two-year, $20,000 loan at 7 percent will cost you $1,491 in interest; the same amount at five years will cost you $3,761— over twice as much!

Check out manufacturer promotional rates—the 0.9–2.9 percent rates you see advertised. These low rates are usually only valid on two- to three-year loans.

Read everything you are asked to sign and ask questions about anything you don't fully understand.

Make sure that an extended warranty has not been added to the purchase price. Dealers will sometimes add this cost without informing the consumer. Extended warranties are generally a bad value. See the "Warranties" chapter for more information.

Credit Unions vs. Banks: Credit unions generally charge fewer and lower fees and offer better rates than banks. In addition, credit unions offer counseling services where consumers can find pricing information on

DON'T BE TONGUE-TIED

Beware of high-pressure phrases like "I've talked to the manager and this is really the best we can do. As it is, we're losing money on this deal." Rarely is this true. Dealers are in the business to make money and most do very well. Don't tolerate a take-it-or-leave-it attitude. Simply repeat that you will only buy when you see the deal you want and that you don't appreciate the dealer pressuring you. Threaten to leave if the dealer continues to pressure you to buy today.

Don't let the dealer answer your questions with a question. If you ask, "Can I get air conditioning with this car?" and the salesperson answers, "If I get you air conditioning in this car, will you buy today?" this response tries to force you to decide to buy before you are ready. Ask the dealer to just answer your question and say that you'll buy when you're ready. It's the dealer's job to answer questions, not yours.

If you are having a difficult time getting what you want, ask the dealer: "Why won't you let me buy a car today?" Most salespeople will be thrown off by this phrase as they are often too busy trying to use it on you. If they respond in frustration, "OK, what do you want?" then you can make straightforward answers to simple questions.

Get a price; don't settle for: "If you're shopping price, go to the other dealers first and then come back." This technique ensures that they don't have to truly negotiate. Your best response is: "I only plan to come back if your price is the lowest, so that's what I need today, your lowest price."

cars or compare monthly payments for financing. You can join a credit union either through your employer, an organization or club, or if you have a relative who is part of a credit union.

Low Rate or Cash Back? Sometimes auto manufacturers offer a choice of below market financing or cash back. The table below will tell you if it is better to take the lower rate or the cash back rebate. For example, say you want to finance $18,000. Your credit union or bank offers you 6.5 percent for an auto loan and the dealer offers either a 4 percent loan or a $1,500 rebate. Which is better? Find your bank or credit union's rate (6.5 percent in the square) on the left and the dealer's low rate (4 percent in the square) on the top of the table. Find where the two intersect on the table and you will find the difference per thousand dollars between the two interest rates (48 in the square). When you multiply this number (48) by the number of thousands you're financing (18 for $18,000), you get $864. Since the dealer's $1,500 rebate is more than the $864 savings if you went with the 4% rate over the 6.5%. So taking your bank's rate (6.5 percent) and the rebate is a better deal than taking the dealer's low rate (4 percent). If the answer had been more than $1,500, then the dealer's rate would have been the better deal. An asterisk (*) in the table means that the bank or credit union's rate is the better deal regardless of dealer discount.

TYPICAL OPERATING COSTS

The table below shows the annual operating costs for some popular vehicle. Costs include operating expenses (fuel, oil, maintenance, and tires) and ownership expenses (insurance, depreciation, financing, taxes and licensing) and are based on keeping the vehicle for 3 years and driving 20,000 miles per year. This information is from Runzheimer International. Runzheimer evaluated 30, 2010 model cars, vans, SUVs and light trucks and determined the most and least expensive to operate among those vehicles. (Source: Runzheimer International, www.runzheimer.com)

Projected Ownership and Operating Costs for Selected 2010 Cars

Most Expensive

Cadillac STS 8-cyl. 4.6L	$23,520
Lincoln Town Car Signature L 8-cyl. 4.6L	$21,232
BMW 550I 8-cyl. 4.8L	$20,781

Least Expensive

Ford Focus SE 4-cyl. 2.0L	$8,861
Chevrolet Aveo 1LT 4-cyl. 1.6L	$7,888
Toyota Corolla 4-cyl. 1.8L	$7,808

Projected Ownership and Operating Costs for Selected 2010 Light Trucks, Vans, and SUVs

Most Expensive

Chevrolet Tahoe LS 4x4 8-cyl. 5.3L	$17,551
Ford E350 XL S.D. 8-cyl. 5.4L	$16,301
Ford Explorer XLT 4x4 6-cyl. 4.0L	$15,255

Least Expensive

Dodge Grand Caravan SE 6-cyl. 3.3L	$12,386
Mercury Mariner 4-cyl. 2.5L	$11,237
Ford Ranger XL 4x2 6ft 4-cyl. 2.3L	$10,331

Runzheimer International is an international management consulting firm specializing in transportation, travel and living cost information.

REBATE VS. LOW RATES (FOUR YEAR LOAN)

Credit Union or Bank Rate	Dealer Rate						
	1%	2%	3%	4%	5%	6%	7%
6%	95	76	58	39	19	*	*
6.5%	103	85	67	48	29	10	*
7%	112	94	76	57	38	19	*
7.5%	121	103	85	66	48	29	10

Based on data from *Home and Family Finances*, a publication of the Credit Union National Association.

LEASING VS. BUYING

Because the unpredictibility of the value of a vehicle at the end of a lease, more and more companies are getting out of the leasing business. That's good news because, in general, leasing costs more than buying outright or financing. When you pay cash or finance a car, you own an asset; leasing leaves you with nothing except all the headaches and responsibilities of ownership with none of the benefits. When you lease you pay a monthly fee for a predetermined time in exchange for the use of a car. However, you also pay for maintenance, insurance, and repairs as if you owned the car. Finally, when it comes time to turn in the car, it has to be in top shape—otherwise, you'll have to pay for repairs or body work.

If you are considering a lease, here are some leasing terms you need to know and some tips to get you through the process:

Capitalized Cost is the price of the car on which the lease is based. Negotiate this as if you were buying the car. Capitalized Cost Reduction is your down payment.

Know the make and model of the vehicle you want. Tell the agent exactly how you want the car equipped. You don't have to pay for options you don't request. Decide in advance how long you will keep the car.

Find out the price of the options on which the lease is based. Typically, they will be full retail price. Their cost can be negotiated (albeit with some difficulty) before you settle on the monthly payment.

Make sure options like a sunroof or stereo are added to the Capitalized Cost. When you purchase dealer-added options, be sure they add the full cost of the option to the Capitalized Cost so that you only pay for the depreciated value of the option, not the full cost.

Find out how much you are required to pay at delivery. Most leases require at least the first month's payment. Others have a security deposit, registration fees, or other "hidden costs." When shopping around, make sure price quotes include security deposit and taxes—sales tax, monthly use tax, or gross receipt tax. Ask how the length of the lease affects your monthly cost.

Find out how the lease price was determined. Lease prices are generally based on the manufacturer's suggested retail price, less the predetermined residual value. The best values are cars with a high expected residual value. To protect themselves, leasers tend to underestimate residual value, but you can do little about this estimate.

Find out the annual mileage limit. Don't accept a contract with a lower limit than you need. Most standard contracts allow 15,000 to 18,000 miles per year. If you go under the allowance one year, you can go over it the next. Watch out for Excess Mileage fees. If you go over, you'll get charged per mile.

Avoid "capitalized cost reduction" or "equity leases." Here the leaser offers to lower the monthly payment by asking you for more money up front—in other words, a down payment.

Ask about early termination. Between 30 and 40 percent of two-year leases are terminated early and 40–60 percent of four-year leases terminate early—this means expensive early termination fees. If you terminate the lease before it is up, what are the financial penalties? Typically, they are very high so watch out. Ask the dealer exactly what you would owe at the end of each year if you wanted out of the lease. Remember, if your car is stolen, the lease will typically be terminated. While your

LEASEWISE

TIP

If you must lease, why haggle when you can let someone else do it for you? LeaseWise, a service from the non-profit Center for the Study of Services, makes dealers bid for your lease. First, they get leasing bids from dealers on the vehicles you're interested in. Next, you'll receive a detailed report with all the bids, the dealer and invoice cost of the vehicle, and a complete explanation of the various bids. Then, you can lease from the lowest bidder or use the report as leverage with another dealer. The service costs $335. For more information, call 800-475-7283, or visit www.checkbook.org.

insurance should cover the value of the car, you still may owe additional amounts per your lease contract.

Avoid maintenance contracts. Getting work done privately is cheaper in the long run. And don't forget, this is a new car with a standard warranty.

Arrange for your own insurance. By shopping around, you can generally find less expensive insurance than what's offered by the leaser.

Ask how quickly you can expect delivery. If your agent can't deliver in a reasonable time, maybe he or she can't meet the price quoted.

Retain your option to buy the car at the end of the lease at a predetermined price. The price should equal the residual value; if it is more then the leaser is trying to make an additional profit. Regardless of how the end-of-lease value is determined, if you want the car, make an offer based on the current "Blue Book" value of the car at the end of the lease.

Residual Value is the value of your car at the end of the lease.

Here's what Automotive Lease Guide estimates the residual value after five years will be for a few 2009 vehicles:

MINI Cooper	46%
Scion xB	36%
Honda CR-V	35%
Toyota Camry	31%
Chevrolet Traverse	17%
Chrys. Sebring convertible	15%

LEASING VS. BUYING

The following table compares the costs of leasing vs. buying the same car over three and six years. Your actual costs may vary, but you can use this format to compare the cars you are considering. Our example assumes the residual value to be 45 percent after three years and 22 percent after six years.

3 Years

	Lease	Finance
MSRP	$29,000.00	$29,000.00
Purchase Cost of Car	$26,100.00	$26,100.00
Down Payment	$3790.00	$3190.00
Monthly Payment	$371.27	$448.26
Total Payments	$13,365.72	$16,137.36[1]
Amount left on loan		$10,062.81
Value of vehicle at 3 yrs.		$13050.00
Overall Cost, first 3 yrs.	$17,155.72	$16340.17
Savings over Leasing		**$815.55**

If you choose to keep the car you financed for six years, the savings over leasing becomes huge!

6 Years

	Lease[2]	Finance[3]
MSRP	$30,450.00	$29,000.00
Cost of Car	$27,405.00	$26,100.00
Down Payment	$3950.00	$3,190.00
Monthly Payment	$389.83	$448.26
Total Payments	$14,033.88	$26,895.60
Value of vehicle at 6 yrs.		$6,496.00
Overall Cost, 6 yrs.	$35,139.60[4]	$23,589.60
Savings over Leasing		**$11,550.00**

Even if you decide to finance two cars over a six year period (to match two leased cars in six years) you save over $2,400.00 by financing vs. leasing.

[1] First 3 years of 5-year loan with 6.5 percent annual percentage rate.
[2] These are the second 3 year lease costs which assume a 5% increase for a similar vehicle.
[3] Five-year loan with 6.5 percent annual percentage rate, no monthly payments in sixth year.
[4] Two 3-year leases.

USING THE INTERNET

The Internet is changing the way car buyers research and shop for cars. But the Internet should be used with caution. Remember that anyone—and we mean *anyone*—can publish a website with no guarantee concerning the accuracy of the information on it. We advise that you only visit websites that have a familiar non-web counterpart. A good example is the Center for Auto Safety's website at www.autosafety.org where you'll find information on auto safety, including publications and newsletters which are typically mailed out to subscribers.

Use the Internet as an information resource. Unfortunately, most automaker websites are nothing more than sophisticated ads with little comparative information.

Good information, like pricing and features, *can* be found online. We've listed some useful websites on this page.

There are also several online car shopping services that have launched. We view most of them with skepticism. Many online car shopping services are tied to a limited, often non-competitive, group of dealers. They may claim the lowest price, but you'll most likely have a dealer calling you with a price that is not much better than what you'd get if you went into a dealership to haggle.

Auto insurance and financing sites are sometimes no better. Don't rely solely on these online services; getting quotes from other sources is the only way to make sure you truly have the best deal.

Finally, clicking a mouse is no substitute for going out and test-driving a car. If you are shopping for a used car, you must check out the actual car before signing on the dotted line. Do not rely on online photos. In fact, online classifieds for cars are no more reliable than looking in a newspaper.

If you do use an online car shopping service, be sure to shop around on your own. Visit dealerships, get quotes from several car shopping services, and research the value of your used car (see www.nadaguides.com). Beware that if you give anyone online your phone number, or email address, you are opening yourself up to unwanted email, junk mail, and even sales calls.

TIP

ON THE WEB

autosafety.org
The Center for Auto Safety (CAS) provides consumers with a voice for auto safety and quality in Washington and to help lemon owners fight back across the country.

carfax.com
Used car buyers will want to visit Carfax. Carfax collects information from numerous sources to provide a vehicle history on a specific vehicle, based on the Vehicle Identification Number (VIN). Carfax can help uncover costly and potentially dangerous hidden problems or confirm the clean history of a vehicle.

consumer.checkbook.org
The Center for the Study of Services (CSS) is an independent, nonprofit consumer organization and the creator of Consumer Checkbook. One of the few car buying services worth using, CSS's CarBargains pits dealers against each other, keeping you from haggling.

nhtsa.gov
The National Highway Traffic Safety Administration (NHTSA) website contains useful information on safety standards, crash tests, recalls, technical service bulletins, child seats, and safety advisories.

fueleconomy.gov
This joint effort by the Department of Energy and the Environmental Protection Agency contains EPA fuel economy ratings for passenger cars and trucks from 1985 to the present, gas saving tips, greenhouse gas and air pollution ratings, energy impact scores, a downloadable Fuel Economy Guide, and a variety of other useful information in a very user-friendly format.

DEPRECIATION

Over the past 20 years, new vehicle depreciation costs have steadily increased. A study conducted by Runzheimer International shows that depreciation and interest now account for just over 50 percent of the costs of owning and operating a vehicle. Recently, however, the increasing cost of depreciation has slowed down. This is due to the relatively stable prices of new vehicles and to the slow increase in finance rates. The higher cost of gasoline consumes a larger percentage of the automotive dollar than ever before. Other costs, including insurance, maintenance, and tires, have remained at relatively steady shares of the automotive dollar.

While there is no foolproof method for predicting retained vehicle value, your best bet is to purchase a popular vehicle model. Chances are it will also be a popular used vehicle model, meaning that the retained value may be higher when you go to sell it.

Most new cars are traded in within four years and are then available on the used car market. The priciest used cars may not be the highest quality. Supply and demand, as well as appearance, are important factors in determining used car prices.

The following table indicates which of the top-selling 2006 cars held their value the best and which did not.

2006 VEHICLES WITH THE BEST AND WORST RESALE VALUE

THE BEST				THE WORST			
Model	2006 Price	2009 Price	Retain. Value	Model	2006 Price	2009 Price	Retain. Value
Scion xB	$13,880	$11,425	82.3%	Dodge Stratus	$21,315	$8,250	38.7%
Toyota Matrix	$15,110	$12,200	80.7%	Ford Taurus	$20,830	$8,225	39.5%
Toyota Corolla	$15,050	$12,000	79.7%	Chevrolet Impala	$25,225	$10,150	40.2%
Lexus IS	$29,990	$23,750	79.2%	Ford Crown Victoria	$24,755	$10,050	40.6%
Honda Element	$19,625	$15,350	78.2%	Chrysler Sebring	$20,425	$8,500	41.6%
Ford Ranger	$16,160	$12,600	78.0%	Chevrolet Malibu	$21,060	$8,775	41.7%
Toyota RAV4	$21,875	$17,000	77.7%	Hyundai Sonata	$17,649	$7,450	42.2%
Jeep Wrangler	$20,380	$15,800	77.5%	Pontiac Grand Prix	$22,435	$10,275	45.8%
Honda Civic	$18,260	$13,850	75.8%	Mercury Gr. Marquis	$24,780	$11,375	45.9%
Scion tC	$16,200	$12,175	75.2%	Dodge Durango	$30,350	$14,225	46.9%
Toyota 4Runner	$29,975	$22,250	74.2%	Ford Five Hundred	$22,230	$10,475	47.1%
Toyota Prius	$21,725	$16,050	73.9%	Chevrolet Uplander	$23,835	$11,275	47.3%
Nissan Pathfinder	$26,500	$19,475	73.5%	Merc.-Benz E-Class	$50,050	$23,875	47.7%
Honda CR-V	$22,500	$16,350	72.7%	Kia Sedona	$22,995	$10,975	47.7%
Nissan Frontier	$19,000	$13,500	71.1%	Chrysler PT Cruiser	$15,405	$7,450	48.4%
Mazda 3	$16,880	$11,975	70.9%	Chrysler Pacifica	$28,365	$13,800	48.7%
Saturn Ion	$11,925	$8,425	70.6%	Cadillac DTS	$41,195	$20,500	49.8%
Toyota Highlander	$25,590	$17,875	69.9%	Dodge Gr. Caravan	$20,615	$10,275	49.8%
Lexus RX	$37,770	$26,175	69.3%	Buick Lucerne	$26,265	$13,175	50.2%
BMW 3-Series	$30,300	$20,825	68.7%	Hyundai Elantra	$13,299	$6,675	50.2%
Nissan Xterra	$22,150	$15,150	68.4%	Kia Spectra	$14,300	$7,200	50.3%
Dodge Charger	$18,939	$12,925	68.2%	Chrysler T & C	$27,860	$14,125	50.7%
Nissan Titan	$27,900	$19,000	68.1%	Chevrolet Trail Blazer	$26,700	$13,550	50.7%
Hummer H3	$29,960	$20,225	67.5%	GMC Envoy	$32,125	$16,575	51.6%
Toyota Camry	$19,545	$13,175	67.4%	Pontiac G6	$20,030	$10,375	51.8%

CORPORATE TWINS

"Corporate twins" refers to vehicles that have different names but share the same mechanics, drivetrain, and chassis. In most cases the vehicles are identical. Sometimes the difference is in body style, price, or options as with the Chevrolet Tahoe and the Cadillac Escalade. Traditionally, corporate twins have been limited mainly to domestic car companies. Today, due to the many car company mergers, corporate twins include cars that were once considered European or Asian coupled with a domestic model name. For example, the Pontiac Vibe and the Toyota Matrix.

CORPORATE TWINS

Chrysler Corp.
Chrysler 300
Dodge Charger

Chrysler Sebring
Dodge Avenger

Chrysler Town &
  Country
Dodge Grand Caravan

Ford Motor Co.
Ford Edge
Lincoln MKX

Ford Escape
Mazda Tribute
Mercury Mariner

Ford Expedition
Lincoln Navigator

Ford Explorer
Mercury Mountaineer

Ford Fusion
Lincoln MKZ
Mercury Milan

General Motors
Buick Lucerne
Cadillac DTS

Cadillac Escalade
Chevrolet Tahoe
GMC Yukon

Cadillac Escalade ESV
Chevrolet Suburban
GMC Yukon XL

Cadillac Escalade EXT
Chevrolet Avalanche

Chevrolet Colorado
GMC Canyon

Chevrolet Equinox
GMC Terrain

Chevrolet Malibu
Pontiac G6
Saturn Aura

Chevrolet Silverado
GMC Sierra

General Motors (cont.)
Chevrolet Traverse
GMC Acadia
Saturn Outlook

Pontiac Vibe
Toyota Matrix

Honda
Acura RL
Honda Accord

Hyundai-Kia
Hyundai Accent
Kia Rio

Hyundai Entourage
Kia Sedona

Hyundai Santa Fe
Kia Rondo

Nissan
Infiniti QX56
Nissan Armada

Porsche
Porsche Cayenne
Volkswagen Touareg

Toyota
Lexus ES
Toyota Camry

Lexus GX
Toyota 4Runner

Lexus LX
Toyota Land Cruiser

Toyota Matrix
Pontiac Vibe

Volkswagen
Porsche Cayenne
Volkswagen Touareg

Ford Escape

Mazda Tribute

Mercury Mariner

T his section provides an overview of the most important features of this year's new models. Nearly all the information you'll need to make a smart choice is concisely presented on one page. (The data is collected for the model expected to be the most popular.) Here's what you'll find and how to interpret the data we've provided:

The Ratings

These are ratings in nine important categories, as well as an overall comparative rating. We have adopted the Olympic rating system with "10" being the best.

Overall Rating: This is the "bottom line." Using a combination of all of the key ratings, this tells how this vehicle stacks up against the others on a scale of 1 to 10. Due to the importance of safety, the combined crash test rating is 20 percent of the overall rating while the other eight ratings are 10 percent each. Vehicles with no front or side crash test results, as of our publication date, cannot be given an overall rating. In other categories, if information is unavailable, an "average" is included in order to develop an overall rating.

Overall Crash Test: This rating represents a combination of the front and side crash test ratings and provides a relative comparison of how this year's models did against each other. We give the best performers a 10 and the worst a 1. Remember to compare crash test results relative to other cars in the same size class. For details, see page 18.

Safety Features: This is an evaluation of how much extra safety is built into the car. We give credit for head and side airbags, roll-sensing side airbags, traction control, brake assist, daytime running lamps, built-in child safety seats, electronic stability control and seat integrated belts. We also include dynamic head restraint and anti-pinch power windows among other important safety features. See the "Safety Checklist" box on each page for more details.

Rollover: Many consumers are aware that vehicles with higher centers of gravity could be more likely to roll over. Comparing the tendency of a vehicle to roll over is very difficult, as there is no agreed upon comparative rating system. Recently, the U.S. government adopted the rating system that we have been using called the static stability formula (SSF). We have compiled the SSF for all of the vehicles. The government provides the SSF rating for some vehicles. For those vehicles not on the government list, we use the SSF formula to provide a rating. The details behind the SSF appear on page 30.

Preventive Maintenance: Each manufacturer suggests a preventive maintenance schedule designed to keep the car in good shape and to protect your rights under the warranty. Those with the lowest estimated PM costs get a 10 and the highest a 1. See pages 39-43 for the estimated costs and more information.

Repair Costs: It is virtually impossible to predict exactly what any new car will cost you in repairs. As such, we take nine typical repairs that you are likely to experience after your warranty expires and compare those costs among this year's models. Those with the lowest cost get a 10 and the highest a 1. See pages 39-43 for specific part repair cost and more information.

Warranty: This is an overall assessment of the manufacturer's basic, powertrain, corrosion, and roadside assistance warranties when compared to all other manufacturer warranties. We give the highest-rated warranties a 10 and the lowest a 1. For details, see the Warranty section.

Fuel Economy: Here we compare the EPA mileage ratings of each car. The misers get a 10 and the guzzlers get a 1. For the purposes of the overall rating we pick the fuel economy rating of what is expected to be the most popular engine and drive train configuration. See page 33 for more information.

Complaints: This is where you'll find how each vehicle stacks up against hundreds of others on the road, based on the U.S. government complaint data for that vehicle. If the car has not been around long enough to have developed a complaint history, it is given a 5 (average). The least complained about cars get a 10 and the most problematic a 1. See the "Complaints Chapter" for details.

Insurance Costs: Insurance companies rate vehicles to determine how much they plan to charge for insurance. Here, you'll find whether you can expect to pay higher or lower insurance premium for what we expect to be the most popular model. We looked at data from various insurance rating programs. Vehicles with a low rating (1 or 3) are more expensive to insure, vehicles with a high rating (8 or 10) are less expensive to insure and those receiving a 5 are typical. This rating will give you a basic idea of the cost to insure the vehicle, but different insurance companies have different rating programs, so it's best to compare prices between companies.

At-a-Glance

Status: Here we tell you if a vehicle is all-new, unchanged, or has recieved appearance change. All-new vehicles (the minority) are brand new from the ground up. Unchanged vehicles are essentially the same, but could have some different color or feature options. Vehicles with an appearance change are those whose internal workings stayed essentially the same, but have updated body panels.

Year Series Started: We generally recommend against buying a car during its first model year of production. Each year the model is made, the production usually improves and as a result there are fewer defects. Therefore, the longer a car has been made, the less likely you are to be plagued with manufacturing and design defects. On the other hand, the newer a car is, the more likely it is to have the latest in features and safety.

Twins: These are cars with different make and model names but share the same mechanics, drive train, and chassis. In some cases the vehicles are identical, in other cases the body style, pricing or options are different.

Body Styles: This is a listing of the various body styles available such as coupe, sedan, wagon, etc. SUVs and minivans are only offered in one body style. Data on the page is for the first style listed.

Seating: This is the number of seating positions in the most popular model. When more than one number is listed (for example, 5/6) it means that different seat configurations are available.

Anti-theft Device: This lists the antitheft devices standard for the vehicle. An *immobilizer* is an electronic device fitted to an automobile which prevents the engine from running unless the correct key (or other token) is present. This prevents the car from being "hot wired" and driven away. A car *alarm* is an electronic device that emits high-volume sound and can sometimes flash the vehicles headlights in an attempt to discourage theft of the vehicle itself, its contents, or both.

Passive devices automatically enter an armed state after the ignition is turned off and doors are closed. Active devices require the user to perform some action like pressing a button to arm and disarm the system.

Parking Index Rating: Using the car's length, wheelbase, and turning circle, we have calculated how easy it will be to maneuver this car in tight spots. This rating of "very easy" to "very hard" is an indicator of how much difficulty you may have parking.

Where Made: Here we tell you where the car was assembled. You'll find that traditional domestic companies often build their vehicles in other countries. Also, many foreign companies build their cars in the U.S.

Fuel Factor

MPG Rating (city/hwy): This is the EPA-rated fuel economy for city and highway driving measured in miles per gallon. Most models have a variety of fuel economy ratings because of different engine and transmission options. We've selected the combination expected to be most popular.

Driving Range: Given the car's expected fuel economy and gas tank size, this value gives you an idea of the number of miles you can expect go on one tank of gas.

Fuel: The type of fuel specified by the manufacturer: regular, premium, E85.

Annual Fuel Cost: This is an estimate based on driving

15,000 miles per year at $2.25/gallon for regular and $2.45/gallon for premium. If the vehicle takes E85 (85% ethanol and 15% gasoline) or gasoline we calculated the annual cost using gasoline.

Greenhouse Gas Emissions: This shows the amount (in tons) of greenhouse gases (carbon dioxide, nitrous oxide, and methane) that a vehicle emits per year along with the CO_2 emitted in producing and distributing the fuel.

Barrels of Oil Used Per Year: This is the number of barrels of petroleum the vehicle will likely use each year. One barrel, once refined, makes about 19.5 gallons of gas.

Competition

Here we tell you how the car stacks up with some of its key competitors. Use this information to broaden your choice of new car possibilities. This list is only a guideline, not an all-inclusive list of every possible alternative.

Price Range

This box contains information on the MSRP. When available, we offer a variety of prices between the base and the most luxurious version of the car. The difference is often substantial. Usually the more expensive versions have fancy trim, larger engines, and lots of automatic equipment. The least expensive

versions usually have manual transmissions and few extra features. In addition to the price range, we provide the expected dealer markup. Be prepared for higher retail prices when you get to the showroom. Manufacturers like to load their cars with factory options, and dealers like to add their own items such as fabric protection and paint sealant. Remember, prices and dealer costs can change during the year. Use these figures for general reference and comparisons, not as a precise indication of exactly how much the car you are interested in will cost. See page 68 for a buying service designed to ensure that you get the very best price.

Safety Checklist

Frontal and Side Crash Test Ratings: Here's where we tell you if the front or side crash

test index was among the best, above average, average, below average or the worst when compared to 2010 cars tested to date. To provide this rating we use the crash test for the vehicles with the best available safety equipment among the models when multiple models were tested.

Airbags

Head Airbag: One of the two types of side airbags, this device protects the head area and can offer extra rollover protection.

Chest/Torso Airbag: The other type of side airbag that protects the chest and torso and provides important protection in side crashes.

Roll Sensing Side Airbags: Some companies offer a special side airbag system which keeps the side airbags inflated longer in the event of a rollover. This

---

TYPES OF AIRBAGS

Since airbags were introduced over 30 years ago, they have been so successful in saving lives that car makers include a variety of types in today's cars. Here's a rundown of the basic types of airbags available. Please note that manufacturers have varying marketing names for these airbags.

Front: These airbags deploy toward the occupant and protect both the driver and front passenger. They are now standard in all vehicles.

Side: These airbags deploy from the side of a seat or from the door and are designed to protect the body in a side impact. They can be placed to protect both the front and rear passengers. Bags mounted in seats offer protection in a wider range of seating positions.

Head: These airbags deploy from above the doors. In many cars, there is one head curtain that stretches from the front to the back of the vehicle. They serve as a shield from spraying glass, and protection in rollovers and can reduce head injuries. Some designs such as Audi's "side guard," remain inflated for five seconds in the event of a sustained rollover.

feature can reduce the likelihood of injury when a vehicle flips.

Out of Position Test: This indicates if the manufacturer has reported to the government that its side airbags meet voluntary requirements designed to reduce the risk of injury to out of position occupants in side crashes with airbags.

Children
Built-In Child Safety Seat: 85% of parents use child safety seats improperly. One reason is because they are so difficult to properly install. To overcome this problem a few manufacturers offer built-in seats.

Automatic Window Reversal: Automatically reverses the window when it contacts something. This important safety feature can prevent severe injury to children who accidentally control the switches..

Crash Avoidance
Frontal Collision Warning: This feature use radar or laser sensors to detect an imminent crash in front of the vehicle. Systems may warn the driver with a light and/or audible chime, precharge the brakes, retract the seat belts removing excess slack, and automatically apply partial or full braking to minimize the crash severity.

Electronic Stability Control: This feature automatically senses when a vehicle may be going out of control and applies the brakes and steers the vehicle in a manner to regain control. It will not work if the vehicle's speed is simply too great for conditions.

Lane Departure Warning: This mechanism is designed to warn a driver when the vehicle begins to move out of its lane (unless a turn signal is on in that direction). The warning may be a light, audible chime, or a vibrating steering wheel.

Brake Assist: Emergency Brake Assist (EBA) detects the speed or force which the driver presses the brake pedal and applies all available power if this speed or force exceeds a certain threshold.

General
Automatic Crash Notification: Using cellular technology and global positioning systems, some vehicles have the ability to send a call for help in the event of airbag deployment or accident. You'll have to pay extra for this feature.

Daytime Running Lights: Some cars offer daytime running lights that can reduce your chances of being in a crash by up to 40 percent by increasing the visibility of your vehicle. We indicate whether daytime running lights are standard, optional, or not available.

Automatic Door-Locking System: In vehicles equipped with ADL, all doors automatically lock either when the shift lever is moved out of 'Park' or when the vehicle reaches a certain speed. ADL improves the likelihood that doors will stay closed in the event of an accident, retaining the structural integrity of the vehicle and lowering the chance of occupant ejection. In addition, they prevent doors from being opened accidentally or by children while the car is in motion.

Safety Belts/Restraints
Adjustable Front Belts: Proper positioning of the safety belt across your chest is critical to obtaining the benefits of buckling up. Some systems allow you to adjust the height of the belt so it crosses your chest properly.

Specifications

Drive: This indicates the type of drive the manufacturer offers. This could be two wheel drive in the front (FWD) or rear (RWD) or all or four wheel drive (AWD/4WD).

Engine: This lists the engine size (liters) and type that is expected to be the most popular and the one on which we based the ratings. The type options are V6 or V8 for six or eight valve layout, I4 for four inline, or CVVT for continuous variable valve timing.

Transmission: This indicates the type of transmission expected to be the most popular. Most drivers today prefer automatic transmissions. The number listed with the transmission (5-sp.) is the number of gears or speeds. Then we list whether it's automatic or manual and in some cases we list the automatic transmission as continuously variable transmission (CVT). CVT changes smoothly and efficiently between gears. This can provide better fuel economy than other transmissions by enabling the engine to run at its most efficient speed.

Tow Rating: Ratings of very low, low, average, high, and very high indicate the vehicle's relative ability to tow trailers or other loads. Some manufacturers do not provide a tow rating.

Head/Leg Room: This tells how roomy the front seat is. The values are given in inches and rated compared to the other 2010 vehicles.

Interior Space: This tells how roomy the car's passenger area should feel. This value is given in cubic feet. Many SUVs do not provide interior space specifications.

Cargo Space: This gives you the cubic feet available for cargo. For minivans, the volume is behind the last row of seats. In cars, it's the trunk space. We rate the roominess of the cargo space compared to all SUVs and cars. For trucks we list the Truck Bed Volume and rate it, small, medium, or large, compared to other truck bed volumes available.

Wheelbase/Length: The wheelbase is the distance between the centers of the front and rear wheels and the length is the distance from front bumper to rear bumper. Wheelbase can effect the ride and length effects how big the car "feels."

DESTINATION CHARGES

TIP

Destination charges are a non-negotiable part of buying a new car, no matter where you purchase it. They are an important factor when comparing prices. You'll find the destination charges on the price sticker attached to the vehicle. According to automakers, destination charges are the cost of shipping a vehicle from its "final assembly point" to the dealership. But, the following table illustrates that there is little correlation between destination charges and where the cars are assembled:

Vehicle	Destination Charge*	Assembly Country
Ford F-150	$975	U.S.A.
Acura TL	$810	Japan
Hyundai Genesis	$750	South Korea
Jeep Patriot	$630	U.S.A.

*Data based on 2010 model year cars.

Ratings—10 Best, 1 Worst

Combo Crash Tests	–
Safety Features	10
Rollover	5
Preventive Maintenance	8
Repair Costs	6
Warranty	5
Fuel Economy	3
Complaints	10
Insurance Costs	8
OVERALL RATING	**–**

Acura MDX

Acura MDX

At-a-Glance

Status	Appearance Change
Year Series Started	2007
Twins	–
Body Styles	SUV
Seating	7/8
Anti-Theft Device	Std. Pass. Immobil. & Pass. Alarm
Parking Index Rating	Average
Where Made	Alliston, Ontario

Fuel Factor

MPG Rating (city/hwy)	Poor-16/21
Driving Range (mi.)	Average-376.3
Fuel Type	Premium
Annual Fuel Cost	Very High-$2427
Greenhouse Gas Emissions (tons/yr.)	High-10.2
Barrels of Oil Used per year	High-19.0

How the Competition Rates

Competitors	Rating	Pg.
BMW X5	8	96
Lexus GX	–	186
Volvo XC90	10	270

Price Range

Price Range	Retail	Markup
Base	$40,990	10%
Base w/ Tech. Pkg. & RES	$46,790	10%
Sport	$47,140	10%
Sport w/ Rear Entertain. System	$48,890	10%

Safety Checklist

Crash Tests:
Frontal . . . . Average
Side . . . . Not Tested

Airbags:
Head . . . . Std. Curtain All Rows
Chest/Torso . . . Std. Row 1 Torso & Pelvis from Seat
Roll-Sensing Side Airbag . . . . Standard
Out-of-Position Test . . . . –

Children:
Built-in Child Safety Seat . . . . –
Automatic Window Reversal. Std. Front and Rear

Crash Avoidance:
Frontal Collision Warning . . . . Optional
Electronic Stability Control . . . . Standard
Lane Departure Warning . . . . –
Brake Assist . . . . Standard

General:
Automatic Crash Notification . . . . –
Daytime Running Lights . . . . Standard
Automatic Door-Locking . . . . Standard

Safety Belt:
Adjustable Front Belt . . . . Standard

Acura MDX

Specifications

Drive	AWD
Engine	3.7-liter V6
Transmission	6-sp. Automatic
Tow Rating (lbs.)	Average-5000
Head/Leg Room (in.)	Cramped-39.2/41.2
Interior Space (cu. ft.)	Very Roomy-142.2
Cargo Space (cu. ft.)	Cramped-15
Wheelbase/Length (in.)	108.3/191.6

*Combines results of both front and side tests in relation to all tests for 2010 vehicles.

Ratings—10 Best, 1 Worst

Combo Crash Tests	5
Safety Features	9
Rollover	4
Preventive Maintenance	8
Repair Costs	6
Warranty	5
Fuel Economy	5
Complaints	10
Insurance Costs	8
OVERALL RATING	**8**

Acura RDX

Acura RDX

At-a-Glance

Status	Unchanged
Year Series Started	2007
Twins	–
Body Styles	SUV
Seating	5
Anti-Theft Device	Std. Pass. Immobil. & Pass. Alarm
Parking Index Rating	Hard
Where Made	Marysville, OH

Fuel Factor

MPG Rating (city/hwy)	Average-19/24
Driving Range (mi.)	Average-377.4
Fuel Type	Premium
Annual Fuel Cost	Average-$2075
Greenhouse Gas Emissions (tons/yr.)	High-8.7
Barrels of Oil Used per year	High-16.3

How the Competition Rates

Competitors	Rating	Pg.
Infiniti FX	–	164
Lexus RX	6	190
Volkswagen Tiguan	6	265

Price Range	Retail	Markup
Base	$32,520	9%
SH-AWD	$34,250	9%
Base w/ Tech. Pkg.	$35,620	9%
SH-AWD w/ Tech. Pkg.	$37,620	9%

Safety Checklist

Crash Tests:
Frontal . . . . Good
Side. . . . . Very Poor
Airbags:
Head . . . . Std. Row 1 & 2 Curtain
Chest/Torso . . . . Std. Row 1 Torso from Seat
Roll-Sensing Side Airbag . . . . Standard
Out-of-Position Test. . . . . . Meets Requirements
Children:
Built-in Child Safety Seat . . . . –
Automatic Window Reversal. Std. Front and Rear
Crash Avoidance:
Frontal Collision Warning . . . . –
Electronic Stability Control . . . . Standard
Lane Departure Warning . . . . –
Brake Assist . . . . Standard
General:
Automatic Crash Notification . . . . –
Daytime Running Lights. . . . . Standard
Automatic Door-Locking . . . . Standard
Safety Belt:
Adjustable Front Belt . . . . Standard

Acura RDX

Specifications

Drive	FWD
Engine	2.3-liter I4
Transmission	5-sp. Automatic
Tow Rating (lbs.)	Very Low-1500
Head/Leg Room (in.)	Cramped-38.7/41.8
Interior Space (cu. ft.)	Average-101.4
Cargo Space (cu. ft.)	Roomy-27.8
Wheelbase/Length (in.)	104.3/182.5

*Combines results of both front and side tests in relation to all tests for 2010 vehicles.

Ratings—10 Best, 1 Worst

Combo Crash Tests	6
Safety Features	8
Rollover	9
Preventive Maintenance	8
Repair Costs	–
Warranty	5
Fuel Economy	5
Complaints	10
Insurance Costs	3
OVERALL RATING	**9**

Acura TL

Acura TL

At-a-Glance

Status. . . . . Unchanged
Year Series Started 2009
Twins . . . . –
Body Styles . . . . Sedan
Seating. 5
Anti-Theft Device. . Std. Pass. Immobil. & Pass. Alarm
Parking Index Rating . . . . Hard
Where Made. . . . . Marysville, OH

Fuel Factor
MPG Rating (city/hwy) Average-18/26
Driving Range (mi.) Average-386.5
Fuel Type. . . . . Premium
Annual Fuel Cost. . . . . Average-$2082
Greenhouse Gas Emissions (tons/yr.) High-8.7
Barrels of Oil Used per year. High-16.3

How the Competition Rates

Competitors	Rating	Pg.
Hyundai Genesis	9	158
Infiniti G	7	165
Lexus ES	6	184

Price Range

Price Range	Retail	Markup
Base	$35,105	9%
SH-AWD	$38,655	9%
Base w/ Tech. Pkg.	$38,835	9%
SH-AWD w/ Tech. Pkg. & HPT	$43,385	9%

Safety Checklist

Crash Tests:
Frontal . . . . Average
Side . . . . Average

Airbags:
Head . . . . Std. Row 1 & 2 Curtain
Chest/Torso. . . Std. Row 1 Torso & Pelvis from Seat
Roll-Sensing Side Airbag . . . . –
Out-of-Position Test. . . . . . . Meets Requirements

Children:
Built-in Child Safety Seat . . . . –
Automatic Window Reversal. Std. Front and Rear

Crash Avoidance:
Frontal Collision Warning . . . . –
Electronic Stability Control . . . . Standard
Lane Departure Warning . . . . –
Brake Assist . . . . Standard

General:
Automatic Crash Notification . . . . –
Daytime Running Lights. . . . . Standard
Automatic Door-Locking. . . . . Standard

Safety Belt:
Adjustable Front Belt . . . . Standard

Acura TL

Specifications

Drive . . . . FWD
Engine 3.5-liter V6
Transmission . . . . 5-sp. Automatic
Tow Rating (lbs.) . . . . –
Head/Leg Room (in.) Cramped-38.4/42.5
Interior Space (cu. ft.). Cramped-98.2
Cargo Space (cu. ft.) Cramped-13.1
Wheelbase/Length (in.) 109.3/195.5

*Combines results of both front and side tests in relation to all tests for 2010 vehicles.

Ratings—10 Best, 1 Worst

Combo Crash Tests	10
Safety Features	8
Rollover	8
Preventive Maintenance	10
Repair Costs	7
Warranty	5
Fuel Economy	7
Complaints	1
Insurance Costs	3
OVERALL RATING	**10**

Acura TSX

Acura TSX

At-a-Glance

Status	Unchanged
Year Series Started	2009
Twins	—
Body Styles	Sedan
Seating	5
Anti-Theft Device	Std. Pass. Immobil. & Pass. Alarm
Parking Index Rating	Easy
Where Made	Sayama, Japan

Fuel Factor

MPG Rating (city/hwy)	Good-21/30
Driving Range (mi.)	Very Long-449.1
Fuel Type	Premium
Annual Fuel Cost	Low-$1792
Greenhouse Gas Emissions (tons/yr.)	Average-7.3
Barrels of Oil Used per year	Average-13.7

How the Competition Rates

Competitors	Rating	Pg.
Chrysler Sebring	9	121
Hyundai Sonata	7	160
Lexus IS	5	188

Price Range

	Retail	Markup
Base Manual Trans.	$29,310	9%
Base w/ Tech. Pkg.	$32,410	9%
V6 Auto. Trans.	$34,850	9%
V6 Auto. Trans. w/Tech. Pkg.	$37,950	9%

Safety Checklist

Crash Tests:
Frontal . . . . Very Good
Side . . . . Very Good

Airbags:
Head . . . . Std. Row 1 & 2 Curtain
Chest/Torso . . . Std. Row 1 Torso & Pelvis from Seat
Roll-Sensing Side Airbag . . . . —
Out-of-Position Test . . . . . . Meets Requirements

Children:
Built-in Child Safety Seat . . . . —
Automatic Window Reversal. Std. Front and Rear

Crash Avoidance:
Frontal Collision Warning . . . . —
Electronic Stability Control . . . . Standard
Lane Departure Warning . . . . —
Brake Assist . . . . Standard

General:
Automatic Crash Notification . . . . —
Daytime Running Lights . . . . Standard
Automatic Door-Locking . . . . Standard

Safety Belt:
Adjustable Front Belt . . . . Standard

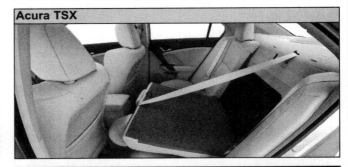

Acura TSX

Specifications

Drive	FWD
Engine	2.4-liter I4
Transmission	5-sp. Automatic
Tow Rating (lbs.)	—
Head/Leg Room (in.)	Cramped-37.6/42.4
Interior Space (cu. ft.)	Cramped-94.5
Cargo Space (cu. ft.)	Cramped-12.6
Wheelbase/Length (in.)	106.4/185.6

*Combines results of both front and side tests in relation to all tests for 2010 vehicles.

Ratings—10 Best, 1 Worst

Combo Crash Tests	–
Safety Features	–
Rollover	7
Preventive Maintenance	–
Repair Costs	–
Warranty	5
Fuel Economy	3
Complaints	–
Insurance Costs	–
OVERALL RATING	–

Acura ZDX

Acura ZDX

Acura ZDX

At-a-Glance

Status	All New
Year Series Started	2010
Twins	–
Body Styles	SUV
Seating	5
Anti-Theft Device	–
Parking Index Rating	Hard
Where Made	Alliston, Ontario
Fuel Factor	
MPG Rating (city/hwy)	Poor-16/22
Driving Range (mi.)	Average-383.0
Fuel Type	Premium
Annual Fuel Cost	High-$2378
Greenhouse Gas Emissions (tons/yr.)	–
Barrels of Oil Used per year	–

How the Competition Rates

Competitors	Rating	Pg.
Dodge Nitro	6	130
Mazda CX-7	6	199
Toyota Venza	6	256

Price Range

	Retail	Markup
Base	$45,495	9%
Technology Package	$49,995	9%
Advance Package	$56,045	9%

Safety Checklist

Crash Tests:
Frontal . . . . –
Side . . . . –
Airbags:
Head . . . . Std. Row 1 & 2 Curtain
   Chest/Torso . . . . Std. Row 1 Torso
Roll-Sensing Side Airbag . . . . Standard
Out-of-Position Test . . . . . . Meets Requirements
Children:
Built-in Child Safety Seat . . . . –
Automatic Window Reversal . . . . Standard
Crash Avoidance:
Frontal Collision Warning . . . . –
Electronic Stability Control . . . . Standard
Lane Departure Warning . . . . –
Brake Assist . . . . Standard
General:
Automatic Crash Notification . . . . –
Daytime Running Lights . . . . Standard
Automatic Door-Locking . . . . –
Safety Belt:
Adjustable Front Belt . . . . Standard

Acura ZDX

Specifications

Drive	AWD
Engine	3.7-liter V6
Transmission	6-sp. Automatic
Tow Rating (lbs.)	Very Low-1500
Head/Leg Room (in.)	Cramped-38/42.6
Interior Space (cu. ft.)	Very Cramped-91.2
Cargo Space (cu. ft.)	Roomy-26.3
Wheelbase/Length (in.)	108.3/192.4

*Combines results of both front and side tests in relation to all tests for 2010 vehicles.

Ratings—10 Best, 1 Worst

Combo Crash Tests	10
Safety Features	9
Rollover	8
Preventive Maintenance	5
Repair Costs	4
Warranty	9
Fuel Economy	8
Complaints	6
Insurance Costs	3
OVERALL RATING	**10**

Audi A4

At-a-Glance

Status. . . . . Unchanged
Year Series Started 2009
Twins . . . . −
Body Styles . . . . Sedan
Seating. 5
Anti-Theft Device. . Std. Pass. Immobil. & Pass. Alarm
Parking Index Rating . . . . Average
Where Made. . . . . Germany
Fuel Factor
  MPG Rating (city/hwy) Good-23/30
  Driving Range (mi.) . . . . Very Long-441.2
  Fuel Type. . . . . Premium
  Annual Fuel Cost . . . . Low-$1693
  Greenhouse Gas Emissions (tons/yr.) . . Average-7.1
  Barrels of Oil Used per year Low-13.2

How the Competition Rates

Competitors	Rating	Pg.
BMW 3 Series	7	92
Mercedes-Benz C-Class	−	203
Volvo S40	9	266

Price Range	Retail	Markup
2.0T FWD Sedan Auto Trans.	$31,450	8%
2.0T quattro Sedan Manual	$32,350	8%
2.0T quattro Sedan Tiptronic	$33,550	8%
2.0T quattro Avant Tiptronic	$35,350	8%

Audi A4

Safety Checklist

Crash Tests:
  Frontal . . . . Very Good
  Side . . . . Very Good
Airbags:
  Head . . . . Std. Row 1 & 2 Curtain
  Chest/Torso Std. Row 1 & Opt. Row 2 Torso from Seat
  Roll-Sensing Side Airbag . . . . −
  Out-of-Position Test. . . . . . . Meets Requirements
Children:
  Built-in Child Safety Seat . . . . −
  Automatic Window Reversal. Std. Front and Rear
Crash Avoidance:
  Frontal Collision Warning . . . . Optional
  Electronic Stability Control . . . . Standard
  Lane Departure Warning . . . . −
  Brake Assist . . . . Standard
General:
  Automatic Crash Notification . . . . −
  Daytime Running Lights. . . . . Standard
  Automatic Door-Locking. . . . . Standard
Safety Belt:
  Adjustable Front Belt . . . . Standard

Audi A4

Specifications

Drive . . . . FWD
Engine. 2.0-liter I4
Transmission . . . . 6-sp. Automatic
Tow Rating (lbs.). . . . . −
Head/Leg Room (in.) Average-40/41.3
Interior Space (cu. ft.) . . . . Very Cramped-91
Cargo Space (cu. ft.). . . . . Very Cramped-12
Wheelbase/Length (in.) 110.6/185.2

*Combines results of both front and side tests in relation to all tests for 2010 vehicles.

Ratings—10 Best, 1 Worst

Combo Crash Tests	–
Safety Features	7
Rollover	10
Preventive Maintenance	7
Repair Costs	3
Warranty	9
Fuel Economy	8
Complaints	10
Insurance Costs	1
OVERALL RATING	**–**

Audi A5

Audi A5

At-a-Glance

Status.	Unchanged
Year Series Started	2008
Twins	–
Body Styles	Coupe
Seating	4
Anti-Theft Device.	Std. Pass. Immobil. & Pass. Alarm
Parking Index Rating	Average
Where Made.	Neckarsulm, Germany

Fuel Factor

MPG Rating (city/hwy)	Good-23/30
Driving Range (mi.)	Very Long-429.3
Fuel Type.	Premium
Annual Fuel Cost	Low-$1740
Greenhouse Gas Emissions (tons/yr.)	Average-8.0
Barrels of Oil Used per year.	Average-14.9

How the Competition Rates

Competitors	Rating	Pg.
BMW 3 Series	7	92
Infiniti G	7	165
Lexus GS	–	185

Price Range

	Retail	Markup
2.0T quattro Coupe Manual	$36,000	8%
2.0T quattro Coupe Tiptronic	$37,200	8%
3.2 quattro Coupe Tiptronic	$44,000	8%
4.2 FSI V8 Coupe Tiptronic	$53,600	8%

Safety Checklist

Crash Tests:
- Frontal. . . . . –
- Side . . . . . –

Airbags:
- Head . . . . . Std. Row 1 & 2 Curtain
- Chest/Torso . . . . . Std. Row 1 Torso from Seat
- Roll-Sensing Side Airbag . . . . . –
- Out-of-Position Test. . . . . Meets Requirements

Children:
- Built-in Child Safety Seat . . . . . –
- Automatic Window Reversal . . . . . Std. Front

Crash Avoidance:
- Frontal Collision Warning . . . . . Optional
- Electronic Stability Control . . . . . Standard
- Lane Departure Warning. . . . . Optional
- Brake Assist . . . . . Standard

General:
- Automatic Crash Notification . . . . . –
- Daytime Running Lights. . . . . Standard
- Automatic Door-Locking. . . . . Standard

Safety Belt:
- Adjustable Front Belt . . . . . –

Audi A5

Specifications

Drive	FWD
Engine.	2.0-liter I4
Transmission	CVT
Tow Rating (lbs.)	–
Head/Leg Room (in.)	Cramped-39/41.3
Interior Space (cu. ft.)	Very Cramped-84
Cargo Space (cu. ft.)	Very Cramped-12
Wheelbase/Length (in.)	108.3/182.09

*Combines results of both front and side tests in relation to all tests for 2010 vehicles.

Ratings—10 Best, 1 Worst

Combo Crash Tests	–
Safety Features	7
Rollover	9
Preventive Maintenance	7
Repair Costs	–
Warranty	9
Fuel Economy	5
Complaints	8
Insurance Costs	5
OVERALL RATING	–

Audi A6

Audi A6

At-a-Glance

Status. . . . . Unchanged
Year Series Started 2005
Twins . . . . –
Body Styles. . . . . Sedan, Wagon
Seating. 5
Anti-Theft Device. . Std. Pass. Immobil. & Pass. Alarm
Parking Index Rating . . . . Hard
Where Made. . . . . Neckarsulm, Germany
Fuel Factor
  MPG Rating (city/hwy) Average-18/26
  Driving Range (mi.) . . . . Very Long-440.8
  Fuel Type. . . . . Premium
  Annual Fuel Cost. . . . . Average-$2082
  Greenhouse Gas Emissions (tons/yr.) High-8.3
  Barrels of Oil Used per year. Average-15.6

How the Competition Rates

Competitors	Rating	Pg.
BMW 7 Series	–	94
Lexus LS	–	189
Volvo S80	–	267

Price Range	Retail	Markup
Premium 3.2 FSI Multitronic FWD	$45,200	8%
Prem. Plus 3.0 TFSI quattro Tiptronic	$52,800	8%
Prestige 3.0 TFSI Avant quattro Tiptron.	$58,160	8%
Prestige 5.2 FSI V10 quattro Tiptronic	$76,100	8%

Safety Checklist

Crash Tests:
  Frontal. . . . . –
  Side . . . . –
Airbags:
  Head . . . . Std. Row 1 & 2 Curtain
  Chest/Torso Std. Row 1 & Opt. Row 2 Torso from Seat
  Roll-Sensing Side Airbag . . . . –
  Out-of-Position Test. . . . . . Meets Requirements
Children:
  Built-in Child Safety Seat . . . . –
  Automatic Window Reversal. Std. Front and Rear
Crash Avoidance:
  Frontal Collision Warning . . . . –
  Electronic Stability Control . . . . Standard
  Lane Departure Warning . . . . –
  Brake Assist . . . . Standard
General:
  Automatic Crash Notification . . . . –
  Daytime Running Lights. . . . . Standard
  Automatic Door-Locking. . . . . Standard
Safety Belt:
  Adjustable Front Belt . . . . Standard

Audi A6

Specifications

Drive . . . . FWD
Engine 3.2-liter V6
Transmission . . . . 6-sp. Automatic
Tow Rating (lbs.). . . . . –
Head/Leg Room (in.) Cramped-38.7/41.3
Interior Space (cu. ft.). Cramped-97.94
Cargo Space (cu. ft.) Cramped-15.9
Wheelbase/Length (in.) 111.9/193.5

*Combines results of both front and side tests in relation to all tests for 2010 vehicles.

Ratings—10 Best, 1 Worst

Combo Crash Tests	5
Safety Features	10
Rollover	4
Preventive Maintenance	–
Repair Costs	–
Warranty	9
Fuel Economy	4
Complaints	9
Insurance Costs	3
OVERALL RATING	**7**

Audi Q5

At-a-Glance

Status	Unchanged
Year Series Started	2009
Twins	–
Body Styles	SUV
Seating	5
Anti-Theft Device	Std. Pass. Immobil. & Pass. Alarm
Parking Index Rating	Average
Where Made	Ingolstadt, Germany

Fuel Factor

MPG Rating (city/hwy)	Poor-18/23
Driving Range (mi.)	Long-395.0
Fuel Type	Premium
Annual Fuel Cost	High-$2180
Greenhouse Gas Emissions (tons/yr.)	High-9.2
Barrels of Oil Used per year	High-17.1

How the Competition Rates

Competitors	Rating	Pg.
Cadillac SRX	5	103
Lexus RX	6	190
Volvo XC60	–	269

Price Range	Retail	Markup
Premium	$37,350	8%
Premium Plus	$41,400	8%
Prestige	$48,850	8%
Prestige S-Line	$51,000	8%

Audi Q5

Safety Checklist

Crash Tests:
Frontal	Poor
Side	Good

Airbags:
Head	Std. Row 1 & 2 Curtain
Chest/Torso	Std. Row 1 & Opt. Row 2 Torso from Seat
Roll-Sensing Side Airbag	Standard
Out-of-Position Test	Meets Requirements

Children:
Built-in Child Safety Seat	–
Automatic Window Reversal	Std. Front and Rear

Crash Avoidance:
Frontal Collision Warning	–
Electronic Stability Control	Standard
Lane Departure Warning	–
Brake Assist	Standard

General:
Automatic Crash Notification	–
Daytime Running Lights	Standard
Automatic Door-Locking	Standard

Safety Belt:
Adjustable Front Belt	Standard

Audi Q5

Specifications

Drive	4WD
Engine	3.2-liter V6
Transmission	6-sp. Automatic
Tow Rating (lbs.)	Average-4400
Head/Leg Room (in.)	Cramped-39.4/41
Interior Space (cu. ft.)	Average-101.5
Cargo Space (cu. ft.)	Roomy-29.1
Wheelbase/Length (in.)	110.5/182.2

*Combines results of both front and side tests in relation to all tests for 2010 vehicles.

Ratings—10 Best, 1 Worst

Combo Crash Tests	6
Safety Features	10
Rollover	3
Preventive Maintenance	9
Repair Costs	2
Warranty	9
Fuel Economy	2
Complaints	7
Insurance Costs	3
OVERALL RATING	**7**

Audi Q7

Audi Q7

At-a-Glance

Status. . . . . Unchanged
Year Series Started 2007
Twins . . . . –
Body Styles. . . . . SUV
Seating. 7
Anti-Theft Device. . Std. Pass. Immobil. & Pass. Alarm
Parking Index Rating . . . . Very Hard
Where Made. . . . . Bratislava, Slovakia
Fuel Factor
  MPG Rating (city/hwy). . . . . Very Poor-14/19
  Driving Range (mi.) Long-419.2
  Fuel Type. . . . . Premium
  Annual Fuel Cost. . . . . Very High-$2739
  Greenhouse Gas Emissions (tons/yr.) Very High-11.4
  Barrels of Oil Used per year . . . . Very High-21.4

How the Competition Rates

Competitors	Rating	Pg.
BMW X5	8	96
Land Rover Range Rover	–	183
Lexus GS	–	185

Price Range	Retail	Markup
Premium 3.6 quattro Tiptronic	$46,900	8%
Premium 3.0 quattro Tiptronic TDI	$50,900	8%
Prem. Plus 3.6 quattro Tiptronic	$52,900	8%
Prestige 4.2 quattro Tiptronic	$61,000	8%

Safety Checklist

Crash Tests:
  Frontal. . . . . Poor
  Side . . . . Very Good
Airbags:
  Head . . . . Std. Curtain All Rows
  Chest/TorsoStd. Row 1 & Opt. Row 2 Torso from Seat
  Roll-Sensing Side Airbag . . . . Standard
  Out-of-Position Test. . . . . . . Meets Requirements
Children:
  Built-in Child Safety Seat . . . . –
  Automatic Window Reversal. Std. Front and Rear
Crash Avoidance:
  Frontal Collision Warning . . . . Optional
  Electronic Stability Control . . . . Standard
  Lane Departure Warning . . . . –
  Brake Assist . . . . Standard
General:
  Automatic Crash Notification . . . . –
  Daytime Running Lights. . . . . Standard
  Automatic Door-Locking. . . . . Standard
Safety Belt:
  Adjustable Front Belt . . . . Standard

Audi Q7

Specifications

Drive . . . . AWD
Engine 3.6-liter V6
Transmission . . . . 6-sp. Automatic
Tow Rating (lbs.). Average-5000
Head/Leg Room (in.) Cramped-39.5/41.3
Interior Space (cu. ft.) . . . . Very Roomy-133.21
Cargo Space (cu. ft.) . . . . Very Cramped-10.9
Wheelbase/Length (in.) 118.2/200.3

*Combines results of both front and side tests in relation to all tests for 2010 vehicles.

Ratings—10 Best, 1 Worst

Combo Crash Tests	–
Safety Features	5
Rollover	7
Preventive Maintenance	10
Repair Costs	2
Warranty	10
Fuel Economy	5
Complaints	3
Insurance Costs	3
OVERALL RATING	**–**

BMW 1 Series

At-a-Glance

Status	Unchanged
Year Series Started	2008
Twins	–
Body Styles	Coupe, Convertible
Seating	4
Anti-Theft Device	Std. Passive Immobil. Only
Parking Index Rating	Very Easy
Where Made	Leipzig, Germany

Fuel Factor

MPG Rating (city/hwy)	Average-18/28
Driving Range (mi.)	Very Short-300.3
Fuel Type	Premium
Annual Fuel Cost	Average-$2028
Greenhouse Gas Emissions (tons/yr.)	High-8.3
Barrels of Oil Used per year	Average-15.6

How the Competition Rates

Competitors	Rating	Pg.
Audi A4	10	86
Mercedes-Benz C-Class	–	203
Nissan Altima Coupe	6	218

Price Range	Retail	Markup
128i Coupe	$29,000	9%
128i Convertible	$34,000	9%
135i Coupe	$35,850	9%
135i Convertible	$40,150	9%

BMW 1 Series

Safety Checklist

Crash Tests:
- Frontal . . . . –
- Side . . . . –

Airbags:
- Head . . . . Std. Row 1 & 2 Curtain
- Chest/Torso . . . . Std. Row 1 Torso from Seat
- Roll-Sensing Side Airbag . . . . –
- Out-of-Position Test . . . . . . Meets Requirements

Children:
- Built-in Child Safety Seat . . . . –
- Automatic Window Reversal . . . . Std. Front

Crash Avoidance:
- Frontal Collision Warning . . . . –
- Electronic Stability Control . . . . Standard
- Lane Departure Warning . . . . –
- Brake Assist . . . . Standard

General:
- Automatic Crash Notification . . . . Optional
- Daytime Running Lights . . . . Optional
- Automatic Door-Locking . . . . Optional

Safety Belt:
- Adjustable Front Belt . . . . –

BMW 1 Series

Specifications

Drive	RWD
Engine	3.0-liter I6
Transmission	6-sp. Automatic
Tow Rating (lbs.)	–
Head/Leg Room (in.)	Very Cramped-37.9/41.4
Interior Space (cu. ft.)	Very Cramped-86
Cargo Space (cu. ft.)	Very Cramped-10
Wheelbase/Length (in.)	104.7/172.2

*Combines results of both front and side tests in relation to all tests for 2010 vehicles.

Ratings—10 Best, 1 Worst

Combo Crash Tests	3
Safety Features	9
Rollover	8
Preventive Maintenance	10
Repair Costs	1
Warranty	10
Fuel Economy	5
Complaints	5
Insurance Costs	3
OVERALL RATING	**7**

BMW 3 Series

BMW 3 Series

At-a-Glance

Status. . . . . Unchanged
Year Series Started 2006
Twins . . . . –
Body Styles . . . . . Sedan, Coupe, Wagon, Convertible
Seating. 5
Anti-Theft Device. . . . . Std. Passive Immobil. Only
Parking Index Rating . . . . Easy
Where Made. . . Leipzig, Germany / Munich, Germany
Fuel Factor
  MPG Rating (city/hwy) Average-18/28
  Driving Range (mi.) Short-345.3
  Fuel Type. . . . . Premium
  Annual Fuel Cost. . . . . Average-$2028
  Greenhouse Gas Emissions (tons/yr.) High-8.3
  Barrels of Oil Used per year. Average-15.6

How the Competition Rates

Competitors	Rating	Pg.
Audi A4	10	86
Mercedes-Benz C-Class	–	203
Volvo S40	9	266

Price Range	Retail	Markup
328i Sedan	$32,850	9%
328xi Coupe	$37,650	9%
335xi Sedan	$42,300	9%
335i Convertible	$50,700	9%

Safety Checklist

Crash Tests:
  Frontal. . . . . Very Poor
  Side . . . . Good
Airbags:
  Head . . . . Std. Row 1 & 2 Curtain
  Chest/Torso . . . . Std. Row 1 Torso from Seat
  Roll-Sensing Side Airbag . . . . Standard
  Out-of-Position Test. . . . . . . Meets Requirements
Children:
  Built-in Child Safety Seat . . . . –
  Automatic Window Reversal. Std. Front and Rear
Crash Avoidance:
  Frontal Collision Warning . . . . –
  Electronic Stability Control . . . . Standard
  Lane Departure Warning . . . . –
  Brake Assist . . . . Standard
General:
  Automatic Crash Notification. . . . . Optional
  Daytime Running Lights . . . . Optional
  Automatic Door-Locking . . . . Optional
Safety Belt:
  Adjustable Front Belt . . . . –

BMW 3 Series

Specifications

Drive. . . . . RWD
Engine. 3.0-liter I6
Transmission . . . . 6-sp. Automatic
Tow Rating (lbs.). . . . . –
Head/Leg Room (in.) Cramped-38.5/41.5
Interior Space (cu. ft.) Cramped-93
Cargo Space (cu. ft.). . . . . Very Cramped-12
Wheelbase/Length (in.) 108.7/178.8

*Combines results of both front and side tests in relation to all tests for 2010 vehicles.

Ratings—10 Best, 1 Worst

Combo Crash Tests	3
Safety Features	8
Rollover	8
Preventive Maintenance	10
Repair Costs	1
Warranty	10
Fuel Economy	5
Complaints	6
Insurance Costs	3
OVERALL RATING	**7**

BMW 5 Series

BMW 5 Series

At-a-Glance

Status. . . . . Unchanged
Year Series Started 2004
Twins . . . . –
Body Styles. Sedan, Wagon
Seating. 5
Anti-Theft Device. . . . . Std. Passive Immobil. Only
Parking Index Rating . . . . Average
Where Made . . . . Dingolfing, Germany
Fuel Factor
  MPG Rating (city/hwy) Average-18/27
  Driving Range (mi.) Long-396.8
  Fuel Type. . . . . Premium
  Annual Fuel Cost. . . . . Average-$2028
  Greenhouse Gas Emissions (tons/yr.) High-8.7
  Barrels of Oil Used per year. High-16.3

How the Competition Rates

Competitors	Rating	Pg.
Infiniti G	7	165
Lexus GS	–	185
Mercedes-Benz E-Class	7	204

Price Range	Retail	Markup
528i Sedan	$45,800	9%
535i Sedan	$51,100	9%
535xi Sports Wagon	$55,800	9%
550i Sedan	$60,400	9%

Safety Checklist

Crash Tests:
  Frontal. . . . . Very Poor
  Side . . . . Good
Airbags:
  Head . . . . Std. Row 1 & 2 Tube with Sail
  Chest/TorsoStd. Row 1 & Opt. Row 2 Torso from Door
  Roll-Sensing Side Airbag . . . . –
  Out-of-Position Test. . . . . . . Meets Requirements
Children:
  Built-in Child Safety Seat . . . . –
  Automatic Window Reversal. Std. Front and Rear
Crash Avoidance:
  Frontal Collision Warning . . . . –
  Electronic Stability Control . . . . Standard
  Lane Departure Warning. . . . . Optional
  Brake Assist . . . . Standard
General:
  Automatic Crash Notification . . . . Standard
  Daytime Running Lights . . . . Optional
  Automatic Door-Locking . . . . Optional
Safety Belt:
  Adjustable Front Belt . . . . –

BMW 5 Series

Specifications

Drive. . . . . RWD
Engine. 3.0-liter I6
Transmission . . . . 6-sp. Automatic
Tow Rating (lbs.). . . . . –
Head/Leg Room (in.) Cramped-39.1/41.5
Interior Space (cu. ft.). Average-99
Cargo Space (cu. ft.). Cramped-14
Wheelbase/Length (in.) 113.7/191.1

*Combines results of both front and side tests in relation to all tests for 2010 vehicles.

Ratings—10 Best, 1 Worst

Combo Crash Tests	–
Safety Features	5
Rollover	9
Preventive Maintenance	10
Repair Costs	1
Warranty	10
Fuel Economy	2
Complaints	–
Insurance Costs	1
OVERALL RATING	–

BMW 7 Series

BMW 7 Series

At-a-Glance

Status	Unchanged
Year Series Started	2009
Twins	–
Body Styles	Sedan
Seating	5
Anti-Theft Device	Std. Passive Immobil. Only
Parking Index Rating	Very Hard
Where Made	Dingolfing, Germany

Fuel Factor

MPG Rating (city/hwy)	Very Poor-14/21
Driving Range (mi.)	Short-357.4
Fuel Type	Premium
Annual Fuel Cost	Very High-$2641
Greenhouse Gas Emissions (tons/yr.)	Very High-10.8
Barrels of Oil Used per year	Very High-20.1

How the Competition Rates

Competitors	Rating	Pg.
Jaguar XF	–	167
Lexus LS	–	189
Mercedes-Benz S-Class	–	208

Price Range	Retail	Markup
750i	$80,455	9%
750xi	$83,455	9%
750Li	$84,355	9%
760Li	$136,600	9%

Safety Checklist

Crash Tests:
Frontal . . . . –
Side . . . . –

Airbags:
Head . . . . Std. Row 1 & 2 Curtain
Chest/Torso . . . . Std. Row 1 Torso from Seat
Roll-Sensing Side Airbag . . . . –
Out-of-Position Test . . . . . . Meets Requirements

Children:
Built-in Child Safety Seat . . . . –
Automatic Window Reversal. Std. Front and Rear

Crash Avoidance:
Frontal Collision Warning . . . . –
Electronic Stability Control . . . . Standard
Lane Departure Warning . . . . Optional
Brake Assist . . . . Standard

General:
Automatic Crash Notification . . . . Standard
Daytime Running Lights . . . . Optional
Automatic Door-Locking . . . . Optional

Safety Belt:
Adjustable Front Belt . . . . –

BMW 7 Series

Specifications

Drive	RWD
Engine	4.4-liter V8
Transmission	6-sp. Automatic
Tow Rating (lbs.)	–
Head/Leg Room (in.)	Average-40.8/41.2
Interior Space (cu. ft.)	Roomy-104
Cargo Space (cu. ft.)	Cramped-14
Wheelbase/Length (in.)	117.7/205.3

*Combines results of both front and side tests in relation to all tests for 2010 vehicles.

Ratings—10 Best, 1 Worst

Combo Crash Tests	–
Safety Features	8
Rollover	3
Preventive Maintenance	10
Repair Costs	2
Warranty	10
Fuel Economy	4
Complaints	7
Insurance Costs	8
OVERALL RATING	–

BMW X3

BMW X3

Safety Checklist

Crash Tests:
Frontal. . . . . –
Side . . . . –
Airbags:
Head . . . . Std. Row 1 & 2 Curtain
Chest/Torso Std. Row 1 & Opt. Row 2 Torso from Door
Roll-Sensing Side Airbag . . . . –
Out-of-Position Test . . . . Meets Requirements
Children:
Built-in Child Safety Seat . . . . –
Automatic Window Reversal. Std. Front and Rear
Crash Avoidance:
Frontal Collision Warning . . . . Optional
Electronic Stability Control . . . . Standard
Lane Departure Warning . . . . –
Brake Assist . . . . Standard
General:
Automatic Crash Notification. . . . . Optional
Daytime Running Lights . . . . Optional
Automatic Door-Locking . . . . Optional
Safety Belt:
Adjustable Front Belt . . . . –

At-a-Glance

Status. . . . . Unchanged
Year Series Started 2004
Twins . . . . –
Body Styles. . . . . SUV
Seating. 5
Anti-Theft Device. . . . . . . Std. Passive Immobil. Only
Parking Index Rating . . . . Average
Where Made . . . . Graz, Austria
Fuel Factor
MPG Rating (city/hwy). Poor-17/24
Driving Range (mi.). Short-346.4
Fuel Type. Premium
Annual Fuel Cost. . . . . High-$2221
Greenhouse Gas Emissions (tons/yr.) High-9.2
Barrels of Oil Used per year. High-17.1

How the Competition Rates

Competitors	Rating	Pg.
Audi Q5	7	89
Infiniti FX	–	164
Porsche Cayenne	–	230

Price Range

Price Range	Retail	Markup
XDrive30i	$38,750	9%

Specifications

Drive 4WD
Engine. 3.0-liter I6
Transmission . . . . 6-sp. Automatic
Tow Rating (lbs.). Average-3500
Head/Leg Room (in.) . . . . . Very Cramped-39.3/40.2
Interior Space (cu. ft.) . . . . –
Cargo Space (cu. ft.) . . . . Very Roomy-71
Wheelbase/Length (in.) 110.1/179.9

*Combines results of both front and side tests in relation to all tests for 2010 vehicles.

Ratings—10 Best, 1 Worst	
Combo Crash Tests	6
Safety Features	9
Rollover	3
Preventive Maintenance	10
Repair Costs	1
Warranty	10
Fuel Economy	2
Complaints	9
Insurance Costs	5
OVERALL RATING	**8**

BMW X5

BMW X5

At-a-Glance

Status	Unchanged
Year Series Started	2007
Twins	–
Body Styles	SUV
Seating	7
Anti-Theft Device	Std. Passive Immobil. Only
Parking Index Rating	Very Hard
Where Made	Spartanburg, SC
Fuel Factor	
MPG Rating (city/hwy)	Very Poor-15/21
Driving Range (mi.)	Average-387.3
Fuel Type	Premium
Annual Fuel Cost	Very High-$2527
Greenhouse Gas Emissions (tons/yr.)	High-10.2
Barrels of Oil Used per year	High-19.0

How the Competition Rates

Competitors	Rating	Pg.
Audi Q7	7	90
Cadillac SRX	5	103
Volvo XC90	10	270

Price Range	Retail	Markup
XDrive30i	$47,500	9%
XDrive35d	$51,200	9%
XDrive48i	$56,200	9%

Safety Checklist

Crash Tests:
Frontal . . . . Poor
Side . . . . Very Good
Airbags:
Head . . . . Std. Row 1 & 2 Curtain
Chest/Torso . . . . Std. Row 1 Torso from Seat
Roll-Sensing Side Airbag . . . . Standard
Out-of-Position Test . . . . . . Meets Requirements
Children:
Built-in Child Safety Seat . . . . –
Automatic Window Reversal . Std. Front and Rear
Crash Avoidance:
Frontal Collision Warning . . . . –
Electronic Stability Control . . . . Standard
Lane Departure Warning . . . . –
Brake Assist . . . . Standard
General:
Automatic Crash Notification . . . . Optional
Daytime Running Lights . . . . Optional
Automatic Door-Locking . . . . Optional
Safety Belt:
Adjustable Front Belt . . . . –

BMW X5

Specifications

Drive	4WD
Engine	3.0-liter I6
Transmission	6-sp. Automatic
Tow Rating (lbs.)	High-6000
Head/Leg Room (in.)	Very Cramped-39.3/40
Interior Space (cu. ft.)	Average-102.4
Cargo Space (cu. ft.)	Average-23.2
Wheelbase/Length (in.)	115.5/191.1

*Combines results of both front and side tests in relation to all tests for 2010 vehicles.

Ratings—10 Best, 1 Worst

Combo Crash Tests	7
Safety Features	10
Rollover	4
Preventive Maintenance	8
Repair Costs	4
Warranty	7
Fuel Economy	4
Complaints	3
Insurance Costs	8
OVERALL RATING	**7**

Buick Enclave

Buick Enclave

At-a-Glance

Status. . . . . Unchanged
Year Series Started 2008
Twins . . . . –
Body Styles. . . . . SUV
Seating 7/8
Anti-Theft Device. . Std. Pass. Immobil. & Pass. Alarm
Parking Index Rating . . . . Very Hard
Where Made . . . . Lansing, MI

Fuel Factor
MPG Rating (city/hwy). Poor-17/24
Driving Range (mi.). . . . . Very Long-430.5
Fuel Type. . . . . Regular
Annual Fuel Cost. . . . . Average-$2070
Greenhouse Gas Emissions (tons/yr.) High-9.6
Barrels of Oil Used per year. High-18.0

How the Competition Rates

Competitors	Rating	Pg.
Acura MDX	–	81
Lexus RX	6	190
Volvo XC90	10	270

Price Range	Retail	Markup
CX FWD	$35,165	6%
CX AWD	$37,165	6%
CXL FWD	$38,330	6%
CXL AWD	$40,330	6%

Safety Checklist

Crash Tests:
Frontal . . . . Average
Side . . . . Very Good
Airbags:
Head . . . . Std. Curtain All Rows
Chest/Torso . . . . Std. Row 1 Torso from Seat
Roll-Sensing Side Airbag . . . . Standard
Out-of-Position Test. . . . . . Meets Requirements
Children:
Built-in Child Safety Seat . . . . –
Automatic Window Reversal. . . . . Std. Front
Crash Avoidance:
Frontal Collision Warning . . . . –
Electronic Stability Control . . . . Standard
Lane Departure Warning . . . . –
Brake Assist . . . . Standard
General:
Automatic Crash Notification . . . . Standard
Daytime Running Lights. . . . . Standard
Automatic Door-Locking. . . . . Standard
Safety Belt:
Adjustable Front Belt . . . . Standard

Buick Enclave

Specifications

Drive . . . . FWD
Engine 3.6-liter V6
Transmission . . . . 6-sp. Automatic
Tow Rating (lbs.). Average-4500
Head/Leg Room (in.). Average-40.4/41.3
Interior Space (cu. ft.). . . . . Very Roomy-153
Cargo Space (cu. ft.). Average-23.2
Wheelbase/Length (in.). 119/201.5

*Combines results of both front and side tests in relation to all tests for 2010 vehicles.

Ratings—10 Best, 1 Worst

Combo Crash Tests	10
Safety Features	10
Rollover	6
Preventive Maintenance	9
Repair Costs	4
Warranty	7
Fuel Economy	4
Complaints	–
Insurance Costs	8
OVERALL RATING	**10**

Buick LaCrosse

Buick LaCrosse

At-a-Glance

Status	All New
Year Series Started	2010
Twins	–
Body Styles	Sedan
Seating	5
Anti-Theft Device	Std. Pass. Immob./Opt. Pass. Immob. & Alarm
Parking Index Rating	Hard
Where Made	Kansas City, MO

Fuel Factor

MPG Rating (city/hwy)	Poor-17/26
Driving Range (mi.)	Short-370.5
Fuel Type	Regular
Annual Fuel Cost	Average-$2011
Greenhouse Gas Emissions (tons/yr.)	High-9.2
Barrels of Oil Used per year	High-17.1

How the Competition Rates

Competitors	Rating	Pg.
Dodge Avenger	6	123
Lexus GS	–	185
Lincoln MKZ	8	194

Price Range	Retail	Markup
CX	$27,085	5%
CXL	$29,645	5%
CXL AWD	$31,820	5%
CXS	$33,015	5%

Safety Checklist

Crash Tests:
Frontal . . . . Very Good
Side . . . . Very Good

Airbags:
Head . . . . Std. Row 1 & 2 Curtain
Chest/Torso Std. Row 1 & Opt. Row 2 Torso from Seat
Roll-Sensing Side Airbag . . . . Standard
Out-of-Position Test . . . . Meets Requirements

Children:
Built-in Child Safety Seat . . . . –
Automatic Window Reversal. Std. Front and Rear

Crash Avoidance:
Frontal Collision Warning . . . . –
Electronic Stability Control . . . . Standard
Lane Departure Warning . . . . –
Brake Assist . . . . Standard

General:
Automatic Crash Notification . . . . Standard
Daytime Running Lights . . . . Standard
Automatic Door-Locking. . . . . Standard

Safety Belt:
Adjustable Front Belt . . . . Standard

Buick LaCrosse

Specifications

Drive	FWD
Engine	3.0-liter V6
Transmission	6-sp. Automatic
Tow Rating (lbs.)	Very Low-1000
Head/Leg Room (in.)	Very Cramped-38/41.7
Interior Space (cu. ft.)	Average-101.7
Cargo Space (cu. ft.)	Cramped-13.3
Wheelbase/Length (in.)	111.7/197

*Combines results of both front and side tests in relation to all tests for 2010 vehicles.

Buick Lucerne

Large

Ratings—10 Best, 1 Worst

Combo Crash Tests	6
Safety Features	7
Rollover	8
Preventive Maintenance	9
Repair Costs	7
Warranty	7
Fuel Economy	4
Complaints	5
Insurance Costs	8
OVERALL RATING	**9**

Buick Lucerne

Buick Lucerne

Safety Checklist

Crash Tests:
Frontal . . . . Very Good
Side. . . . . Very Poor

Airbags:
Head . . . . Std. Row 1 & 2 Curtain
Chest/Torso . . . . Std. Row 1 Torso from Seat
Roll-Sensing Side Airbag . . . . –
Out-of-Position Test. . . . . . Meets Requirements

Children:
Built-in Child Safety Seat . . . . –
Automatic Window Reversal . . . . –

Crash Avoidance:
Frontal Collision Warning . . . . –
Electronic Stability Control . . . . Standard
Lane Departure Warning. . . . . Optional
Brake Assist . . . . Optional

General:
Automatic Crash Notification . . . . Standard
Daytime Running Lights. . . . . Standard
Automatic Door-Locking. . . . . Standard

Safety Belt:
Adjustable Front Belt . . . . Standard

At-a-Glance

Status. . . . . Unchanged
Year Series Started 2006
Twins. . . . . Cadillac DTS
Body Styles . . . . Sedan
Seating 5/6
Anti-Theft Device Std. Pass. Immob./Opt. Pass. Immob. & Alarm
Parking Index Rating . . . . Very Hard
Where Made . . . . Detroit, MI

Fuel Factor
MPG Rating (city/hwy). Poor-17/26
Driving Range (mi.) Average-372.5
Fuel Type. Regular/E85
Annual Fuel Cost. . . . . Average-$2011
Greenhouse Gas Emissions (tons/yr.) High-9.2
Barrels of Oil Used per year. High-17.1

How the Competition Rates

Competitors	Rating	Pg.
Chrysler 300	8	119
Dodge Charger	8	126
Lincoln MKS	6	191

Price Range	Retail	Markup
CX	$29,230	5%
CXL	$32,730	5%
CXL SE	$33,230	5%
Super	$39,230	5%

Buick Lucerne

Specifications

Drive . . . . FWD
Engine 3.9-liter V6
Transmission . . . . 4-sp. Automatic
Tow Rating (lbs.). . . . . Very Low-1000
Head/Leg Room (in.) Average-39.5/42.5
Interior Space (cu. ft.). Roomy-108
Cargo Space (cu. ft.) Average-17
Wheelbase/Length (in.) 115.6/203.2

*Combines results of both front and side tests in relation to all tests for 2010 vehicles.

Ratings—10 Best, 1 Worst

Combo Crash Tests	8
Safety Features	10
Rollover	8
Preventive Maintenance	4
Repair Costs	2
Warranty	7
Fuel Economy	5
Complaints	3
Insurance Costs	1
OVERALL RATING	**7**

Cadillac CTS

Cadillac CTS

At-a-Glance

Status	Unchanged
Year Series Started	2003
Twins	—
Body Styles	Sedan, Wagon
Seating	5
Anti-Theft Device	Std. Pass. Immob./Opt. Pass. Immob. & Alarm
Parking Index Rating	Easy
Where Made	Lansing, MI

Fuel Factor

MPG Rating (city/hwy)	Average-18/27
Driving Range (mi.)	Average-381.2
Fuel Type	Regular
Annual Fuel Cost	Average-$1913
Greenhouse Gas Emissions (tons/yr.)	High-8.3
Barrels of Oil Used per year	Average-15.6

How the Competition Rates

Competitors	Rating	Pg.
Acura TL	9	83
Infiniti G	7	165
Lexus ES	6	184

Price Range	Retail	Markup
3.0	$36,730	6%
3.0 Wagon AWD	$41,730	6%
3.6 AWD	$45,725	6%
V	$60,720	8%

Safety Checklist

Crash Tests:
- Frontal . . . . Average
- Side . . . . Very Good

Airbags:
- Head . . . . Std. Row 1 & 2 Curtain
- Chest/Torso . . . . Std. Row 1 Torso from Seat
- Roll-Sensing Side Airbag . . . . Standard
- Out-of-Position Test . . . . . . Meets Requirements

Children:
- Built-in Child Safety Seat . . . . —
- Automatic Window Reversal . . . . Std. Front

Crash Avoidance:
- Frontal Collision Warning . . . . —
- Electronic Stability Control . . . . Standard
- Lane Departure Warning . . . . —
- Brake Assist . . . . Standard

General:
- Automatic Crash Notification . . . . Standard
- Daytime Running Lights . . . . Standard
- Automatic Door-Locking . . . . Standard

Safety Belt:
- Adjustable Front Belt . . . . Standard

Cadillac CTS

Specifications

Drive	RWD
Engine	3.0-liter V6
Transmission	6-sp. Automatic
Tow Rating (lbs.)	Very Low-1000
Head/Leg Room (in.)	Cramped-38.8/42.2
Interior Space (cu. ft.)	Cramped-98
Cargo Space (cu. ft.)	Cramped-13.6
Wheelbase/Length (in.)	113.4/191.6

*Combines results of both front and side tests in relation to all tests for 2010 vehicles.

Cadillac DTS

Ratings—10 Best, 1 Worst

Combo Crash Tests	2
Safety Features	9
Rollover	7
Preventive Maintenance	8
Repair Costs	2
Warranty	7
Fuel Economy	3
Complaints	8
Insurance Costs	8
OVERALL RATING	**6**

Cadillac DTS

Cadillac DTS

At-a-Glance

Status. . . . . Unchanged
Year Series Started 2006
Twins. . . . . Buick Lucerne
Body Styles . . . . Sedan
Seating 5/6
Anti-Theft Device. . Std. Pass. Immobil. & Pass. Alarm
Parking Index Rating . . . . Very Hard
Where Made . . . . Detroit, MI

Fuel Factor
MPG Rating (city/hwy). Poor-15/23
Driving Range (mi.). . . . . Very Short-329.0
Fuel Type. . . . . Regular
Annual Fuel Cost. . . . . High-$2260
Greenhouse Gas Emissions (tons/yr.). . . . High-10.2
Barrels of Oil Used per year. High-19.0

How the Competition Rates

Competitors	Rating	Pg.
BMW 7 Series	–	94
Lincoln Town Car	7	195
Mercedes-Benz S-Class	–	208

Price Range

	Retail	Markup
Base	$46,280	6%
Luxury Package	$59,475	6%

Safety Checklist

Crash Tests:
Frontal. . . . . Poor
Side. . . . . Very Poor
Airbags:
Head . . . . Std. Row 1 & 2 Curtain
Chest/Torso . . . . Std. Row 1 Torso from Seat
Roll-Sensing Side Airbag . . . . –
Out-of-Position Test. . . . . . Meets Requirements
Children:
Built-in Child Safety Seat . . . . –
Automatic Window Reversal. . . . . Std. Front
Crash Avoidance:
Frontal Collision Warning . . . . Optional
Electronic Stability Control . . . . Standard
Lane Departure Warning. . . . . Optional
Brake Assist . . . . Standard
General:
Automatic Crash Notification . . . . Standard
Daytime Running Lights. . . . . Standard
Automatic Door-Locking. . . . . Standard
Safety Belt:
Adjustable Front Belt . . . . Standard

Cadillac DTS

Specifications

Drive . . . . FWD
Engine 4.6-liter V8
Transmission . . . . 4-sp. Automatic
Tow Rating (lbs.). . . . . Very Low-1000
Head/Leg Room (in.). Average-39.2/42.5
Interior Space (cu. ft.). . . . . Very Roomy-132
Cargo Space (cu. ft.). Average-18.8
Wheelbase/Length (in.) 115.6/207.6

*Combines results of both front and side tests in relation to all tests for 2010 vehicles.

Cadillac Escalade

Ratings—10 Best, 1 Worst

Combo Crash Tests	10
Safety Features	10
Rollover	1
Preventive Maintenance	6
Repair Costs	2
Warranty	7
Fuel Economy	1
Complaints	6
Insurance Costs	1
OVERALL RATING	**6**

Cadillac Escalade

Cadillac Escalade

At-a-Glance

Status . . . . Unchanged
Year Series Started 2002
Twins . . . . Chevrolet Tahoe, GMC Yukon
Body Styles. . . . . SUV
Seating 7/8
Anti-Theft Device. . Std. Pass. Immobil. & Pass. Alarm
Parking Index Rating . . . . Hard
Where Made . . . . Arlington, TX

Fuel Factor
MPG Rating (city/hwy). . . . . Very Poor-13/20
Driving Range (mi.) Long-401.2
Fuel Type Premium/E85
Annual Fuel Cost. . . . . Very High-$2819
Greenhouse Gas Emissions (tons/yr.) Very High-12.2
Barrels of Oil Used per year . . . . Very High-22.8

How the Competition Rates

Competitors	Rating	Pg.
Land Rover Range Rover	–	183
Lincoln MKT	–	192
Nissan Armada	–	219

Price Range

	Retail	Markup
Base RWD	$62,495	8%
Hybrid RWD	$73,425	8%
Platinum AWD	$84,125	8%

Safety Checklist

Crash Tests:
Frontal . . . . Very Good
Side . . . . Very Good
Airbags:
Head . . . . Std. Curtain All Rows
Chest/Torso . . . . Std. Row 1 Torso from Seat
Roll-Sensing Side Airbag . . . . Standard
Out-of-Position Test. . . . . . Meets Requirements
Children:
Built-in Child Safety Seat . . . . –
Automatic Window Reversal . . . . Std. Front
Crash Avoidance:
Frontal Collision Warning . . . . –
Electronic Stability Control . . . . Standard
Lane Departure Warning . . . . –
Brake Assist . . . . Standard
General:
Automatic Crash Notification . . . . Standard
Daytime Running Lights. . . . . Standard
Automatic Door-Locking. . . . . Standard
Safety Belt:
Adjustable Front Belt . . . . Standard

Cadillac Escalade

Specifications

Drive . . . . AWD
Engine 6.2-liter V8
Transmission . . . . 6-sp. Automatic
Tow Rating (lbs.) . . . . Very High-8100
Head/Leg Room (in.). Average-40.3/41.3
Interior Space (cu. ft.) Roomy-108.9
Cargo Space (cu. ft.). . . . . Very Roomy-60.3
Wheelbase/Length (in.) 116/202.5

*Combines results of both front and side tests in relation to all tests for 2010 vehicles.

Cadillac SRX

Mid-Size SUV

Ratings—10 Best, 1 Worst

Combo Crash Tests	4
Safety Features	10
Rollover	3
Preventive Maintenance	8
Repair Costs	1
Warranty	7
Fuel Economy	5
Complaints	–
Insurance Costs	5
OVERALL RATING	**5**

Cadillac SRX

Cadillac SRX

Cadillac SRX

At-a-Glance

Status. . . . . All New
Year Series Started 2010
Twins . . . . –
Body Styles. . . . . SUV
Seating 5
Anti-Theft Device. . Std. Pass. Immobil. & Pass. Alarm
Parking Index Rating . . . . Hard
Where Made. . . . . Ramos Arizpe, Mexico

Fuel Factor
  MPG Rating (city/hwy) Average-18/25
  Driving Range (mi.) . . . . Very Long-432.5
  Fuel Type. . . . . Regular
  Annual Fuel Cost. . . . . Average-$1967
  Greenhouse Gas Emissions (tons/yr.) High-8.7
  Barrels of Oil Used per year. High-16.3

How the Competition Rates

Competitors	Rating	Pg.
Acura MDX	–	81
Lexus RX	6	190
Volvo XC90	10	270

Price Range	Retail	Markup
Hybrid Platinum 4WD	$87,725	8%
Base FWD	$33,330	6%
Luxury AWD	$39,405	6%
Performance FWD	$41,350	6%

Safety Checklist

Crash Tests:
  Frontal. . . . . Poor
  Side . . . . Good
Airbags:
  Head . . . . Std. Row 1 & 2 Curtain
  Chest/Torso . . . . Std. Row 1 Torso from Seat
  Roll-Sensing Side Airbag . . . . Standard
  Out-of-Position Test. . . . . . Meets Requirements
Children:
  Built-in Child Safety Seat . . . . –
  Automatic Window Reversal. Std. Front and Rear
Crash Avoidance:
  Frontal Collision Warning . . . . –
  Electronic Stability Control . . . . Standard
  Lane Departure Warning . . . . –
  Brake Assist . . . . Standard
General:
  Automatic Crash Notification . . . . Standard
  Daytime Running Lights . . . . Standard
  Automatic Door-Locking. . . . . Standard
Safety Belt:
  Adjustable Front Belt . . . . Standard

Cadillac SRX

Specifications

Drive . . . . FWD
Engine 3.0-liter V6
Transmission . . . . 6-sp. Automatic
Tow Rating (lbs.) Low-2500
Head/Leg Room (in.) Cramped-39.7/41.2
Interior Space (cu. ft.) Average-100.6
Cargo Space (cu. ft.) Roomy-29.2
Wheelbase/Length (in.) 110.5/190.3

*Combines results of both front and side tests in relation to all tests for 2010 vehicles.

Ratings—10 Best, 1 Worst

Combo Crash Tests	2
Safety Features	10
Rollover	8
Preventive Maintenance	6
Repair Costs	1
Warranty	7
Fuel Economy	5
Complaints	5
Insurance Costs	1
OVERALL RATING	**5**

Cadillac STS

Cadillac STS

Cadillac STS

At-a-Glance

Status. . . . . Unchanged
Year Series Started 2005
Twins . . . . —
Body Styles . . . . Sedan
Seating. 5
Anti-Theft Device. . Std. Pass. Immobil. & Pass. Alarm
Parking Index Rating . . . . Average
Where Made . . . . Lansing, MI

Fuel Factor
  MPG Rating (city/hwy) Poor-18/27
  Driving Range (mi.) Short-357.0
  Fuel Type. . . . . Regular
  Annual Fuel Cost. . . . . Average-$1985
  Greenhouse Gas Emissions (tons/yr.) High-8.7
  Barrels of Oil Used per year. High-16.3

How the Competition Rates

Competitors	Rating	Pg.
BMW 7 Series	—	94
Infiniti M	—	166
Lexus LS	—	189

Price Range	Retail	Markup
Premium AWD	$47,540	6%
Base V6	$46,845	6%
Base V8	$56,345	6%

Safety Checklist

Crash Tests:
  Frontal. . . . . Very Poor
  Side. . . . . Poor
Airbags:
  Head . . . . Std. Row 1 & 2 Curtain
  Chest/Torso . . . . Std. Row 1 Torso from Seat
  Roll-Sensing Side Airbag . . . . —
  Out-of-Position Test. . . . . . . Meets Requirements
Children:
  Built-in Child Safety Seat . . . . —
  Automatic Window Reversal. Std. Front and Rear
Crash Avoidance:
  Frontal Collision Warning . . . . Optional
  Electronic Stability Control . . . . Standard
  Lane Departure Warning. . . . . Optional
  Brake Assist . . . . Standard
General:
  Automatic Crash Notification . . . . Standard
  Daytime Running Lights. . . . . Standard
  Automatic Door-Locking. . . . . Standard
Safety Belt:
  Adjustable Front Belt . . . . Standard

Cadillac STS

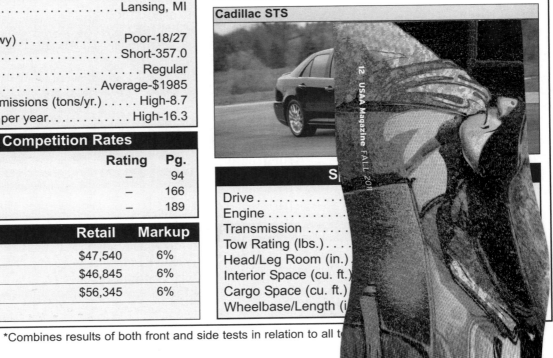

S...

Drive . . . .
Engine . . . .
Transmission . . . . . .
Tow Rating (lbs.) . . . .
Head/Leg Room (in.) .
Interior Space (cu. ft.)
Cargo Space (cu. ft.)
Wheelbase/Length (i...

*Combines results of both front and side tests in relation to all t...

	Avalanche	Escalade EXT
...rst		
	10	10
	9	10
	2	2
...ance	6	6
	3	1
	6	7
	2	1
	3	10
	8	1
...TING	7	7

...a-Glance

....	Unchanged
....	2002
......	Cadillac Escalade EXT
....	Pickup
....	5
Pass.	Immobil. & Pass. Alarm
....	Very Hard
....	Silao, Mexico
....	Very Poor-15/21
....	Very Long-542.2
....	Regular/E85
....	High-$2346
...sions (tons/yr.)	Very High-10.8
...year	Very High-20.1

...mpetition Rates

	Rating	Pg.
	9	136
	7	154
	–	255

	Retail	Markup
	$35,725	8%
	$38,830	8%
	$41,880	8%

Chevrolet Avalanche

Safety Checklist

Crash Tests:
Frontal . . . . Very Good
Side . . . . Very Good

Airbags:
Head . . . . Std. Row 1 & 2 Curtain
Chest/Torso . . . . Std. Row 1 Torso from Seat
Roll-Sensing Side Airbag . . . . Standard
Out-of-Position Test . . . . . . Meets Requirements

Children:
Built-in Child Safety Seat . . . . –
Automatic Window Reversal . . . . –

Crash Avoidance:
Frontal Collision Warning . . . . –
Electronic Stability Control . . . . Standard
Lane Departure Warning . . . . –
Brake Assist . . . . Standard

General:
Automatic Crash Notification . . . . Standard
Daytime Running Lights . . . . Standard
Automatic Door-Locking . . . . Standard

Safety Belt:
Adjustable Front Belt . . . . Standard

Cadillac Excalade EXT

Specifications

Drive . . . . RWD
Engine 5.3-liter V8
Transmission . . . . 6-sp. Automatic
Tow Rating (lbs.) . . . . Very High-7900
Head/Leg Room (in.) Roomy-41.1/41.3
Interior Space (cu. ft.) . . . . –
Cargo Space (cu. ft.) . . . . Very Roomy-45.5
Wheelbase/Length (in.) 130/221.3

...mbines results of both front and side tests in relation to all tests for 2010 vehicles.

Ratings—10 Best, 1 Worst

Combo Crash Tests	1
Safety Features	1
Rollover	6
Preventive Maintenance	3
Repair Costs	7
Warranty	6
Fuel Economy	9
Complaints	4
Insurance Costs	3
OVERALL RATING	**3**

Chevrolet Aveo

Chevrolet Aveo

At-a-Glance

Status. . . . . Unchanged
Year Series Started 2004
Twins . . . . –
Body Styles. . . . . Sedan, Hatchback
Seating. 5
Anti-Theft Device . Opt. Pass. Immob. & Alarm or Alarm Only
Parking Index Rating . . . . Very Easy
Where Made . . . . Bupyong, South Korea
Fuel Factor
  MPG Rating (city/hwy) . . . . Very Good-25/34
  Driving Range (mi.). . . . . Very Short-337.7
  Fuel Type. . . . . Regular
  Annual Fuel Cost . . . . Very Low-$1427
  Greenhouse Gas Emissions (tons/yr.) Low-6.6
  Barrels of Oil Used per year Low-12.2

How the Competition Rates

Competitors	Rating	Pg.
Honda Fit	8	150
Hyundai Accent	8	156
Nissan Versa	5	228

Price Range

	Retail	Markup
LTZ 4WD	$48,865	8%
LS	$11,965	5%
LT	$14,100	5%

Safety Checklist

Crash Tests:
  Frontal. . . . . Poor
  Side. . . . . Very Poor
Airbags:
  Head. . . . . Std. Row 1 Combo
  Chest/Torso . . . . . . Std. Row 1 Combo from Seat
  Roll-Sensing Side Airbag . . . . –
  Out-of-Position Test. . . . . . . Meets Requirements
Children:
  Built-in Child Safety Seat . . . . –
  Automatic Window Reversal . . . . –
Crash Avoidance:
  Frontal Collision Warning . . . . –
  Electronic Stability Control . . . . –
  Lane Departure Warning . . . . –
  Brake Assist . . . . –
General:
  Automatic Crash Notification . . . . Standard
  Daytime Running Lights. . . . . Standard
  Automatic Door-Locking . . . . –
Safety Belt:
  Adjustable Front Belt . . . . Standard

Chevrolet Aveo

Specifications

Drive . . . . FWD
Engine. 1.6-liter I4
Transmission . . . . 4-sp. Automatic
Tow Rating (lbs.). . . . . –
Head/Leg Room (in.) Cramped-39.3/41.3
Interior Space (cu. ft.) . . . . Very Cramped-90.2
Cargo Space (cu. ft.) . . . . Very Cramped-12.4
Wheelbase/Length (in.) 97.6/169.7

*Combines results of both front and side tests in relation to all tests for 2010 vehicles.

...t, 1 Worst

...ests	4
	7
	10
...tenance	–
	–
	6
	5
	–
...s	3
...RATING	6

...At-a-Glance

. . . .	All New
. . . .	2010
. . . .	–
. . . .	Coupe
. . . .	4
...td. Pass. Immobil. & Pass. Alarm	
. . . .	Average
. . . .	Oshawa, Ontario
...vy)	Average-18/29
. . . .	Long-412.4
. . . .	Regular
. . . .	Average-$1866
...missions (tons/yr.)	High-8.3
...per year.	Average-15.6

Competition Rates

	Rating	Pg.
	4	125
	7	140

	Retail	Markup
	$22,245	5%
	$23,880	5%
	$30,245	5%

Chevrolet Camaro

Safety Checklist

Crash Tests:
Frontal . . . . Very Poor
Side . . . . Very Good
Airbags:
Head . . . . Std. Row 1 & 2 Curtain
Chest/Torso . . . . Std. Row 1 Torso from Seat
Roll-Sensing Side Airbag . . . . –
Out-of-Position Test . . . . . . Meets Requirements
Children:
Built-in Child Safety Seat . . . . –
Automatic Window Reversal . . . . Std. Front
Crash Avoidance:
Frontal Collision Warning . . . . –
Electronic Stability Control . . . . Standard
Lane Departure Warning . . . . –
Brake Assist . . . . Standard
General:
Automatic Crash Notification . . . . Standard
Daytime Running Lights . . . . Standard
Automatic Door-Locking . . . . Standard
Safety Belt:
Adjustable Front Belt . . . . –

Chevrolet Camaro

Specifications

Drive . . . . RWD
Engine 3.6-liter V6
Transmission . . . . 6-sp. Automatic
Tow Rating (lbs.) . . . . –
Head/Leg Room (in.) . . . . . Very Cramped-37.4/42.4
Interior Space (cu. ft.) . . . . Very Cramped-81.4
Cargo Space (cu. ft.) . . . . Very Cramped-11.3
Wheelbase/Length (in.) 112.3/190.4

*Combines results of both front and side tests in relation to all tests for 2010 vehicles.

Ratings—10 Best, 1 Worst

Combo Crash Tests	3
Safety Features	2
Rollover	7
Preventive Maintenance	9
Repair Costs	5
Warranty	6
Fuel Economy	9
Complaints	1
Insurance Costs	1
OVERALL RATING	**4**

Chevrolet Cobalt

Chevrolet Cobalt

At-a-Glance

Status . . . . Unchanged
Year Series Started 2005
Twins . . . . –
Body Styles . . . . Sedan, Coupe
Seating 5
Anti-Theft Device Std. Pass. Immob./Opt. Pass. Immob. & Alarm
Parking Index Rating . . . . Easy
Where Made . . . . Lordstown, OH

Fuel Factor
MPG Rating (city/hwy) . . . . Very Good-24/33
Driving Range (mi.) Short-361.1
Fuel Type . . . . Regular
Annual Fuel Cost . . . . Very Low-$1480
Greenhouse Gas Emissions (tons/yr.) Low-6.8
Barrels of Oil Used per year Low-12.7

How the Competition Rates

Competitors	Rating	Pg.
Ford Focus	6	138
Honda Civic	8	146
Toyota Corolla	5	246

Price Range

	Retail	Markup
Base Coupe	$14,990	5%
LS Sedan	$15,670	5%
LT Sedan	$16,470	5%

Safety Checklist

Crash Tests:
Frontal . . . . Average
Side . . . . Very Poor
Airbags:
Head . . . . Std. Row 1 & 2 Curtain
Chest/Torso . . . . –
Roll-Sensing Side Airbag . . . . –
Out-of-Position Test . . . . . . Meets Requirements
Children:
Built-in Child Safety Seat . . . . –
Automatic Window Reversal . . . . –
Crash Avoidance:
Frontal Collision Warning . . . . –
Electronic Stability Control . . . . Optional
Lane Departure Warning . . . . –
Brake Assist . . . . Optional
General:
Automatic Crash Notification . . . . Standard
Daytime Running Lights . . . . Standard
Automatic Door-Locking . . . . Optional
Safety Belt:
Adjustable Front Belt . . . . Standard

Chevrolet Cobalt

Specifications

Drive . . . . FWD
Engine 2.2-liter I4
Transmission . . . . 4-sp. Automatic
Tow Rating (lbs.) . . . . Very Low-1000
Head/Leg Room (in.) Cramped-38.5/41.8
Interior Space (cu. ft.) . . . . Very Cramped-87.1
Cargo Space (cu. ft.) Cramped-13.9
Wheelbase/Length (in.) 103.3/180.3

*Combines results of both front and side tests in relation to all tests for 2010 vehicles.

st, 1 Worst	Colorado	Canyon
Tests	1	1
s	3	3
	3	3
ntenance	9	9
	3	2
	6	6
	4	4
	9	5
s	5	5
RATING	3	2

Chevrolet Colorado

Safety Checklist

Crash Tests:
Frontal . . . . Poor
Side . . . . Very Poor
Airbags:
Head . . . . Std. Row 1 & 2 Curtain
Chest/Torso . . . . –
Roll-Sensing Side Airbag . . . . –
Out-of-Position Test . . . . Meets Requirements
Children:
Built-in Child Safety Seat . . . . –
Automatic Window Reversal . . . . –
Crash Avoidance:
Frontal Collision Warning . . . . –
Electronic Stability Control . . . . Standard
Lane Departure Warning . . . . –
Brake Assist . . . . Standard
General:
Automatic Crash Notification . . . . Standard
Daytime Running Lights . . . . Standard
Automatic Door-Locking . . . . Optional
Safety Belt:
Adjustable Front Belt . . . . Standard

At-a-Glance

. . . . Unchanged
. . . . 2007
. . . . GMC Canyon
. . Crew, Regular, Extended Cabs
. . . . 5/6
d. Pass. Immob./Opt. Pass. Immob. & Alarm
) . . . . Very Hard
. . . . Shreveport, LA
wy) Poor-17/23
. . . . Average-377.5
. . . . Regular
. . . . Average-$2103
missions (tons/yr.) High-9.6
per year. High-18.0

Competition Rates

	Rating	Pg.
	7	127
	3	141
	2	254

	Retail	Markup
	$24,535	5%
D	$16,985	5%
Z85	$21,615	6%
D Z71	$25,025	6%

Chevrolet Colorado

Specifications

Drive . . . . RWD
Engine 3.7-liter I5
Transmission . . . . 4-sp. Automatic
Tow Rating (lbs.) Low-3000
Head/Leg Room (in.) . . . . Very Roomy-39.6/44
Interior Space (cu. ft.) . . . . –
Cargo Space (cu. ft.) . . . . Very Roomy-37
Wheelbase/Length (in.) 126/207.1

*Combines results of both front and side tests in relation to all tests for 2010 vehicles.

Ratings—10 Best, 1 Worst

Combo Crash Tests	–
Safety Features	2
Rollover	10
Preventive Maintenance	10
Repair Costs	1
Warranty	6
Fuel Economy	3
Complaints	2
Insurance Costs	5
OVERALL RATING	–

Chevrolet Corvette

Chevrolet Corvette

Chevrolet Corvette

At-a-Glance

Status . . . . Unchanged
Year Series Started 2005
Twins . . . . –
Body Styles . . . . Coupe, Convertible
Seating 2
Anti-Theft Device. . Std. Pass. Immobil. & Pass. Alarm
Parking Index Rating . . . . Average
Where Made . . . . Bowling Green, KY
Fuel Factor
  MPG Rating (city/hwy) Poor-15/25
  Driving Range (mi.). . . . . Very Short-329.3
  Fuel Type. . . . . Premium
  Annual Fuel Cost. . . . . High-$2353
  Greenhouse Gas Emissions (tons/yr.) High-10.2
  Barrels of Oil Used per year. High-19.0

How the Competition Rates

Competitors	Rating	Pg.
Audi A5	–	87
Dodge Avenger	6	123
Ford Mustang	7	140

Price Range	Retail	Markup
LT Crew Cab 4WD Z71	$28,915	6%
Base Coupe	$48,930	10%
GS Convertible	$58,580	10%
Z06 Coupe	$74,285	10%

Safety Checklist

Crash Tests:
  Frontal. . . . . –
  Side . . . . –
Airbags:
  Head . . . . Std. Row 1 Combo
  Chest/Torso . . . . . . Std. Row 1 Combo from Seat
  Roll-Sensing Side Airbag . . . . –
  Out-of-Position Test. . . . . . . Meets Requirements
Children:
  Built-in Child Safety Seat . . . . –
  Automatic Window Reversal . . . . –
Crash Avoidance:
  Frontal Collision Warning . . . . –
  Electronic Stability Control . . . . Standard
  Lane Departure Warning . . . . –
  Brake Assist . . . . –
General:
  Automatic Crash Notification . . . . Standard
  Daytime Running Lights. . . . . Standard
  Automatic Door-Locking. . . . . Standard
Safety Belt:
  Adjustable Front Belt . . . . –

Chevrolet Corvette

Specifications

Drive. . . . . RWD
Engine 6.2-liter V8
Transmission . . . . 6-sp. Automatic
Tow Rating (lbs.). . . . . –
Head/Leg Room (in.) Cramped-38/43
Interior Space (cu. ft.) . . . . Very Cramped-52
Cargo Space (cu. ft.). . . . . Very Cramped-12
Wheelbase/Length (in.) 105.7/174.6

*Combines results of both front and side tests in relation to all tests for 2010 vehicles.

st, 1 Worst	Equinox	Terrain
Tests	4	4
s	9	9
	3	3
ntenance	8	8
	2	2
	6	6
	8	8
	3	–
s	8	5
RATING	6	6

Chevrolet Equinox

Safety Checklist

Crash Tests:
- Frontal . . . . Average
- Side . . . . Poor

Airbags:
- Head . . . . Std. Row 1 & 2 Curtain
- Chest/Torso . . . . Std. Row 1 Torso from Seat
- Roll-Sensing Side Airbag . . . . Standard
- Out-of-Position Test . . . . . . Meets Requirements

Children:
- Built-in Child Safety Seat . . . . –
- Automatic Window Reversal . . . . –

Crash Avoidance:
- Frontal Collision Warning . . . . –
- Electronic Stability Control . . . . Standard
- Lane Departure Warning . . . . –
- Brake Assist . . . . Standard

General:
- Automatic Crash Notification . . . . Standard
- Daytime Running Lights . . . . Standard
- Automatic Door-Locking . . . . Standard

Safety Belt:
- Adjustable Front Belt . . . . Standard

At-a-Glance	
. . . . Appearance Change
. . . . 2005
. . . . GMC Terrain
. . . . SUV
. . . . 5
Std. Pass. Immobil. & Pass. Alarm
. . . . Hard
. . . . Ingersoll, Ontario
wy) Good-22/32
. . . . Very Long-481.3
. . . . Regular
. . . . Very Low-$1582
missions (tons/yr.) . . Average-7.1
per year Low-13.2

Competition Rates

	Rating	Pg.
	–	159
	6	200
	2	223

	Retail	Markup
	$106,880	8%
	$22,440	6%
	$25,110	6%
	$28,045	6%

Chevrolet Equinox

Specifications

- Drive . . . . FWD
- Engine 2.4-liter I4
- Transmission . . . . 6-sp. Automatic
- Tow Rating (lbs.) . . . . Very Low-1500
- Head/Leg Room (in.) Cramped-39.8/41.2
- Interior Space (cu. ft.) Average-99.7
- Cargo Space (cu. ft.) Roomy-31.4
- Wheelbase/Length (in.) 112.5/187.8

*Combines results of both front and side tests in relation to all tests for 2010 vehicles.

Ratings—10 Best, 1 Worst

Combo Crash Tests	5
Safety Features	7
Rollover	5
Preventive Maintenance	9
Repair Costs	5
Warranty	6
Fuel Economy	8
Complaints	3
Insurance Costs	3
OVERALL RATING	**7**

Chevrolet HHR

At-a-Glance

Status	Unchanged
Year Series Started	2006
Twins	–
Body Styles	SUV
Seating	5
Anti-Theft Device	Std. Pass. Immob./Opt. Pass. Immob. & Alarm
Parking Index Rating	Easy
Where Made	Ramos Arizpe, Mexico

Fuel Factor

MPG Rating (city/hwy)	Good-22/30
Driving Range (mi.)	Long-405.0
Fuel Type	Regular/E85
Annual Fuel Cost	Low-$1620
Greenhouse Gas Emissions (tons/yr.)	Average-7.3
Barrels of Oil Used per year	Average-13.7

How the Competition Rates

Competitors	Rating	Pg.
Honda Element	7	149
Jeep Compass	5	169
Suzuki Grand Vitara	1	240

Price Range	Retail	Markup
LTZ AWD	$29,795	6%
LS	$18,720	5%
LT	$19,720	5%
LT Panel Van	$20,030	5%

Chevrolet HHR

Safety Checklist

Crash Tests:

Frontal	Good
Side	Very Poor

Airbags:

Head	Std. Row 1 & 2 Curtain
Chest/Torso	–
Roll-Sensing Side Airbag	Standard
Out-of-Position Test	Meets Requirements

Children:

Built-in Child Safety Seat	–
Automatic Window Reversal	–

Crash Avoidance:

Frontal Collision Warning	–
Electronic Stability Control	Standard
Lane Departure Warning	–
Brake Assist	Standard

General:

Automatic Crash Notification	Standard
Daytime Running Lights	Standard
Automatic Door-Locking	Standard

Safety Belt:

Adjustable Front Belt	Standard

Chevrolet HHR

Specifications

Drive	FWD
Engine	2.2-liter I4
Transmission	4-sp. Automatic
Tow Rating (lbs.)	Very Low-1000
Head/Leg Room (in.)	Cramped-39.6/40.6
Interior Space (cu. ft.)	Cramped-97.4
Cargo Space (cu. ft.)	Roomy-25.2
Wheelbase/Length (in.)	103.6/176.2

*Combines results of both front and side tests in relation to all tests for 2010 vehicles.

st, 1 Worst	
ests	9
	6
	7
tenance	9
	4
	6
	5
	5
	8
ATING	9

Chevrolet Impala

Safety Checklist

Crash Tests:
Frontal . . . . Very Good
Side . . . . Average
Airbags:
Head . . . . Std. Row 1 & 2 Curtain
Chest/Torso . . . . Std. Row 1 Torso from Seat
Roll-Sensing Side Airbag . . . . −
Out-of-Position Test . . . . . . Meets Requirements
Children:
Built-in Child Safety Seat . . . . −
Automatic Window Reversal . . . . −
Crash Avoidance:
Frontal Collision Warning . . . . −
Electronic Stability Control . . . . Standard
Lane Departure Warning . . . . −
Brake Assist . . . . −
General:
Automatic Crash Notification . . . . Standard
Daytime Running Lights . . . . Standard
Automatic Door-Locking . . . . Standard
Safety Belt:
Adjustable Front Belt . . . . Standard

t-a-Glance	
. . . . Unchanged	
. . . . 1999	
. . . . −	
. . . . Sedan	
. . . . 5/6	
Pass. Immob./Opt. Pass. Immob. & Alarm	
. . . . Hard	
. . . . Oshawa, Ontario	
y) Average-18/29	
. . . . Average-379.8	
. . . . Regular	
. . . . Average-$1866	
issions (tons/yr.) High-8.3	
er year. Average-15.6	

Chevrolet Impala

Competition Rates	Rating	Pg.
	9	121
	9	139
	7	222

	Retail	Markup
	$26,255	5%
	$23,890	5%
	$25,055	5%
	$29,630	5%

Specifications

Drive . . . . FWD
Engine 3.5-liter V6
Transmission . . . . 4-sp. Automatic
Tow Rating (lbs.) . . . . Very Low-1000
Head/Leg Room (in.) Average-39.4/42.3
Interior Space (cu. ft.) Roomy-104.5
Cargo Space (cu. ft.) Average-18.6
Wheelbase/Length (in.) 110.5/200.4

Combines results of both front and side tests in relation to all tests for 2010 vehicles.

Ratings—10 Best, 1 Worst

Combo Crash Tests	7
Safety Features	7
Rollover	7
Preventive Maintenance	9
Repair Costs	5
Warranty	6
Fuel Economy	8
Complaints	8
Insurance Costs	3
OVERALL RATING	**9**

Chevrolet Malibu

Chevrolet Malibu

At-a-Glance

Status	Unchanged
Year Series Started	2008
Twins	Pontiac G6, Saturn Aura
Body Styles	Sedan
Seating	5
Anti-Theft Device	Std. Pass. Immobil. & Pass. Alarm
Parking Index Rating	Very Hard
Where Made	Kansas City, MO / Orion Township, MI

Fuel Factor

MPG Rating (city/hwy)	Good-22/30
Driving Range (mi.)	Long-407.5
Fuel Type	Premium/E85
Annual Fuel Cost	Low-$1740
Greenhouse Gas Emissions (tons/yr.)	Average-7.3
Barrels of Oil Used per year	Average-13.7

How the Competition Rates

Competitors	Rating	Pg.
Honda Accord	8	144
Nissan Altima	9	217
Toyota Camry	7	245

Price Range

Price Range	Retail	Markup
LS	$21,825	6%
LT	$22,715	6%
Hybrid	$25,925	6%

Safety Checklist

Crash Tests:
Frontal	Good
Side	Good

Airbags:
Head	Std. Row 1 & 2 Curtain
Chest/Torso	Std. Row 1 Torso from Seat
Roll-Sensing Side Airbag	–
Out-of-Position Test	Meets Requirements

Children:
Built-in Child Safety Seat	–
Automatic Window Reversal	Std. Driver

Crash Avoidance:
Frontal Collision Warning	–
Electronic Stability Control	Standard
Lane Departure Warning	–
Brake Assist	Standard

General:
Automatic Crash Notification	Standard
Daytime Running Lights	Standard
Automatic Door-Locking	Standard

Safety Belt:
Adjustable Front Belt	Standard

Chevrolet Malibu

Specifications

Drive	FWD
Engine	2.4-liter I4
Transmission	4-sp. Automatic
Tow Rating (lbs.)	Very Low-1000
Head/Leg Room (in.)	Average-39.4/42.2
Interior Space (cu. ft.)	Cramped-97.7
Cargo Space (cu. ft.)	Cramped-15.1
Wheelbase/Length (in.)	112.3/191.8

*Combines results of both front and side tests in relation to all tests for 2010 vehicles.

Ratings—10 Best, 1 Worst	Silverado	Sierra
Combo Crash Tests	9	9
Safety Features	9	9
Rollover	3	3
Preventive Maintenance	6	6
Repair Costs	4	5
Warranty	6	6
Fuel Economy	2	2
Complaints	8	7
Insurance Costs	8	5
OVERALL RATING	**8**	**8**

Chevrolet Silverado

GMC Sierra

At-a-Glance

Status . . . . Appearance Change
Year Series Started 1999
Twins . . . . GMC Sierra
Body Styles . . . . Crew, Regular, Extended Cabs
Seating 5/6
Anti-Theft Device Std. Pass. Immob./Opt. Pass. Immob. & Alarm
Parking Index Rating . . . . Very Hard
Where Made . . . . Fort Wayne, IN
Fuel Factor
  MPG Rating (city/hwy) . . . . Very Poor-15/21
  Driving Range (mi.) . . . . Very Long-447.5
  Fuel Type Regular/E85
  Annual Fuel Cost . . . . High-$2353
  Greenhouse Gas Emissions (tons/yr.) Very High-10.8
  Barrels of Oil Used per year . . . . Very High-20.1

How the Competition Rates

Competitors	Rating	Pg.
Dodge Ram Pickup	–	131
Ford F-150	9	136
Toyota Tundra	–	255

Price Range

Price Range	Retail	Markup
LTZ	$26,605	6%
W/T Regular Cab 2WD WB119	$20,850	5%
LS Crew Cab 2WD	$30,360	8%
LT Extended Cab 4WD 143.5WB	$32,275	8%

Safety Checklist

Crash Tests:
  Frontal . . . . Very Good
  Side . . . . Good
Airbags:
  Head . . . . Std. Row 1 & 2 Curtain
  Chest/Torso . . . . Std. Row 1 Torso from Seat
  Roll-Sensing Side Airbag . . . . Standard
  Out-of-Position Test . . . . Meets Requirements
Children:
  Built-in Child Safety Seat . . . . –
  Automatic Window Reversal . . . . –
Crash Avoidance:
  Frontal Collision Warning . . . . –
  Electronic Stability Control . . . . Standard
  Lane Departure Warning . . . . –
  Brake Assist . . . . Standard
General:
  Automatic Crash Notification . . . . Standard
  Daytime Running Lights . . . . Standard
  Automatic Door-Locking . . . . Standard
Safety Belt:
  Adjustable Front Belt . . . . Standard

Chevrolet Silverado

Specifications

Drive 4WD
Engine 5.3-liter V8
Transmission . . . . 6-sp. Automatic
Tow Rating (lbs.) . . . . Very High-9500
Head/Leg Room (in.) Roomy-41.2/41.3
Interior Space (cu. ft.) . . . . –
Cargo Space (cu. ft.) . . . . Very Roomy-60.7
Wheelbase/Length (in.) 143.5/230

*Combines results of both front and side tests in relation to all tests for 2010 vehicles.

Ratings—10 Best, 1 Worst	Suburban	Escalade ESV	Yukon XL
Combo Crash Tests	10	10	10
Safety Features	9	10	9
Rollover	1	1	1
Preventive Maintenance	7	6	7
Repair Costs	4	2	4
Warranty	6	7	6
Fuel Economy	2	1	1
Complaints	5	8	7
Insurance Costs	8	1	8
OVERALL RATING	7	7	8

Chevrolet Suburban

Cadillac Escalade ESV

At-a-Glance

Status	Unchanged
Year Series Started	2000
Twins	Cadillac Escalade ESV, GMC Yukon XL
Body Styles	SUV
Seating	9
Anti-Theft Device	Std. Pass. Immobil. & Active Alarm
Parking Index Rating	Very Hard
Where Made	Arlington, TX

Fuel Factor

MPG Rating (city/hwy)	Very Poor-15/21
Driving Range (mi.)	Very Long-542.2
Fuel Type	Regular/E85
Annual Fuel Cost	High-$2353
Greenhouse Gas Emissions (tons/yr.)	Very High-10.8
Barrels of Oil Used per year	Very High-20.1

How the Competition Rates

Competitors	Rating	Pg.
Ford Expedition	6	134
Nissan Armada	–	219
Toyota Sequoia	–	252

Price Range	Retail	Markup
Hybrid Crew Cab 4WD	$41,490	6%
1500 LS RWD	$40,635	8%
1500 LT RWD	$44,145	8%
2500 LT 4WD	$48,580	8%

Safety Checklist

Crash Tests:
Frontal . . . . Very Good
Side . . . . Very Good

Airbags:
Head . . . . Std. Curtain All Rows
Chest/Torso . . . . Std. Row 1 Torso from Seat
Roll-Sensing Side Airbag . . . . Standard
Out-of-Position Test . . . . . . Meets Requirements

Children:
Built-in Child Safety Seat . . . . –
Automatic Window Reversal . . . . –

Crash Avoidance:
Frontal Collision Warning . . . . –
Electronic Stability Control . . . . Standard
Lane Departure Warning . . . . –
Brake Assist . . . . Standard

General:
Automatic Crash Notification . . . . Standard
Daytime Running Lights . . . . Standard
Automatic Door-Locking . . . . Standard

Safety Belt:
Adjustable Front Belt . . . . Standard

GMC Yukon XL

Specifications

Drive	RWD
Engine	5.3-liter V8
Transmission	6-sp. Automatic
Tow Rating (lbs.)	Very High-7900
Head/Leg Room (in.)	Roomy-41.1/41.3
Interior Space (cu. ft.)	Very Roomy-137.4
Cargo Space (cu. ft.)	Very Roomy-45.8
Wheelbase/Length (in.)	130/222.4

*Combines results of both front and side tests in relation to all tests for 2010 vehicles.

Ratings—10 Best, 1 Worst	Tahoe	Yukon
Combo Crash Tests	10	10
Safety Features	9	9
Rollover	1	1
Preventive Maintenance	7	7
Repair Costs	4	3
Warranty	6	6
Fuel Economy	2	2
Complaints	7	5
Insurance Costs	8	8
OVERALL RATING	8	7

Chevrolet Tahoe

GMC Yukon

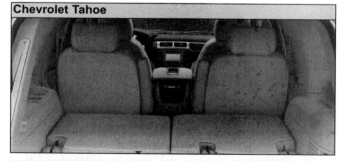

Safety Checklist

Crash Tests:
Frontal . . . . Very Good
Side . . . . Very Good
Airbags:
Head . . . . Std. Curtain All Rows
Chest/Torso . . . . Std. Row 1 Torso from Seat
Roll-Sensing Side Airbag . . . . Standard
Out-of-Position Test . . . . . Meets Requirements
Children:
Built-in Child Safety Seat . . . . –
Automatic Window Reversal . . . . –
Crash Avoidance:
Frontal Collision Warning . . . . –
Electronic Stability Control . . . . Standard
Lane Departure Warning . . . . –
Brake Assist . . . . Standard
General:
Automatic Crash Notification . . . . Standard
Daytime Running Lights . . . . Standard
Automatic Door-Locking . . . . Standard
Safety Belt:
Adjustable Front Belt . . . . Standard

At-a-Glance

Status . . . . Unchanged
Year Series Started 2000
Twins . . . . Cadillac Escalade, GMC Yukon
Body Styles . . . . SUV
Seating 9
Anti-Theft Device. . Std. Pass. Immobil. & Pass. Alarm
Parking Index Rating . . . . Hard
Where Made . . . . Janesville, WI/Arlington, TX
Fuel Factor
MPG Rating (city/hwy) . . . . Very Poor-15/21
Driving Range (mi.) . . . . Very Long-447.5
Fuel Type Regular/E85
Annual Fuel Cost . . . . High-$2353
Greenhouse Gas Emissions (tons/yr.) Very High-10.8
Barrels of Oil Used per year . . . . . . Very High-20.1

How the Competition Rates

Competitors	Rating	Pg.
Ford Expedition	6	134
Nissan Armada	–	219
Toyota Sequoia	–	252

Price Range

Price Range	Retail	Markup
1500 LTZ 4WD	$55,625	8%
LS RWD	$37,280	8%
LT RWD	$42,130	8%
Hybrid 4WD	$53,525	6%

Specifications

Drive 4WD
Engine 5.3-liter V6
Transmission . . . . 6-sp. Automatic
Tow Rating (lbs.) . . . . Very High-8200
Head/Leg Room (in.) Roomy-41.1/41.3
Interior Space (cu. ft.) . . . . –
Cargo Space (cu. ft.) Average-16.9
Wheelbase/Length (in.) 116/202

*Combines results of both front and side tests in relation to all tests for 2010 vehicles.

Ratings—10 Best, 1 Worst

Combo Crash Tests	7
Safety Features	10
Rollover	4
Preventive Maintenance	8
Repair Costs	4
Warranty	6
Fuel Economy	4
Complaints	10
Insurance Costs	8
OVERALL RATING	**9**

Chevrolet Traverse

Chevrolet Traverse

At-a-Glance

Status. . . . . Unchanged
Year Series Started 2009
Twins . . . . GMC Acadia, Saturn Outlook
Body Styles. . . . . SUV
Seating 7/8
Anti-Theft Device. . Std. Pass. Immobil. & Pass. Alarm
Parking Index Rating . . . . Very Hard
Where Made . . . . Spring Hill, TN

Fuel Factor
MPG Rating (city/hwy). Poor-17/24
Driving Range (mi.) . . . . Very Long-430.5
Fuel Type. . . . . Regular
Annual Fuel Cost. . . . . Average-$2070
Greenhouse Gas Emissions (tons/yr.) High-9.6
Barrels of Oil Used per year. High-18.0

How the Competition Rates

Competitors	Rating	Pg.
Ford Flex	6	137
Jeep Grand Cherokee	5	170
Lincoln MKT	–	192

Price Range

Price Range	Retail	Markup
LTZ 4WD	$53,615	8%
LS FWD	$29,224	6%
LT FWD	$31,745	6%
LT AWD	$33,745	6%

Safety Checklist

Crash Tests:
  Frontal . . . . Average
  Side . . . . Very Good
Airbags:
  Head . . . . Std. Curtain All Rows
  Chest/Torso . . . . Std. Row 1 Torso from Seat
  Roll-Sensing Side Airbag . . . . Standard
  Out-of-Position Test. . . . . . Meets Requirements
Children:
  Built-in Child Safety Seat . . . . –
  Automatic Window Reversal. . . . . Std. Front
Crash Avoidance:
  Frontal Collision Warning . . . . –
  Electronic Stability Control . . . . Standard
  Lane Departure Warning . . . . –
  Brake Assist . . . . Standard
General:
  Automatic Crash Notification . . . . Standard
  Daytime Running Lights. . . . . Standard
  Automatic Door-Locking. . . . . Standard
Safety Belt:
  Adjustable Front Belt . . . . Standard

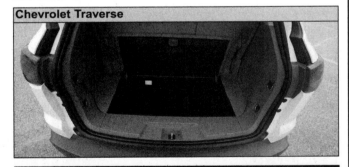

Chevrolet Traverse

Specifications

Drive . . . . FWD
Engine 3.6-liter V6
Transmission . . . . 6-sp. Automatic
Tow Rating (lbs.). High-5200
Head/Leg Room (in.) Average-40.4/41.3
Interior Space (cu. ft.) . . . . Very Roomy-153.1
Cargo Space (cu. ft.). Roomy-24.4
Wheelbase/Length (in.) 118.9/205

*Combines results of both front and side tests in relation to all tests for 2010 vehicles.

Ratings—10 Best, 1 Worst

Combo Crash Tests	10
Safety Features	1
Rollover	7
Preventive Maintenance	8
Repair Costs	8
Warranty	4
Fuel Economy	5
Complaints	5
Insurance Costs	5
OVERALL RATING	**8**

Chrysler 300

Chrysler 300

At-a-Glance

Status	Unchanged
Year Series Started	2005
Twins	Dodge Charger
Body Styles	Sedan
Seating	5
Anti-Theft Device	Std. Pass. Immobil. & Pass. Alarm
Parking Index Rating	Hard
Where Made	Brampton, Ontario / Graz, Austria

Fuel Factor

MPG Rating (city/hwy)	Average-18/26
Driving Range (mi.)	Average-376.1
Fuel Type	Regular
Annual Fuel Cost	Average-$1938
Greenhouse Gas Emissions (tons/yr.)	High-8.7
Barrels of Oil Used per year	High-16.3

How the Competition Rates

Competitors	Rating	Pg.
Buick Lucerne	9	99
Cadillac DTS	6	101
Lincoln MKS	6	191

Price Range

	Retail	Markup
LTZ AWD	$39,985	6%
Touring	$26,915	7%
Touring Sign. Series AWD	$33,390	7%
Limited	$35,535	8%

Safety Checklist

Crash Tests:
Frontal	Very Good
Side	Very Good

Airbags:
Head	Std. Row 1 & 2 Curtain
Chest/Torso	—
Roll-Sensing Side Airbag	—
Out-of-Position Test	Meets Requirements

Children:
Built-in Child Safety Seat	—
Automatic Window Reversal	Opt. Front

Crash Avoidance:
Frontal Collision Warning	—
Electronic Stability Control	Optional
Lane Departure Warning	—
Brake Assist	Optional

General:
Automatic Crash Notification	—
Daytime Running Lights	Optional
Automatic Door-Locking	Standard

Safety Belt:
Adjustable Front Belt	Standard

Chrysler 300

Specifications

Drive	RWD
Engine	2.7-liter V6
Transmission	4-sp. Automatic
Tow Rating (lbs.)	Very Low-1000
Head/Leg Room (in.)	Cramped-38.7/41.8
Interior Space (cu. ft.)	Roomy-106.6
Cargo Space (cu. ft.)	Cramped-15.6
Wheelbase/Length (in.)	120/196.8

*Combines results of both front and side tests in relation to all tests for 2010 vehicles.

Ratings—10 Best, 1 Worst

Combo Crash Tests	1
Safety Features	1
Rollover	5
Preventive Maintenance	7
Repair Costs	9
Warranty	4
Fuel Economy	5
Complaints	4
Insurance Costs	3
OVERALL RATING	**2**

Chrysler PT Cruiser

Chrysler PT Cruiser

At-a-Glance

Status . . . . Unchanged
Year Series Started 2000
Twins . . . . –
Body Styles . . . . Hatchback
Seating 5
Anti-Theft Device. . Std. Pass. Immobil. & Pass. Alarm
Parking Index Rating . . . . Average
Where Made. . . . . Toluca, Mexico
Fuel Factor
  MPG Rating (city/hwy) Average-19/24
  Driving Range (mi.). . . . . Very Short-314.5
  Fuel Type. . . . . Regular
  Annual Fuel Cost. . . . . Average-$1932
  Greenhouse Gas Emissions (tons/yr.) High-8.7
  Barrels of Oil Used per year. High-16.3

How the Competition Rates

Competitors	Rating	Pg.
Dodge Caliber	7	124
Subaru Impreza	4	237
Toyota Matrix	5	249

Price Range	Retail	Markup
300C WPC Exec. Series LWB	$48,340	8%
Classic	$18,275	6%

Safety Checklist

Crash Tests:
  Frontal. . . . . Very Poor
  Side. . . . . Poor
Airbags:
  Head . . . . Std. Row 1 Combo
  Chest/Torso . . . . . . Std. Row 1 Combo from Seat
  Roll-Sensing Side Airbag . . . . –
  Out-of-Position Test. . . . . . Meets Requirements
Children:
  Built-in Child Safety Seat . . . . –
  Automatic Window Reversal . . . . –
Crash Avoidance:
  Frontal Collision Warning . . . . –
  Electronic Stability Control . . . . –
  Lane Departure Warning . . . . –
  Brake Assist . . . . –
General:
  Automatic Crash Notification . . . . –
  Daytime Running Lights . . . . Optional
  Automatic Door-Locking. . . . . Standard
Safety Belt:
  Adjustable Front Belt . . . . Standard

Chrysler PT Cruiser

Specifications

Drive . . . . FWD
Engine. 2.4-liter I4
Transmission . . . . 4-sp. Auto. w/Overdrive
Tow Rating (lbs.) . . . . Very Low-1000
Head/Leg Room (in.) . . . . . Very Cramped-39.2/40.6
Interior Space (cu. ft.) Average-99
Cargo Space (cu. ft.) Average-21.6
Wheelbase/Length (in.) 103/168.9

*Combines results of both front and side tests in relation to all tests for 2010 vehicles.

Ratings—10 Best, 1 Worst

Combo Crash Tests	7
Safety Features	3
Rollover	7
Preventive Maintenance	9
Repair Costs	10
Warranty	4
Fuel Economy	7
Complaints	7
Insurance Costs	3
OVERALL RATING	**9**

Chrysler Sebring

Chrysler Sebring

At-a-Glance

Status	Unchanged
Year Series Started	2007
Twins	Dodge Avenger
Body Styles	Sedan, Convertible
Seating	5
Anti-Theft Device	Std. Pass. Immobil. & Pass. Alarm
Parking Index Rating	Average
Where Made	Sterling Heights, MI

Fuel Factor

MPG Rating (city/hwy)	Good-21/30
Driving Range (mi.)	Long-410.3
Fuel Type	Regular
Annual Fuel Cost	Low-$1668
Greenhouse Gas Emissions (tons/yr.)	Average-7.7
Barrels of Oil Used per year	Average-14.3

How the Competition Rates

Competitors	Rating	Pg.
Chevrolet Malibu	9	114
Ford Fusion	9	139
Nissan Maxima	7	222

Price Range

	Retail	Markup
Touring	$20,120	4%
Limited	$22,115	4%
LX Convertible	$27,850	4%

Safety Checklist

Crash Tests:
Frontal . . . . Very Good
Side . . . . Poor
Airbags:
Head . . . . Std. Row 1 & 2 Curtain
Chest/Torso . . . . Std. Row 1 Torso from Seat
Roll-Sensing Side Airbag . . . . −
Out-of-Position Test . . . . Meets Requirements
Children:
Built-in Child Safety Seat . . . . −
Automatic Window Reversal . . . . Opt. Front
Crash Avoidance:
Frontal Collision Warning . . . . −
Electronic Stability Control . . . . Optional
Lane Departure Warning . . . . −
Brake Assist . . . . Optional
General:
Automatic Crash Notification . . . . −
Daytime Running Lights . . . . Optional
Automatic Door-Locking . . . . Standard
Safety Belt:
Adjustable Front Belt . . . . Standard

Chrysler Sebring

Specifications

Drive	FWD
Engine	2.4-liter I4
Transmission	6-sp. Auto. w/Overdrive
Tow Rating (lbs.)	Very Low-1000
Head/Leg Room (in.)	Roomy-40.1/42.4
Interior Space (cu. ft.)	Average-100.9
Cargo Space (cu. ft.)	Cramped-13.6
Wheelbase/Length (in.)	108.9/190.6

*Combines results of both front and side tests in relation to all tests for 2010 vehicles.

Chrysler Town and Country — Minivan

Ratings—10 Best, 1 Worst

Rating	
Combo Crash Tests	7
Safety Features	6
Rollover	4
Preventive Maintenance	8
Repair Costs	10
Warranty	4
Fuel Economy	4
Complaints	5
Insurance Costs	10
OVERALL RATING	**8**

Chrysler Town and Country

Chrysler Town and Country

At-a-Glance

Status. . . . . Unchanged
Year Series Started 2008
Twins . . . . Dodge Grand Caravan
Body Styles . . . . Minivan
Seating. 7
Anti-Theft Device. . Std. Pass. Immobil. & Pass. Alarm
Parking Index Rating . . . . Very Hard
Where Made . . . . Windsor, Ontario

Fuel Factor
MPG Rating (city/hwy). Poor-17/24
Driving Range (mi.) Long-397.2
Fuel Type. Regular/E85
Annual Fuel Cost. . . . . Average-$2039
Greenhouse Gas Emissions (tons/yr.) High-9.6
Barrels of Oil Used per year High-18

How the Competition Rates

Competitors	Rating	Pg.
Honda Odyssey	6	152
Kia Rondo	5	178
Volkswagen Routan	5	264

Price Range	Retail	Markup
Limited Convertible	$34,705	5%
LX	$25,175	4%
Touring	$28,425	5%
Limited	$35,060	6%

Safety Checklist

Crash Tests:
Frontal . . . . Good
Side . . . . Very Good
Airbags:
Head . . . . Std. Curtain All Rows
Chest/Torso . . . . –
Roll-Sensing Side Airbag . . . . Standard
Out-of-Position Test. . . . . . . Meets Requirements
Children:
Built-in Child Safety Seat . . . . Optional
Automatic Window Reversal . . . . Opt. Driver
Crash Avoidance:
Frontal Collision Warning . . . . –
Electronic Stability Control . . . . Standard
Lane Departure Warning . . . . –
Brake Assist . . . . Standard
General:
Automatic Crash Notification . . . . –
Daytime Running Lights . . . . Optional
Automatic Door-Locking. . . . . Standard
Safety Belt:
Adjustable Front Belt . . . . Standard

Chrysler Town and Country

Specifications

Drive . . . . FWD
Engine 3.3-liter V6
Transmission . . . . 4-sp. Automatic
Tow Rating (lbs.). . . . . Very Low-1800
Head/Leg Room (in.) Cramped-39.8/40.6
Interior Space (cu. ft.) . . . . Very Roomy-162.1
Cargo Space (cu. ft.) Roomy-32.3
Wheelbase/Length (in.) 121.2/202.5

*Combines results of both front and side tests in relation to all tests for 2010 vehicles.

Dodge Avenger

Ratings—10 Best, 1 Worst

Combo Crash Tests	6
Safety Features	3
Rollover	6
Preventive Maintenance	9
Repair Costs	9
Warranty	4
Fuel Economy	7
Complaints	2
Insurance Costs	3
OVERALL RATING	**6**

Dodge Avenger

Dodge Avenger

At-a-Glance

Status. . . . . Unchanged
Year Series Started 2008
Twins. . . . . Chrysler Sebring
Body Styles . . . . Sedan
Seating. 5
Anti-Theft Device. . Std. Pass. Immobil. & Pass. Alarm
Parking Index Rating . . . . Average
Where Made. . . . . Sterling Heights, MI
Fuel Factor
  MPG Rating (city/hwy) Good-21/30
  Driving Range (mi.) Long-410.3
  Fuel Type. . . . . Regular
  Annual Fuel Cost . . . . Low-$1668
  Greenhouse Gas Emissions (tons/yr.) . . Average-7.7
  Barrels of Oil Used per year. Average-14.3

How the Competition Rates

Competitors	Rating	Pg.
Chevrolet Impala	9	113
Ford Fusion	9	139
Nissan Maxima	7	222

Price Range

	Retail	Markup
SXT	$20,230	4%
R/T	$21,730	4%

Safety Checklist

Crash Tests:
  Frontal . . . . Average
  Side . . . . Average
Airbags:
  Head . . . . Std. Row 1 & 2 Curtain
  Chest/Torso . . . . Std. Row 1 Torso from Seat
  Roll-Sensing Side Airbag . . . . –
  Out-of-Position Test. . . . . . Meets Requirements
Children:
  Built-in Child Safety Seat . . . . –
  Automatic Window Reversal . . . . Opt. Front
Crash Avoidance:
  Frontal Collision Warning . . . . –
  Electronic Stability Control . . . . Optional
  Lane Departure Warning . . . . –
  Brake Assist . . . . Optional
General:
  Automatic Crash Notification . . . . –
  Daytime Running Lights . . . . Optional
  Automatic Door-Locking. . . . . Standard
Safety Belt:
  Adjustable Front Belt . . . . Standard

Dodge Avenger

Specifications

Drive . . . . FWD
Engine. 2.4-liter I4
Transmission . . . . 4-sp. Auto. w/Overdrive
Tow Rating (lbs.) . . . . Very Low-1000
Head/Leg Room (in.) Roomy-40/42.4
Interior Space (cu. ft.) Average-100.5
Cargo Space (cu. ft.) Cramped-13.4
Wheelbase/Length (in.) 108.9/190.9

*Combines results of both front and side tests in relation to all tests for 2010 vehicles.

Dodge Caliber

Ratings—10 Best, 1 Worst

Combo Crash Tests	6
Safety Features	2
Rollover	4
Preventive Maintenance	8
Repair Costs	10
Warranty	4
Fuel Economy	8
Complaints	5
Insurance Costs	5
OVERALL RATING	**7**

Dodge Caliber

Dodge Caliber

Safety Checklist

Crash Tests:
Frontal . . . . Average
Side . . . . Good
Airbags:
Head . . . . Std. Row 1 & 2 Curtain
Chest/Torso . . . . Opt. Row 1 Torso from Seat
Roll-Sensing Side Airbag . . . . −
Out-of-Position Test. . . . . . Meets Requirements
Children:
Built-in Child Safety Seat . . . . −
Automatic Window Reversal . . . . −
Crash Avoidance:
Frontal Collision Warning . . . . −
Electronic Stability Control . . . . Optional
Lane Departure Warning . . . . −
Brake Assist . . . . Optional
General:
Automatic Crash Notification . . . . −
Daytime Running Lights . . . . Optional
Automatic Door-Locking . . . . Optional
Safety Belt:
Adjustable Front Belt . . . . Standard

At-a-Glance

Status. . . . . Unchanged
Year Series Started 2006
Twins . . . . −
Body Styles . . . . Hatchback
Seating. 5
Anti-Theft Device. . Std. Pass. Immobil. & Pass. Alarm
Parking Index Rating . . . . Very Easy
Where Made . . . . Belvidere, IL
Fuel Factor
MPG Rating (city/hwy) Good-23/27
Driving Range (mi.). . . . . Very Short-335.1
Fuel Type. . . . . Regular
Annual Fuel Cost . . . . Low-$1643
Greenhouse Gas Emissions (tons/yr.) . . Average-7.3
Barrels of Oil Used per year. Average-13.7

How the Competition Rates

Competitors	Rating	Pg.
Chevrolet HHR	7	112
Subaru Impreza	4	237
Toyota Matrix	5	249

Price Range

Price Range	Retail	Markup
SE	$16,915	6%
SXT	$18,345	6%
R/T	$20,960	7%

Dodge Caliber

Specifications

Drive . . . . FWD
Engine. 2.0-liter I4
Transmission . . . . CVT
Tow Rating (lbs.). . . . . Very Low-1000
Head/Leg Room (in.). Average-39.8/41.8
Interior Space (cu. ft.). Cramped-96.2
Cargo Space (cu. ft.). Average-18.4
Wheelbase/Length (in.) 103.7/173.8

*Combines results of both front and side tests in relation to all tests for 2010 vehicles.

Dodge Challenger Large

Ratings—10 Best, 1 Worst

Combo Crash Tests	7
Safety Features	1
Rollover	7
Preventive Maintenance	5
Repair Costs	6
Warranty	4
Fuel Economy	4
Complaints	2
Insurance Costs	3
OVERALL RATING	**4**

Dodge Challenger

At-a-Glance

Status. . . . . Unchanged
Year Series Started 2009
Twins . . . . –
Body Styles . . . . Coupe
Seating 5
Anti-Theft Device. . Std. Pass. Immobil. & Pass. Alarm
Parking Index Rating . . . . Hard
Where Made. . . . . Toluca, Mexico

Fuel Factor
  MPG Rating (city/hwy). Poor-17/25
  Driving Range (mi.). Short-357.5
  Fuel Type. . . . . Regular
  Annual Fuel Cost. . . . . Average-$2039
  Greenhouse Gas Emissions (tons/yr.) High-9.2
  Barrels of Oil Used per year. High-17.1

How the Competition Rates

Competitors	Rating	Pg.
Chevrolet Camaro	6	107
Ford Mustang	7	140

Price Range

Price Range	Retail	Markup
SRT4	$25,205	7%
SE	$22,735	2%
R/T	$30,860	4%
SRT8	$41,230	5%

Dodge Challenger

Safety Checklist

Crash Tests:
  Frontal . . . . Good
  Side. . . . . Average
Airbags:
  Head . . . . Std. Row 1 & 2 Curtain
  Chest/Torso . . . . –
  Roll-Sensing Side Airbag . . . . –
  Out-of-Position Test. . . . . . . Meets Requirements
Children:
  Built-in Child Safety Seat . . . . –
  Automatic Window Reversal . . . . –
Crash Avoidance:
  Frontal Collision Warning . . . . –
  Electronic Stability Control . . . . Optional
  Lane Departure Warning . . . . –
  Brake Assist . . . . Optional
General:
  Automatic Crash Notification . . . . –
  Daytime Running Lights . . . . Optional
  Automatic Door-Locking. . . . . Standard
Safety Belt:
  Adjustable Front Belt . . . . –

Dodge Challenger

Specifications

Drive . . . . RWD
Engine 3.5-liter V6
Transmission . . . . 5-sp. Auto. w/Overdrive
Tow Rating (lbs.). . . . . –
Head/Leg Room (in.) Average-39.3/42
Interior Space (cu. ft.) . . . . Very Cramped-91.5
Cargo Space (cu. ft.) Average-16.2
Wheelbase/Length (in.). 116/197.7

*Combines results of both front and side tests in relation to all tests for 2010 vehicles.

Ratings—10 Best, 1 Worst

Combo Crash Tests	10
Safety Features	1
Rollover	7
Preventive Maintenance	8
Repair Costs	8
Warranty	4
Fuel Economy	5
Complaints	5
Insurance Costs	1
OVERALL RATING	**8**

Dodge Charger

Dodge Charger

At-a-Glance

Status. . . . . Unchanged
Year Series Started 2006
Twins . . . . Chrysler 300
Body Styles . . . . Sedan
Seating. 5
Anti-Theft Device. . Std. Pass. Immobil. & Pass. Alarm
Parking Index Rating . . . . Hard
Where Made. . . . . Brampton, Ontario
Fuel Factor
  MPG Rating (city/hwy) Average-18/26
  Driving Range (mi.) Average-376.1
  Fuel Type. . . . . Regular
  Annual Fuel Cost. . . . . Average-$1938
  Greenhouse Gas Emissions (tons/yr.) High-8.7
  Barrels of Oil Used per year. High-16.3

How the Competition Rates

Competitors	Rating	Pg.
Cadillac STS	5	104
Chrysler 300	8	119
Ford Taurus	8	142

Price Range

Price Range	Retail	Markup
Base	$24,390	3%
SXT AWD	$26,150	3%
R/T	$31,370	4%

Safety Checklist

Crash Tests:
  Frontal . . . . Very Good
  Side . . . . Very Good
Airbags:
  Head . . . . Std. Row 1 & 2 Curtain
  Chest/Torso . . . . –
  Roll-Sensing Side Airbag . . . . –
  Out-of-Position Test. . . . . . Meets Requirements
Children:
  Built-in Child Safety Seat . . . . –
  Automatic Window Reversal . . . . Opt. Front
Crash Avoidance:
  Frontal Collision Warning . . . . –
  Electronic Stability Control . . . . Optional
  Lane Departure Warning . . . . –
  Brake Assist . . . . Optional
General:
  Automatic Crash Notification . . . . –
  Daytime Running Lights . . . . Optional
  Automatic Door-Locking. . . . . Standard
Safety Belt:
  Adjustable Front Belt . . . . Standard

Dodge Charger

Specifications

Drive. . . . . RWD
Engine 2.7-liter V6
Transmission . . . . 4-sp. Automatic
Tow Rating (lbs.). Low-2000
Head/Leg Room (in.) Cramped-38.7/41.8
Interior Space (cu. ft.). Roomy-104
Cargo Space (cu. ft.). Average-16.2
Wheelbase/Length (in.). 120/200.1

*Combines results of both front and side tests in relation to all tests for 2010 vehicles.

Dodge Dakota | Compact Pickup

Ratings—10 Best, 1 Worst

Combo Crash Tests	9
Safety Features	1
Rollover	3
Preventive Maintenance	8
Repair Costs	9
Warranty	4
Fuel Economy	2
Complaints	6
Insurance Costs	8
OVERALL RATING	**7**

Dodge Dakota

Dodge Dakota

At-a-Glance

Status. . . . . Unchanged
Year Series Started 2005
Twins . . . . −
Body Styles . . . . Crew, Extended Cabs
Seating 5/6
Anti-Theft Device . . . . . Opt. Pass. Immobil. & Alarm
Parking Index Rating . . . . Very Hard
Where Made. Warren, MI

Fuel Factor
MPG Rating (city/hwy) . . . . Very Poor-15/20
Driving Range (mi.) Average-371.8
Fuel Type. Regular/E85
Annual Fuel Cost. . . . . High-$2396
Greenhouse Gas Emissions (tons/yr.) Very High-10.8
Barrels of Oil Used per year . . . . . . Very High-20.1

How the Competition Rates

Competitors	Rating	Pg.
Chevrolet Colorado	3	109
Ford Ranger	3	141
Toyota Tacoma	2	254

Price Range	Retail	Markup
SRT-8	$38,180	5%
ST Ext. Cab RWD	$22,755	5%
Bighorn Ext. Cab 4WD	$27,880	6%
TRX Crew Cab 4WD	$31,365	6%

Safety Checklist

Crash Tests:
Frontal . . . . Very Good
Side . . . . Good
Airbags:
Head . . . . Opt. Row 1 & 2 Curtain
Chest/Torso . . . . −
Roll-Sensing Side Airbag . . . . −
Out-of-Position Test. . . . . . Meets Requirements
Children:
Built-in Child Safety Seat . . . . −
Automatic Window Reversal . . . . −
Crash Avoidance:
Frontal Collision Warning . . . . −
Electronic Stability Control . . . . −
Lane Departure Warning . . . . −
Brake Assist . . . . −
General:
Automatic Crash Notification . . . . −
Daytime Running Lights . . . . Optional
Automatic Door-Locking. . . . . Standard
Safety Belt:
Adjustable Front Belt . . . . Standard

Dodge Dakota

Specifications

Drive . . . . RWD
Engine 3.7-liter V6
Transmission . . . . 4-sp. Automatic
Tow Rating (lbs.). Average-4500
Head/Leg Room (in.) Average-39.9/41.9
Interior Space (cu. ft.) Average-102.3
Cargo Space (cu. ft.) . . . . Very Roomy-46.6
Wheelbase/Length (in.) 131.3/218.5

*Combines results of both front and side tests in relation to all tests for 2010 vehicles.

Ratings—10 Best, 1 Worst

Combo Crash Tests	7
Safety Features	6
Rollover	4
Preventive Maintenance	4
Repair Costs	10
Warranty	4
Fuel Economy	4
Complaints	5
Insurance Costs	10
OVERALL RATING	**7**

Dodge Grand Caravan

Dodge Grand Caravan

At-a-Glance

Status	Unchanged
Year Series Started	2008
Twins	Chrysler Town and Country
Body Styles	Minivan
Seating	7
Anti-Theft Device	Std. Pass. Immobil. & Pass. Alarm
Parking Index Rating	Very Hard
Where Made	Windsor, Ontario

Fuel Factor

MPG Rating (city/hwy)	Poor-17/24
Driving Range (mi.)	Long-391.4
Fuel Type	Regular/E85
Annual Fuel Cost	Average-$2070
Greenhouse Gas Emissions (tons/yr.)	High-9.6
Barrels of Oil Used per year	High-18.0

How the Competition Rates

Competitors	Rating	Pg.
Honda Odyssey	6	152
Toyota Sienna	1	253
Volkswagen Routan	5	264

Price Range	Retail	Markup
Laramie Crew Cab 4WD	$33,180	6%
Cargo Van	$21,800	4%
SE	$23,175	4%
SXT	$26,480	5%

Safety Checklist

Crash Tests:
Frontal	Good
Side	Very Good

Airbags:
Head	Std. Curtain All Rows
Chest/Torso	–
Roll-Sensing Side Airbag	Standard
Out-of-Position Test	Meets Requirements

Children:
Built-in Child Safety Seat	Optional
Automatic Window Reversal	Opt. Driver

Crash Avoidance:
Frontal Collision Warning	–
Electronic Stability Control	Standard
Lane Departure Warning	–
Brake Assist	Standard

General:
Automatic Crash Notification	–
Daytime Running Lights	Optional
Automatic Door-Locking	Standard

Safety Belt:
Adjustable Front Belt	Standard

Dodge Grand Caravan

Specifications

Drive	FWD
Engine	3.3-liter V6
Transmission	4-sp. Automatic
Tow Rating (lbs.)	Very Low-1800
Head/Leg Room (in.)	Cramped-39.8/40.6
Interior Space (cu. ft.)	Very Roomy-163.5
Cargo Space (cu. ft.)	Roomy-32.3
Wheelbase/Length (in.)	121.2/202.5

*Combines results of both front and side tests in relation to all tests for 2010 vehicles.

Ratings—10 Best, 1 Worst

Combo Crash Tests	6
Safety Features	9
Rollover	3
Preventive Maintenance	10
Repair Costs	10
Warranty	4
Fuel Economy	5
Complaints	1
Insurance Costs	8
OVERALL RATING	**7**

Dodge Journey

Dodge Journey

At-a-Glance

Status	Unchanged
Year Series Started	2009
Twins	–
Body Styles	SUV
Seating	4/5/7
Anti-Theft Device	Std. Pass. Immobil. & Pass. Alarm
Parking Index Rating	Hard
Where Made	Toluca, Mexico

Fuel Factor

MPG Rating (city/hwy)	Average-19/25
Driving Range (mi.)	Very Long-436.7
Fuel Type	Regular
Annual Fuel Cost	Average-$1901
Greenhouse Gas Emissions (tons/yr.)	High-8.7
Barrels of Oil Used per year	High-16.3

How the Competition Rates

Competitors	Rating	Pg.
Chevrolet Equinox	6	111
Ford Explorer	5	135
Kia Borrego	8	174

Price Range

Price Range	Retail	Markup
SE	$20,490	3%
SXT AWD	$26,280	5%
R/T	$26,445	5%

Safety Checklist

Crash Tests:
Frontal .... Average
Side .... Good

Airbags:
Head .... Std. Curtain All Rows
Chest/Torso .... Std. Row 1 Torso from Seat
Roll-Sensing Side Airbag .... Standard
Out-of-Position Test ...... Meets Requirements

Children:
Built-in Child Safety Seat .... Optional
Automatic Window Reversal .... Opt. Driver

Crash Avoidance:
Frontal Collision Warning .... –
Electronic Stability Control .... Standard
Lane Departure Warning .... –
Brake Assist .... Standard

General:
Automatic Crash Notification .... –
Daytime Running Lights .... Optional
Automatic Door-Locking............. Standard

Safety Belt:
Adjustable Front Belt .... Standard

Dodge Journey

Specifications

Drive	FWD
Engine	2.4-liter I4
Transmission	4-sp. Auto. w/Overdrive
Tow Rating (lbs.)	Very Low-1000
Head/Leg Room (in.)	Cramped-40.8/39.2
Interior Space (cu. ft.)	Very Roomy-125.62
Cargo Space (cu. ft.)	Very Cramped-10.7
Wheelbase/Length (in.)	113.8/192.4

*Combines results of both front and side tests in relation to all tests for 2010 vehicles.

Ratings—10 Best, 1 Worst	
Combo Crash Tests	7
Safety Features	5
Rollover	2
Preventive Maintenance	7
Repair Costs	8
Warranty	4
Fuel Economy	3
Complaints	3
Insurance Costs	10
OVERALL RATING	**6**

Dodge Nitro

Dodge Nitro

At-a-Glance

Status.	Unchanged
Year Series Started	2007
Twins	–
Body Styles	4-Door
Seating	5
Anti-Theft Device	Opt. Pass. Immobil. & Alarm
Parking Index Rating	Easy
Where Made	Toldeo, OH
Fuel Factor	
MPG Rating (city/hwy)	Poor-16/22
Driving Range (mi.)	Short-355.6
Fuel Type	Regular
Annual Fuel Cost	High-$2221
Greenhouse Gas Emissions (tons/yr.)	High-10.2
Barrels of Oil Used per year	High-19.0

How the Competition Rates

Competitors	Rating	Pg.
Hummer H3	6	155
Nissan Xterra	3	229
Toyota Highlander	4	248

Price Range	Retail	Markup
R/T AWD	$28,195	5%
SE RWD	$21,590	2%
SXT 2WD	$23,235	3%
SE 4WD	$23,250	3%

Safety Checklist

Crash Tests:
Frontal . . . . Good
Side . . . . Average

Airbags:
Head . . . . Std. Row 1 & 2 Curtain
Chest/Torso . . . . –
Roll-Sensing Side Airbag . . . . Standard
Out-of-Position Test . . . . . . Meets Requirements

Children:
Built-in Child Safety Seat . . . . –
Automatic Window Reversal . . . . Opt. Driver

Crash Avoidance:
Frontal Collision Warning . . . . –
Electronic Stability Control . . . . Standard
Lane Departure Warning . . . . –
Brake Assist . . . . Standard

General:
Automatic Crash Notification . . . . –
Daytime Running Lights . . . . Optional
Automatic Door-Locking . . . . Standard

Safety Belt:
Adjustable Front Belt . . . . Standard

Dodge Nitro

Specifications

Drive	RWD
Engine	3.7-liter V6
Transmission	4-sp. Auto. w/Overdrive
Tow Rating (lbs.)	Low-2000
Head/Leg Room (in.)	Very Cramped-40.6/38.3
Interior Space (cu. ft.)	Average-102.5
Cargo Space (cu. ft.)	Roomy-32.1
Wheelbase/Length (in.)	108.8/178.9

*Combines results of both front and side tests in relation to all tests for 2010 vehicles.

Ratings—10 Best, 1 Worst

Combo Crash Tests	–
Safety Features	2
Rollover	2
Preventive Maintenance	6
Repair Costs	9
Warranty	4
Fuel Economy	2
Complaints	10
Insurance Costs	5
OVERALL RATING	–

Dodge Ram

Dodge Ram

At-a-Glance

Status	Unchanged
Year Series Started	2009
Twins	–
Body Styles	Crew, Regular, Extended Cabs
Seating	5/6
Anti-Theft Device	Opt. Pass. Immobil. & Alarm
Parking Index Rating	Very Hard
Where Made	Warren, MI

Fuel Factor

MPG Rating (city/hwy)	Very Poor-14/20
Driving Range (mi.)	Long-420.8
Fuel Type	Regular/E85
Annual Fuel Cost	Very High-$2502
Greenhouse Gas Emissions (tons/yr.)	Very High-11.4
Barrels of Oil Used per year	Very High-21.4

How the Competition Rates

Competitors	Rating	Pg.
Chevrolet Silverado	8	115
Ford F-150	9	136
Toyota Tundra	–	255

Price Range

Price Range	Retail	Markup
SXT 4WD	$24,895	3%
ST Reg. Cab SWB RWD	$20,610	6%
TRX Reg. Cab LWB RWD	$25,705	8%
SLT Quad Cab SWB 4WD	$32,085	8%

Safety Checklist

Crash Tests:
Frontal . . . . Average
Side . . . . –
Airbags:
Head . . . . Std. Row 1 & 2 Curtain
Chest/Torso . . . . –
Roll-Sensing Side Airbag . . . . –
Out-of-Position Test . . . . Meets Requirements
Children:
Built-in Child Safety Seat . . . . –
Automatic Window Reversal . . . . Opt. Front
Crash Avoidance:
Frontal Collision Warning . . . . –
Electronic Stability Control . . . . Standard
Lane Departure Warning . . . . –
Brake Assist . . . . Standard
General:
Automatic Crash Notification . . . . –
Daytime Running Lights . . . . Optional
Automatic Door-Locking . . . . Standard
Safety Belt:
Adjustable Front Belt . . . . Standard

Dodge Ram

Specifications

Drive	RWD
Engine	5.7-liter V8
Transmission	5-sp. Automatic
Tow Rating (lbs.)	High-7200
Head/Leg Room (in.)	Average-41/41
Interior Space (cu. ft.)	Very Roomy-125.3
Cargo Space (cu. ft.)	Very Roomy-50.3
Wheelbase/Length (in.)	140.5/229

*Combines results of both front and side tests in relation to all tests for 2010 vehicles.

Ratings—10 Best, 1 Worst	
Combo Crash Tests	2
Safety Features	8
Rollover	4
Preventive Maintenance	5
Repair Costs	3
Warranty	3
Fuel Economy	5
Complaints	8
Insurance Costs	10
OVERALL RATING	**4**

Ford Edge

Ford Edge

At-a-Glance

Status	Unchanged
Year Series Started	2007
Twins	Lincoln MKX
Body Styles	SUV
Seating	5
Anti-Theft Device	Std. Pass. Immobil. & Pass. Alarm
Parking Index Rating	Hard
Where Made	Oakville, Ontario

Fuel Factor

MPG Rating (city/hwy)	Average-18/25
Driving Range (mi.)	Long-391.3
Fuel Type	Regular
Annual Fuel Cost	Average-$1967
Greenhouse Gas Emissions (tons/yr.)	High-9.2
Barrels of Oil Used per year	High-17.1

How the Competition Rates

Competitors	Rating	Pg.
Dodge Journey	7	129
Hyundai Veracruz	4	162
Kia Borrego	8	174

Price Range	Retail	Markup
Laramie Crew Cab 4WD	$42,650	9%
SE FWD	$26,920	6%
SEL AWD	$31,770	8%
Limited FWD	$32,720	8%

Safety Checklist

Crash Tests:
Frontal	Very Poor
Side	Poor

Airbags:
Head	Std. Row 1 & 2 Curtain
Chest/Torso	Std. Row 1 Torso from Seat
Roll-Sensing Side Airbag	Standard
Out-of-Position Test	Meets Requirements

Children:
Built-in Child Safety Seat	−
Automatic Window Reversal	Std. Driver

Crash Avoidance:
Frontal Collision Warning	−
Electronic Stability Control	Standard
Lane Departure Warning	−
Brake Assist	−

General:
Automatic Crash Notification	Optional
Daytime Running Lights	Optional
Automatic Door-Locking	Standard

Safety Belt:
Adjustable Front Belt	Standard

Ford Edge

Specifications

Drive	FWD
Engine	3.5-liter V6
Transmission	6-sp. Automatic
Tow Rating (lbs.)	Average-3500
Head/Leg Room (in.)	Cramped-40/40.7
Interior Space (cu. ft.)	−
Cargo Space (cu. ft.)	Roomy-32.2
Wheelbase/Length (in.)	111.2/185.7

*Combines results of both front and side tests in relation to all tests for 2010 vehicles.

Ratings—10 Best, 1 Worst

Combo Crash Tests	4
Safety Features	8
Rollover	1
Preventive Maintenance	5
Repair Costs	10
Warranty	3
Fuel Economy	7
Complaints	6
Insurance Costs	10
OVERALL RATING	**6**

Ford Escape

At-a-Glance

Status. . . . . Unchanged
Year Series Started 2005
Twins. . . . . Mazda Tribute, Mercury Mariner
Body Styles. . . . . SUV
Seating. 5
Anti-Theft Device. . Std. Pass. Immobil. & Pass. Alarm
Parking Index Rating . . . . Easy
Where Made . . . . Kansas City, MO

Fuel Factor
MPG Rating (city/hwy) Good-21/28
Driving Range (mi.) Average-390.4
Fuel Type. . . . . Regular
Annual Fuel Cost . . . . Low-$1712
Greenhouse Gas Emissions (tons/yr.) . . Average-8.0
Barrels of Oil Used per year. Average-14.9

How the Competition Rates

Competitors	Rating	Pg.
Honda CR-V	10	148
Kia Sportage	5	182
Toyota RAV4	4	251

Price Range	Retail	Markup
Sport AWD	$35,770	8%
XLS FWD	$20,515	6%
XLT FWD	$23,540	7%
Limited 4WD	$27,020	8%

Ford Escape

Safety Checklist

Crash Tests:
Frontal . . . . Average
Side . . . . Poor
Airbags:
Head . . . . Std. Row 1 & 2 Curtain
Chest/Torso . . . . Std. Row 1 Torso from Seat
Roll-Sensing Side Airbag . . . . Standard
Out-of-Position Test. . . . . . Meets Requirements
Children:
Built-in Child Safety Seat . . . . —
Automatic Window Reversal . . . . —
Crash Avoidance:
Frontal Collision Warning . . . . —
Electronic Stability Control . . . . Standard
Lane Departure Warning . . . . —
Brake Assist . . . . —
General:
Automatic Crash Notification. . . . . Optional
Daytime Running Lights . . . . Optional
Automatic Door-Locking. . . . . Standard
Safety Belt:
Adjustable Front Belt . . . . Standard

Ford Escape

Specifications

Drive . . . . FWD
Engine. 2.4-liter I4
Transmission . . . . 6-sp. Automatic
Tow Rating (lbs.). . . . . Very Low-1500
Head/Leg Room (in.). Average-40.4/41.6
Interior Space (cu. ft.) Average-99.4
Cargo Space (cu. ft.). Roomy-31.4
Wheelbase/Length (in.) 103.1/174.7

*Combines results of both front and side tests in relation to all tests for 2010 vehicles.

Ratings—10 Best, 1 Worst	Expedition	Navigator
Combo Crash Tests	9	9
Safety Features	8	8
Rollover	2	2
Preventive Maintenance	5	5
Repair Costs	6	3
Warranty	3	6
Fuel Economy	1	2
Complaints	5	5
Insurance Costs	8	8
OVERALL RATING	**6**	**6**

Lincoln Navigator

At-a-Glance

Status. . . . . Unchanged
Year Series Started 2003
Twins . . . . Lincoln Navigator
Body Styles. . . . . SUV
Seating. 5/6/7
Anti-Theft Device. . Std. Pass. Immobil. & Pass. Alarm
Parking Index Rating . . . . Very Hard
Where Made. . . . . Louisville, Kentucky
Fuel Factor
  MPG Rating (city/hwy). . . . . Very Poor-12/17
  Driving Range (mi.) Average-387.3
  Fuel Type. Regular/E85
  Annual Fuel Cost. . . . . Very High-$2928
  Greenhouse Gas Emissions (tons/yr.) Very High-13.1
  Barrels of Oil Used per year . . . . Very High-24.5

How the Competition Rates

Competitors	Rating	Pg.
Chevrolet Suburban	7	116
Nissan Armada	–	219
Toyota Sequoia	–	252

Price Range	Retail	Markup
Limited Hybrid 4WD	$34,010	8%
XLT SSV 2WD	$32,855	7%
XLT 4WD	$37,985	7%
Limited 2WD	$42,660	8%

Ford Expedition

Safety Checklist

Crash Tests:
  Frontal . . . . Good
  Side . . . . Very Good
Airbags:
  Head . . . . Std. Curtain All Rows
  Chest/Torso . . . . Std. Row 1 Torso from Seat
  Roll-Sensing Side Airbag . . . . Standard
  Out-of-Position Test. . . . . . Meets Requirements
Children:
  Built-in Child Safety Seat . . . . –
  Automatic Window Reversal . . . . Std. Driver
Crash Avoidance:
  Frontal Collision Warning . . . . –
  Electronic Stability Control . . . . Standard
  Lane Departure Warning . . . . –
  Brake Assist . . . . –
General:
  Automatic Crash Notification. . . . . Optional
  Daytime Running Lights . . . . Optional
  Automatic Door-Locking. . . . . Standard
Safety Belt:
  Adjustable Front Belt . . . . Standard

Ford Expedition

Specifications

Drive 4WD
Engine 5.4-liter V8
Transmission . . . . 6-sp. Automatic
Tow Rating (lbs.) . . . . Very High-9000
Head/Leg Room (in.) Cramped-39.6/41.1
Interior Space (cu. ft.) . . . . –
Cargo Space (cu. ft.) Average-18.6
Wheelbase/Length (in.). 119/206.5

*Combines results of both front and side tests in relation to all tests for 2010 vehicles.

Ratings—10 Best, 1 Worst

	Explorer	Mountaineer
Combo Crash Tests	6	6
Safety Features	8	8
Rollover	1	1
Preventive Maintenance	5	5
Repair Costs	7	7
Warranty	3	3
Fuel Economy	1	1
Complaints	6	5
Insurance Costs	10	10
OVERALL RATING	**5**	**5**

Ford Explorer

Mercury Mountaineer

At-a-Glance

Status. . . . . Unchanged
Year Series Started 2006
Twins . . . . Mercury Mountaineer
Body Styles. . . . . SUV
Seating 7/8
Anti-Theft Device. . Std. Pass. Immobil. & Pass. Alarm
Parking Index Rating . . . . Average
Where Made . . . . Louisville, Kentucky / St. Louis, MO
Fuel Factor
  MPG Rating (city/hwy). . . . . Very Poor-13/19
  Driving Range (mi.). . . . . Very Short-341.0
  Fuel Type. . . . . Regular
  Annual Fuel Cost. . . . . Very High-$2673
  Greenhouse Gas Emissions (tons/yr.) Very High-12.2
  Barrels of Oil Used per year . . . . Very High-22.8

How the Competition Rates

Competitors	Rating	Pg.
Dodge Journey	7	129
Nissan Pathfinder	–	224
Toyota 4Runner	–	243

Price Range	Retail	Markup
King Ranch 4WD	$48,090	8%
XLT 2WD	$28,880	7%
XLT 4WD	$31,200	7%
Limited 2WD	$35,880	8%

Safety Checklist

Crash Tests:
  Frontal. . . . . Average
  Side . . . . Good
Airbags:
  Head . . . . Std. Row 1 & 2 Curtain
  Chest/Torso . . . . Std. Row 1 Torso from Seat
  Roll-Sensing Side Airbag . . . . Standard
  Out-of-Position Test. . . . . . . Meets Requirements
Children:
  Built-in Child Safety Seat . . . . –
  Automatic Window Reversal . . . . Opt. Driver
Crash Avoidance:
  Frontal Collision Warning . . . . –
  Electronic Stability Control . . . . Standard
  Lane Departure Warning . . . . –
  Brake Assist . . . . –
General:
  Automatic Crash Notification. . . . . Optional
  Daytime Running Lights . . . . Optional
  Automatic Door-Locking. . . . . Standard
Safety Belt:
  Adjustable Front Belt . . . . Standard

Ford Explorer

Specifications

Drive 4WD
Engine 4.0-liter V6
Transmission . . . . 5-sp. Automatic
Tow Rating (lbs.). Average-5115
Head/Leg Room (in.) Roomy-39.8/42.4
Interior Space (cu. ft.) . . . . –
Cargo Space (cu. ft.) Cramped-13.6
Wheelbase/Length (in.) 113.7/193.4

*Combines results of both front and side tests in relation to all tests for 2010 vehicles.

Ratings—10 Best, 1 Worst

Combo Crash Tests	10
Safety Features	7
Rollover	2
Preventive Maintenance	8
Repair Costs	8
Warranty	3
Fuel Economy	2
Complaints	10
Insurance Costs	8
OVERALL RATING	**9**

Ford F-150

Ford F-150

At-a-Glance

Status. . . . . Unchanged
Year Series Started 2009
Twins . . . . −
Body Styles . . . SuperCab, Regular, SuperCrew Cabs
Seating 5/6
Anti-Theft Device. . Std. Pass. Immobil. & Pass. Alarm
Parking Index Rating . . . . Very Hard
Where Made . . . . Dearborn, MI / Kansas City, KS

Fuel Factor
MPG Rating (city/hwy) . . . . Very Poor-15/21
Driving Range (mi.) . . . . Very Long-447.5
Fuel Type Regular/E85
Annual Fuel Cost. . . . . High-$2353
Greenhouse Gas Emissions (tons/yr.) Very High-10.8
Barrels of Oil Used per year . . . . . . Very High-20.1

How the Competition Rates

Competitors	Rating	Pg.
Chevrolet Silverado	8	115
Nissan Titan	−	227
Toyota Tundra	−	255

Price Range

Price Range	Retail	Markup
Limited AWD	$41,675	9%
XL Regular Cab 2WD 126WB	$21,380	7%
STX Supercab 4WD 145WB	$30,150	10%
FX4 Supercrew 4WD 145WB	$37,450	11%

Safety Checklist

Crash Tests:
  Frontal . . . . Very Good
  Side . . . . Very Good
Airbags:
  Head . . . . Std. Row 1 & 2 Curtain
  Chest/Torso . . . . Std. Row 1 Torso from Seat
  Roll-Sensing Side Airbag . . . . Standard
  Out-of-Position Test. . . . . . Meets Requirements
Children:
  Built-in Child Safety Seat . . . . −
  Automatic Window Reversal . . . . −
Crash Avoidance:
  Frontal Collision Warning . . . . −
  Electronic Stability Control . . . . Standard
  Lane Departure Warning . . . . −
  Brake Assist . . . . −
General:
  Automatic Crash Notification. . . . . Optional
  Daytime Running Lights . . . . Optional
  Automatic Door-Locking . . . . Optional
Safety Belt:
  Adjustable Front Belt . . . . −

Ford F-150

Specifications

Drive . . . . RWD
Engine 4.6-liter V8
Transmission . . . . 6-sp. Auto. w/Overdrive
Tow Rating (lbs.) . . . . Very High-8100
Head/Leg Room (in.) Roomy-41/41.4
Interior Space (cu. ft.) . . . . −
Cargo Space (cu. ft.) . . . . Very Roomy-66
Wheelbase/Length (in.) 144.5/231.7

*Combines results of both front and side tests in relation to all tests for 2010 vehicles.

Ratings—10 Best, 1 Worst

Combo Crash Tests	7
Safety Features	9
Rollover	4
Preventive Maintenance	6
Repair Costs	4
Warranty	3
Fuel Economy	4
Complaints	–
Insurance Costs	5
OVERALL RATING	**6**

Ford Flex

Ford Flex

At-a-Glance

Status	Unchanged
Year Series Started	2009
Twins	–
Body Styles	SUV
Seating	6/7
Anti-Theft Device	Std. Pass. Immobil. & Pass. Alarm
Parking Index Rating	Very Hard
Where Made	Oakville, Ontario

Fuel Factor

MPG Rating (city/hwy)	Poor-17/24
Driving Range (mi.)	Short-364.0
Fuel Type	Regular
Annual Fuel Cost	Average-$2070
Greenhouse Gas Emissions (tons/yr.)	High-9.2
Barrels of Oil Used per year	High-17.1

How the Competition Rates

Competitors	Rating	Pg.
Chevrolet Traverse	9	118
GMC Acadia	8	143
Jeep Commander	–	168

Price Range

	Retail	Markup
Harley Davidson Supercrew 4WD 145WB	$45,835	11%
SE FWD	$28,550	6%
SEL AWD	$33,175	7%
Limited FWD	$37,220	8%

Safety Checklist

Crash Tests:

Frontal	Good
Side	Good

Airbags:

Head	Std. Curtain All Rows
Chest/Torso	Std. Row 1 Torso from Seat
Roll-Sensing Side Airbag	Standard
Out-of-Position Test	Meets Requirements

Children:

Built-in Child Safety Seat	–
Automatic Window Reversal	–

Crash Avoidance:

Frontal Collision Warning	–
Electronic Stability Control	Standard
Lane Departure Warning	–
Brake Assist	Standard

General:

Automatic Crash Notification	Optional
Daytime Running Lights	Optional
Automatic Door-Locking	Standard

Safety Belt:

Adjustable Front Belt	Standard

Ford Flex

Specifications

Drive	FWD
Engine	3.5-liter V6
Transmission	6-sp. Automatic
Tow Rating (lbs.)	Average-4500
Head/Leg Room (in.)	Roomy-41.8/40.8
Interior Space (cu. ft.)	Very Roomy-155.8
Cargo Space (cu. ft.)	Average-20
Wheelbase/Length (in.)	117.9/201.8

*Combines results of both front and side tests in relation to all tests for 2010 vehicles.

Ratings—10 Best, 1 Worst

Combo Crash Tests	2
Safety Features	4
Rollover	6
Preventive Maintenance	5
Repair Costs	9
Warranty	3
Fuel Economy	9
Complaints	9
Insurance Costs	3
OVERALL RATING	**6**

Ford Focus

Ford Focus

At-a-Glance

Status. . . . . Unchanged
Year Series Started 2005
Twins . . . . –
Body Styles. Sedan, Coupe
Seating. 5
Anti-Theft Device. . Std. Pass. Immobil. & Pass. Alarm
Parking Index Rating . . . . Very Easy
Where Made . . . . Wayne, MI
Fuel Factor
  MPG Rating (city/hwy) . . . . Very Good-24/34
  Driving Range (mi.) Average-373.4
  Fuel Type. . . . . Regular
  Annual Fuel Cost . . . . Very Low-$1464
  Greenhouse Gas Emissions (tons/yr.) Low-6.6
  Barrels of Oil Used per year Low-12.2

How the Competition Rates

Competitors	Rating	Pg.
Honda Civic	8	146
Kia Forte	7	175
Toyota Corolla	5	246

Price Range	Retail	Markup
Limited Ecoboost AWD	$42,065	8%
S Sedan	$15,995	6%
SE Coupe	$16,875	7%
SEL Sedan	$18,485	8%

Safety Checklist

Crash Tests:
  Frontal. . . . . Very Poor
  Side. . . . . Poor
Airbags:
  Head . . . . Std. Row 1 & 2 Curtain
  Chest/Torso . . . . Std. Row 1 Torso from Seat
  Roll-Sensing Side Airbag . . . . –
  Out-of-Position Test. . . . . . . Meets Requirements
Children:
  Built-in Child Safety Seat . . . . –
  Automatic Window Reversal . . . . –
Crash Avoidance:
  Frontal Collision Warning . . . . –
  Electronic Stability Control . . . . Standard
  Lane Departure Warning . . . . –
  Brake Assist . . . . –
General:
  Automatic Crash Notification. . . . . Optional
  Daytime Running Lights . . . . Optional
  Automatic Door-Locking . . . . Optional
Safety Belt:
  Adjustable Front Belt . . . . Standard

Ford Focus

Specifications

Drive . . . . FWD
Engine. 2.0-liter I4
Transmission . . . . 4-sp. Automatic
Tow Rating (lbs.) . . . . –
Head/Leg Room (in.) Cramped-39.2/41.7
Interior Space (cu. ft.). Cramped-93.4
Cargo Space (cu. ft.) Cramped-13.8
Wheelbase/Length (in.). 102.9/175

*Combines results of both front and side tests in relation to all tests for 2010 vehicles.

Ratings—10 Best, 1 Worst

Combo Crash Tests	7
Safety Features	5
Rollover	8
Preventive Maintenance	6
Repair Costs	9
Warranty	3
Fuel Economy	8
Complaints	10
Insurance Costs	3
OVERALL RATING	**9**

Ford Fusion

Ford Fusion

At-a-Glance

Status . . . . Appearance Change
Year Series Started 2006
Twins . . . . Lincoln MKZ, Mercury Milan
Body Styles . . . . Sedan
Seating 5
Anti-Theft Device. . Std. Pass. Immobil. & Pass. Alarm
Parking Index Rating . . . . Average
Where Made . . . . Hermosillo, Mexico
Fuel Factor
MPG Rating (city/hwy) . . . . Very Good-22/31
Driving Range (mi.) . . . . Very Long-471.1
Fuel Type Regular/E85
Annual Fuel Cost . . . . Very Low-$1505
Greenhouse Gas Emissions (tons/yr.) . . Average-7.3
Barrels of Oil Used per year. Average-13.7

How the Competition Rates

Competitors	Rating	Pg.
Chevrolet Malibu	9	114
Hyundai Sonata	7	160
Toyota Camry	7	245

Price Range	Retail	Markup
SES Sedan	$18,485	8%
S 4-cyl.	$19,270	7%
SEL 4-cyl.	$23,975	9%
Hybrid	$27,270	9%

Safety Checklist

Crash Tests:
Frontal . . . . Very Good
Side. . . . . Poor
Airbags:
Head . . . . Std. Row 1 & 2 Curtain
Chest/Torso . . . . Std. Row 1 Torso from Seat
Roll-Sensing Side Airbag . . . . −
Out-of-Position Test. . . . . . . Meets Requirements
Children:
Built-in Child Safety Seat . . . . −
Automatic Window Reversal . . . . Std. Driver
Crash Avoidance:
Frontal Collision Warning . . . . −
Electronic Stability Control . . . . Standard
Lane Departure Warning . . . . −
Brake Assist . . . . −
General:
Automatic Crash Notification. . . . . Optional
Daytime Running Lights . . . . Optional
Automatic Door-Locking. . . . . Standard
Safety Belt:
Adjustable Front Belt . . . . Standard

Ford Fusion

Specifications

Drive . . . . FWD
Engine. 2.5-liter I4
Transmission . . . . 6-sp. Automatic
Tow Rating (lbs.) . . . . −
Head/Leg Room (in.) Cramped-38.7/42.3
Interior Space (cu. ft.) Average-100.3
Cargo Space (cu. ft.) Average-16.5
Wheelbase/Length (in.) 107.4/190.6

*Combines results of both front and side tests in relation to all tests for 2010 vehicles.

Ratings—10 Best, 1 Worst

Combo Crash Tests	9
Safety Features	2
Rollover	10
Preventive Maintenance	4
Repair Costs	10
Warranty	3
Fuel Economy	3
Complaints	5
Insurance Costs	1
OVERALL RATING	**7**

Ford Mustang

At-a-Glance

Status . . . . Appearance Change
Year Series Started 2005
Twins . . . . –
Body Styles . . . . Coupe, Convertible
Seating 4
Anti-Theft Device . . Std. Pass. Immobil. & Pass. Alarm
Parking Index Rating . . . . Very Easy
Where Made . . . . Flat Rock, MI

Fuel Factor
  MPG Rating (city/hwy) Poor-16/24
  Driving Range (mi.) . . . . Very Short-301.2
  Fuel Type . . . . Regular
  Annual Fuel Cost . . . . High-$2152
  Greenhouse Gas Emissions (tons/yr.) High-9.6
  Barrels of Oil Used per year High-18.0

How the Competition Rates

Competitors	Rating	Pg.
Chevrolet Camaro	6	107
Dodge Challenger	4	125
Hyundai Elantra	8	157

Price Range

Price Range	Retail	Markup
Sport V6 AWD	$27,675	9%
Base Coupe	$20,995	8%
GT Coupe	$27,995	9%
GT Convertible	$32,995	9%

Ford Mustang

Safety Checklist

Crash Tests:
  Frontal . . . . Very Good
  Side . . . . Good
Airbags:
  Head . . . . Std. Row 1 Combo
  Chest/Torso . . . . . . Std. Row 1 Combo from Seat
  Roll-Sensing Side Airbag . . . . –
  Out-of-Position Test . . . . . . Meets Requirements
Children:
  Built-in Child Safety Seat . . . . –
  Automatic Window Reversal . . . . Opt. Front
Crash Avoidance:
  Frontal Collision Warning . . . . –
  Electronic Stability Control . . . . Standard
  Lane Departure Warning . . . . –
  Brake Assist . . . . –
General:
  Automatic Crash Notification . . . . Optional
  Daytime Running Lights . . . . Optional
  Automatic Door-Locking . . . . Standard
Safety Belt:
  Adjustable Front Belt . . . . –

Ford Mustang

Specifications

Drive . . . . RWD
Engine 4.0-liter V6
Transmission . . . . 5-sp. Automatic
Tow Rating (lbs.) . . . . Very Low-1000
Head/Leg Room (in.) Cramped-38.5/42.4
Interior Space (cu. ft.) . . . . Very Cramped-83.3
Cargo Space (cu. ft.) Cramped-13.4
Wheelbase/Length (in.) 107.1/188.1

*Combines results of both front and side tests in relation to all tests for 2010 vehicles.

Ford Ranger

Ratings—10 Best, 1 Worst

Combo Crash Tests	3
Safety Features	2
Rollover	2
Preventive Maintenance	5
Repair Costs	10
Warranty	3
Fuel Economy	3
Complaints	8
Insurance Costs	5
OVERALL RATING	**3**

Ford Ranger

Safety Checklist

Crash Tests:
Frontal . . . . Poor
Side . . . . Very Poor

Airbags:
Head . . . . Std. Row 1 Combo
Chest/Torso . . . . . . Std. Row 1 Combo from Seat
Roll-Sensing Side Airbag . . . . −
Out-of-Position Test . . . . . . Meets Requirements

Children:
Built-in Child Safety Seat . . . . −
Automatic Window Reversal . . . . −

Crash Avoidance:
Frontal Collision Warning . . . . −
Electronic Stability Control . . . . Standard
Lane Departure Warning . . . . −
Brake Assist . . . . −

General:
Automatic Crash Notification . . . . −
Daytime Running Lights . . . . Optional
Automatic Door-Locking . . . . −

Safety Belt:
Adjustable Front Belt . . . . Standard

Ford Ranger

At-a-Glance

Status . . . . Unchanged
Year Series Started 1998
Twins . . . . −
Body Styles . . . . Regular, Super Cabs
Seating 2/3
Anti-Theft Device . . Std. Pass. Immobil. & Pass. Alarm
Parking Index Rating . . . . Average
Where Made . . . . St. Paul, MN

Fuel Factor
MPG Rating (city/hwy) Poor-16/21
Driving Range (mi.) . . . . Very Short-304.6
Fuel Type . . . . Regular
Annual Fuel Cost . . . . High-$2223
Greenhouse Gas Emissions (tons/yr.) High-10.2
Barrels of Oil Used per year High-19.0

How the Competition Rates

Competitors	Rating	Pg.
Chevrolet Colorado	3	109
Dodge Dakota	7	127
Toyota Tacoma	2	254

Price Range

Price Range	Retail	Markup
Shelby GT500 Convertible	$51,325	11%
XL Regular Cab 2WD SWB	$17,440	6%
XLT Regular Cab 2WD SWB	$18,580	7%
XLT Supercab 4WD 4D	$24,730	8%

Ford Ranger

Specifications

Drive . . . . RWD
Engine 4.0-liter V6
Transmission . . . . 5-sp. Automatic
Tow Rating (lbs.) High-6000
Head/Leg Room (in.) Average-39.2/42.4
Interior Space (cu. ft.) . . . . −
Cargo Space (cu. ft.) . . . . Very Roomy-72.7
Wheelbase/Length (in.) 111.5/189.4

*Combines results of both front and side tests in relation to all tests for 2010 vehicles.

Ratings—10 Best, 1 Worst

Combo Crash Tests	9
Safety Features	9
Rollover	7
Preventive Maintenance	10
Repair Costs	3
Warranty	3
Fuel Economy	5
Complaints	3
Insurance Costs	8
OVERALL RATING	**8**

Ford Taurus

Safety Checklist

Crash Tests:
Frontal . . . . Good
Side . . . . Very Good

Airbags:
Head . . . . Std. Row 1 & 2 Curtain
Chest/Torso . . . . Std. Row 1 Torso from Seat
Roll-Sensing Side Airbag . . . . Standard
Out-of-Position Test . . . . . . Meets Requirements

Children:
Built-in Child Safety Seat . . . . —
Automatic Window Reversal . . . . Opt. Front

Crash Avoidance:
Frontal Collision Warning . . . . Optional
Electronic Stability Control . . . . Standard
Lane Departure Warning . . . . —
Brake Assist . . . . Standard

General:
Automatic Crash Notification. . . . . Optional
Daytime Running Lights . . . . Optional
Automatic Door-Locking. . . . . Standard

Safety Belt:
Adjustable Front Belt . . . . Standard

Ford Taurus

At-a-Glance

Status. . . . . Unchanged
Year Series Started 2008
Twins . . . . —
Body Styles . . . . Sedan
Seating 5/6
Anti-Theft Device. . Std. Pass. Immobil. & Pass. Alarm
Parking Index Rating . . . . Very Hard
Where Made . . . . Chicago, IL

Fuel Factor
MPG Rating (city/hwy) Average-18/28
Driving Range (mi.) Long-407.5
Fuel Type. . . . . Regular
Annual Fuel Cost. . . . . Average-$1888
Greenhouse Gas Emissions (tons/yr.) High-8.3
Barrels of Oil Used per year. Average-15.6

How the Competition Rates

Competitors	Rating	Pg.
Chevrolet Malibu	9	114
Dodge Charger	8	126
Lincoln MKS	6	191

Price Range	Retail	Markup
Sport Supercab 4WD 4D	$25,570	8%
SE	$25,170	9%
SEL AWD	$29,020	9%
Limited	$31,170	9%

Ford Taurus

Specifications

Drive . . . . FWD
Engine 3.5-liter V6
Transmission . . . . 6-sp. Automatic
Tow Rating (lbs.) . . . . Very Low-1000
Head/Leg Room (in.) Cramped-39/41.9
Interior Space (cu. ft.) Average-102.2
Cargo Space (cu. ft.) Average-20.1
Wheelbase/Length (in.) 112.9/202.9

*Combines results of both front and side tests in relation to all tests for 2010 vehicles.

Ratings—10 Best, 1 Worst

Combo Crash Tests	7
Safety Features	10
Rollover	4
Preventive Maintenance	9
Repair Costs	4
Warranty	6
Fuel Economy	4
Complaints	4
Insurance Costs	8
OVERALL RATING	**8**

GMC Acadia

GMC Acadia

At-a-Glance

Status. . . . . Unchanged
Year Series Started 2007
Twins . . . . Chevrolet Traverse, Saturn Outlook
Body Styles. . . . . SUV
Seating 7/8
Anti-Theft Device. . Std. Pass. Immobil. & Pass. Alarm
Parking Index Rating . . . . Very Hard
Where Made . . . . Lansing, MI

Fuel Factor
MPG Rating (city/hwy) Poor-17/24
Driving Range (mi.) . . . . Very Long-430.5
Fuel Type. . . . . Regular
Annual Fuel Cost. . . . . Average-$2070
Greenhouse Gas Emissions (tons/yr.) High-9.6
Barrels of Oil Used per year. High-18.0

How the Competition Rates

Competitors	Rating	Pg.
Ford Flex	6	137
Jeep Grand Cherokee	5	170
Lincoln MKT	–	192

Price Range	Retail	Markup
SHO AWD	$37,170	9%
SL FWD	$31,740	6%
SLE FWD	$34,315	6%
SLE AWD	$36,315	6%

Safety Checklist

Crash Tests:
Frontal . . . . Average
Side . . . . Very Good
Airbags:
Head . . . . Std. Curtain All Rows
Chest/Torso . . . . Std. Row 1 Torso from Seat
Roll-Sensing Side Airbag . . . . Standard
Out-of-Position Test. . . . . . . Meets Requirements
Children:
Built-in Child Safety Seat . . . . –
Automatic Window Reversal. . . . . Std. Front
Crash Avoidance:
Frontal Collision Warning . . . . –
Electronic Stability Control . . . . Standard
Lane Departure Warning . . . . –
Brake Assist . . . . Standard
General:
Automatic Crash Notification . . . . Standard
Daytime Running Lights . . . . Standard
Automatic Door-Locking. . . . . Standard
Safety Belt:
Adjustable Front Belt . . . . Standard

GMC Acadia

Specifications

Drive . . . . FWD
Engine 3.6-liter V6
Transmission . . . . 6-sp. Automatic
Tow Rating (lbs.). High-5200
Head/Leg Room (in.) Average-40.4/41.3
Interior Space (cu. ft.) . . . . Very Roomy-154
Cargo Space (cu. ft.) Roomy-24.1
Wheelbase/Length (in.) 118.9/201.1

*Combines results of both front and side tests in relation to all tests for 2010 vehicles.

Ratings—10 Best, 1 Worst

Combo Crash Tests	6
Safety Features	7
Rollover	9
Preventive Maintenance	10
Repair Costs	9
Warranty	2
Fuel Economy	7
Complaints	1
Insurance Costs	5
OVERALL RATING	**8**

Honda Accord

Honda Accord

At-a-Glance

Status	Unchanged
Year Series Started	2008
Twins	Acura RL
Body Styles	Sedan
Seating	5
Anti-Theft Device	Opt. Pass. Immob. & Alarm/Opt Pass. Immob.
Parking Index Rating	Hard
Where Made	Marysville, OH

Fuel Factor

MPG Rating (city/hwy)	Good-21/31
Driving Range (mi.)	Very Long-454.5
Fuel Type	Regular
Annual Fuel Cost	Low-$1649
Greenhouse Gas Emissions (tons/yr.)	Average-7.3
Barrels of Oil Used per year	Average-13.7

How the Competition Rates

Competitors	Rating	Pg.
Ford Fusion	9	139
Nissan Altima	9	217
Toyota Camry	7	245

Price Range	Retail	Markup
LX Manual Trans.	$21,055	10%
LX-P Auto. Trans.	$22,855	10%
EX w/ Nav & Lthr. Auto. Trans.	$28,830	10%
EX V6 w/ Nav & Lthr.	$31,105	10%

Safety Checklist

Crash Tests:
Frontal . . . . Very Good
Side . . . . Very Poor

Airbags:
Head . . . . Std. Row 1 & 2 Curtain
Chest/Torso . . . Std. Row 1 Torso & Pelvis from Seat
Roll-Sensing Side Airbag . . . . −
Out-of-Position Test . . . . . . Meets Requirements

Children:
Built-in Child Safety Seat . . . . −
Auto. Window Reversal . . . Std. Fr. (Driver only in LX)

Crash Avoidance:
Frontal Collision Warning . . . . −
Electronic Stability Control . . . . Standard
Lane Departure Warning . . . . −
Brake Assist . . . . Standard

General:
Automatic Crash Notification . . . . −
Daytime Running Lights . . . . Standard
Automatic Door-Locking . . . . Standard

Safety Belt:
Adjustable Front Belt . . . . Standard

Honda Accord

Specifications

Drive	FWD
Engine	2.4-liter I4
Transmission	5-sp. Automatic
Tow Rating (lbs.)	−
Head/Leg Room (in.)	Very Roomy-41.4/42.5
Interior Space (cu. ft.)	Roomy-106
Cargo Space (cu. ft.)	Cramped-14
Wheelbase/Length (in.)	110.2/194.1

*Combines results of both front and side tests in relation to all tests for 2010 vehicles.

Honda Accord Coupe

Ratings—10 Best, 1 Worst

Combo Crash Tests	8
Safety Features	6
Rollover	9
Preventive Maintenance	10
Repair Costs	9
Warranty	2
Fuel Economy	7
Complaints	1
Insurance Costs	1
OVERALL RATING	**8**

Honda Accord Coupe

Honda Accord Coupe

At-a-Glance

Status. . . . . Unchanged
Year Series Started 2008
Twins . . . . –
Body Styles . . . . Coupe
Seating. 5
Anti-Theft Device. . Std. Pass. Immobil. & Pass. Alarm
Parking Index Rating . . . . Average
Where Made. . . . . Marysville, OH

Fuel Factor
 MPG Rating (city/hwy) Good-21/31
 Driving Range (mi.) . . . . Very Long-454.5
 Fuel Type. . . . . Regular
 Annual Fuel Cost . . . . Low-$1649
 Greenhouse Gas Emissions (tons/yr.) . . Average-7.3
 Barrels of Oil Used per year. Average-13.7

How the Competition Rates

Competitors	Rating	Pg.
Hyundai Genesis	9	158
Infiniti G	7	165
Volkswagen CC	6	260

Price Range

Price Range	Retail	Markup
LX Manual Trans.	$22,555	10%
EX Auto. Trans.	$24,680	10%
EX w/Nav. & Lthr. Auto. Trans.	$28,880	10%
EX V6 w/Nav. & Lthr. Auto. Trans.	$31,305	10%

Safety Checklist

Crash Tests:
 Frontal . . . . Very Good
 Side . . . . Average
Airbags:
 Head . . . . Std. Row 1 & 2 Curtain
 Chest/Torso. . . Std. Row 1 Torso & Pelvis from Seat
 Roll-Sensing Side Airbag . . . . –
 Out-of-Position Test. . . . . . Meets Requirements
Children:
 Built-in Child Safety Seat . . . . –
 Auto. Window Reversal. . Std. Fr. (Driver only in LX)
Crash Avoidance:
 Frontal Collision Warning . . . . –
 Electronic Stability Control . . . . Standard
 Lane Departure Warning . . . . –
 Brake Assist . . . . Standard
General:
 Automatic Crash Notification . . . . –
 Daytime Running Lights. . . . . Standard
 Automatic Door-Locking. . . . . Standard
Safety Belt:
 Adjustable Front Belt . . . . –

Honda Accord Coupe

Specifications

Drive. . . . . FWD
Engine 2.4-liter I4
Transmission . . . . 5-sp. Automatic
Tow Rating (lbs.) . . . . –
Head/Leg Room (in.) Average-39.1/42.2
Interior Space (cu. ft.) . . . . Very Cramped-89.7
Cargo Space (cu. ft.). . . . . Very Cramped-11.9
Wheelbase/Length (in.) 107.9/190.9

*Combines results of both front and side tests in relation to all tests for 2010 vehicles.

Ratings—10 Best, 1 Worst

Combo Crash Tests	6
Safety Features	4
Rollover	8
Preventive Maintenance	10
Repair Costs	9
Warranty	2
Fuel Economy	10
Complaints	4
Insurance Costs	5
OVERALL RATING	**8**

Honda Civic

Honda Civic

At-a-Glance

Status	Unchanged
Year Series Started	2006
Twins	–
Body Styles	Sedan
Seating	5
Anti-Theft Device	Opt. Pass. Immob. & Alarm/Opt Pass. Immobil.
Parking Index Rating	Easy
Where Made	East Liberty, OH / Alliston, Ontario
Fuel Factor	
MPG Rating (city/hwy)	Very Good-25/36
Driving Range (mi.)	Average-382.6
Fuel Type	Regular
Annual Fuel Cost	Very Low-$1397
Greenhouse Gas Emissions (tons/yr.)	Low-6.3
Barrels of Oil Used per year	Low-11.8

How the Competition Rates

Competitors	Rating	Pg.
Chevrolet Cobalt	4	108
Nissan Sentra	7	226
Suzuki Kizashi	–	241

Price Range	Retail	Markup
DX Manual Trans.	$15,655	8%
LX-S Auto. Trans	$19,005	9%
EX w/ Nav. & XM Auto. Trans.	$22,255	9%
Hybrid w/ Lthr., Nav. & XM	$27,000	9%

Safety Checklist

Crash Tests:
Frontal . . . . Good
Side . . . . Average

Airbags:
Head . . . . Std. Row 1 & 2 Curtain
Chest/Torso . . . Std. Row 1 Torso & Pelvis from Seat
Roll-Sensing Side Airbag . . . . –
Out-of-Position Test . . . . . . Meets Requirements

Children:
Built-in Child Safety Seat . . . . –
Auto. Window Reversal . . Opt. Driver (None in DX)

Crash Avoidance:
Frontal Collision Warning . . . . –
Electronic Stability Control . . . . Optional
Lane Departure Warning . . . . –
Brake Assist . . . . Optional

General:
Automatic Crash Notification . . . . –
Daytime Running Lights . . . . Standard
Automatic Door-Locking . . . . Optional

Safety Belt:
Adjustable Front Belt . . . . Standard

Honda Civic

Specifications

Drive	FWD
Engine	1.8-liter I4
Transmission	5-sp. Automatic
Tow Rating (lbs.)	–
Head/Leg Room (in.)	Average-39.4/42.2
Interior Space (cu. ft.)	Very Cramped-90.9
Cargo Space (cu. ft.)	Very Cramped-12
Wheelbase/Length (in.)	106.3/177.3

*Combines results of both front and side tests in relation to all tests for 2010 vehicles.

Honda Civic Coupe

Ratings—10 Best, 1 Worst

Combo Crash Tests	7
Safety Features	4
Rollover	8
Preventive Maintenance	10
Repair Costs	9
Warranty	2
Fuel Economy	10
Complaints	4
Insurance Costs	1
OVERALL RATING	**8**

Honda Civic Coupe

Honda Civic Coupe

At-a-Glance

Status. . . . . Unchanged
Year Series Started 2006
Twins . . . . —
Body Styles . . . . Coupe
Seating 5
Anti-Theft Device. . Opt. Pass. Immob. & Alarm/Opt Pass. Immobil.
Parking Index Rating . . . . Very Easy
Where Made. . . . . Alliston, Ontario

Fuel Factor
MPG Rating (city/hwy) . . . . Very Good-25/36
Driving Range (mi.) Average-382.6
Fuel Type. . . . . Regular
Annual Fuel Cost . . . . Very Low-$1397
Greenhouse Gas Emissions (tons/yr.) Low-6.3
Barrels of Oil Used per year Low-11.8

How the Competition Rates

Competitors	Rating	Pg.
Ford Focus	6	138
Mazda 3	6	196
Scion tC	3	232

Price Range

	Retail	Markup
DX Manual Trans.	$15,455	8%
EX-L Manual Trans.	$21,005	9%
EX w/ Nav. & XM Auto. Trans.	$22,255	9%
Si w/Nav., XM & Perf. Tires Manual	$24,255	9%

Safety Checklist

Crash Tests:
  Frontal . . . . Very Good
  Side. . . . . Poor
Airbags:
  Head . . . . Std. Row 1 & 2 Curtain
  Chest/Torso. . . Std. Row 1 Torso & Pelvis from Seat
  Roll-Sensing Side Airbag . . . . —
  Out-of-Position Test. . . . . . . Meets Requirements
Children:
  Built-in Child Safety Seat . . . . —
  Auto. Window Reversal . . Opt. Driver (None in DX)
Crash Avoidance:
  Frontal Collision Warning . . . . —
  Electronic Stability Control . . . . Optional
  Lane Departure Warning . . . . —
  Brake Assist . . . . Optional
General:
  Automatic Crash Notification . . . . —
  Daytime Running Lights. . . . . Standard
  Automatic Door-Locking . . . . Optional
Safety Belt:
  Adjustable Front Belt . . . . —

Honda Civic Coupe

Specifications

Drive. . . . . FWD
Engine 1.8-liter I4
Transmission. . . . . 5-sp. Automatic
Tow Rating (lbs.) . . . . —
Head/Leg Room (in.) Cramped-38/42.6
Interior Space (cu. ft.) . . . . Very Cramped-83.7
Cargo Space (cu. ft.). . . . . Very Cramped-11.5
Wheelbase/Length (in.) 104.3/175.5

*Combines results of both front and side tests in relation to all tests for 2010 vehicles.

Ratings—10 Best, 1 Worst

Combo Crash Tests	7
Safety Features	9
Rollover	3
Preventive Maintenance	10
Repair Costs	7
Warranty	2
Fuel Economy	7
Complaints	10
Insurance Costs	10
OVERALL RATING	**10**

Honda CR-V

Honda CR-V

At-a-Glance

Status	Unchanged
Year Series Started	2007
Twins	–
Body Styles	SUV
Seating	5
Anti-Theft Device	Opt. Pass. Immob. & Alarm/Opt Pass. Immobil.
Parking Index Rating	Easy
Where Made	East Liberty, OH

Fuel Factor

MPG Rating (city/hwy)	Good-21/27
Driving Range (mi.)	Short-357.0
Fuel Type	Regular
Annual Fuel Cost	Low-$1736
Greenhouse Gas Emissions (tons/yr.)	Average-8.0
Barrels of Oil Used per year	Average-14.9

How the Competition Rates

Competitors	Rating	Pg.
Ford Escape	6	133
Hyundai Tucson	–	161
Kia Sportage	5	182

Price Range	Retail	Markup
LX 2WD	$21,545	7%
EX 4WD	$25,095	7%
EX-L 2WD	$26,495	8%
EX-L 4WD w/Nav.	$29,745	8%

Safety Checklist

Crash Tests:
Frontal	Very Good
Side	Poor

Airbags:
Head	Std. Row 1 & 2 Curtain
Chest/Torso	Std. Row 1 Torso from Seat
Roll-Sensing Side Airbag	Standard
Out-of-Position Test	Meets Requirements

Children:
Built-in Child Safety Seat	–
Automatic Window Reversal	Std. Driver

Crash Avoidance:
Frontal Collision Warning	–
Electronic Stability Control	Standard
Lane Departure Warning	–
Brake Assist	Standard

General:
Automatic Crash Notification	–
Daytime Running Lights	Standard
Automatic Door-Locking	Standard

Safety Belt:
Adjustable Front Belt	Standard

Honda CR-V

Specifications

Drive	4WD
Engine	2.4-liter I4
Transmission	5-sp. Automatic
Tow Rating (lbs.)	Very Low-1500
Head/Leg Room (in.)	Roomy-40.9/41.3
Interior Space (cu. ft.)	Average-103.8
Cargo Space (cu. ft.)	Very Roomy-35.7
Wheelbase/Length (in.)	103.1/179.3

*Combines results of both front and side tests in relation to all tests for 2010 vehicles.

Ratings—10 Best, 1 Worst

Combo Crash Tests	6
Safety Features	7
Rollover	2
Preventive Maintenance	10
Repair Costs	9
Warranty	2
Fuel Economy	6
Complaints	3
Insurance Costs	8
OVERALL RATING	**7**

Honda Element

Honda Element

At-a-Glance

Status. . . . . Unchanged
Year Series Started 2003
Twins . . . . –
Body Styles 4-Door
Seating 4
Anti-Theft Device. . . . . Std. Passive Immobil. Only
Parking Index Rating . . . . Very Easy
Where Made . . . . East Liberty, OH
Fuel Factor
  MPG Rating (city/hwy) Average-20/25
  Driving Range (mi.). Short-349.5
  Fuel Type. . . . . Regular
  Annual Fuel Cost. . . . . Average-$1843
  Greenhouse Gas Emissions (tons/yr.) High-8.3
  Barrels of Oil Used per year. Average-15.6

How the Competition Rates

Competitors	Rating	Pg.
Chevrolet HHR	7	112
Jeep Wrangler	–	173
Suzuki Grand Vitara	1	240

Price Range	Retail	Markup
LX FWD	$20,525	7%
LX 4WD	$21,775	7%
EX w/ Nav.	$24,335	7%
EX 4WD w/ Nav.	$25,585	7%

Safety Checklist

Crash Tests:
  Frontal . . . . Good
  Side. . . . . Poor
Airbags:
  Head . . . . Std. Row 1 & 2 Curtain
  Chest/Torso . . . . Std. Row 1 Torso from Seat
  Roll-Sensing Side Airbag . . . . Standard
  Out-of-Position Test. . . . . . . Meets Requirements
Children:
  Built-in Child Safety Seat . . . . –
  Automatic Window Reversal . . . . Std. Driver
Crash Avoidance:
  Frontal Collision Warning . . . . –
  Electronic Stability Control . . . . Standard
  Lane Departure Warning . . . . –
  Brake Assist . . . . Standard
General:
  Automatic Crash Notification . . . . –
  Daytime Running Lights. . . . . Standard
  Automatic Door-Locking . . . . –
Safety Belt:
  Adjustable Front Belt . . . . –

Honda Element

Specifications

Drive. . . . . FWD
Engine 2.4-liter I4
Transmission. . . . . 5-sp. Automatic
Tow Rating (lbs.) . . . . Very Low-1500
Head/Leg Room (in.) . . . . Very Roomy-43.3/41
Interior Space (cu. ft.) Average-103.6
Cargo Space (cu. ft.) Roomy-25.1
Wheelbase/Length (in.). 101.4/169.9

*Combines results of both front and side tests in relation to all tests for 2010 vehicles.

Ratings—10 Best, 1 Worst

Combo Crash Tests	7
Safety Features	2
Rollover	6
Preventive Maintenance	10
Repair Costs	7
Warranty	2
Fuel Economy	10
Complaints	8
Insurance Costs	5
OVERALL RATING	**8**

Honda Fit

At-a-Glance

Status. . . . . Unchanged
Year Series Started 2009
Twins . . . . –
Body Styles . . . . Hatchback
Seating 5
Anti-Theft Device. . Opt. Pass. Immob. & Alarm/Opt Pass. Immobil.
Parking Index Rating . . . . Very Easy
Where Made. . . . . Suzuka, Japan
Fuel Factor
MPG Rating (city/hwy) . . . . Very Good-27/33
Driving Range (mi.). . . . . Very Short-311.7
Fuel Type. . . . . Regular
Annual Fuel Cost. . . . . Very Low-$1377
Greenhouse Gas Emissions (tons/yr.) Low-6.1
Barrels of Oil Used per year Low-11.4

How the Competition Rates

Competitors	Rating	Pg.
Chevrolet Aveo	3	106
Hyundai Accent	8	156
Nissan Versa	5	228

Price Range	Retail	Markup
Base Manual Transmission	$14,900	4%
Base Automatic Transmission	$15,700	4%
Sport Automatic Transmission	$17,260	4%
Sport VSA w/ NAV Auto. Trans.	$19,110	4%

Honda Fit

Safety Checklist

Crash Tests:
Frontal . . . . Very Good
Side. . . . . Poor
Airbags:
Head . . . . Std. Row 1 & 2 Curtain
Chest/Torso . . . . Std. Row 1 Torso from Seat
Roll-Sensing Side Airbag . . . . –
Out-of-Position Test. . . . . . . Meets Requirements
Children:
Built-in Child Safety Seat . . . . –
Automatic Window Reversal . . . . Std. Driver
Crash Avoidance:
Frontal Collision Warning . . . . –
Electronic Stability Control . . . . Optional
Lane Departure Warning . . . . –
Brake Assist . . . . Optional
General:
Automatic Crash Notification . . . . –
Daytime Running Lights. . . . . Standard
Automatic Door-Locking . . . . –
Safety Belt:
Adjustable Front Belt . . . . Standard

Honda Fit

Specifications

Drive. . . . . FWD
Engine 1.5-liter I4
Transmission. . . . . 5-sp. Automatic
Tow Rating (lbs.) . . . . –
Head/Leg Room (in.) Average-40.4/41.3
Interior Space (cu. ft.) . . . . Very Cramped-90.8
Cargo Space (cu. ft.). Average-20.6
Wheelbase/Length (in.). 98.4/161.6

*Combines results of both front and side tests in relation to all tests for 2010 vehicles.

Honda Insight

Ratings—10 Best, 1 Worst

Combo Crash Tests	2
Safety Features	3
Rollover	7
Preventive Maintenance	–
Repair Costs	–
Warranty	2
Fuel Economy	10
Complaints	–
Insurance Costs	5
OVERALL RATING	**4**

Honda Insight

Honda Insight

Safety Checklist

Crash Tests:
Frontal . . . . Poor
Side . . . . Very Poor
Airbags:
Head . . . . Std. Row 1 & 2 Curtain
Chest/Torso . . . . Std. Row 1 Torso from Seat
Roll-Sensing Side Airbag . . . . –
Out-of-Position Test . . . . Meets Requirements
Children:
Built-in Child Safety Seat . . . . –
Automatic Window Reversal . . . . Std. Driver
Crash Avoidance:
Frontal Collision Warning . . . . –
Electronic Stability Control . . . . Optional
Lane Departure Warning . . . . –
Brake Assist . . . . Optional
General:
Automatic Crash Notification . . . . –
Daytime Running Lights . . . . Standard
Automatic Door-Locking . . . . Standard
Safety Belt:
Adjustable Front Belt . . . . Standard

At-a-Glance

Status . . . . All New
Year Series Started 2010
Twins . . . . –
Body Styles . . . . Hatchback
Seating 5
Anti-Theft Device . . Std. Pass. Immobil. & Pass. Alarm
Parking Index Rating . . . . Very Easy
Where Made . . . . Suzuka, Japan
Fuel Factor
MPG Rating (city/hwy) . . . . Very Good-40/43
Driving Range (mi.) . . . . Very Long-437.7
Fuel Type . . . . Regular
Annual Fuel Cost . . . . Very Low-$981
Greenhouse Gas Emissions (tons/yr.) . Very Low-4.5
Barrels of Oil Used per year . . . . Very Low-8.3

How the Competition Rates

Competitors	Rating	Pg.
Kia Soul	6	181
Scion xD	4	234
Toyota Prius	5	250

Price Range

Price Range	Retail	Markup
LX	$19,800	6%
EX	$21,300	6%
EX w/ NAV	$23,100	6%

Specifications

Drive . . . . FWD
Engine 1.3-liter I4
Transmission . . . . CVT
Tow Rating (lbs.) . . . . –
Head/Leg Room (in.) Cramped-38.4/42.3
Interior Space (cu. ft.) . . . . Very Cramped-85
Cargo Space (cu. ft.) Cramped-15.9
Wheelbase/Length (in.) 100.4/172.3

*Combines results of both front and side tests in relation to all tests for 2010 vehicles.

Ratings—10 Best, 1 Worst	
Combo Crash Tests	6
Safety Features	8
Rollover	5
Preventive Maintenance	9
Repair Costs	5
Warranty	2
Fuel Economy	3
Complaints	4
Insurance Costs	10
OVERALL RATING	**6**

Honda Odyssey

Honda Odyssey

At-a-Glance

Status	Unchanged
Year Series Started	2005
Twins	–
Body Styles	Minivan
Seating	7/8
Anti-Theft Device	Opt. Pass. Immob. & Alarm/Opt Pass. Immobil.
Parking Index Rating	Hard
Where Made	Lincoln, AL

Fuel Factor

MPG Rating (city/hwy)	Poor-16/23
Driving Range (mi.)	Average-389.3
Fuel Type	Regular
Annual Fuel Cost	High-$2185
Greenhouse Gas Emissions (tons/yr.)	High-10.2
Barrels of Oil Used per year	High-19.0

How the Competition Rates

Competitors	Rating	Pg.
Kia Sedona	5	179
Toyota Sienna	1	253
Volkswagen Routan	5	264

Price Range	Retail	Markup
LX	$26,805	10%
EX w/Entertain. System	$31,505	10%
EX w/Entertain. System & Nav.	$37,205	10%
Touring w/Entertain. System & Nav.	$40,755	10%

Safety Checklist

Crash Tests:

Frontal	Very Good
Side	Very Good

Airbags:

Head	Std. Curtain All Rows
Chest/Torso	Std. Row 1 Torso from Seat
Roll-Sensing Side Airbag	Standard
Out-of-Position Test	Meets Requirements

Children:

Built-in Child Safety Seat	–
Automatic Window Reversal	Std. Driver

Crash Avoidance:

Frontal Collision Warning	–
Electronic Stability Control	Standard
Lane Departure Warning	–
Brake Assist	Standard

General:

Automatic Crash Notification	–
Daytime Running Lights	Standard
Automatic Door-Locking	Standard

Safety Belt:

Adjustable Front Belt	Standard

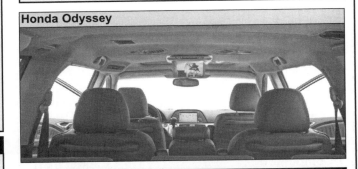

Honda Odyssey

Specifications

Drive	FWD
Engine	3.5-liter V6
Transmission	5-sp. Automatic
Tow Rating (lbs.)	Average-3500
Head/Leg Room (in.)	Average-40.9/40.8
Interior Space (cu. ft.)	Very Roomy-171.4
Cargo Space (cu. ft.)	Very Roomy-38.4
Wheelbase/Length (in.)	118.1/202.1

*Combines results of both front and side tests in relation to all tests for 2010 vehicles.

Ratings—10 Best, 1 Worst

Combo Crash Tests	7
Safety Features	9
Rollover	3
Preventive Maintenance	8
Repair Costs	5
Warranty	2
Fuel Economy	3
Complaints	10
Insurance Costs	8
OVERALL RATING	**7**

Honda Pilot

At-a-Glance

Status. . . . . Unchanged
Year Series Started 2009
Twins . . . . –
Body Styles. . . . . SUV
Seating. 8
Anti-Theft Device. . Opt. Pass. Immob. & Alarm/Opt Pass. Immobil.
Parking Index Rating . . . . Hard
Where Made. . . . . Lincoln, AL

Fuel Factor

MPG Rating (city/hwy) Poor-16/22
Driving Range (mi.) Average-383.0
Fuel Type. . . . . Regular
Annual Fuel Cost. . . . . High-$2221
Greenhouse Gas Emissions (tons/yr.) High-10.2
Barrels of Oil Used per year. High-19.0

How the Competition Rates

Competitors	Rating	Pg.
Ford Explorer	5	135
Nissan Pathfinder	–	224
Toyota 4Runner	–	243

Price Range	Retail	Markup
LX 2WD	$27,895	10%
EX 4WD	$32,345	10%
EX-L 2WD w/DVD	$35,445	10%
Touring 4WD w/DVD	$40,245	10%

Honda Pilot

Safety Checklist

Crash Tests:
Frontal . . . . Average
Side . . . . Good
Airbags:
Head . . . . Std. Curtain All Rows
Chest/Torso. . . Std. Row 1 Torso & Pelvis from Seat
Roll-Sensing Side Airbag . . . . Standard
Out-of-Position Test. . . . . . . Meets Requirements
Children:
Built-in Child Safety Seat . . . . –
Automatic Window Reversal . . . . Std. Driver
Crash Avoidance:
Frontal Collision Warning . . . . –
Electronic Stability Control . . . . Standard
Lane Departure Warning . . . . –
Brake Assist . . . . Standard
General:
Automatic Crash Notification . . . . –
Daytime Running Lights. . . . . Standard
Automatic Door-Locking. . . . . Standard
Safety Belt:
Adjustable Front Belt . . . . Standard

Honda Pilot

Specifications

Drive. 4WD
Engine. 3.5-liter V6
Transmission . . . . 5-sp. Automatic
Tow Rating (lbs.) Average-4500
Head/Leg Room (in.). Average-40/41.4
Interior Space (cu. ft.). . . . . Very Roomy-153.7
Cargo Space (cu. ft.). Average-18
Wheelbase/Length (in.). 109.2/190.9

*Combines results of both front and side tests in relation to all tests for 2010 vehicles.

Ratings—10 Best, 1 Worst

Combo Crash Tests	7
Safety Features	8
Rollover	5
Preventive Maintenance	8
Repair Costs	7
Warranty	2
Fuel Economy	2
Complaints	6
Insurance Costs	8
OVERALL RATING	**7**

Honda Ridgeline

Honda Ridgeline

Honda Ridgeline

At-a-Glance

Status . . . . Unchanged
Year Series Started 2006
Twins . . . . –
Body Styles . . . . Crew Cab
Seating 5
Anti-Theft Device . . Opt. Pass. Immob. & Alarm/Opt Pass. Immobil.
Parking Index Rating . . . . Very Hard
Where Made . . . . Alliston, Ontario
Fuel Factor
  MPG Rating (city/hwy) . . . . Very Poor-15/20
  Driving Range (mi.) Average-371.8
  Fuel Type . . . . Regular
  Annual Fuel Cost . . . . High-$2396
  Greenhouse Gas Emissions (tons/yr.) Very High-10.8
  Barrels of Oil Used per year . . . . Very High-20.1

How the Competition Rates

Competitors	Rating	Pg.
Chevrolet Avalanche	7	105
Nissan Titan	–	227
Toyota Tacoma	2	254

Price Range	Retail	Markup
RT Crew Cab	$28,450	10%
RTS Crew Cab	$31,555	10%
RTL Crew Cab w/ Leather	$34,430	10%
RTL Crew Cab w/ Leather & Nav.	$36,780	10%

Safety Checklist

Crash Tests:
  Frontal . . . . Very Good
  Side . . . . Poor
Airbags:
  Head . . . . Std. Row 1 & 2 Curtain
  Chest/Torso . . . . Std. Row 1 Torso from Seat
  Roll-Sensing Side Airbag . . . . Standard
  Out-of-Position Test . . . . Meets Requirements
Children:
  Built-in Child Safety Seat . . . . –
  Automatic Window Reversal . . . . Std. Driver
Crash Avoidance:
  Frontal Collision Warning . . . . –
  Electronic Stability Control . . . . Standard
  Lane Departure Warning . . . . –
  Brake Assist . . . . Standard
General:
  Automatic Crash Notification . . . . –
  Daytime Running Lights . . . . Standard
  Automatic Door-Locking . . . . Standard
Safety Belt:
  Adjustable Front Belt . . . . Standard

Honda Ridgeline

Specifications

Drive 4WD
Engine 3.5-liter V6
Transmission . . . . 5-sp. Automatic
Tow Rating (lbs.) Average-5000
Head/Leg Room (in.) Average-40.7/40.8
Interior Space (cu. ft.) Roomy-112
Cargo Space (cu. ft.) . . . . Very Cramped-8.5
Wheelbase/Length (in.) 122/207

*Combines results of both front and side tests in relation to all tests for 2010 vehicles.

Ratings—10 Best, 1 Worst

Combo Crash Tests	7
Safety Features	7
Rollover	1
Preventive Maintenance	8
Repair Costs	5
Warranty	7
Fuel Economy	2
Complaints	6
Insurance Costs	8
OVERALL RATING	**6**

Hummer H3

Hummer H3

At-a-Glance

Status	Unchanged
Year Series Started	2006
Twins	–
Body Styles	SUV, Crew Cab Pickup
Seating	5
Anti-Theft Device	Std. Pass. Immobil. & Pass. Alarm
Parking Index Rating	Average
Where Made	Shreveport, LA

Fuel Factor

MPG Rating (city/hwy)	Very Poor-14/18
Driving Range (mi.)	Short-357.8
Fuel Type	Regular
Annual Fuel Cost	Very High-$2604
Greenhouse Gas Emissions (tons/yr.)	Very High-11.4
Barrels of Oil Used per year	Very High-21.4

How the Competition Rates

Competitors	Rating	Pg.
Dodge Nitro	6	130
Nissan Pathfinder	–	224
Toyota FJ Cruiser	1	247

Price Range

	Retail	Markup
Base	$33,390	8%
Alpha Sport	$41,705	8%
X Sport	$43,130	8%

Safety Checklist

Crash Tests:
Frontal . . . . Average
Side . . . . Very Good

Airbags:
Head . . . . Std. Row 1 & 2 Curtain
Chest/Torso . . . . –
Roll-Sensing Side Airbag . . . . Standard
Out-of-Position Test . . . . Meets Requirements

Children:
Built-in Child Safety Seat . . . . –
Automatic Window Reversal . . . . –

Crash Avoidance:
Frontal Collision Warning . . . . –
Electronic Stability Control . . . . Standard
Lane Departure Warning . . . . –
Brake Assist . . . . Standard

General:
Automatic Crash Notification . . . . Standard
Daytime Running Lights . . . . Standard
Automatic Door-Locking . . . . Standard

Safety Belt:
Adjustable Front Belt . . . . Standard

Hummer H3

Specifications

Drive	4WD
Engine	3.7-liter I5
Transmission	4-sp. Automatic
Tow Rating (lbs.)	Average-4500
Head/Leg Room (in.)	Roomy-40.7/41.9
Interior Space (cu. ft.)	–
Cargo Space (cu. ft.)	Roomy-25
Wheelbase/Length (in.)	111.9/187.5

*Combines results of both front and side tests in relation to all tests for 2010 vehicles.

Ratings—10 Best, 1 Worst

Combo Crash Tests	5
Safety Features	1
Rollover	6
Preventive Maintenance	3
Repair Costs	10
Warranty	10
Fuel Economy	10
Complaints	9
Insurance Costs	3
OVERALL RATING	**8**

Hyundai Accent

Hyundai Accent

Hyundai Accent

At-a-Glance

Status. . . . . Unchanged
Year Series Started 2006
Twins . . . . Kia Rio
Body Styles . . . . Hatchback
Seating. 5
Anti-Theft Device . . . . Opt. Active Alarm Only
Parking Index Rating . . . . Very Easy
Where Made . . . . Ulsan, South Korea

Fuel Factor
 MPG Rating (city/hwy) . . . . Very Good-27/36
 Driving Range (mi.). Short-362.0
 Fuel Type. . . . . Regular
 Annual Fuel Cost . . . . Very Low-$1331
 Greenhouse Gas Emissions (tons/yr.) Low-6.1
 Barrels of Oil Used per year Low-11.4

How the Competition Rates

Competitors	Rating	Pg.
Chevrolet Aveo	3	106
Honda Fit	8	150
Nissan Versa	5	228

Price Range	Retail	Markup
Blue Coupe	$9,970	2%
GS Coupe Auto. Trans.	$12,995	3%
GLS Sedan Manual Trans.	$13,645	3%
GLS Sedan Auto. Trans.	$14,645	3%

Safety Checklist

Crash Tests:
 Frontal . . . . Good
 Side. . . . . Very Poor

Airbags:
 Head . . . . Std. Row 1 & 2 Curtain
 Chest/Torso . . . . Std. Row 1 Torso from Seat
 Roll-Sensing Side Airbag . . . . −
 Out-of-Position Test. . . . . . Meets Requirements

Children:
 Built-in Child Safety Seat . . . . −
 Automatic Window Reversal . . . . −

Crash Avoidance:
 Frontal Collision Warning . . . . −
 Electronic Stability Control . . . . −
 Lane Departure Warning . . . . −
 Brake Assist . . . . −

General:
 Automatic Crash Notification . . . . −
 Daytime Running Lights . . . . −
 Automatic Door-Locking . . . . −

Safety Belt:
 Adjustable Front Belt . . . . Standard

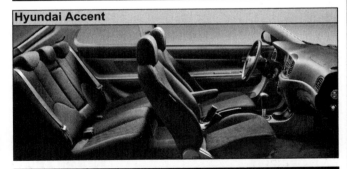

Hyundai Accent

Specifications

Drive. . . . . FWD
Engine 1.8-liter I4
Transmission . . . . 4-sp. Automatic
Tow Rating (lbs.) . . . . −
Head/Leg Room (in.) Roomy-39.6/42.8
Interior Space (cu. ft.) Cramped-92.2
Cargo Space (cu. ft.). Cramped-15.9
Wheelbase/Length (in.). 98.4/159.3

*Combines results of both front and side tests in relation to all tests for 2010 vehicles.

Hyundai Elantra Compact

Ratings—10 Best, 1 Worst	
Combo Crash Tests	5
Safety Features	2
Rollover	8
Preventive Maintenance	3
Repair Costs	10
Warranty	10
Fuel Economy	10
Complaints	5
Insurance Costs	3
OVERALL RATING	**8**

Hyundai Elantra

Hyundai Elantra

At-a-Glance

Status	Unchanged
Year Series Started	2007
Twins	–
Body Styles	Sedan
Seating	5
Anti-Theft Device	Opt. Active Alarm Only
Parking Index Rating	Very Easy
Where Made	Ulsan, South Korea
Fuel Factor	
MPG Rating (city/hwy)	Very Good-26/34
Driving Range (mi.)	Long-407.1
Fuel Type	Regular
Annual Fuel Cost	Very Low-$1393
Greenhouse Gas Emissions (tons/yr.)	Low-6.3
Barrels of Oil Used per year	Low-11.8

How the Competition Rates

Competitors	Rating	Pg.
Honda Civic	8	146
Nissan Sentra	7	226
Toyota Corolla	5	246

Price Range	Retail	Markup
Blue	$14,145	3%
GLS 2.0 PZEV	$16,895	3%
SE 2.0	$17,845	4%
SE 2.0 PZEV	$17,845	4%

Safety Checklist

Crash Tests:
Frontal . . . . Good
Side . . . . Poor
Airbags:
Head . . . . Std. Row 1 & 2 Curtain
Chest/Torso . . . . Std. Row 1 Torso from Seat
Roll-Sensing Side Airbag . . . . –
Out-of-Position Test . . . . Meets Requirements
Children:
Built-in Child Safety Seat . . . . –
Automatic Window Reversal . . . . Opt. Driver
Crash Avoidance:
Frontal Collision Warning . . . . –
Electronic Stability Control . . . . Optional
Lane Departure Warning . . . . –
Brake Assist . . . . Optional
General:
Automatic Crash Notification . . . . –
Daytime Running Lights . . . . –
Automatic Door-Locking . . . . –
Safety Belt:
Adjustable Front Belt . . . . Standard

Hyundai Elantra

Specifications

Drive	FWD
Engine	2.0-liter CVVT
Transmission	4-sp. Automatic
Tow Rating (lbs.)	Very Low-750
Head/Leg Room (in.)	Very Roomy-40/43.5
Interior Space (cu. ft.)	Cramped-97.9
Cargo Space (cu. ft.)	Cramped-14.2
Wheelbase/Length (in.)	104.3/177.4

*Combines results of both front and side tests in relation to all tests for 2010 vehicles.

Ratings—10 Best, 1 Worst	
Combo Crash Tests	8
Safety Features	7
Rollover	9
Preventive Maintenance	–
Repair Costs	–
Warranty	10
Fuel Economy	5
Complaints	6
Insurance Costs	3
OVERALL RATING	9

Hyundai Genesis

Hyundai Genesis

At-a-Glance

Status	Unchanged
Year Series Started	2009
Twins	–
Body Styles	Sedan, Coupe
Seating	5
Anti-Theft Device	Std. Pass. Immobil. & Active Alarm
Parking Index Rating	Average
Where Made	Ulsan, South Korea
Fuel Factor	
MPG Rating (city/hwy)	Average-18/27
Driving Range (mi.)	Long-408.7
Fuel Type	Regular
Annual Fuel Cost	Average-$1913
Greenhouse Gas Emissions (tons/yr.)	High-8.7
Barrels of Oil Used per year	High-16.3

How the Competition Rates

Competitors	Rating	Pg.
Acura TL	9	83
Lexus ES	6	184
Volkswagen CC	6	260

Price Range	Retail	Markup
Base 2.0T Manual Transmission	$22,000	5%
Premium 2.0T Automatic Trans.	$25,500	5%
Grand Touring 3.8 Manual Trans.	$27,500	6%
Track 3.8 Automatic Transmission	$31,000	7%

Safety Checklist

Crash Tests:
Frontal . . . . Average
Side . . . . Very Good

Airbags:
Head . . . . Std. Row 1 & 2 Curtain
Chest/Torso . . . . Std. Row 1 & 2 Torso from Seat
Roll-Sensing Side Airbag . . . . –
Out-of-Position Test . . . . . . Meets Requirements

Children:
Built-in Child Safety Seat . . . . –
Automatic Window Reversal . . . . Std. Front

Crash Avoidance:
Frontal Collision Warning . . . . –
Electronic Stability Control . . . . Standard
Lane Departure Warning . . . . –
Brake Assist . . . . Standard

General:
Automatic Crash Notification . . . . –
Daytime Running Lights . . . . Optional
Automatic Door-Locking . . . . Standard

Safety Belt:
Adjustable Front Belt . . . . Standard

Hyundai Genesis

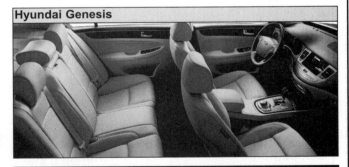

Specifications

Drive	FWD
Engine	3.8-liter V6
Transmission	6-sp. Automatic
Tow Rating (lbs.)	–
Head/Leg Room (in.)	Very Roomy-40.4/44.3
Interior Space (cu. ft.)	Roomy-109
Cargo Space (cu. ft.)	Cramped-16
Wheelbase/Length (in.)	115.6/195.9

*Combines results of both front and side tests in relation to all tests for 2010 vehicles.

Hyundai Santa Fe

Ratings—10 Best, 1 Worst

Combo Crash Tests	–
Safety Features	7
Rollover	3
Preventive Maintenance	4
Repair Costs	6
Warranty	10
Fuel Economy	7
Complaints	4
Insurance Costs	8

OVERALL RATING —

Hyundai Santa Fe

Hyundai Santa Fe (2009)

At-a-Glance

Status . . . . Appearance Change
Year Series Started 2007
Twins . . . . Kia Rondo
Body Styles . . . . SUV
Seating 5
Anti-Theft Device . . . . Std. Active Alarm Only
Parking Index Rating . . . . Easy
Where Made . . . . Montgomery, AL

Fuel Factor
MPG Rating (city/hwy) Good-22/27
Driving Range (mi.) . . . . Very Long-475.2
Fuel Type . . . . Regular
Annual Fuel Cost . . . . Low-$1688
Greenhouse Gas Emissions (tons/yr.) High-8.3
Barrels of Oil Used per year Average-15.6

How the Competition Rates

Competitors	Rating	Pg.
Mazda CX-7	6	199
Nissan Rogue	5	225
Subaru Tribeca	5	239

Price Range

	Retail	Markup
GLS Manual Trans.	$21,695	4%
GLS AWD Auto. Trans.	$24,695	4%
SE AWD	$26,595	5%
Limited AWD	$30,545	7%

Safety Checklist

Crash Tests:
Frontal . . . . Average
Side . . . . –

Airbags:
Head . . . . Std. Row 1 & 2 Curtain
Chest/Torso . . . . Std. Row 1 Torso from Seat
Roll-Sensing Side Airbag . . . . Standard
Out-of-Position Test . . . . . . Meets Requirements

Children:
Built-in Child Safety Seat . . . . –
Automatic Window Reversal . . . . Std. Driver

Crash Avoidance:
Frontal Collision Warning . . . . –
Electronic Stability Control . . . . Standard
Lane Departure Warning . . . . –
Brake Assist . . . . Standard

General:
Automatic Crash Notification . . . . –
Daytime Running Lights . . . . –
Automatic Door-Locking . . . . Optional

Safety Belt:
Adjustable Front Belt . . . . Standard

Hyundai Santa Fe (2009)

Specifications

Drive . . . . FWD
Engine . . . . 2.4-liter CVVT
Transmission . . . . 6-sp. Automatic
Tow Rating (lbs.) Low-2000
Head/Leg Room (in.) Roomy-40.2/42.6
Interior Space (cu. ft.) Roomy-108.3
Cargo Space (cu. ft.) . . . . Very Roomy-34.2
Wheelbase/Length (in.) 106.3/184.1

*Combines results of both front and side tests in relation to all tests for 2010 vehicles.

Ratings—10 Best, 1 Worst

Combo Crash Tests	5
Safety Features	4
Rollover	8
Preventive Maintenance	3
Repair Costs	9
Warranty	10
Fuel Economy	8
Complaints	4
Insurance Costs	3
OVERALL RATING	**7**

Hyundai Sonata

Hyundai Sonata

At-a-Glance

Status . . . . Unchanged
Year Series Started 2006
Twins . . . . –
Body Styles . . . . Sedan
Seating 5
Anti-Theft Device . . . . Std. Active Alarm Only
Parking Index Rating . . . . Easy
Where Made. . . . . Montgomery, AL
Fuel Factor
  MPG Rating (city/hwy) Good-22/32
  Driving Range (mi.) . . . . Very Long-453.1
  Fuel Type. . . . . Regular
  Annual Fuel Cost . . . . Very Low-$1582
  Greenhouse Gas Emissions (tons/yr.) . . Average-7.3
  Barrels of Oil Used per year. Average-13.7

How the Competition Rates

Competitors	Rating	Pg.
Mazda 6	8	198
Toyota Camry	7	245
Volkswagen Passat	6	263

Price Range

Price Range	Retail	Markup
GLS Manual Transmission	$18,700	4%
SE Automatic Transmission	$22,050	6%
SE V6 Automatic Transmission	$24,050	6%
Limited V6 Automatic Transmission	$26,550	7%

Safety Checklist

Crash Tests:
  Frontal . . . . Average
  Side . . . . Average
Airbags:
  Head . . . . Std. Row 1 & 2 Curtain
  Chest/Torso . . . . Std. Row 1 Torso from Seat
  Roll-Sensing Side Airbag . . . . –
  Out-of-Position Test. . . . . . . Meets Requirements
Children:
  Built-in Child Safety Seat . . . . –
  Automatic Window Reversal . . . . Std. Driver
Crash Avoidance:
  Frontal Collision Warning . . . . –
  Electronic Stability Control . . . . Standard
  Lane Departure Warning . . . . –
  Brake Assist . . . . Standard
General:
  Automatic Crash Notification . . . . –
  Daytime Running Lights . . . . –
  Automatic Door-Locking . . . . Optional
Safety Belt:
  Adjustable Front Belt . . . . Standard

Hyundai Sonata

Specifications

Drive. . . . . FWD
Engine . . . . 2.4-liter CVVT
Transmission . . . . 5-sp. Automatic
Tow Rating (lbs.) . . . . Very Low-1000
Head/Leg Room (in.) . . . . Very Roomy-40.1/43.7
Interior Space (cu. ft.) Roomy-105
Cargo Space (cu. ft.) Cramped-16
Wheelbase/Length (in.) 107.4/188.9

*Combines results of both front and side tests in relation to all tests for 2010 vehicles.

Ratings—10 Best, 1 Worst

Combo Crash Tests	–
Safety Features	
Rollover	4
Preventive Maintenance	7
Repair Costs	9
Warranty	10
Fuel Economy	8
Complaints	–
Insurance Costs	8
OVERALL RATING	–

Hyundai Tucson

Hyundai Tucson

At-a-Glance

Status	All New
Year Series Started	2010
Twins	–
Body Styles	SUV
Seating	5
Anti-Theft Device	–
Parking Index Rating	Very Easy
Where Made	Ulsan, South Korea
Fuel Factor	
MPG Rating (city/hwy)	Good-23/31
Driving Range (mi.)	Average-377.0
Fuel Type	Regular
Annual Fuel Cost	Very Low-$1556
Greenhouse Gas Emissions (tons/yr.)	–
Barrels of Oil Used per year	–

How the Competition Rates

Competitors	Rating	Pg.
Honda CR-V	10	148
Suzuki Grand Vitara	1	240
Toyota RAV4	4	251

Price Range	Retail	Markup
GLS Manual Transmission	$18,995	6%
GLS w/ Navi. FWD	$23,695	7%
Limited FWD	$24,345	7%
Limited w/ Premium Pkg. AWD	$28,695	8%

Safety Checklist

Crash Tests:
Frontal. –
Side –
Airbags:
Head . Std. Row 1 & 2 Curtain
Chest/Torso . Std. Row 1 Torso
Roll-Sensing Side Airbag . Standard
Out-of-Position Test . Meets Requirements
Children:
Built-in Child Safety Seat . –
Automatic Window Reversal . –
Crash Avoidance:
Frontal Collision Warning . –
Electronic Stability Control . Standard
Lane Departure Warning . –
Brake Assist . Standard
General:
Automatic Crash Notification . –
Daytime Running Lights . Optional
Automatic Door-Locking . –
Safety Belt:
Adjustable Front Belt . Standard

Hyundai Tucson

Specifications

Drive	FWD
Engine	2.4-liter I4
Transmission	6-sp. Automatic
Tow Rating (lbs.)	–
Head/Leg Room (in.)	Average-39.4/42.1
Interior Space (cu. ft.)	Average-101.9
Cargo Space (cu. ft.)	Roomy-25.7
Wheelbase/Length (in.)	103.9/173.2

*Combines results of both front and side tests in relation to all tests for 2010 vehicles.

Ratings—10 Best, 1 Worst

Combo Crash Tests	4
Safety Features	4
Rollover	4
Preventive Maintenance	4
Repair Costs	5
Warranty	10
Fuel Economy	4
Complaints	1
Insurance Costs	8
OVERALL RATING	**4**

Hyundai Veracruz

Hyundai Veracruz

At-a-Glance

Status	Unchanged
Year Series Started	2008
Twins	–
Body Styles	SUV
Seating	7/8
Anti-Theft Device	Opt. Pass. Immobil. & Active Alarm
Parking Index Rating	Average
Where Made	Ulsan, South Korea

Fuel Factor

MPG Rating (city/hwy)	Poor-17/23
Driving Range (mi.)	Long-396.8
Fuel Type	Regular
Annual Fuel Cost	Average-$2103
Greenhouse Gas Emissions (tons/yr.)	High-9.6
Barrels of Oil Used per year	High-18.0

How the Competition Rates

Competitors	Rating	Pg.
Acura MDX	–	81
Nissan Pathfinder	–	224
Toyota Highlander	4	248

Price Range

Price Range	Retail	Markup
GLS FWD	$28,145	5%
GLS AWD	$30,045	5%
Limited FWD	$34,195	8%
Limited AWD	$35,895	8%

Safety Checklist

Crash Tests:
Frontal . . . . Poor
Side . . . . Average

Airbags:
Head . . . . Std. Curtain All Rows
Chest/Torso . . . . Std. Row 1 Torso from Seat
Roll-Sensing Side Airbag . . . . –
Out-of-Position Test . . . . Meets Requirements

Children:
Built-in Child Safety Seat . . . . –
Automatic Window Reversal . . . . Std. Driver

Crash Avoidance:
Frontal Collision Warning . . . . –
Electronic Stability Control . . . . Standard
Lane Departure Warning . . . . –
Brake Assist . . . . Standard

General:
Automatic Crash Notification . . . . –
Daytime Running Lights . . . . –
Automatic Door-Locking . . . . Standard

Safety Belt:
Adjustable Front Belt . . . . Standard

Hyundai Veracruz

Specifications

Drive	FWD
Engine	3.8-liter V6
Transmission	6-sp. Automatic
Tow Rating (lbs.)	Average-3500
Head/Leg Room (in.)	Roomy-40.3/42.6
Interior Space (cu. ft.)	Very Roomy-137.2
Cargo Space (cu. ft.)	Cramped-13.4
Wheelbase/Length (in.)	110.4/190.6

*Combines results of both front and side tests in relation to all tests for 2010 vehicles.

Ratings—10 Best, 1 Worst

Combo Crash Tests	4
Safety Features	9
Rollover	6
Preventive Maintenance	5
Repair Costs	4
Warranty	8
Fuel Economy	3
Complaints	10
Insurance Costs	5
OVERALL RATING	**7**

Infiniti EX

Infiniti EX

At-a-Glance

Status. . . . . Unchanged
Year Series Started 2008
Twins . . . . –
Body Styles. . . . . Wagon
Seating. 5
Anti-Theft Device. . Std. Pass. Immobil. & Pass. Alarm
Parking Index Rating . . . . Easy
Where Made . . . . Tochigi, Japan

Fuel Factor
MPG Rating (city/hwy) Poor-16/23
Driving Range (mi.). Short-370.8
Fuel Type. . . . . Premium
Annual Fuel Cost. . . . . High-$2340
Greenhouse Gas Emissions (tons/yr.) High-9.6
Barrels of Oil Used per year. High-18.0

How the Competition Rates

Competitors	Rating	Pg.
Subaru Outback	7	238
Volkswagen Passat	6	263
Volvo V70	–	268

Price Range	Retail	Markup
Base RWD	$33,800	8%
Base AWD	$35,200	8%
Journey RWD	$36,000	8%
Journey AWD	$37,400	8%

Safety Checklist

Crash Tests:
Frontal. . . . . Very Poor
Side . . . . Very Good
Airbags:
Head . . . . Std. Row 1 & 2 Curtain
Chest/Torso. . . Std. Row 1 Torso & Pelvis from Seat
Roll-Sensing Side Airbag . . . . –
Out-of-Position Test. . . . . . . Meets Requirements
Children:
Built-in Child Safety Seat . . . . –
Automatic Window Reversal. . . . . Std. Front
Crash Avoidance:
Frontal Collision Warning . . . . Optional
Electronic Stability Control . . . . Standard
Lane Departure Warning. . . . . Optional
Brake Assist . . . . Standard
General:
Automatic Crash Notification . . . . –
Daytime Running Lights . . . . –
Automatic Door-Locking. . . . . Standard
Safety Belt:
Adjustable Front Belt . . . . Standard

Infiniti EX

Specifications

Drive. . . . . AWD
Engine. 3.5-liter V6
Transmission . . . . 5-sp. Auto. w/Overdrive
Tow Rating (lbs.) . . . . –
Head/Leg Room (in.) . . . . Very Roomy-40.5/44.3
Interior Space (cu. ft.). Roomy-107.1
Cargo Space (cu. ft.). Average-18.6
Wheelbase/Length (in.) 110.2/182.3

*Combines results of both front and side tests in relation to all tests for 2010 vehicles.

Ratings—10 Best, 1 Worst

Combo Crash Tests	–
Safety Features	10
Rollover	4
Preventive Maintenance	6
Repair Costs	3
Warranty	8
Fuel Economy	3
Complaints	–
Insurance Costs	5
OVERALL RATING	**–**

Infiniti FX

At-a-Glance

Status. . . . . Unchanged
Year Series Started 2009
Twins . . . . –
Body Styles. . . . . SUV
Seating. 5
Anti-Theft Device. . Std. Pass. Immobil. & Pass. Alarm
Parking Index Rating . . . . Average
Where Made . . . . Tochigi, Japan
Fuel Factor
  MPG Rating (city/hwy). Poor-16/23
  Driving Range (mi.) . . . . Very Long-441.2
  Fuel Type. . . . . Premium
  Annual Fuel Cost. . . . . High-$2346
  Greenhouse Gas Emissions (tons/yr.) High-9.6
  Barrels of Oil Used per year. High-18.0

How the Competition Rates

Competitors	Rating	Pg.
BMW X5	8	96
Lexus GX	–	186
Mercedes-Benz M-Class	6	207

Price Range	Retail	Markup
FX35 RWD	$42,400	8%
FX35 AWD	$43,850	8%
FX50 AWD	$58,400	8%

Infiniti FX

Safety Checklist

Crash Tests:
  Frontal. . . . . –
  Side . . . . –
Airbags:
  Head . . . . Std. Row 1 & 2 Curtain
  Chest/Torso. . . Std. Row 1 Torso & Pelvis from Seat
  Roll-Sensing Side Airbag . . . . Standard
  Out-of-Position Test. . . . . . Meets Requirements
Children:
  Built-in Child Safety Seat . . . . –
  Automatic Window Reversal Std. Front, Opt. Rear
Crash Avoidance:
  Frontal Collision Warning . . . . Optional
  Electronic Stability Control . . . . Standard
  Lane Departure Warning. . . . . Optional
  Brake Assist . . . . Standard
General:
  Automatic Crash Notification . . . . –
  Daytime Running Lights . . . . –
  Automatic Door-Locking. . . . . Standard
Safety Belt:
  Adjustable Front Belt . . . . Standard

Infiniti FX

Specifications

Drive . . . . RWD
Engine. 3.5-liter V6
Transmission . . . . 7-sp. Auto. w/Overdrive
Tow Rating (lbs.) Average-3500
Head/Leg Room (in.) . . . . Very Roomy-39.3/44.7
Interior Space (cu. ft.). Average-102.5
Cargo Space (cu. ft.). Roomy-24.8
Wheelbase/Length (in.). 113.6/191.3

*Combines results of both front and side tests in relation to all tests for 2010 vehicles.

Ratings—10 Best, 1 Worst

Combo Crash Tests	5
Safety Features	7
Rollover	8
Preventive Maintenance	7
Repair Costs	2
Warranty	8
Fuel Economy	6
Complaints	7
Insurance Costs	3
OVERALL RATING	**7**

Infiniti G

Infiniti G

At-a-Glance

Status . . . . Appearance Change
Year Series Started 2003
Twins . . . . –
Body Styles . . . . Sedan, Coupe, Convertible
Seating 5
Anti-Theft Device . . Std. Pass. Immobil. & Pass. Alarm
Parking Index Rating . . . . Easy
Where Made . . . . Tochigi, Japan
Fuel Factor
 MPG Rating (city/hwy) Average-19/27
 Driving Range (mi.) . . . . Very Long-438.0
 Fuel Type . . . . Premium
 Annual Fuel Cost . . . . Average-$1847
 Greenhouse Gas Emissions (tons/yr.) . . . . –
 Barrels of Oil Used per year . . . . –

How the Competition Rates

Competitors	Rating	Pg.
Acura TL	9	83
Cadillac CTS	7	100
Lexus GS	–	185

Price Range	Retail	Markup
Base Sedan	$33,250	9%
Journey Sedan	$34,450	9%
G37X Sedan AWD	$36,050	9%
Sport Coupe Manual Transmission	$40,400	9%

Safety Checklist

Crash Tests:
 Frontal . . . . Very Poor
 Side . . . . Very Good
Airbags:
 Head . . . . Std. Row 1 & 2 Curtain
 Chest/Torso . . . Std. Row 1 Torso & Pelvis from Seat
 Roll-Sensing Side Airbag . . . . –
 Out-of-Position Test . . . . Meets Requirements
Children:
 Built-in Child Safety Seat . . . . –
 Automatic Window Reversal Std. Front, Opt. Rear
Crash Avoidance:
 Frontal Collision Warning . . . . –
 Electronic Stability Control . . . . Standard
 Lane Departure Warning . . . . –
 Brake Assist . . . . Standard
General:
 Automatic Crash Notification . . . . –
 Daytime Running Lights . . . . –
 Automatic Door-Locking . . . . Standard
Safety Belt:
 Adjustable Front Belt . . . . Standard

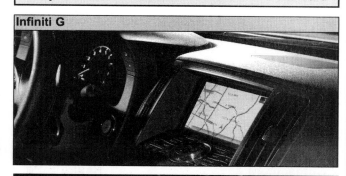

Infiniti G

Specifications

Drive . . . . RWD
Engine 3.7-liter V6
Transmission . . . . 7-sp. Automatic
Tow Rating (lbs.) . . . . –
Head/Leg Room (in.) . . . . Very Roomy-40.5/43.9
Interior Space (cu. ft.) Average-99
Cargo Space (cu. ft.) Cramped-13.5
Wheelbase/Length (in.) 112.2/187

*Combines results of both front and side tests in relation to all tests for 2010 vehicles.

Ratings—10 Best, 1 Worst

Combo Crash Tests	–
Safety Features	8
Rollover	6
Preventive Maintenance	6
Repair Costs	2
Warranty	8
Fuel Economy	4
Complaints	4
Insurance Costs	3
OVERALL RATING	–

Infiniti M

Infiniti M

At-a-Glance

Status	Unchanged
Year Series Started	2006
Twins	–
Body Styles	Sedan
Seating	5
Anti-Theft Device	Std. Pass. Immobil. & Pass. Alarm
Parking Index Rating	Average
Where Made	Tochigi, Japan

Fuel Factor

MPG Rating (city/hwy)	Poor-17/25
Driving Range (mi.)	Long-397.2
Fuel Type	Premium
Annual Fuel Cost	High-$2190
Greenhouse Gas Emissions (tons/yr.)	High-9.6
Barrels of Oil Used per year	High-18.0

How the Competition Rates

Competitors	Rating	Pg.
BMW 7 Series	–	94
Cadillac STS	5	104
Jaguar XF	–	167

Price Range	Retail	Markup
Base M35 RWD	$45,800	8%
X M35 AWD	$47,950	8%
Base M45 RWD	$52,150	8%
X M45 AWD	$54,650	8%

Safety Checklist

Crash Tests:
Frontal . . . . –
Side . . . . –

Airbags:
Head . . . . Std. Row 1 & 2 Curtain
Chest/Torso . . . Std. Row 1 Torso & Pelvis from Seat
Roll-Sensing Side Airbag . . . . –
Out-of-Position Test . . . . . . Meets Requirements

Children:
Built-in Child Safety Seat . . . . –
Automatic Window Reversal. Std. Front and Rear

Crash Avoidance:
Frontal Collision Warning . . . . –
Electronic Stability Control . . . . Standard
Lane Departure Warning . . . . Optional
Brake Assist . . . . Standard

General:
Automatic Crash Notification . . . . –
Daytime Running Lights . . . . –
Automatic Door-Locking . . . . Standard

Safety Belt:
Adjustable Front Belt . . . . Standard

Infiniti M

Specifications

Drive	RWD
Engine	3.5-liter V6
Transmission	7-sp. Auto. w/Overdrive
Tow Rating (lbs.)	–
Head/Leg Room (in.)	Very Roomy-39.6/44.2
Interior Space (cu. ft.)	Roomy-105.2
Cargo Space (cu. ft.)	Cramped-14.9
Wheelbase/Length (in.)	114.2/194.1

*Combines results of both front and side tests in relation to all tests for 2010 vehicles.

Ratings—10 Best, 1 Worst

Combo Crash Tests	–
Safety Features	4
Rollover	8
Preventive Maintenance	8
Repair Costs	2
Warranty	4
Fuel Economy	4
Complaints	1
Insurance Costs	1
OVERALL RATING	**–**

Jaguar XF

Jaguar XF

At-a-Glance

Status. . . . . Unchanged
Year Series Started 2009
Twins . . . . –
Body Styles . . . . Sedan
Seating. 5
Anti-Theft Device . Std. Pass. Immobil. & Active Alarm
Parking Index Rating . . . . Hard
Where Made . . . . Castle Bromwich, UK
Fuel Factor
  MPG Rating (city/hwy). Poor-16/25
  Driving Range (mi.). Short-351.3
  Fuel Type. . . . . Premium
  Annual Fuel Cost. . . . . High-$2277
  Greenhouse Gas Emissions (tons/yr.) High-9.6
  Barrels of Oil Used per year. High-18.0

How the Competition Rates

Competitors	Rating	Pg.
BMW 7 Series	–	94
Lexus LS	–	189
Mercedes-Benz S-Class	–	208

Price Range	Retail	Markup
Base	$51,150	10%
Premium	$56,150	10%
Supercharged	$67,150	10%
XFR	$79,150	10%

Safety Checklist

Crash Tests:
  Frontal. . . . . –
  Side . . . . –
Airbags:
  Head . . . . Std. Row 1 & 2 Curtain
  Chest/Torso . . . . Std. Row 1 Torso from Seat
  Roll-Sensing Side Airbag . . . . –
  Out-of-Position Test . . . . –
Children:
  Built-in Child Safety Seat . . . . –
  Automatic Window Reversal. Std. Front and Rear
Crash Avoidance:
  Frontal Collision Warning . . . . –
  Electronic Stability Control . . . . Standard
  Lane Departure Warning . . . . –
  Brake Assist . . . . Standard
General:
  Automatic Crash Notification . . . . –
  Daytime Running Lights . . . . Optional
  Automatic Door-Locking. . . . . Standard
Safety Belt:
  Adjustable Front Belt . . . . Standard

Jaguar XF

Specifications

Drive . . . . RWD
Engine. 4.2-liter V8
Transmission. . . . . 6-sp. Automatic
Tow Rating (lbs.) . . . . –
Head/Leg Room (in.) Cramped-39/41.5
Interior Space (cu. ft.). Cramped-95
Cargo Space (cu. ft.) Average-17
Wheelbase/Length (in.) 114.5/195.3

*Combines results of both front and side tests in relation to all tests for 2010 vehicles.

Ratings—10 Best, 1 Worst

Combo Crash Tests	–
Safety Features	5
Rollover	1
Preventive Maintenance	7
Repair Costs	8
Warranty	4
Fuel Economy	2
Complaints	2
Insurance Costs	5
OVERALL RATING	–

Jeep Commander

Jeep Commander

At-a-Glance

Status. . . . . Unchanged
Year Series Started 2007
Twins . . . . –
Body Styles. . . . . SUV
Seating 7
Anti-Theft Device. . Std. Pass. Immobil. & Pass. Alarm
Parking Index Rating . . . . Hard
Where Made . . . . Detroit, MI
Fuel Factor
  MPG Rating (city/hwy). . . . . Very Poor-14/19
  Driving Range (mi.). . . . . Very Short-335.1
  Fuel Type. . . . . Regular
  Annual Fuel Cost. . . . . Very High-$2550
  Greenhouse Gas Emissions (tons/yr.) Very High-11.4
  Barrels of Oil Used per year . . . . Very High-21.4

How the Competition Rates

Competitors	Rating	Pg.
Chevrolet Tahoe	8	117
Lincoln MKT	–	192
Toyota FJ Cruiser	1	247

Price Range	Retail	Markup
Sport 2WD	$31,575	5%
Sport 4WD	$33,575	5%
Limited 2WD	$40,210	7%
Limited 4WD	$42,830	7%

Safety Checklist

Crash Tests:
  Frontal . . . . Very Good
  Side . . . . –
Airbags:
  Head . . . . Std. Curtain All Rows
  Chest/Torso . . . . –
  Roll-Sensing Side Airbag . . . . Standard
  Out-of-Position Test. . . . . . . Meets Requirements
Children:
  Built-in Child Safety Seat . . . . –
  Automatic Window Reversal. . . . . Std. Front
Crash Avoidance:
  Frontal Collision Warning . . . . –
  Electronic Stability Control . . . . Standard
  Lane Departure Warning . . . . –
  Brake Assist . . . . Standard
General:
  Automatic Crash Notification . . . . –
  Daytime Running Lights . . . . Optional
  Automatic Door-Locking. . . . . Standard
Safety Belt:
  Adjustable Front Belt . . . . Standard

Jeep Commander

Specifications

Drive. 4WD
Engine. 3.7-liter V6
Transmission . . . . 5-sp. Auto. w/Overdrive
Tow Rating (lbs.) Average-3500
Head/Leg Room (in.) . . . . Very Roomy-42.1/41.7
Interior Space (cu. ft.). –
Cargo Space (cu. ft.). . . . . Very Cramped-7.5
Wheelbase/Length (in.). 109.5/188.5

*Combines results of both front and side tests in relation to all tests for 2010 vehicles.

Ratings—10 Best, 1 Worst

Combo Crash Tests	1
Safety Features	6
Rollover	3
Preventive Maintenance	6
Repair Costs	10
Warranty	4
Fuel Economy	6
Complaints	8
Insurance Costs	8
OVERALL RATING	**5**

Jeep Compass

Jeep Compass

At-a-Glance

Status	Unchanged
Year Series Started	2007
Twins	–
Body Styles	SUV
Seating	5
Anti-Theft Device	Std. Pass. Immobil. & Pass. Alarm
Parking Index Rating	Very Easy
Where Made	Belvidere, IL

Fuel Factor

MPG Rating (city/hwy)	Average-21/24
Driving Range (mi.)	Very Short-300.4
Fuel Type	Regular
Annual Fuel Cost	Low-$1820
Greenhouse Gas Emissions (tons/yr.)	High-8.3
Barrels of Oil Used per year	Average-15.6

How the Competition Rates

Competitors	Rating	Pg.
Acura RDX	8	82
Honda CR-V	10	148
Subaru Forester	6	236

Price Range

Price Range	Retail	Markup
Sport FWD	$18,720	3%
Sport 4WD	$20,470	3%
Limited FWD	$23,385	4%
Limited 4WD	$25,135	4%

Safety Checklist

Crash Tests:
Frontal . . . . Very Poor
Side . . . . Poor

Airbags:
Head . . . . Std. Row 1 & 2 Curtain
Chest/Torso . . . . Opt. Row 1 Torso from Seat
Roll-Sensing Side Airbag . . . . Standard
Out-of-Position Test . . . . . . Meets Requirements

Children:
Built-in Child Safety Seat . . . . –
Automatic Window Reversal . . . . –

Crash Avoidance:
Frontal Collision Warning . . . . –
Electronic Stability Control . . . . Standard
Lane Departure Warning . . . . –
Brake Assist . . . . Standard

General:
Automatic Crash Notification . . . . –
Daytime Running Lights . . . . Optional
Automatic Door-Locking . . . . Optional

Safety Belt:
Adjustable Front Belt . . . . Standard

Jeep Compass

Specifications

Drive	4WD
Engine	2.4-liter I4
Transmission	CVT
Tow Rating (lbs.)	Very Low-1000
Head/Leg Room (in.)	Average-40.7/40.6
Interior Space (cu. ft.)	Average-101.3
Cargo Space (cu. ft.)	Average-22.7
Wheelbase/Length (in.)	103.7/173.4

*Combines results of both front and side tests in relation to all tests for 2010 vehicles.

Ratings—10 Best, 1 Worst

Combo Crash Tests	7
Safety Features	5
Rollover	2
Preventive Maintenance	2
Repair Costs	8
Warranty	4
Fuel Economy	2
Complaints	5
Insurance Costs	10
OVERALL RATING	**5**

Jeep Grand Cherokee

Jeep Grand Cherokee

At-a-Glance

Status	Unchanged
Year Series Started	2005
Twins	–
Body Styles	SUV
Seating	5
Anti-Theft Device	Std. Pass. Immobil. & Pass. Alarm
Parking Index Rating	Hard
Where Made	Detroit, MI / Graz, Austria

Fuel Factor

MPG Rating (city/hwy)	Very Poor-15/20
Driving Range (mi.)	Very Short-357.0
Fuel Type	Regular
Annual Fuel Cost	High-$2396
Greenhouse Gas Emissions (tons/yr.)	Very High-10.8
Barrels of Oil Used per year	Very High-20.1

How the Competition Rates

Competitors	Rating	Pg.
Chevrolet Tahoe	8	117
Ford Expedition	6	134
Lincoln MKT	–	192

Price Range	Retail	Markup
Laredo 2WD	$30,710	5%
Limited 2WD	$37,480	6%
Limited 4WD	$39,420	6%
SRT8 4WD	$43,325	7%

Safety Checklist

Crash Tests:
Frontal	Very Good
Side	Poor

Airbags:
Head	Std. Row 1 & 2 Curtain
Chest/Torso	–
Roll-Sensing Side Airbag	Standard
Out-of-Position Test	Meets Requirements

Children:
Built-in Child Safety Seat	–
Automatic Window Reversal	Opt. Front

Crash Avoidance:
Frontal Collision Warning	–
Electronic Stability Control	Standard
Lane Departure Warning	–
Brake Assist	Standard

General:
Automatic Crash Notification	–
Daytime Running Lights	Optional
Automatic Door-Locking	Standard

Safety Belt:
Adjustable Front Belt	Standard

Jeep Grand Cherokee

Specifications

Drive	4WD
Engine	3.7-liter V6
Transmission	5-sp. Automatic
Tow Rating (lbs.)	Average-3500
Head/Leg Room (in.)	Average-39.7/41.7
Interior Space (cu. ft.)	Roomy-105.6
Cargo Space (cu. ft.)	Very Roomy-35.5
Wheelbase/Length (in.)	109.5/188

*Combines results of both front and side tests in relation to all tests for 2010 vehicles.

Ratings—10 Best, 1 Worst

Combo Crash Tests	8
Safety Features	5
Rollover	1
Preventive Maintenance	6
Repair Costs	9
Warranty	4
Fuel Economy	2
Complaints	8
Insurance Costs	10
OVERALL RATING	**7**

Jeep Liberty

Jeep Liberty

At-a-Glance

Status. . . . . Unchanged
Year Series Started 2008
Twins . . . . –
Body Styles. . . . . SUV
Seating. 5
Anti-Theft Device . . . . . . Opt. Pass. Immobil. & Alarm
Parking Index Rating . . . . Easy
Where Made . . . . Toledo, OH

Fuel Factor
MPG Rating (city/hwy) . . . . Very Poor-15/21
Driving Range (mi.). . . . . Very Short-335.7
Fuel Type. . . . . , Regular
Annual Fuel Cost. . . . . High-$2353
Greenhouse Gas Emissions (tons/yr.) Very High-10.8
Barrels of Oil Used per year . . . . Very High-20.1

How the Competition Rates

Competitors	Rating	Pg.
Ford Escape	6	133
Kia Sportage	5	182
Toyota RAV4	4	251

Price Range

Price Range	Retail	Markup
Sport 2WD	$23,255	3%
Sport 4WD	$24,865	3%
Limited 2WD	$27,125	4%
Limited 4WD	$28,735	4%

Safety Checklist

Crash Tests:
Frontal . . . . Very Good
Side. . . . . Average
Airbags:
Head . . . . Std. Row 1 & 2 Curtain
Chest/Torso . . . . –
Roll-Sensing Side Airbag . . . . Standard
Out-of-Position Test. . . . . . Meets Requirements
Children:
Built-in Child Safety Seat . . . . –
Automatic Window Reversal . . . . Opt. Driver
Crash Avoidance:
Frontal Collision Warning . . . . –
Electronic Stability Control . . . . Standard
Lane Departure Warning . . . . –
Brake Assist . . . . Standard
General:
Automatic Crash Notification . . . . –
Daytime Running Lights . . . . Optional
Automatic Door-Locking. . . . . Standard
Safety Belt:
Adjustable Front Belt . . . . Standard

Jeep Liberty

Specifications

Drive. 4WD
Engine. 3.7-liter V6
Transmission . . . . 4-sp. Auto. w/Overdrive
Tow Rating (lbs.) Average-5000
Head/Leg Room (in.) Average-40.4/40.8
Interior Space (cu. ft.). Roomy-104.7
Cargo Space (cu. ft.) Roomy-25.2
Wheelbase/Length (in.). 106.1/176.1

*Combines results of both front and side tests in relation to all tests for 2010 vehicles.

Jeep Patriot

Small SUV

Ratings—10 Best, 1 Worst

Combo Crash Tests	4
Safety Features	6
Rollover	3
Preventive Maintenance	5
Repair Costs	10
Warranty	4
Fuel Economy	6
Complaints	6
Insurance Costs	8
OVERALL RATING	**6**

Jeep Patriot

Jeep Patriot

At-a-Glance

Status.	Unchanged
Year Series Started	2007
Twins	–
Body Styles	SUV
Seating	5
Anti-Theft Device. . Std. Pass. Immobil. & Pass. Alarm
Parking Index Rating	Very Easy
Where Made	Belvidere, IL

Fuel Factor

MPG Rating (city/hwy)	Average-21/24
Driving Range (mi.)	Very Short-300.4
Fuel Type.	Regular
Annual Fuel Cost	Low-$1820
Greenhouse Gas Emissions (tons/yr.)	High-8.3
Barrels of Oil Used per year.	Average-15.6

How the Competition Rates

Competitors	Rating	Pg.
Ford Escape	6	133
Honda CR-V	10	148
Kia Sportage	5	182

Price Range	Retail	Markup
Sport FWD	$17,795	2%
Sport 4WD	$19,545	3%
Limited FWD	$22,800	4%
Limited 4WD	$24,550	4%

Safety Checklist

Crash Tests:
Frontal	Average
Side	Poor

Airbags:
Head	Std. Row 1 & 2 Curtain
Chest/Torso	Opt. Row 1 Torso from Seat
Roll-Sensing Side Airbag	Standard
Out-of-Position Test	Meets Requirements

Children:
Built-in Child Safety Seat	–
Automatic Window Reversal	–

Crash Avoidance:
Frontal Collision Warning	–
Electronic Stability Control	Standard
Lane Departure Warning	–
Brake Assist	Standard

General:
Automatic Crash Notification	–
Daytime Running Lights	Optional
Automatic Door-Locking	Optional

Safety Belt:
Adjustable Front Belt	Standard

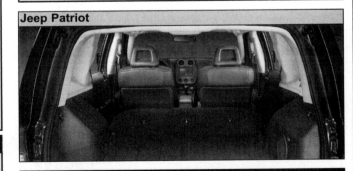

Jeep Patriot

Specifications

Drive	4WD
Engine	2.4-liter I4
Transmission	CVT
Tow Rating (lbs.)	Very Low-1000
Head/Leg Room (in.)	Average-41/40.6
Interior Space (cu. ft.)	Average-101.7
Cargo Space (cu. ft.)	Average-23
Wheelbase/Length (in.)	103.7/173.6

*Combines results of both front and side tests in relation to all tests for 2010 vehicles.

Ratings—10 Best, 1 Worst

Combo Crash Tests	–
Safety Features	1
Rollover	2
Preventive Maintenance	8
Repair Costs	10
Warranty	4
Fuel Economy	2
Complaints	1
Insurance Costs	10
OVERALL RATING	–

Jeep Wrangler

Jeep Wrangler

At-a-Glance

Status	Unchanged
Year Series Started	2007
Twins	–
Body Styles	SUV
Seating	4
Anti-Theft Device	Std. Pass. Immobil. & Pass. Alarm
Parking Index Rating	Very Easy
Where Made	Toledo, OH

Fuel Factor

MPG Rating (city/hwy)	Very Poor-15/19
Driving Range (mi.)	Very Short-308.2
Fuel Type	Regular
Annual Fuel Cost	Very High-$2444
Greenhouse Gas Emissions (tons/yr.)	Very High-10.8
Barrels of Oil Used per year	Very High-20.1

How the Competition Rates

Competitors	Rating	Pg.
Chevrolet HHR	7	112
Honda Element	7	149
Suzuki Grand Vitara	1	240

Price Range	Retail	Markup
Sport 4WD	$21,165	3%
Unlimted Sport 2WD	$23,410	3%
Sahara 4WD	$26,255	6%
Unlimited Rubicon	$32,050	7%

Safety Checklist

Crash Tests:
Frontal . . . . Poor
Side . . . . –

Airbags:
Head . . . . Opt. Row 1 Combo
Chest/Torso . . . . . . Opt. Row 1 Combo from Seat
Roll-Sensing Side Airbag . . . . –
Out-of-Position Test . . . . Meets Requirements

Children:
Built-in Child Safety Seat . . . . –
Automatic Window Reversal . . . . –

Crash Avoidance:
Frontal Collision Warning . . . . –
Electronic Stability Control . . . . Standard
Lane Departure Warning . . . . –
Brake Assist . . . . Standard

General:
Automatic Crash Notification . . . . –
Daytime Running Lights . . . . –
Automatic Door-Locking . . . . Optional

Safety Belt:
Adjustable Front Belt . . . . Standard

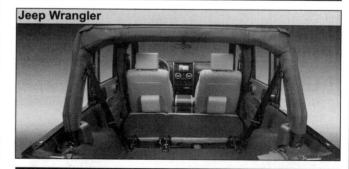

Jeep Wrangler

Specifications

Drive	4WD
Engine	3.8-liter V6
Transmission	4-sp. Auto. w/Overdrive
Tow Rating (lbs.)	Average-3500
Head/Leg Room (in.)	Roomy-41.3/41
Interior Space (cu. ft.)	Average-102.9
Cargo Space (cu. ft.)	Average-17.15
Wheelbase/Length (in.)	95.4/152.8

*Combines results of both front and side tests in relation to all tests for 2010 vehicles.

Ratings—10 Best, 1 Worst

Combo Crash Tests	9
Safety Features	8
Rollover	2
Preventive Maintenance	–
Repair Costs	–
Warranty	8
Fuel Economy	3
Complaints	8
Insurance Costs	5
OVERALL RATING	**8**

Kia Borrego

Kia Borrego

At-a-Glance

Status	Unchanged
Year Series Started	2009
Twins	–
Body Styles	SUV
Seating	7
Anti-Theft Device	Std. Pass. Immobil. & Active Alarm
Parking Index Rating	Average
Where Made	Hwasung, South Korea

Fuel Factor

MPG Rating (city/hwy)	Poor-16/21
Driving Range (mi.)	Short-369.2
Fuel Type	Regular
Annual Fuel Cost	High-$2260
Greenhouse Gas Emissions (tons/yr.)	High-10.2
Barrels of Oil Used per year	High-19.0

How the Competition Rates

Competitors	Rating	Pg.
Acura MDX	–	81
Honda Pilot	7	153
Mazda CX-7	6	199

Price Range	Retail	Markup
LX 2WD V6	$26,245	7%
EX 2WD V8	$30,995	8%
LX 4WD V8	$30,995	7%
EX 4WD V8	$32,995	9%

Safety Checklist

Crash Tests:
Frontal	Very Good
Side	Good

Airbags:
Head	Std. Curtain All Rows
Chest/Torso	Std. Row 1 Torso from Seat
Roll-Sensing Side Airbag	Standard
Out-of-Position Test	Meets Requirements

Children:
Built-in Child Safety Seat	–
Automatic Window Reversal	Opt. Driver

Crash Avoidance:
Frontal Collision Warning	–
Electronic Stability Control	Standard
Lane Departure Warning	–
Brake Assist	Standard

General:
Automatic Crash Notification	–
Daytime Running Lights	–
Automatic Door-Locking	Standard

Safety Belt:
Adjustable Front Belt	Standard

Kia Borrego

Specifications

Drive	4WD
Engine	3.8-liter V6
Transmission	5-sp. Automatic
Tow Rating (lbs.)	Average-5000
Head/Leg Room (in.)	Average-40/41.7
Interior Space (cu. ft.)	Very Roomy-156.8
Cargo Space (cu. ft.)	Very Cramped-12.4
Wheelbase/Length (in.)	114/192.1

*Combines results of both front and side tests in relation to all tests for 2010 vehicles.

Kia Forte

Ratings—10 Best, 1 Worst

Combo Crash Tests	4
Safety Features	4
Rollover	8
Preventive Maintenance	–
Repair Costs	–
Warranty	8
Fuel Economy	9
Complaints	–
Insurance Costs	5
OVERALL RATING	**7**

Kia Forte

At-a-Glance

Status. . . . . All New
Year Series Started 2010
Twins . . . . –
Body Styles . . . . Sedan, Coupe
Seating 5
Anti-Theft Device . . . . –
Parking Index Rating . . . . Very Easy
Where Made . . . . Hwasung, South Korea

Fuel Factor
MPG Rating (city/hwy) . . . . Very Good-25/34
Driving Range (mi.) Average-388.8
Fuel Type. . . . . Regular
Annual Fuel Cost . . . . Very Low-$1427
Greenhouse Gas Emissions (tons/yr.) Low-6.6
Barrels of Oil Used per year Low-12.2

How the Competition Rates

Competitors	Rating	Pg.
Chevrolet Cobalt	4	108
Honda Civic	8	146
Subaru Impreza	4	237

Price Range

	Retail	Markup
LX Manual Transmission	$13,695	2%
LX Automatic Transmission	$14,695	2%
EX Automatic Transmission	$16,795	5%
SX Automatic Transmission	$18,195	5%

Safety Checklist

Crash Tests:
  Frontal . . . . Average
  Side. . . . . Very Poor
Airbags:
  Head . . . . Std. Row 1 & 2 Curtain
  Chest/Torso . . . . Std. Row 1 Torso from Seat
  Roll-Sensing Side Airbag . . . . –
  Out-of-Position Test. . . . . . . Meets Requirements
Children:
  Built-in Child Safety Seat . . . . –
  Automatic Window Reversal . . . . –
Crash Avoidance:
  Frontal Collision Warning . . . . –
  Electronic Stability Control . . . . Standard
  Lane Departure Warning . . . . –
  Brake Assist . . . . Optional
General:
  Automatic Crash Notification . . . . –
  Daytime Running Lights . . . . –
  Automatic Door-Locking. . . . . Standard
Safety Belt:
  Adjustable Front Belt . . . . Standard

Kia Forte

Specifications

Drive. . . . . FWD
Engine 2.0-liter I4
Transmission . . . . 4-sp. Automatic
Tow Rating (lbs.) . . . . –
Head/Leg Room (in.) Roomy-40/43.3
Interior Space (cu. ft.) Cramped-96.8
Cargo Space (cu. ft.) Cramped-14.7
Wheelbase/Length (in.). 104.3/178.3

*Combines results of both front and side tests in relation to all tests for 2010 vehicles.

Ratings—10 Best, 1 Worst	
Combo Crash Tests	7
Safety Features	4
Rollover	7
Preventive Maintenance	3
Repair Costs	7
Warranty	8
Fuel Economy	8
Complaints	8
Insurance Costs	3
OVERALL RATING	8

Kia Optima

Kia Optima

At-a-Glance

Status. . . . . Unchanged
Year Series Started 2007
Twins . . . . −
Body Styles . . . . Sedan
Seating. 5
Anti-Theft Device . Opt. Pass. Immobil. & Active Alarm
Parking Index Rating . . . . Easy
Where Made . . . . Hwasung, South Korea
Fuel Factor
  MPG Rating (city/hwy) Good-22/32
  Driving Range (mi.) Long-419.8
  Fuel Type. . . . . Regular
  Annual Fuel Cost . . . . Very Low-$1582
  Greenhouse Gas Emissions (tons/yr.) . . Average-7.3
  Barrels of Oil Used per year. Average-13.7

How the Competition Rates

Competitors	Rating	Pg.
Honda Accord	8	144
Mercury Milan	9	211
Mitsubishi Galant	9	213

Price Range	Retail	Markup
LX Manual Trans.	$17,995	6%
EX I4 Auto. Trans	$20,995	7%
EX V6 Auto. Trans.	$21,995	8%
SX V6 Auto. Trans.	$22,795	8%

Safety Checklist

Crash Tests:
  Frontal . . . . Good
  Side. . . . . Average
Airbags:
  Head . . . . Std. Row 1 & 2 Curtain
  Chest/Torso . . . . Std. Row 1 Torso from Seat
  Roll-Sensing Side Airbag . . . . −
  Out-of-Position Test. . . . . . Meets Requirements
Children:
  Built-in Child Safety Seat . . . . −
  Automatic Window Reversal. . . . . Opt. Driver
Crash Avoidance:
  Frontal Collision Warning . . . . −
  Electronic Stability Control . . . . Standard
  Lane Departure Warning . . . . −
  Brake Assist . . . . Optional
General:
  Automatic Crash Notification . . . . −
  Daytime Running Lights . . . . −
  Automatic Door-Locking . . . . Optional
Safety Belt:
  Adjustable Front Belt . . . . Standard

Kia Optima

Specifications

Drive. . . . . FWD
Engine 2.4-liter I4
Transmission . . . . 5-sp. Auto. w/Overdrive
Tow Rating (lbs.) . . . . −
Head/Leg Room (in.) . . . . Very Roomy-39.8/43.7
Interior Space (cu. ft.). Roomy-104.2
Cargo Space (cu. ft.) Cramped-15
Wheelbase/Length (in.) 107.1/189

*Combines results of both front and side tests in relation to all tests for 2010 vehicles.

Kia Rio

Ratings—10 Best, 1 Worst

Combo Crash Tests	2
Safety Features	1
Rollover	6
Preventive Maintenance	1
Repair Costs	10
Warranty	8
Fuel Economy	10
Complaints	8
Insurance Costs	3
OVERALL RATING	**5**

Kia Rio

Kia Rio

At-a-Glance

Status. . . . . Unchanged
Year Series Started 2006
Twins. Hyundai Accent
Body Styles. . . . . Sedan, Hatchback
Seating. 5
Anti-Theft Device . . . . Opt. Active Alarm Only
Parking Index Rating . . . . Very Easy
Where Made . . . . Sohari, South Korea

Fuel Factor

MPG Rating (city/hwy) . . . . Very Good-27/36
Driving Range (mi.). Short-362.0
Fuel Type. . . . . Regular
Annual Fuel Cost . . . . Very Low-$1331
Greenhouse Gas Emissions (tons/yr.) Low-6.1
Barrels of Oil Used per year Low-11.4

How the Competition Rates

Competitors	Rating	Pg.
Chevrolet Aveo	3	106
Honda Fit	8	150
Hyundai Accent	8	156

Price Range

	Retail	Markup
Base Manual Trans.	$11,695	4%
LX Auto. Trans.	$14,695	5%
SX Auto Trans.	$15,795	5%
Rio5 SX Auto. Trans.	$16,095	5%

Safety Checklist

Crash Tests:
 Frontal. . . . . Poor
 Side. . . . . Very Poor
Airbags:
 Head . . . . Std. Row 1 & 2 Curtain
  Chest/Torso . . . . . . Std. Row 1 Torso from Seat
 Roll-Sensing Side Airbag . . . . –
 Out-of-Position Test. . . . . . . Meets Requirements
Children:
 Built-in Child Safety Seat . . . . –
 Automatic Window Reversal . . . . –
Crash Avoidance:
 Frontal Collision Warning . . . . –
 Electronic Stability Control . . . . –
 Lane Departure Warning . . . . –
 Brake Assist . . . . –
General:
 Automatic Crash Notification . . . . –
 Daytime Running Lights . . . . –
 Automatic Door-Locking . . . . –
Safety Belt:
 Adjustable Front Belt . . . . Standard

Kia Rio

Specifications

Drive. . . . . FWD
Engine 1.6-liter I4
Transmission . . . . 4-sp. Auto. w/Overdrive
Tow Rating (lbs.) . . . . –
Head/Leg Room (in.) Roomy-39.5/42.8
Interior Space (cu. ft.) Cramped-92.2
Cargo Space (cu. ft.). . . . . Very Cramped-11.9
Wheelbase/Length (in.) 98.4/167.3

*Combines results of both front and side tests in relation to all tests for 2010 vehicles.

Kia Rondo

Ratings—10 Best, 1 Worst

Combo Crash Tests	4
Safety Features	4
Rollover	6
Preventive Maintenance	4
Repair Costs	7
Warranty	8
Fuel Economy	6
Complaints	2
Insurance Costs	8
OVERALL RATING	**5**

Kia Rondo

Kia Rondo

At-a-Glance

Status	Unchanged
Year Series Started	2007
Twins	Hyundai Santa Fe
Body Styles	Minivan
Seating	7
Anti-Theft Device	Opt. Active Alarm Only
Parking Index Rating	Easy
Where Made	Gwanju, South Korea

Fuel Factor

MPG Rating (city/hwy)	Average-20/27
Driving Range (mi.)	Short-360.0
Fuel Type	Regular
Annual Fuel Cost	Low-$1789
Greenhouse Gas Emissions (tons/yr.)	High-8.3
Barrels of Oil Used per year	Average-15.6

How the Competition Rates

Competitors	Rating	Pg.
Chevrolet HHR	7	112
Honda Element	7	149
Mazda 5	4	197

Price Range

	Retail	Markup

Safety Checklist

Crash Tests:
- Frontal . . . . Good
- Side . . . . Poor

Airbags:
- Head . . . . Std. Curtain All Rows
- Chest/Torso . . . . Std. Row 1 Torso from Seat
- Roll-Sensing Side Airbag . . . . –
- Out-of-Position Test . . . . . . Meets Requirements

Children:
- Built-in Child Safety Seat . . . . –
- Automatic Window Reversal . . . . –

Crash Avoidance:
- Frontal Collision Warning . . . . –
- Electronic Stability Control . . . . Standard
- Lane Departure Warning . . . . –
- Brake Assist . . . . Standard

General:
- Automatic Crash Notification . . . . –
- Daytime Running Lights . . . . Optional
- Automatic Door-Locking . . . . –

Safety Belt:
- Adjustable Front Belt . . . . Standard

Kia Rondo

Specifications

Drive	FWD
Engine	2.4-liter I4
Transmission	4-sp. Automatic
Tow Rating (lbs.)	Very Low-680
Head/Leg Room (in.)	Roomy-41.6/41.3
Interior Space (cu. ft.)	Roomy-107.8
Cargo Space (cu. ft.)	Roomy-31.7
Wheelbase/Length (in.)	106.3/179

*Combines results of both front and side tests in relation to all tests for 2010 vehicles.

Kia Sedona

Ratings—10 Best, 1 Worst

Combo Crash Tests	7
Safety Features	3
Rollover	5
Preventive Maintenance	2
Repair Costs	5
Warranty	8
Fuel Economy	4
Complaints	3
Insurance Costs	8
OVERALL RATING	**5**

Kia Sedona

Kia Sedona

At-a-Glance

Status. . . . . Unchanged
Year Series Started 2006
Twins . . . . —
Body Styles . . . . Minivan
Seating. 7
Anti-Theft Device . Opt. Pass. Immobil. & Active Alarm
Parking Index Rating . . . . Hard
Where Made . . . . Sohari, South Korea

Fuel Factor
MPG Rating (city/hwy) Poor-17/23
Driving Range (mi.) Long-406.4
Fuel Type. . . . . Regular
Annual Fuel Cost. . . . . Average-$2103
Greenhouse Gas Emissions (tons/yr.) High-9.6
Barrels of Oil Used per year. High-18.0

How the Competition Rates

Competitors	Rating	Pg.
Honda Odyssey	6	152
Toyota Sienna	1	253
Volkswagen Routan	5	264

Price Range

	Retail	Markup
Base	$22,195	4%
LX	$24,195	6%
EX	$28,695	8%

Safety Checklist

Crash Tests:
Frontal . . . . Good
Side . . . . Very Good
Airbags:
Head . . . . Std. Curtain All Rows
Chest/Torso . . . . Std. Row 1 Torso from Seat
Roll-Sensing Side Airbag . . . . —
Out-of-Position Test . . . . . . Meets Requirements
Children:
Built-in Child Safety Seat . . . . —
Automatic Window Reversal . . . . —
Crash Avoidance:
Frontal Collision Warning . . . . —
Electronic Stability Control . . . . Standard
Lane Departure Warning . . . . —
Brake Assist . . . . Standard
General:
Automatic Crash Notification . . . . —
Daytime Running Lights . . . . —
Automatic Door-Locking . . . . —
Safety Belt:
Adjustable Front Belt . . . . Standard

Kia Sedona

Specifications

Drive. . . . . FWD
Engine. 3.8-liter V6
Transmission . . . . 5-sp. Auto. w/Overdrive
Tow Rating (lbs.) Average-3500
Head/Leg Room (in.) Roomy-40.9/41.7
Interior Space (cu. ft.) . . . . Very Roomy-161.6
Cargo Space (cu. ft.) Cramped-12.9
Wheelbase/Length (in.) 118.9/189.4

*Combines results of both front and side tests in relation to all tests for 2010 vehicles.

Ratings—10 Best, 1 Worst

Combo Crash Tests	−
Safety Features	
Rollover	4
Preventive Maintenance	2
Repair Costs	−
Warranty	8
Fuel Economy	7
Complaints	−
Insurance Costs	10
OVERALL RATING	−

Kia Sorento

Kia Sorento

At-a-Glance

Status	All New
Year Series Started	2010
Twins	−
Body Styles	SUV
Seating	5/7
Anti-Theft Device	−
Parking Index Rating	Easy
Where Made	West Point, GA

Fuel Factor

MPG Rating (city/hwy)	Good-21/28
Driving Range (mi.)	Very Long-425.9
Fuel Type	Regular
Annual Fuel Cost	Low-$1712
Greenhouse Gas Emissions (tons/yr.)	−
Barrels of Oil Used per year	−

How the Competition Rates

Competitors	Rating	Pg.
Nissan Rogue	5	225
Subaru Tribeca	5	239
Volvo XC60	−	269

Price Range	Retail	Markup
Base AWD	$28,295	

Safety Checklist

Crash Tests:
Frontal	−
Side	−

Airbags:
Head	Std. Row 1 Curtain
Chest/Torso	Std. Row 1 Torso from Seat
Roll-Sensing Side Airbag	Standard
Out-of-Position Test	Meets Requirements

Children:
Built-in Child Safety Seat	−
Automatic Window Reversal	−

Crash Avoidance:
Frontal Collision Warning	−
Electronic Stability Control	Standard
Lane Departure Warning	−
Brake Assist	−

General:
Automatic Crash Notification	−
Daytime Running Lights	−
Automatic Door-Locking	−

Safety Belt:
Adjustable Front Belt	−

Kia Sorento

Specifications

Drive	FWD
Engine	2.4-liter I4
Transmission	6-sp. Auto. w/Overdrive
Tow Rating (lbs.)	Low-2000
Head/Leg Room (in.)	Cramped-39.2/41.3
Interior Space (cu. ft.)	Average-103.9
Cargo Space (cu. ft.)	Very Cramped-9.1
Wheelbase/Length (in.)	106.3/183.9

*Combines results of both front and side tests in relation to all tests for 2010 vehicles.

Ratings—10 Best, 1 Worst

Combo Crash Tests	5
Safety Features	3
Rollover	4
Preventive Maintenance	–
Repair Costs	–
Warranty	8
Fuel Economy	9
Complaints	–
Insurance Costs	10
OVERALL RATING	**6**

Kia Soul

Kia Soul

At-a-Glance

Status	All New
Year Series Started	2010
Twins	–
Body Styles	Hatchback
Seating	5
Anti-Theft Device	–
Parking Index Rating	Very Easy
Where Made	Hwasung, South Korea

Fuel Factor

MPG Rating (city/hwy)	Very Good-24/30
Driving Range (mi.)	Very Short-334.9
Fuel Type	Regular
Annual Fuel Cost	Very Low-$1536
Greenhouse Gas Emissions (tons/yr.)	Average-7.1
Barrels of Oil Used per year	Low-13.2

How the Competition Rates

Competitors	Rating	Pg.
Mini Cooper	6	212
Nissan Cube	5	220
Scion xB	1	233

Price Range

	Retail	Markup
Base Manual Transmission	$13,300	4%
+ Automatic Transmission	$15,900	7%
Sport Automatic Transmission	$17,900	7%
! Automatic Transmission	$17,900	7%

Safety Checklist

Crash Tests:
Frontal . . . . Good
Side . . . . Poor
Airbags:
Head . . . . Std. Row 1 & 2 Curtain
Chest/Torso . . . . Std. Row 1 Torso from Seat
Roll-Sensing Side Airbag . . . . –
Out-of-Position Test . . . . . . Meets Requirements
Children:
Built-in Child Safety Seat . . . . –
Automatic Window Reversal . . . . –
Crash Avoidance:
Frontal Collision Warning . . . . –
Electronic Stability Control . . . . Standard
Lane Departure Warning . . . . –
Brake Assist . . . . Optional
General:
Automatic Crash Notification . . . . –
Daytime Running Lights . . . . –
Automatic Door-Locking . . . . –
Safety Belt:
Adjustable Front Belt . . . . Standard

Kia Soul

Specifications

Drive	FWD
Engine	2.0-liter I4
Transmission	4-sp. Auto. w/Overdrive
Tow Rating (lbs.)	–
Head/Leg Room (in.)	Roomy-40.2/42.1
Interior Space (cu. ft.)	Average-102
Cargo Space (cu. ft.)	Average-19.3
Wheelbase/Length (in.)	100.4/161.6

*Combines results of both front and side tests in relation to all tests for 2010 vehicles.

Kia Sportage

Ratings—10 Best, 1 Worst

Combo Crash Tests	3
Safety Features	3
Rollover	2
Preventive Maintenance	4
Repair Costs	9
Warranty	8
Fuel Economy	6
Complaints	8
Insurance Costs	8
OVERALL RATING	**5**

Kia Sportage

At-a-Glance

Status	Unchanged
Year Series Started	2006
Twins	—
Body Styles	SUV
Seating	5
Anti-Theft Device	Opt. Active Alarm Only
Parking Index Rating	Very Easy
Where Made	Gwanju, South Korea

Fuel Factor

MPG Rating (city/hwy)	Average-20/25
Driving Range (mi.)	Average-378.0
Fuel Type	Regular
Annual Fuel Cost	Average-$1843
Greenhouse Gas Emissions (tons/yr.)	High-8.3
Barrels of Oil Used per year	Average-15.6

How the Competition Rates

Competitors	Rating	Pg.
Ford Escape	6	133
Honda CR-V	10	148
Toyota RAV4	4	251

Price Range

Price Range	Retail	Markup
LX 2WD Manual Trans.	$16,995	5%
LX V6 2WD Auto. Trans.	$20,995	7%
LX V6 4WD Auto. Trans.	$22,495	7%
EX V6 4WD Auto. Trans.	$23,495	7%

Safety Checklist

Crash Tests:
- Frontal . . . . Poor
- Side . . . . Very Poor

Airbags:
- Head . . . . Std. Row 1 & 2 Curtain
- Chest/Torso . . . . Std. Row 1 Torso from Seat
- Roll-Sensing Side Airbag . . . . —
- Out-of-Position Test . . . . . . Meets Requirements

Children:
- Built-in Child Safety Seat . . . . —
- Automatic Window Reversal . . . . —

Crash Avoidance:
- Frontal Collision Warning . . . . —
- Electronic Stability Control . . . . Standard
- Lane Departure Warning . . . . —
- Brake Assist . . . . Standard

General:
- Automatic Crash Notification . . . . —
- Daytime Running Lights . . . . —
- Automatic Door-Locking . . . . —

Safety Belt:
- Adjustable Front Belt . . . . Standard

Kia Sportage

Specifications

Drive	FWD
Engine	2.0-liter I4
Transmission	4-sp. Auto. w/Overdrive
Tow Rating (lbs.)	Very Low-1000
Head/Leg Room (in.)	Roomy-40.7/42.1
Interior Space (cu. ft.)	Average-103.9
Cargo Space (cu. ft.)	Roomy-23.6
Wheelbase/Length (in.)	103.5/171.3

*Combines results of both front and side tests in relation to all tests for 2010 vehicles.

Ratings—10 Best, 1 Worst

Combo Crash Tests	–
Safety Features	7
Rollover	1
Preventive Maintenance	4
Repair Costs	1
Warranty	4
Fuel Economy	1
Complaints	4
Insurance Costs	1

OVERALL RATING — –

Land Rover Range Rover

Land Rover Range Rover

At-a-Glance

Status . . . . Unchanged
Year Series Started 2006
Twins . . . . –
Body Styles . . . . SUV
Seating 5
Anti-Theft Device . Std. Pass. Immobil. & Active Alarm
Parking Index Rating . . . . Hard
Where Made . . . . Souhil, UK

Fuel Factor
MPG Rating (city/hwy) . . . . Very Poor-12/18
Driving Range (mi.) Average-389.6
Fuel Type . . . . Premium
Annual Fuel Cost . . . . Very High-$3081
Greenhouse Gas Emissions (tons/yr.) Very High-13.1
Barrels of Oil Used per year . . . . . . Very High-24.5

How the Competition Rates

Competitors	Rating	Pg.
Audi Q7	7	90
Cadillac Escalade	6	102
Mercedes-Benz GL-Class	–	205

Price Range	Retail	Markup
HSE	$78,425	10%
Supercharged	$94,275	10%

Safety Checklist

Crash Tests:
  Frontal . . . . –
  Side . . . . –
Airbags:
  Head . . . . Std. Row 1 & 2 Curtain
  Chest/Torso . . . . Std. Row 1 Torso from Seat
  Roll-Sensing Side Airbag . . . . Standard
  Out-of-Position Test . . . . –
Children:
  Built-in Child Safety Seat . . . . –
  Automatic Window Reversal. Std. Front and Rear
Crash Avoidance:
  Frontal Collision Warning . . . . –
  Electronic Stability Control . . . . Standard
  Lane Departure Warning . . . . –
  Brake Assist . . . . Standard
General:
  Automatic Crash Notification . . . . –
  Daytime Running Lights . . . . Optional
  Automatic Door-Locking . . . . Standard
Safety Belt:
  Adjustable Front Belt . . . . Standard

Land Rover Range Rover

Specifications

Drive 4WD
Engine 5.0-liter V8
Transmission . . . . 6-sp. Automatic
Tow Rating (lbs.) Average-3500
Head/Leg Room (in.) . . . . Very Cramped-39.3/38.9
Interior Space (cu. ft.) . . . . –
Cargo Space (cu. ft.) . . . . Very Roomy-35.1
Wheelbase/Length (in.) 113.3/195.8

*Combines results of both front and side tests in relation to all tests for 2010 vehicles.

Lexus ES

Lexus ES 350

Ratings—10 Best, 1 Worst

Combo Crash Tests	6
Safety Features	10
Rollover	7
Preventive Maintenance	1
Repair Costs	1
Warranty	7
Fuel Economy	6
Complaints	4
Insurance Costs	5
OVERALL RATING	**6**

Lexus ES 350

At-a-Glance

Status. . . . . Unchanged
Year Series Started 2007
Twins . . . . Toyota Camry
Body Styles . . . . Sedan
Seating. 5
Anti-Theft Device. . Std. Pass. Immobil. & Pass. Alarm
Parking Index Rating . . . . Average
Where Made. . . . . Kyushu, Japan
Fuel Factor
  MPG Rating (city/hwy) Average-19/27
  Driving Range (mi.) Long-405.6
  Fuel Type. . . . . Premium
  Annual Fuel Cost. . . . . Average-$1984
  Greenhouse Gas Emissions (tons/yr.) High-8.3
  Barrels of Oil Used per year. Average-15.6

How the Competition Rates

Competitors	Rating	Pg.
Acura TL	9	83
Cadillac STS	5	104
Infiniti G	7	165

Price Range	Retail	Markup
Base	$35,175	10%

Safety Checklist

Crash Tests:
  Frontal . . . . Good
  Side. . . . . Average
Airbags:
  Head . . . . Std. Row 1 & 2 Curtain
  Chest/Torso . . . . Std. Row 1 & 2 Torso from Seat
  Roll-Sensing Side Airbag . . . . –
  Out-of-Position Test. . . . . . . Meets Requirements
Children:
  Built-in Child Safety Seat . . . . –
  Automatic Window Reversal. Std. Front and Rear
Crash Avoidance:
  Frontal Collision Warning . . . . Optional
  Electronic Stability Control . . . . Standard
  Lane Departure Warning . . . . –
  Brake Assist . . . . Standard
General:
  Automatic Crash Notification . . . . Standard
  Daytime Running Lights. . . . . Standard
  Automatic Door-Locking. . . . . Standard
Safety Belt:
  Adjustable Front Belt . . . . Standard

Lexus ES 350

Specifications

Drive. . . . . FWD
Engine. 3.5-liter V6
Transmission . . . . 6-sp. Automatic
Tow Rating (lbs.) . . . . –
Head/Leg Room (in.) . . . . Very Cramped-37.4/42.2
Interior Space (cu. ft.) Cramped-95.4
Cargo Space (cu. ft.) Cramped-14.8
Wheelbase/Length (in.) 109.3/191.7

*Combines results of both front and side tests in relation to all tests for 2010 vehicles.

Ratings—10 Best, 1 Worst

Combo Crash Tests	–
Safety Features	10
Rollover	8
Preventive Maintenance	1
Repair Costs	1
Warranty	7
Fuel Economy	5
Complaints	7
Insurance Costs	3
OVERALL RATING	–

Lexus GS 350

Lexus GS 450

At-a-Glance

Status. . . . . Unchanged
Year Series Started 2006
Twins . . . . –
Body Styles . . . . Sedan
Seating. 5
Anti-Theft Device. . Std. Pass. Immobil. & Pass. Alarm
Parking Index Rating . . . . Easy
Where Made . . . . Tahara, Japan
Fuel Factor
  MPG Rating (city/hwy) Average-19/26
  Driving Range (mi.) Long-406.4
  Fuel Type. . . . . Premium
  Annual Fuel Cost. . . . . Average-$2012
  Greenhouse Gas Emissions (tons/yr.) High-8.3
  Barrels of Oil Used per year. Average-15.6

How the Competition Rates

Competitors	Rating	Pg.
BMW 5 Series	7	93
Hyundai Genesis	9	158
Mercedes-Benz E-Class	7	204

Price Range	Retail	Markup
350 RWD	$45,600	11%
350 AWD	$47,550	11%
460	$54,070	11%
450h	$57,450	11%

Safety Checklist

Crash Tests:
  Frontal. . . . . –
  Side . . . . –
Airbags:
  Head . . . . Std. Row 1 & 2 Curtain
  Chest/TorsoStd. Row 1 & Opt. Row 2 Torso from Seat
  Roll-Sensing Side Airbag . . . . –
  Out-of-Position Test. . . . . . . Meets Requirements
Children:
  Built-in Child Safety Seat . . . . –
  Automatic Window Reversal. Std. Front and Rear
Crash Avoidance:
  Frontal Collision Warning . . . . Optional
  Electronic Stability Control . . . . Standard
  Lane Departure Warning . . . . –
  Brake Assist . . . . Standard
General:
  Automatic Crash Notification . . . . Standard
  Daytime Running Lights. . . . . Standard
  Automatic Door-Locking. . . . . Standard
Safety Belt:
  Adjustable Front Belt . . . . Standard

Lexus GS 460

Specifications

Drive . . . . RWD
Engine. 3.5-liter V6
Transmission . . . . 6-sp. Automatic
Tow Rating (lbs.) . . . . –
Head/Leg Room (in.) Average-37.8/43.5
Interior Space (cu. ft.). Roomy-109.1
Cargo Space (cu. ft.). Cramped-12.7
Wheelbase/Length (in.) 112.2/190

*Combines results of both front and side tests in relation to all tests for 2010 vehicles.

Ratings—10 Best, 1 Worst

Combo Crash Tests	–
Safety Features	10
Rollover	1
Preventive Maintenance	1
Repair Costs	6
Warranty	7
Fuel Economy	2
Complaints	10
Insurance Costs	8
OVERALL RATING	**–**

Lexus GX 460

Lexus GX 460

At-a-Glance

Status . . . . Appearance Change
Year Series Started 2003
Twins 4Runner
Body Styles. . . . . SUV
Seating. 7
Anti-Theft Device. . Std. Pass. Immobil. & Pass. Alarm
Parking Index Rating . . . . Average
Where Made . . . . Tahara, Japan

Fuel Factor
  MPG Rating (city/hwy). . . . . Very Poor-15/20
  Driving Range (mi.) Average-389
  Fuel Type. . . . . Premium
  Annual Fuel Cost. . . . . Very High-$2574
  Greenhouse Gas Emissions (tons/yr.) . . . . –
  Barrels of Oil Used per year . . . . –

How the Competition Rates

Competitors	Rating	Pg.
Audi Q5	7	89
Hummer H3	6	155
Volvo XC90	10	270

Price Range	Retail	Markup
Base	$51,970	15%
Premium	$56,765	15%

Safety Checklist

Crash Tests:
  Frontal. . . . . –
  Side . . . . –
Airbags:
  Head . . . . Std. Curtain All Rows
  Chest/Torso . Std. Row 1 & Opt. Row 2 Torso from Seat
  Roll-Sensing Side Airbag . . . . Standard
  Out-of-Position Test. . . . . . . Meets Requirements
Children:
  Built-in Child Safety Seat . . . . –
  Automatic Window Reversal. Std. Front and Rear
Crash Avoidance:
  Frontal Collision Warning . . . . Optional
  Electronic Stability Control . . . . Standard
  Lane Departure Warning . . . . –
  Brake Assist . . . . Standard
General:
  Automatic Crash Notification . . . . Standard
  Daytime Running Lights . . . . Standard
  Automatic Door-Locking. . . . . Standard
Safety Belt:
  Adjustable Front Belt . . . . Standard

Lexus GX 460

Specifications

Drive. 4WD
Engine. 4.6-liter V8
Transmission . . . . 6-sp. Automatic
Tow Rating (lbs.) High-6500
Head/Leg Room (in.) . . . . Very Cramped-38/41.7
Interior Space (cu. ft.) . . . . Very Roomy-129.7
Cargo Space (cu. ft.). . . . . Very Cramped-4.2
Wheelbase/Length (in.). 109.8/189.2

*Combines results of both front and side tests in relation to all tests for 2010 vehicles.

Ratings—10 Best, 1 Worst

Combo Crash Tests	9
Safety Features	10
Rollover	6
Preventive Maintenance	–
Repair Costs	–
Warranty	7
Fuel Economy	10
Complaints	–
Insurance Costs	3
OVERALL RATING	**10**

Lexus HS 250

Lexus HS 250

At-a-Glance

Status. . . . . All New
Year Series Started 2010
Twins . . . . –
Body Styles . . . . Sedan
Seating. 5
Anti-Theft Device. . Std. Pass. Immobil. & Pass. Alarm
Parking Index Rating . . . . Average
Where Made. . . . . Kyushu, Japan
Fuel Factor
  MPG Rating (city/hwy) . . . . Very Good-35/34
  Driving Range (mi.) . . . . Very Long-500.9
  Fuel Type. . . . . Regular
  Annual Fuel Cost . . . . Very Low-$1172
  Greenhouse Gas Emissions (tons/yr.) . Very Low-5.3
  Barrels of Oil Used per year . . . . Very Low-9.8

How the Competition Rates

Competitors	Rating	Pg.
Acura TSX	10	84
Chevrolet Malibu	9	114
Ford Fusion	9	139

Price Range

Price Range	Retail	Markup
Base	$34,200	10%
Premium	$36,970	10%

Safety Checklist

Crash Tests:
  Frontal . . . . Good
  Side . . . . Very Good
Airbags:
  Head . . . . Std. Row 1 & 2 Curtain
  Chest/Torso . . . . Std. Row 1 & 2 Torso from Seat
  Roll-Sensing Side Airbag . . . . –
  Out-of-Position Test. . . . . . Meets Requirements
Children:
  Built-in Child Safety Seat . . . . –
  Automatic Window Reversal. Std. Front and Rear
Crash Avoidance:
  Frontal Collision Warning . . . . Optional
  Electronic Stability Control . . . . Standard
  Lane Departure Warning . . . . –
  Brake Assist . . . . Standard
General:
  Automatic Crash Notification . . . . Standard
  Daytime Running Lights. . . . . Standard
  Automatic Door-Locking. . . . . Standard
Safety Belt:
  Adjustable Front Belt . . . . Standard

Lexus HS 250

Specifications

Drive. . . . . FWD
Engine 2.4-liter I4
Transmission . . . . ECVT
Tow Rating (lbs.) . . . . –
Head/Leg Room (in.) Cramped-38/42.6
Interior Space (cu. ft.) . . . . Very Cramped-90.2
Cargo Space (cu. ft.). . . . . Very Cramped-12.1
Wheelbase/Length (in.). 106.3/184.8

*Combines results of both front and side tests in relation to all tests for 2010 vehicles.

Ratings—10 Best, 1 Worst

Combo Crash Tests	3
Safety Features	9
Rollover	8
Preventive Maintenance	1
Repair Costs	1
Warranty	7
Fuel Economy	7
Complaints	10
Insurance Costs	1
OVERALL RATING	**5**

Lexus IS 250

Lexus IS 350

At-a-Glance

Status	Unchanged
Year Series Started	2006
Twins	–
Body Styles	Sedan, Coupe, Convertible
Seating	5
Anti-Theft Device	Std. Pass. Immobil. & Pass. Alarm
Parking Index Rating	Very Easy
Where Made	Tahara, Japan / Kyushu, Japan

Fuel Factor

MPG Rating (city/hwy)	Good-21/29
Driving Range (mi.)	Long-410.0
Fuel Type	Premium
Annual Fuel Cost	Low-$1814
Greenhouse Gas Emissions (tons/yr.)	Average-7.7
Barrels of Oil Used per year	Average-14.3

How the Competition Rates

Competitors	Rating	Pg.
Acura TSX	10	84
BMW 5 Series	7	93
Infiniti G	7	165

Price Range	Retail	Markup
250 Manual Trans.	$32,145	11%
350	$37,595	11%
250C Convertible Automatic Trans.	$39,660	11%
F	$58,460	11%

Safety Checklist

Crash Tests:

Frontal	Poor
Side	Poor

Airbags:

Head	Std. Row 1 & 2 Curtain
Chest/Torso	Std. Row 1 Torso from Seat
Roll-Sensing Side Airbag	–
Out-of-Position Test	Meets Requirements

Children:

Built-in Child Safety Seat	–
Automatic Window Reversal	Std. Front and Rear

Crash Avoidance:

Frontal Collision Warning	Optional
Electronic Stability Control	Standard
Lane Departure Warning	–
Brake Assist	Standard

General:

Automatic Crash Notification	Standard
Daytime Running Lights	Standard
Automatic Door-Locking	Standard

Safety Belt:

Adjustable Front Belt	Standard

Lexus IS 350

Specifications

Drive	RWD
Engine	2.5-liter V6
Transmission	6-sp. Automatic
Tow Rating (lbs.)	–
Head/Leg Room (in.)	Roomy-39/43.9
Interior Space (cu. ft.)	Very Cramped-88.3
Cargo Space (cu. ft.)	Cramped-13
Wheelbase/Length (in.)	107.5/180.3

*Combines results of both front and side tests in relation to all tests for 2010 vehicles.

Ratings—10 Best, 1 Worst

Combo Crash Tests	–
Safety Features	10
Rollover	8
Preventive Maintenance	1
Repair Costs	1
Warranty	7
Fuel Economy	3
Complaints	10
Insurance Costs	1
OVERALL RATING	**–**

Lexus LS 460

Lexus LS 600

At-a-Glance

Status	Unchanged
Year Series Started	2007
Twins	–
Body Styles	Sedan
Seating	5
Anti-Theft Device	Std. Pass. Immobil. & Pass. Alarm
Parking Index Rating	Average
Where Made	Tahara, Japan

Fuel Factor

MPG Rating (city/hwy)	Poor-16/24
Driving Range (mi.)	Long-417.9
Fuel Type	Premium
Annual Fuel Cost	High-$2278
Greenhouse Gas Emissions (tons/yr.)	High-9.6
Barrels of Oil Used per year	High-18.0

How the Competition Rates

Competitors	Rating	Pg.
BMW 7 Series	–	94
Jaguar XF	–	167
Mercedes-Benz S-Class	–	208

Price Range	Retail	Markup
460 RWD	$64,680	12%
460 AWD	$68,205	12%
460 L RWD	$70,225	12%
460 L AWD	$73,750	12%

Safety Checklist

Crash Tests:
- Frontal . . . . –
- Side . . . . –

Airbags:
- Head . . . . Std. Row 1 & 2 Curtain
- Chest/Torso . Std. Row 1 & Opt. Row 2 Torso from Seat
- Roll-Sensing Side Airbag . . . . –
- Out-of-Position Test . . . . . . Meets Requirements

Children:
- Built-in Child Safety Seat . . . . –
- Automatic Window Reversal . Std. Front and Rear

Crash Avoidance:
- Frontal Collision Warning . . . . Optional
- Electronic Stability Control . . . . Standard
- Lane Departure Warning . . . . –
- Brake Assist . . . . Standard

General:
- Automatic Crash Notification . . . . Standard
- Daytime Running Lights . . . . Standard
- Automatic Door-Locking . . . . Standard

Safety Belt:
- Adjustable Front Belt . . . . Standard

Lexus LS 460

Specifications

Drive	RWD
Engine	4.6-liter V8
Transmission	8-sp. Automatic
Tow Rating (lbs.)	–
Head/Leg Room (in.)	Average-38/43.7
Interior Space (cu. ft.)	Average-103
Cargo Space (cu. ft.)	Average-18
Wheelbase/Length (in.)	116.9/199.2

*Combines results of both front and side tests in relation to all tests for 2010 vehicles.

Ratings—10 Best, 1 Worst

Combo Crash Tests	6
Safety Features	10
Rollover	3
Preventive Maintenance	1
Repair Costs	–
Warranty	7
Fuel Economy	4
Complaints	–
Insurance Costs	8
OVERALL RATING	**6**

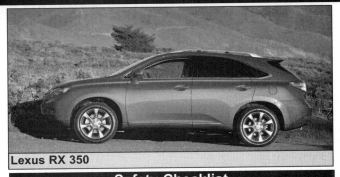

Lexus RX 350

Lexus RX 450

At-a-Glance

Status	All New
Year Series Started	2010
Twins	–
Body Styles	SUV
Seating	5
Anti-Theft Device	Std. Pass. Immobil. & Pass. Alarm
Parking Index Rating	Hard
Where Made	Kyushu, Japan / Cambridge, Ontario

Fuel Factor

MPG Rating (city/hwy)	Poor-18/24
Driving Range (mi.)	Average-389.4
Fuel Type	Premium
Annual Fuel Cost	High-$2145
Greenhouse Gas Emissions (tons/yr.)	High-9.2
Barrels of Oil Used per year	High-17.1

How the Competition Rates

Competitors	Rating	Pg.
Acura ZDX	–	85
Audi Q5	7	89
Mercedes-Benz GLK-Class	–	206

Price Range	Retail	Markup
350 FWD	$36,800	12%
350 AWD	$38,200	12%
Hybrid 450H FWD	$41,660	10%
Hybrid 450H AWD	$43,250	10%

Safety Checklist

Crash Tests:
Frontal	Average
Side	Good

Airbags:
Head	Std. Row 1 & 2 Curtain
Chest/Torso	Std. Row 1 Pelvis/Std. Row 1&2 Torso fr. St.
Roll-Sensing Side Airbag	Standard
Out-of-Position Test	Meets Requirements

Children:
Built-in Child Safety Seat	–
Automatic Window Reversal	Std. Front and Rear

Crash Avoidance:
Frontal Collision Warning	Optional
Electronic Stability Control	Standard
Lane Departure Warning	–
Brake Assist	Standard

General:
Automatic Crash Notification	Standard
Daytime Running Lights	Standard
Automatic Door-Locking	Standard

Safety Belt:
Adjustable Front Belt	Standard

Lexus RX 450

Specifications

Drive	AWD
Engine	3.5-liter V6
Transmission	6-sp. Automatic
Tow Rating (lbs.)	Average-3500
Head/Leg Room (in.)	Roomy-39.1/43.1
Interior Space (cu. ft.)	Very Roomy-139.7
Cargo Space (cu. ft.)	Very Roomy-40
Wheelbase/Length (in.)	107.9/187.8

*Combines results of both front and side tests in relation to all tests for 2010 vehicles.

Lincoln MKS

Ratings—10 Best, 1 Worst

Combo Crash Tests	7
Safety Features	10
Rollover	6
Preventive Maintenance	6
Repair Costs	2
Warranty	6
Fuel Economy	4
Complaints	2
Insurance Costs	1
OVERALL RATING	**6**

Lincoln MKS

Lincoln MKS

At-a-Glance

Status. . . . . Unchanged
Year Series Started 2009
Twins . . . . –
Body Styles . . . . Sedan
Seating. 5
Anti-Theft Device. . Std. Pass. Immobil. & Pass. Alarm
Parking Index Rating . . . . Very Hard
Where Made . . . . Chicago, IL

Fuel Factor
 MPG Rating (city/hwy) Poor-17/24
 Driving Range (mi.) Average-371.8
 Fuel Type. . . . . Regular
 Annual Fuel Cost. . . . . Average-$2070
 Greenhouse Gas Emissions (tons/yr.) High-9.6
 Barrels of Oil Used per year. High-18.0

How the Competition Rates

Competitors	Rating	Pg.
Buick Lucerne	9	99
Cadillac STS	5	104
Chrysler 300	8	119

Price Range

Price Range	Retail	Markup
Base FWD	$40,870	8%
Base AWD	$42,760	9%
Ecoboost AWD	$47,760	9%

Safety Checklist

Crash Tests:
 Frontal . . . . Average
 Side . . . . Very Good
Airbags:
 Head . . . . Std. Row 1 & 2 Curtain
 Chest/Torso . . . . Std. Row 1 Torso from Seat
 Roll-Sensing Side Airbag . . . . Standard
 Out-of-Position Test. . . . . . Meets Requirements
Children:
 Built-in Child Safety Seat . . . . –
 Automatic Window Reversal. Std. Front and Rear
Crash Avoidance:
 Frontal Collision Warning . . . . Optional
 Electronic Stability Control . . . . Standard
 Lane Departure Warning . . . . –
 Brake Assist . . . . Standard
General:
 Automatic Crash Notification . . . . Standard
 Daytime Running Lights . . . . –
 Automatic Door-Locking. . . . . Standard
Safety Belt:
 Adjustable Front Belt . . . . Standard

Lincoln MKS

Specifications

Drive. . . . . FWD
Engine. 3.5-liter V6
Transmission . . . . 6-sp. Automatic
Tow Rating (lbs.) . . . . Very Low-1000
Head/Leg Room (in.) Average-39.7/41.9
Interior Space (cu. ft.) Roomy-105.8
Cargo Space (cu. ft.) Average-18.7
Wheelbase/Length (in.) 112.9/204.1

*Combines results of both front and side tests in relation to all tests for 2010 vehicles.

Ratings—10 Best, 1 Worst

Combo Crash Tests	–
Safety Features	10
Rollover	4
Preventive Maintenance	–
Repair Costs	–
Warranty	6
Fuel Economy	4
Complaints	–
Insurance Costs	10
OVERALL RATING	**–**

Lincoln MKT

Lincoln MKT

At-a-Glance

Status	All New
Year Series Started	2010
Twins	–
Body Styles	SUV
Seating	6/7
Anti-Theft Device	Std. Pass. Immobil. & Pass. Alarm
Parking Index Rating	Very Hard
Where Made	Oakville, Ontario

Fuel Factor

MPG Rating (city/hwy)	Poor-17/23
Driving Range (mi.)	Short-358.3
Fuel Type	Regular
Annual Fuel Cost	Average-$2103
Greenhouse Gas Emissions (tons/yr.)	High-9.6
Barrels of Oil Used per year	High-18.0

How the Competition Rates

Competitors	Rating	Pg.
Audi Q7	7	90
Cadillac Escalade	6	102
Nissan Armada	–	219

Price Range

Price Range	Retail	Markup
Base FWD	$44,200	8%
Base AWD	$46,195	9%
Ecoboost AWD	$49,200	9%

Safety Checklist

Crash Tests:
Frontal . . . . –
Side . . . . –

Airbags:
Head . . . . Std. Curtain All Rows
Chest/Torso . . . . Std. Row 1 Torso from Seat
Roll-Sensing Side Airbag . . . . Standard
Out-of-Position Test . . . . . . Meets Requirements

Children:
Built-in Child Safety Seat . . . . –
Automatic Window Reversal . Std. Front and Rear

Crash Avoidance:
Frontal Collision Warning . . . . Optional
Electronic Stability Control . . . . Standard
Lane Departure Warning . . . . –
Brake Assist . . . . Standard

General:
Automatic Crash Notification . . . . Optional
Daytime Running Lights . . . . –
Automatic Door-Locking . . . . Standard

Safety Belt:
Adjustable Front Belt . . . . Standard

Lincoln MKT

Specifications

Drive	FWD
Engine	3.5-liter V6
Transmission	6-sp. Automatic
Tow Rating (lbs.)	Average-4500
Head/Leg Room (in.)	Average-40.1/41.3
Interior Space (cu. ft.)	Very Roomy-141.9
Cargo Space (cu. ft.)	Average-17.9
Wheelbase/Length (in.)	117.9/207.6

*Combines results of both front and side tests in relation to all tests for 2010 vehicles.

Ratings—10 Best, 1 Worst

Combo Crash Tests	2
Safety Features	9
Rollover	4
Preventive Maintenance	5
Repair Costs	3
Warranty	6
Fuel Economy	4
Complaints	9
Insurance Costs	8
OVERALL RATING	**5**

Lincoln MKX

Lincoln MKX

At-a-Glance

Status. . . . . Unchanged
Year Series Started 2007
Twins. . . . . Ford Edge
Body Styles. . . . . SUV
Seating. 5
Anti-Theft Device. . Std. Pass. Immobil. & Pass. Alarm
Parking Index Rating . . . . Hard
Where Made . . . . Oakville, Ontario

Fuel Factor
MPG Rating (city/hwy) Poor-17/23
Driving Range (mi.) Average-385.2
Fuel Type. . . . . Regular
Annual Fuel Cost. . . . . Average-$2103
Greenhouse Gas Emissions (tons/yr.) High-9.6
Barrels of Oil Used per year. High-18.0

How the Competition Rates

Competitors	Rating	Pg.
Cadillac SRX	5	103
Hyundai Veracruz	4	162
Nissan Murano	2	223

Price Range	Retail	Markup
Base FWD	$38,345	9%
Base AWD	$40,195	9%

Safety Checklist

Crash Tests:
Frontal. . . . . Very Poor
Side. . . . . Poor
Airbags:
Head . . . . Std. Row 1 & 2 Curtain
Chest/Torso . . . . Std. Row 1 Torso from Seat
Roll-Sensing Side Airbag . . . . Standard
Out-of-Position Test. . . . . . . Meets Requirements
Children:
Built-in Child Safety Seat . . . . –
Automatic Window Reversal. . . . . Std. Front
Crash Avoidance:
Frontal Collision Warning . . . . –
Electronic Stability Control . . . . Standard
Lane Departure Warning . . . . –
Brake Assist . . . . –
General:
Automatic Crash Notification . . . . Standard
Daytime Running Lights . . . . Optional
Automatic Door-Locking. . . . . Standard
Safety Belt:
Adjustable Front Belt . . . . Standard

Lincoln MKX

Specifications

Drive. . . . . AWD
Engine. 3.5-liter V6
Transmission . . . . 6-sp. Automatic
Tow Rating (lbs.) Average-3500
Head/Leg Room (in.) Cramped-40/40.7
Interior Space (cu. ft.). –
Cargo Space (cu. ft.) Roomy-32.3
Wheelbase/Length (in.) 111.2/186.5

*Combines results of both front and side tests in relation to all tests for 2010 vehicles.

Ratings—10 Best, 1 Worst

Combo Crash Tests	7
Safety Features	6
Rollover	8
Preventive Maintenance	6
Repair Costs	3
Warranty	6
Fuel Economy	5
Complaints	10
Insurance Costs	5
OVERALL RATING	8

Lincoln MKZ

Lincoln MKZ

At-a-Glance

Status . . . . Appearance Change
Year Series Started 2006
Twins . . . . Ford Fusion, Mercury Milan
Body Styles . . . . Sedan
Seating 5
Anti-Theft Device . . Std. Pass. Immobil. & Pass. Alarm
Parking Index Rating . . . . Average
Where Made . . . . Hermosillo, Mexico
Fuel Factor
  MPG Rating (city/hwy) Average-18/27
  Driving Range (mi.) Short-370.6
  Fuel Type . . . . Regular
  Annual Fuel Cost . . . . Average-$1913
  Greenhouse Gas Emissions (tons/yr.) High-8.7
  Barrels of Oil Used per year High-16.3

How the Competition Rates

Competitors	Rating	Pg.
Buick LaCrosse	10	98
Dodge Avenger	6	123
Nissan Maxima	7	222

Price Range	Retail	Markup
Base FWD	$34,115	9%
Base AWD	$36,005	9%

Safety Checklist

Crash Tests:
  Frontal . . . . Very Good
  Side . . . . Poor
Airbags:
  Head . . . . Std. Row 1 & 2 Curtain
  Chest/Torso . . . . Std. Row 1 Torso from Seat
  Roll-Sensing Side Airbag . . . . −
  Out-of-Position Test . . . . . . Meets Requirements
Children:
  Built-in Child Safety Seat . . . . −
  Automatic Window Reversal . . . . Std. Front
Crash Avoidance:
  Frontal Collision Warning . . . . −
  Electronic Stability Control . . . . Standard
  Lane Departure Warning . . . . −
  Brake Assist . . . . −
General:
  Automatic Crash Notification . . . . Standard
  Daytime Running Lights . . . . Optional
  Automatic Door-Locking . . . . Standard
Safety Belt:
  Adjustable Front Belt . . . . Standard

Lincoln MKZ

Specifications

Drive . . . . FWD
Engine 3.5-liter V6
Transmission . . . . 6-sp. Automatic
Tow Rating (lbs.) . . . . −
Head/Leg Room (in.) Cramped-38.7/42.3
Interior Space (cu. ft.) Average-99
Cargo Space (cu. ft.) Average-16.5
Wheelbase/Length (in.) 107.4/189.8

*Combines results of both front and side tests in relation to all tests for 2010 vehicles.

Ratings—10 Best, 1 Worst

Combo Crash Tests	7
Safety Features	2
Rollover	9
Preventive Maintenance	6
Repair Costs	6
Warranty	6
Fuel Economy	3
Complaints	7
Insurance Costs	8
OVERALL RATING	**7**

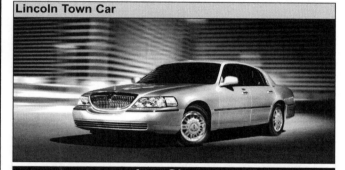
Lincoln Town Car

At-a-Glance

Status	Unchanged
Year Series Started	1998
Twins	–
Body Styles	Sedan
Seating	5
Anti-Theft Device	Std. Pass. Immobil. & Pass. Alarm
Parking Index Rating	Very Hard
Where Made	St. Thomas, Ontario

Fuel Factor

MPG Rating (city/hwy)	Poor-16/24
Driving Range (mi.)	Short-357.6
Fuel Type	Regular/E85
Annual Fuel Cost	High-$2152
Greenhouse Gas Emissions (tons/yr.)	High-9.6
Barrels of Oil Used per year	High-18.0

How the Competition Rates

Competitors	Rating	Pg.
Cadillac DTS	6	101
Chrysler 300	8	119
Mercury Grand Marquis	6	209

Price Range	Retail	Markup
Executive	$45,635	9%
Signature Limited	$46,525	9%
Executive L	$47,790	9%
Signature L	$52,195	9%

Lincoln Town Car

Safety Checklist

Crash Tests:
Frontal . . . . Good
Side . . . . Good

Airbags:
Head . . . . Std. Row 1 Combo
Chest/Torso . . . . . . Std. Row 1 Combo from Seat
Roll-Sensing Side Airbag . . . . –
Out-of-Position Test . . . . Meets Requirements

Children:
Built-in Child Safety Seat . . . . –
Automatic Window Reversal . . . . Std. Driver

Crash Avoidance:
Frontal Collision Warning . . . . –
Electronic Stability Control . . . . Standard
Lane Departure Warning . . . . –
Brake Assist . . . . –

General:
Automatic Crash Notification . . . . –
Daytime Running Lights . . . . Optional
Automatic Door-Locking . . . . Standard

Safety Belt:
Adjustable Front Belt . . . . Standard

Lincoln Town Car

Specifications

Drive	RWD
Engine	4.6-liter V8
Transmission	4-sp. Auto. w/Overdrive
Tow Rating (lbs.)	Very Low-1500
Head/Leg Room (in.)	Average-39.4/41.7
Interior Space (cu. ft.)	Roomy-108.7
Cargo Space (cu. ft.)	Average-21
Wheelbase/Length (in.)	117.7/215.4

*Combines results of both front and side tests in relation to all tests for 2010 vehicles.

Ratings—10 Best, 1 Worst

Combo Crash Tests	6
Safety Features	2
Rollover	7
Preventive Maintenance	6
Repair Costs	6
Warranty	2
Fuel Economy	9
Complaints	8
Insurance Costs	3
OVERALL RATING	**6**

Mazda 3

Mazda 3

At-a-Glance

Status . . . . Appearance Change
Year Series Started 2004
Twins . . . . –
Body Styles. . . . . Sedan, Hatchback
Seating 5
Anti-Theft Device. . Std. Pass. Immobil. & Pass. Alarm
Parking Index Rating . . . . Easy
Where Made. . . . . Hiroshima, Japan
Fuel Factor
  MPG Rating (city/hwy) . . . . . . Very Good-24/33
  Driving Range (mi.) Long-396.7
  Fuel Type. . . . . Regular
  Annual Fuel Cost . . . . Very Low-$1480
  Greenhouse Gas Emissions (tons/yr.) Low-6.8
  Barrels of Oil Used per year Low-12.7

How the Competition Rates

Competitors	Rating	Pg.
Mitsubishi Lancer	5	214
Scion tC	3	232
Subaru Impreza	4	237

Price Range

Price Range	Retail	Markup
i SV Manual Transmission	$15,045	7%
i Automatic Transmission	$16,825	7%
S Automatic Transmission	$19,540	7%
Mazdaspeed3	$23,195	7%

Safety Checklist

Crash Tests:
  Frontal . . . . Good
  Side . . . . Average
Airbags:
  Head . . . . Std. Row 1 & 2 Curtain
  Chest/Torso . . . . Std. Row 1 Torso from Seat
  Roll-Sensing Side Airbag . . . . –
  Out-of-Position Test. . . . . . Meets Requirements
Children:
  Built-in Child Safety Seat . . . . –
  Automatic Window Reversal . . . . Std. Driver
Crash Avoidance:
  Frontal Collision Warning . . . . –
  Electronic Stability Control . . . . Optional
  Lane Departure Warning . . . . –
  Brake Assist . . . . Optional
General:
  Automatic Crash Notification . . . . –
  Daytime Running Lights . . . . –
  Automatic Door-Locking . . . . –
Safety Belt:
  Adjustable Front Belt . . . . Standard

Mazda 3

Specifications

Drive. . . . . FWD
Engine 2.0-liter I4
Transmission. . . . . 5-sp. Automatic
Tow Rating (lbs.) . . . . –
Head/Leg Room (in.) Cramped-38.9/42
Interior Space (cu. ft.) Cramped-94.1
Cargo Space (cu. ft.) . . . . Very Cramped-11.8
Wheelbase/Length (in.) 103.9/180.7

*Combines results of both front and side tests in relation to all tests for 2010 vehicles.

Ratings—10 Best, 1 Worst

Combo Crash Tests	3
Safety Features	4
Rollover	5
Preventive Maintenance	6
Repair Costs	8
Warranty	2
Fuel Economy	7
Complaints	3
Insurance Costs	5
OVERALL RATING	**4**

Mazda 5

Mazda 5

At-a-Glance

Status . . . . Unchanged
Year Series Started 2006
Twins . . . . −
Body Styles . . . . Minivan
Seating 6
Anti-Theft Device . . Std. Pass. Immobil. & Pass. Alarm
Parking Index Rating . . . . Easy
Where Made . . . . Hiroshima, Japan

Fuel Factor
MPG Rating (city/hwy) Good-21/27
Driving Range (mi.) Short-371.0
Fuel Type . . . . Regular
Annual Fuel Cost . . . . Low-$1736
Greenhouse Gas Emissions (tons/yr.) . . Average-8.0
Barrels of Oil Used per year Average-14.9

How the Competition Rates

Competitors	Rating	Pg.
Chevrolet HHR	7	112
Honda Element	7	149
Kia Rondo	5	178

Price Range

	Retail	Markup
Base Manual Transmission	$17,995	7%
Base Automatic Transmission	$19,435	7%

Safety Checklist

Crash Tests:
  Frontal . . . . Average
  Side . . . . Poor
Airbags:
  Head . . . . Std. Curtain All Rows
  Chest/Torso . . . . Std. Row 1 Torso from Seat
  Roll-Sensing Side Airbag . . . . −
  Out-of-Position Test . . . . . . Meets Requirements
Children:
  Built-in Child Safety Seat . . . . −
  Automatic Window Reversal . . . . −
Crash Avoidance:
  Frontal Collision Warning . . . . −
  Electronic Stability Control . . . . Standard
  Lane Departure Warning . . . . −
  Brake Assist . . . . Standard
General:
  Automatic Crash Notification . . . . −
  Daytime Running Lights . . . . Optional
  Automatic Door-Locking . . . . −
Safety Belt:
  Adjustable Front Belt . . . . Standard

Mazda 5

Specifications

Drive . . . . FWD
Engine 2.3-liter I4
Transmission . . . . 5-sp. Auto. w/Overdrive
Tow Rating (lbs.) . . . . −
Head/Leg Room (in.) Average-40.7/40.7
Interior Space (cu. ft.) Cramped-97.7
Cargo Space (cu. ft.) . . . . Very Roomy-44.4
Wheelbase/Length (in.) 108.3/181.5

*Combines results of both front and side tests in relation to all tests for 2010 vehicles.

Ratings—10 Best, 1 Worst

Combo Crash Tests	8
Safety Features	5
Rollover	9
Preventive Maintenance	6
Repair Costs	8
Warranty	2
Fuel Economy	7
Complaints	4
Insurance Costs	5
OVERALL RATING	**8**

Mazda 6

Mazda 6

At-a-Glance

Status. . . . . Unchanged
Year Series Started 2009
Twins . . . . —
Body Styles . . . . Sedan
Seating. 5
Anti-Theft Device. . Std. Pass. Immobil. & Pass. Alarm
Parking Index Rating . . . . Easy
Where Made. . . . . Flat Rock, MI
Fuel Factor
  MPG Rating (city/hwy) Good-21/30
  Driving Range (mi.) . . . . Very Long-449.1
  Fuel Type. . . . . Regular
  Annual Fuel Cost . . . . Low-$1668
  Greenhouse Gas Emissions (tons/yr.) . . Average-7.7
  Barrels of Oil Used per year. Average-14.3

How the Competition Rates

Competitors	Rating	Pg.
Mitsubishi Galant	9	213
Nissan Altima	9	217
Toyota Camry	7	245

Price Range	Retail	Markup
i Manual Transmission	$19,320	8%
i Automatic Transmission	$20,320	8%
S Automatic Transmissino	$26,450	8%

Safety Checklist

Crash Tests:
  Frontal . . . . Good
  Side . . . . Good
Airbags:
  Head . . . . Std. Row 1 & 2 Curtain
  Chest/Torso . . . . Std. Row 1 Torso from Seat
  Roll-Sensing Side Airbag . . . . —
  Out-of-Position Test. . . . . . Meets Requirements
Children:
  Built-in Child Safety Seat . . . . —
  Automatic Window Reversal. . . . . Std. Front
Crash Avoidance:
  Frontal Collision Warning . . . . —
  Electronic Stability Control . . . . Standard
  Lane Departure Warning . . . . —
  Brake Assist . . . . Standard
General:
  Automatic Crash Notification . . . . —
  Daytime Running Lights . . . . Optional
  Automatic Door-Locking. . . . . —
Safety Belt:
  Adjustable Front Belt . . . . Standard

Mazda 6

Specifications

Drive. . . . . FWD
Engine 2.5-liter I4
Transmission. . . . . 5-sp. Automatic
Tow Rating (lbs.) . . . . —
Head/Leg Room (in.) Average-39.4/42.5
Interior Space (cu. ft.). Average-101.9
Cargo Space (cu. ft.). Average-16.6
Wheelbase/Length (in.). 109.8/193.7

*Combines results of both front and side tests in relation to all tests for 2010 vehicles.

Ratings—10 Best, 1 Worst

Combo Crash Tests	6
Safety Features	8
Rollover	5
Preventive Maintenance	7
Repair Costs	5
Warranty	2
Fuel Economy	6
Complaints	2
Insurance Costs	8
OVERALL RATING	**6**

Mazda CX-7

Mazda CX-7

At-a-Glance

Status	Unchanged
Year Series Started	2007
Twins	–
Body Styles	SUV
Seating	5
Anti-Theft Device	Std. Pass. Immobil. & Pass. Alarm
Parking Index Rating	Average
Where Made	Hiroshima, Japan

Fuel Factor

MPG Rating (city/hwy)	Average-20/28
Driving Range (mi.)	Average-376.4
Fuel Type	Regular
Annual Fuel Cost	Low-$1765
Greenhouse Gas Emissions (tons/yr.)	Average-8.0
Barrels of Oil Used per year	Average-14.9

How the Competition Rates

Competitors	Rating	Pg.
Honda Pilot	7	153
Nissan Murano	2	223
Toyota Highlander	4	248

Price Range

	Retail	Markup
i SV FWD	$21,550	5%
i Sport FWD	$22,340	5%
s Touring AWD	$27,500	7%
s Grand Touring AWD	$32,885	7%

Safety Checklist

Crash Tests:
Frontal .... Good
Side............................ Poor

Airbags:
Head .... Std. Row 1 & 2 Curtain
Chest/Torso .... Std. Row 1 Torso from Seat
Roll-Sensing Side Airbag .... Standard
Out-of-Position Test....... Meets Requirements

Children:
Built-in Child Safety Seat .... –
Automatic Window Reversal......... Std. Front

Crash Avoidance:
Frontal Collision Warning .... –
Electronic Stability Control .... Standard
Lane Departure Warning .... –
Brake Assist .... Standard

General:
Automatic Crash Notification .... –
Daytime Running Lights .... Optional
Automatic Door-Locking.................. –

Safety Belt:
Adjustable Front Belt .... Standard

Mazda CX-7

Specifications

Drive	FWD
Engine	2.5-liter I4
Transmission	5-sp. Automatic
Tow Rating (lbs.)	Very Low-1500
Head/Leg Room (in.)	Average-39.7/41.7
Interior Space (cu. ft.)	Average-101.7
Cargo Space (cu. ft.)	Roomy-29.9
Wheelbase/Length (in.)	108.3/184.3

*Combines results of both front and side tests in relation to all tests for 2010 vehicles.

Ratings—10 Best, 1 Worst

Combo Crash Tests	7
Safety Features	8
Rollover	4
Preventive Maintenance	6
Repair Costs	3
Warranty	2
Fuel Economy	3
Complaints	9
Insurance Costs	8
OVERALL RATING	**6**

Mazda CX-9

Mazda CX-9

At-a-Glance

Status	Unchanged
Year Series Started	2007
Twins	–
Body Styles	SUV
Seating	7
Anti-Theft Device	Std. Pass. Immobil. & Pass. Alarm
Parking Index Rating	Hard
Where Made	Hiroshima, Japan

Fuel Factor

MPG Rating (city/hwy)	Poor-16/22
Driving Range (mi.)	Short-366.6
Fuel Type	Regular
Annual Fuel Cost	High-$2221
Greenhouse Gas Emissions (tons/yr.)	High-10.2
Barrels of Oil Used per year	High-19.0

How the Competition Rates

Competitors	Rating	Pg.
Acura MDX	–	81
Chevrolet Equinox	6	111
Nissan Murano	2	223

Price Range

Price Range	Retail	Markup
FWD	$28,635	8%
AWD	$30,035	8%

Safety Checklist

Crash Tests:
Frontal . . . . Good
Side . . . . Average

Airbags:
Head . . . . Std. Curtain All Rows
Chest/Torso . . . . Std. Row 1 Torso from Seat
Roll-Sensing Side Airbag . . . . Standard
Out-of-Position Test . . . . . . Meets Requirements

Children:
Built-in Child Safety Seat . . . . –
Automatic Window Reversal . . . . Std. Front

Crash Avoidance:
Frontal Collision Warning . . . . –
Electronic Stability Control . . . . Standard
Lane Departure Warning . . . . –
Brake Assist . . . . Standard

General:
Automatic Crash Notification . . . . –
Daytime Running Lights . . . . Optional
Automatic Door-Locking . . . . –

Safety Belt:
Adjustable Front Belt . . . . Standard

Mazda CX-9

Specifications

Drive	FWD
Engine	3.7-liter V6
Transmission	6-sp. Automatic
Tow Rating (lbs.)	Low-2000
Head/Leg Room (in.)	Cramped-39.6/40.9
Interior Space (cu. ft.)	Very Roomy-139.4
Cargo Space (cu. ft.)	Average-17.2
Wheelbase/Length (in.)	113.2/200.2

*Combines results of both front and side tests in relation to all tests for 2010 vehicles.

Ratings—10 Best, 1 Worst

Combo Crash Tests	–
Safety Features	1
Rollover	10
Preventive Maintenance	6
Repair Costs	8
Warranty	2
Fuel Economy	7
Complaints	10
Insurance Costs	8
OVERALL RATING	**–**

Mazda MX-5 Miata

Mazda MX-5 Miata

At-a-Glance

Status . . . . Appearance Change
Year Series Started 2006
Twins . . . . –
Body Styles. . . . . Two Seater Convertible
Seating. 2
Anti-Theft Device. . Std. Pass. Immobil. & Pass. Alarm
Parking Index Rating . . . . Very Easy
Where Made. . . . . Hiroshima, Japan
Fuel Factor
  MPG Rating (city/hwy) Good-21/28
  Driving Range (mi.). . . . . Very Short-300.5
  Fuel Type. . . . . Premium
  Annual Fuel Cost. . . . . Average-$1838
  Greenhouse Gas Emissions (tons/yr.) . . Average-8.0
  Barrels of Oil Used per year. Average-14.9

How the Competition Rates

Competitors	Rating	Pg.
Ford Mustang	7	140
Hyundai Genesis	9	158
Nissan 370Z	–	216

Price Range

Price Range	Retail	Markup
Base 5-sp. Manual Transmission	$22,810	8%
Base Automatic Transmission	$25,070	8%
Hardtop Convertible 6-sp. Trans.	$26,850	8%
Hardtop Convertible Auto. Trans.	$27,950	8%

Safety Checklist

Crash Tests:
  Frontal. . . . . –
  Side . . . . –
Airbags:
  Head . . . . Std. Row 1 Combo
  Chest/Torso . . . . . . Std. Row 1 Combo from Seat
  Roll-Sensing Side Airbag . . . . –
  Out-of-Position Test. . . . . . . Meets Requirements
Children:
  Built-in Child Safety Seat . . . . –
  Automatic Window Reversal . . . . –
Crash Avoidance:
  Frontal Collision Warning . . . . –
  Electronic Stability Control . . . . Optional
  Lane Departure Warning . . . . –
  Brake Assist . . . . Optional
General:
  Automatic Crash Notification . . . . –
  Daytime Running Lights . . . . Optional
  Automatic Door-Locking. . . . . –
Safety Belt:
  Adjustable Front Belt . . . . –

Mazda MX-5 Miata

Specifications

Drive . . . . RWD
Engine 2.0-liter I4
Transmission. . . . . 6-sp. Automatic
Tow Rating (lbs.) . . . . –
Head/Leg Room (in.). Cramped-37.4/43.1
Interior Space (cu. ft.). . . . . –
Cargo Space (cu. ft.). . . . . Very Cramped-5.3
Wheelbase/Length (in.). 91.7/157.3

*Combines results of both front and side tests in relation to all tests for 2010 vehicles.

Ratings—10 Best, 1 Worst

Combo Crash Tests	4
Safety Features	7
Rollover	1
Preventive Maintenance	6
Repair Costs	10
Warranty	2
Fuel Economy	7
Complaints	2
Insurance Costs	10
OVERALL RATING	**5**

Mazda Tribute

Mazda Tribute

At-a-Glance

Status. . . . . Unchanged
Year Series Started 2001
Twins . . . . Ford Escape, Mercury Mariner
Body Styles. . . . . SUV
Seating. 5
Anti-Theft Device. . Std. Pass. Immobil. & Pass. Alarm
Parking Index Rating . . . . Easy
Where Made . . . . Kansas City, MO
Fuel Factor
  MPG Rating (city/hwy) Good-21/28
  Driving Range (mi.) Long-414.1
  Fuel Type. . . . . Regular
  Annual Fuel Cost . . . . Low-$1712
  Greenhouse Gas Emissions (tons/yr.) . . Average-8.0
  Barrels of Oil Used per year. Average-14.9

How the Competition Rates

Competitors	Rating	Pg.
Honda CR-V	10	148
Jeep Compass	5	169
Suzuki Grand Vitara	1	240

Price Range

Price Range	Retail	Markup
i FWD Manual Trans.	$20,090	7%
i 4WD	$23,885	7%
S FWD	$26,850	7%
S 4WD	$28,600	7%

Safety Checklist

Crash Tests:
  Frontal . . . . Average
  Side. . . . . Poor
Airbags:
  Head . . . . Std. Row 1 & 2 Curtain
  Chest/Torso . . . . Std. Row 1 Torso from Seat
  Roll-Sensing Side Airbag . . . . Standard
  Out-of-Position Test. . . . . . Meets Requirements
Children:
  Built-in Child Safety Seat . . . . −
  Automatic Window Reversal . . . . −
Crash Avoidance:
  Frontal Collision Warning . . . . −
  Electronic Stability Control . . . . Standard
  Lane Departure Warning . . . . −
  Brake Assist . . . . −
General:
  Automatic Crash Notification . . . . −
  Daytime Running Lights. . . . . Standard
  Automatic Door-Locking. . . . . Standard
Safety Belt:
  Adjustable Front Belt . . . . Standard

Mazda Tribute

Specifications

Drive. . . . . FWD
Engine 2.5-liter I4
Transmission . . . . 6-sp. Automatic
Tow Rating (lbs.) . . . . Very Low-1500
Head/Leg Room (in.) . . . . Very Cramped-40.4/39.2
Interior Space (cu. ft.). Average-99.4
Cargo Space (cu. ft.) Roomy-31.4
Wheelbase/Length (in.) 103.1/174.9

*Combines results of both front and side tests in relation to all tests for 2010 vehicles.

Ratings—10 Best, 1 Worst

Combo Crash Tests	–
Safety Features	7
Rollover	8
Preventive Maintenance	4
Repair Costs	2
Warranty	3
Fuel Economy	4
Complaints	6
Insurance Costs	3
OVERALL RATING	**–**

Mercedes Benz C-Class

Mercedes Benz C-Class

At-a-Glance

Status. . . . . Unchanged
Year Series Started 2008
Twins . . . . –
Body Styles . . . . Sedan
Seating. 5
Anti-Theft Device . Std. Pass. Immobil. & Active Alarm
Parking Index Rating . . . . Easy
Where Made. . . . . Bremen, Germany
Fuel Factor
  MPG Rating (city/hwy). Poor-17/25
  Driving Range (mi.). Short-345.6
  Fuel Type. . . . . Premium
  Annual Fuel Cost. . . . . High-$2190
  Greenhouse Gas Emissions (tons/yr.) High-9.2
  Barrels of Oil Used per year. High-17.1

How the Competition Rates

Competitors	Rating	Pg.
Audi A4	10	86
BMW 3 Series	7	92
Volvo S40	9	266

Price Range	Retail	Markup
C300 Sport	$33,600	8%
C300 Luxury 4Matic	$37,300	8%
C350	$39,750	8%
C63 AMG	$57,350	8%

Safety Checklist

Crash Tests:
  Frontal. . . . . –
  Side . . . . –
Airbags:
  Head . . . . Std. Row 1 & 2 Curtain
  Chest/Torso. . . Std. Row 1 Torso & Pelvis from Seat
  Roll-Sensing Side Airbag . . . . –
  Out-of-Position Test . . . . –
Children:
  Built-in Child Safety Seat . . . . –
  Automatic Window Reversal. Std. Front and Rear
Crash Avoidance:
  Frontal Collision Warning . . . . –
  Electronic Stability Control . . . . Standard
  Lane Departure Warning . . . . –
  Brake Assist . . . . Standard
General:
  Automatic Crash Notification . . . . Standard
  Daytime Running Lights. . . . . Standard
  Automatic Door-Locking. . . . . Standard
Safety Belt:
  Adjustable Front Belt . . . . Standard

Mercedes Benz C-Class

Specifications

Drive . . . . RWD
Engine. 3.5-liter V6
Transmission . . . . 7-sp. Automatic
Tow Rating (lbs.) . . . . –
Head/Leg Room (in.) . . . . Very Cramped-37.1/41.7
Interior Space (cu. ft.) . . . . Very Cramped-88.2
Cargo Space (cu. ft.). . . . . Very Cramped-12.4
Wheelbase/Length (in.). 108.7/182.3

*Combines results of both front and side tests in relation to all tests for 2010 vehicles.

Ratings—10 Best, 1 Worst

Combo Crash Tests	5
Safety Features	10
Rollover	8
Preventive Maintenance	7
Repair Costs	–
Warranty	3
Fuel Economy	5
Complaints	–
Insurance Costs	3
OVERALL RATING	**7**

Mercedes Benz E-Class

At-a-Glance

```
Status. . . . . . . . . . . . . . . . . . . . . . . . . . . . . All New
Year Series Started . . . . . . . . . . . . . . . . . . . . 2010
Twins . . . . . . . . . . . . . . . . . . . . . . . . . . . . . . . . –
Body Styles . . . . . . . . . . . . . . . . . . . . . Sedan, Coupe
Seating. . . . . . . . . . . . . . . . . . . . . . . . . . . . . . . 5
Anti-Theft Device . Std. Pass. Immobil. & Active Alarm
Parking Index Rating . . . . . . . . . . . . . . . . . . Average
Where Made . . . . . . . . . . . . . . . . . . . . . . Germany
```

Fuel Factor
```
MPG Rating (city/hwy) . . . . . . . . . . . Average-18/26
Driving Range (mi.) . . . . . . . . . . . Very Long-440.8
Fuel Type . . . . . . . . . . . . . . . . . . . . . . . . . Premium
Annual Fuel Cost. . . . . . . . . . . . . . Average-$2082
Greenhouse Gas Emissions (tons/yr.) . . . . . High-8.7
Barrels of Oil Used per year. . . . . . . . . . High-16.3
```

How the Competition Rates

Competitors	Rating	Pg.
BMW 5 Series	7	93
Infiniti G	7	165
Lexus GS	–	185

Price Range

	Retail	Markup
E350 Coupe	$48,050	8%
E350 Luxury Sedan 4Matic	$51,100	8%
E550 Sport	$56,300	8%
E550 Sport Sedan 4Matic	$58,800	8%

Mercedes Benz E-Class

Safety Checklist

Crash Tests:
```
Frontal. . . . . . . . . . . . . . . . . . . . . . . . . Very Poor
Side . . . . . . . . . . . . . . . . . . . . . . . . . . Very Good
```
Airbags:
```
Head . . . . . . . . . . . . . . . . Std. Row 1 & 2 Curtain
Chest/Torso . . . . Std. Row 1 & 2 Torso from Seat
Roll-Sensing Side Airbag . . . . . . . . . . . . Standard
Out-of-Position Test . . . . . . . . . . . . . . . . . . . . . –
```
Children:
```
Built-in Child Safety Seat . . . . . . . . . . . . . . . . . –
Automatic Window Reversal. Std. Front and Rear
```
Crash Avoidance:
```
Frontal Collision Warning . . . . . . . . . . . . Optional
Electronic Stability Control . . . . . . . . . . Standard
Lane Departure Warning. . . . . . . . . . . . . Optional
Brake Assist . . . . . . . . . . . . . . . . . . . . . Standard
```
General:
```
Automatic Crash Notification . . . . . . . . Standard
Daytime Running Lights. . . . . . . . . . . . . Standard
Automatic Door-Locking. . . . . . . . . . . . . Standard
```
Safety Belt:
```
Adjustable Front Belt . . . . . . . . . . . . . . Standard
```

Mercedes Benz E-Class

Specifications

```
Drive . . . . . . . . . . . . . . . . . . . . . . . . . . . . . . . . RWD
Engine. . . . . . . . . . . . . . . . . . . . . . . . . . . 3.5-liter V6
Transmission . . . . . . . . . . . . . . . . . . . 7-sp. Automatic
Tow Rating (lbs.). . . . . . . . . . . . . . Very Low-1654.2
Head/Leg Room (in.) . . . . . . . . Very Cramped-37.9/41.3
Interior Space (cu. ft.). . . . . . . . . . . . . . Cramped-97
Cargo Space (cu. ft.). . . . . . . . . . . . . . Cramped-15.9
Wheelbase/Length (in.) . . . . . . . . . . . 113.1/191.7
```

*Combines results of both front and side tests in relation to all tests for 2010 vehicles.

Mercedes Benz GL-Class

Ratings—10 Best, 1 Worst

Combo Crash Tests	–
Safety Features	10
Rollover	2
Preventive Maintenance	5
Repair Costs	1
Warranty	3
Fuel Economy	1
Complaints	4
Insurance Costs	3
OVERALL RATING	**–**

Mercedes Benz GL-Class

Mercedes Benz GL-Class

At-a-Glance

Status . . . . Appearance Change
Year Series Started 2007
Twins . . . . –
Body Styles . . . . SUV
Seating 7
Anti-Theft Device . Std. Pass. Immobil. & Active Alarm
Parking Index Rating . . . . Very Hard
Where Made . . . . Tuscaloosa, AL
Fuel Factor
  MPG Rating (city/hwy) . . . . Very Poor-13/17
  Driving Range (mi.) Average-383.8
  Fuel Type . . . . Premium
  Annual Fuel Cost . . . . Very High-$2992
  Greenhouse Gas Emissions (tons/yr.) Very High-13.1
  Barrels of Oil Used per year . . . . Very High-24.5

How the Competition Rates

Competitors	Rating	Pg.
Ford Expedition	6	134
Nissan Armada	–	219
Toyota Sequoia	–	252

Price Range	Retail	Markup
GL450	$60,950	8%
GL550	$82,850	8%

Safety Checklist

Crash Tests:
  Frontal . . . . –
  Side . . . . –
Airbags:
  Head . . . . Std. Curtain All Rows
    Chest/Torso . . . Std. Row 1 & 2 Torso from Seat
  Roll-Sensing Side Airbag . . . . Standard
  Out-of-Position Test . . . . –
Children:
  Built-in Child Safety Seat . . . . –
  Automatic Window Reversal . Std. Front and Rear
Crash Avoidance:
  Frontal Collision Warning . . . . –
  Electronic Stability Control . . . . Standard
  Lane Departure Warning . . . . –
  Brake Assist . . . . Standard
General:
  Automatic Crash Notification . . . . Standard
  Daytime Running Lights . . . . Standard
  Automatic Door-Locking . . . . Standard
Safety Belt:
  Adjustable Front Belt . . . . Standard

Specifications

Drive . . . . AWD
Engine 4.7-liter V8
Transmission . . . . 7-sp. Automatic
Tow Rating (lbs.) High-7500
Head/Leg Room (in.) Cramped-40.1/40.3
Interior Space (cu. ft.) . . . . –
Cargo Space (cu. ft.) Cramped-14.3
Wheelbase/Length (in.) 121.1/200.6

*Combines results of both front and side tests in relation to all tests for 2010 vehicles.

Ratings—10 Best, 1 Worst

Combo Crash Tests	–
Safety Features	10
Rollover	3
Preventive Maintenance	–
Repair Costs	–
Warranty	3
Fuel Economy	3
Complaints	–
Insurance Costs	5
OVERALL RATING	–

Mercedes Benz GLK-Class

At-a-Glance

Status	All New
Year Series Started	2010
Twins	–
Body Styles	SUV
Seating	5
Anti-Theft Device	Std. Pass. Immobil. & Active Alarm
Parking Index Rating	Average
Where Made	Bremen, Germany

Fuel Factor

MPG Rating (city/hwy)	Poor-16/22
Driving Range (mi.)	Very Short-317.3
Fuel Type	Premium
Annual Fuel Cost	High-$2385
Greenhouse Gas Emissions (tons/yr.)	High-10.2
Barrels of Oil Used per year	High-19.0

How the Competition Rates

Competitors	Rating	Pg.
Acura ZDX	–	85
Audi Q5	7	89
Lexus RX	6	190

Price Range	Retail	Markup
GLK350	$33,900	8%
GLK350 4Matic	$35,900	8%

Mercedes Benz GLK-Class

Safety Checklist

Crash Tests:
Frontal . . . . –
Side . . . . –

Airbags:
Head . . . . Std. Row 1 & 2 Curtain
Chest/Torso . . . . Std. Row 1 & 2 Torso from Seat
Roll-Sensing Side Airbag . . . . Standard
Out-of-Position Test . . . . –

Children:
Built-in Child Safety Seat . . . . –
Automatic Window Reversal . Std. Front and Rear

Crash Avoidance:
Frontal Collision Warning . . . . –
Electronic Stability Control . . . . Standard
Lane Departure Warning . . . . –
Brake Assist . . . . Standard

General:
Automatic Crash Notification . . . . Standard
Daytime Running Lights . . . . Standard
Automatic Door-Locking . . . . Standard

Safety Belt:
Adjustable Front Belt . . . . Standard

Mercedes Benz GLK-Class

Specifications

Drive	RWD
Engine	3.5-liter V6
Transmission	7-sp. Automatic
Tow Rating (lbs.)	Average-3500
Head/Leg Room (in.)	Average-39.8/41.8
Interior Space (cu. ft.)	Average-102.9
Cargo Space (cu. ft.)	Average-23.3
Wheelbase/Length (in.)	108.5/178.3

*Combines results of both front and side tests in relation to all tests for 2010 vehicles.

Mercedes Benz M-Class | Mid-Size SUV

Ratings—10 Best, 1 Worst

Combo Crash Tests	7
Safety Features	10
Rollover	3
Preventive Maintenance	4
Repair Costs	–
Warranty	3
Fuel Economy	2
Complaints	7
Insurance Costs	5
OVERALL RATING	**6**

Mercedes Benz M-Class

Mercedes Benz M-Class

At-a-Glance

Status. . . . . Unchanged
Year Series Started 2006
Twins . . . . –
Body Styles. . . . . SUV
Seating. 5
Anti-Theft Device . Std. Pass. Immobil. & Active Alarm
Parking Index Rating . . . . Hard
Where Made . . . . Tuscaloosa, AL

Fuel Factor
MPG Rating (city/hwy). . . . . Very Poor-15/20
Driving Range (mi.) . . . . Very Long-424.2
Fuel Type. . . . . Premium
Annual Fuel Cost. . . . . Very High-$2574
Greenhouse Gas Emissions (tons/yr.) High-10.2
Barrels of Oil Used per year. High-19.0

How the Competition Rates

Competitors	Rating	Pg.
BMW X5	8	96
Infiniti FX	–	164
Porsche Cayenne	–	230

Price Range	Retail	Markup
ML350	$45,700	8%
ML350CDI	$49,700	8%
ML550	$56,750	8%
ML63AMG	$91,050	8%

Safety Checklist

Crash Tests:
Frontal . . . . Average
Side . . . . Very Good
Airbags:
Head . . . . Std. Row 1 & 2 Curtain
Chest/Torso . . . . Std. Row 1 & 2 Torso from Seat
Roll-Sensing Side Airbag . . . . Standard
Out-of-Position Test. . . . . . . Meets Requirements
Children:
Built-in Child Safety Seat . . . . –
Automatic Window Reversal. Std. Front and Rear
Crash Avoidance:
Frontal Collision Warning . . . . –
Electronic Stability Control . . . . Standard
Lane Departure Warning . . . . –
Brake Assist . . . . Standard
General:
Automatic Crash Notification . . . . Standard
Daytime Running Lights. . . . . Standard
Automatic Door-Locking. . . . . Standard
Safety Belt:
Adjustable Front Belt . . . . Standard

Mercedes Benz M-Class

Specifications

Drive. . . . . AWD
Engine. 3.5-liter V6
Transmission . . . . 7-sp. Automatic
Tow Rating (lbs.) High-7200
Head/Leg Room (in.) Average-39.9/42.2
Interior Space (cu. ft.). . . . . Very Roomy-162.1
Cargo Space (cu. ft.) Roomy-29.4
Wheelbase/Length (in.) 114.7/188.2

*Combines results of both front and side tests in relation to all tests for 2010 vehicles.

Ratings—10 Best, 1 Worst

Combo Crash Tests	–
Safety Features	10
Rollover	8
Preventive Maintenance	6
Repair Costs	1
Warranty	3
Fuel Economy	3
Complaints	9
Insurance Costs	1
OVERALL RATING	–

Mercedes Benz S-Class

Mercedes Benz S-Class

At-a-Glance

Status. . . . . Unchanged
Year Series Started 2007
Twins . . . . –
Body Styles . . . . Sedan
Seating. 5
Anti-Theft Device . Std. Pass. Immobil. & Active Alarm
Parking Index Rating . . . . Very Hard
Where Made . . . . Sindelfingen, Germany

Fuel Factor
MPG Rating (city/hwy). Poor-15/23
Driving Range (mi.) . . . . Very Long-423.2
Fuel Type. . . . . Premium
Annual Fuel Cost. . . . . Very High-$2446
Greenhouse Gas Emissions (tons/yr.) High-10.2
Barrels of Oil Used per year. High-19.0

How the Competition Rates

Competitors	Rating	Pg.
BMW 7 Series	–	94
Jaguar XF	–	167
Lexus LS	–	189

Price Range	Retail	Markup
S400 HV	$87,950	8%
S550 4matic	$94,600	8%
S600	$149,700	8%
S63 AMG	$201,150	8%

Safety Checklist

Crash Tests:
Frontal. . . . . –
Side . . . . –
Airbags:
Head . . . . Std. Row 1 & 2 Curtain
Chest/Torso . . . . . Std. Row 1 & 2 Torso from Seat
Roll-Sensing Side Airbag . . . . Standard
Out-of-Position Test. . . . . . . Meets Requirements
Children:
Built-in Child Safety Seat . . . . –
Automatic Window Reversal. Std. Front and Rear
Crash Avoidance:
Frontal Collision Warning . . . . Optional
Electronic Stability Control . . . . Standard
Lane Departure Warning. . . . . Optional
Brake Assist . . . . Standard
General:
Automatic Crash Notification . . . . Standard
Daytime Running Lights. . . . . Standard
Automatic Door-Locking. . . . . Standard
Safety Belt:
Adjustable Front Belt . . . . Standard

Mercedes Benz S-Class

Specifications

Drive . . . . RWD
Engine. 5.5-liter V8
Transmission. . . . . 7-sp. Automatic
Tow Rating (lbs.) . . . . –
Head/Leg Room (in.) . . . . Very Cramped-37.8/41.9
Interior Space (cu. ft.) . . . . Very Roomy-125
Cargo Space (cu. ft.). Average-19.8
Wheelbase/Length (in.). 124.6/206.5

*Combines results of both front and side tests in relation to all tests for 2010 vehicles.

Mercury Grand Marquis Large

Ratings—10 Best, 1 Worst

Combo Crash Tests	7
Safety Features	1
Rollover	9
Preventive Maintenance	5
Repair Costs	7
Warranty	3
Fuel Economy	2
Complaints	7
Insurance Costs	10
OVERALL RATING	**6**

Mercury Grand Marquis

Mercury Grand Marquis

At-a-Glance

Status	Unchanged
Year Series Started	1999
Twins	–
Body Styles	Sedan
Seating	6
Anti-Theft Device	Std. Pass. Immobil. & Pass. Alarm
Parking Index Rating	Very Hard
Where Made	St. Thomas, Ontario

Fuel Factor

MPG Rating (city/hwy)	Very Poor-14/19
Driving Range (mi.)	Very Short-301.7
Fuel Type	Regular/E85
Annual Fuel Cost	Very High-$2550
Greenhouse Gas Emissions (tons/yr.)	High-9.6
Barrels of Oil Used per year	High-18.0

How the Competition Rates

Competitors	Rating	Pg.
Buick Lucerne	9	99
Cadillac DTS	6	101
Chrysler 300	8	119

Price Range	Retail	Markup
LS	$29,410	6%

Safety Checklist

Crash Tests:
Frontal . . . . Good
Side . . . . Good
Airbags:
Head . . . . Std. Row 1 Combo
Chest/Torso . . . . . . Std. Row 1 Combo from Seat
Roll-Sensing Side Airbag . . . . –
Out-of-Position Test . . . . . . Meets Requirements
Children:
Built-in Child Safety Seat . . . . –
Automatic Window Reversal . . . . –
Crash Avoidance:
Frontal Collision Warning . . . . –
Electronic Stability Control . . . . –
Lane Departure Warning . . . . –
Brake Assist . . . . –
General:
Automatic Crash Notification . . . . –
Daytime Running Lights . . . . Optional
Automatic Door-Locking . . . . Standard
Safety Belt:
Adjustable Front Belt . . . . Standard

Mercury Grand Marquis

Specifications

Drive	RWD
Engine	4.6-liter V8
Transmission	4-sp. Automatic
Tow Rating (lbs.)	Very Low-1500
Head/Leg Room (in.)	Average-39.5/41.6
Interior Space (cu. ft.)	Roomy-107.4
Cargo Space (cu. ft.)	Average-20.6
Wheelbase/Length (in.)	114.7/211.1

*Combines results of both front and side tests in relation to all tests for 2010 vehicles.

Ratings—10 Best, 1 Worst

Combo Crash Tests	4
Safety Features	8
Rollover	1
Preventive Maintenance	4
Repair Costs	10
Warranty	3
Fuel Economy	6
Complaints	9
Insurance Costs	10
OVERALL RATING	**6**

Mercury Mariner

Mercury Mariner

At-a-Glance

Status. . . . . Unchanged
Year Series Started 2006
Twins. . . . . Ford Escape, Mazda Tribute
Body Styles. . . . . SUV
Seating 5
Anti-Theft Device. . Std. Pass. Immobil. & Pass. Alarm
Parking Index Rating . . . . Easy
Where Made . . . . . Claycomo, MO / Kansas City, KS

Fuel Factor
MPG Rating (city/hwy) Average-20/26
Driving Range (mi.). Short-368.2
Fuel Type. Regular/E85
Annual Fuel Cost . . . . Low-$1815
Greenhouse Gas Emissions (tons/yr.) High-8.3
Barrels of Oil Used per year. Average-15.6

How the Competition Rates

Competitors	Rating	Pg.
Honda CR-V	10	148
Jeep Patriot	6	172
Toyota RAV4	4	251

Price Range	Retail	Markup
Base FWD	$23,035	7%
Premier FWD	$25,105	7%
Premier 4WD	$26,855	8%
Hybrid 4WD	$31,745	8%

Safety Checklist

Crash Tests:
Frontal . . . . Average
Side. . . . . Poor
Airbags:
Head . . . . Std. Row 1 & 2 Curtain
Chest/Torso . . . . . . Std. Row 1 Torso from Seat
Roll-Sensing Side Airbag . . . . Standard
Out-of-Position Test. . . . . . Meets Requirements
Children:
Built-in Child Safety Seat . . . . −
Automatic Window Reversal . . . . −
Crash Avoidance:
Frontal Collision Warning . . . . −
Electronic Stability Control . . . . Standard
Lane Departure Warning . . . . −
Brake Assist . . . . −
General:
Automatic Crash Notification. . . . . Optional
Daytime Running Lights . . . . Optional
Automatic Door-Locking. . . . . Standard
Safety Belt:
Adjustable Front Belt . . . . Standard

Mercury Mariner

Specifications

Drive 4WD
Engine. 2.5-liter I4
Transmission . . . . 6-sp. Auto. w/Overdrive
Tow Rating (lbs.). . . . . Very Low-1500
Head/Leg Room (in.). Average-40.4/41.6
Interior Space (cu. ft.) Average-99.4
Cargo Space (cu. ft.) Roomy-31.4
Wheelbase/Length (in.) 103.1/175.1

*Combines results of both front and side tests in relation to all tests for 2010 vehicles.

Mercury Milan

Ratings—10 Best, 1 Worst

Combo Crash Tests	7
Safety Features	4
Rollover	8
Preventive Maintenance	6
Repair Costs	9
Warranty	3
Fuel Economy	8
Complaints	10
Insurance Costs	5
OVERALL RATING	**9**

Mercury Milan

At-a-Glance

Status . . . . Appearance Change
Year Series Started 2006
Twins . . . . Ford Fusion, Lincoln MKZ
Body Styles . . . . Sedan
Seating 5
Anti-Theft Device . . Std. Pass. Immobil. & Pass. Alarm
Parking Index Rating . . . . Average
Where Made . . . . Hermosillo, Mexico
Fuel Factor
  MPG Rating (city/hwy) Average-23/31
  Driving Range (mi.) Average-383.7
  Fuel Type Regular/E85
  Annual Fuel Cost . . . . Average-$1847
  Greenhouse Gas Emissions (tons/yr.) . . Average-7.3
  Barrels of Oil Used per year Average-13.7

How the Competition Rates

Competitors	Rating	Pg.
Hyundai Sonata	7	160
Mitsubishi Galant	9	213
Toyota Camry	7	245

Price Range

	Retail	Markup
Base 4-cyl.	$21,180	8%
Premier 4-cyl.	$24,320	9%
Hybrid	$27,500	9%
Premier V6 AWD	$27,800	9%

Safety Checklist

Crash Tests:
  Frontal . . . . Very Good
  Side . . . . Poor
Airbags:
  Head . . . . Std. Row 1 & 2 Curtain
  Chest/Torso . . . . Std. Row 1 Torso from Seat
  Roll-Sensing Side Airbag . . . . –
  Out-of-Position Test . . . . . . Meets Requirements
Children:
  Built-in Child Safety Seat . . . . –
  Automatic Window Reversal . . . . Std. Driver
Crash Avoidance:
  Frontal Collision Warning . . . . –
  Electronic Stability Control . . . . Standard
  Lane Departure Warning . . . . –
  Brake Assist . . . . –
General:
  Automatic Crash Notification . . . . Optional
  Daytime Running Lights . . . . –
  Automatic Door-Locking . . . . Standard
Safety Belt:
  Adjustable Front Belt . . . . Standard

Mercury Milan

Specifications

Drive . . . . FWD
Engine 2.4-liter I4
Transmission . . . . 6-sp. Automatic
Tow Rating (lbs.) . . . . –
Head/Leg Room (in.) Cramped-38.7/42.3
Interior Space (cu. ft.) Average-101
Cargo Space (cu. ft.) Average-16.5
Wheelbase/Length (in.) 107.4/189

*Combines results of both front and side tests in relation to all tests for 2010 vehicles.

Ratings—10 Best, 1 Worst

Combo Crash Tests	1
Safety Features	3
Rollover	8
Preventive Maintenance	8
Repair Costs	6
Warranty	10
Fuel Economy	9
Complaints	2
Insurance Costs	5
OVERALL RATING	**6**

Mini Coooper

Mini Coooper

At-a-Glance

Status. . . . . Unchanged
Year Series Started 2002
Twins . . . . −
Body Styles . . . . Convertible, Hatchback
Seating 4
Anti-Theft Device. . . . . . . Std. Passive Immobil. Only
Parking Index Rating . . . . Very Easy
Where Made . . . . Oxford, England
Fuel Factor
  MPG Rating (city/hwy) . . . . . Very Good-25/33
  Driving Range (mi.). Short-370.4
  Fuel Type. . . . . Premium
  Annual Fuel Cost . . . . Very Low-$1550
  Greenhouse Gas Emissions (tons/yr.) Low-6.6
  Barrels of Oil Used per year Low-12.2

How the Competition Rates

Competitors	Rating	Pg.
Kia Soul	6	181
Nissan Cube	5	220
Scion xD	4	234

Price Range	Retail	Markup
Base Coupe	$18,800	11%
S Coupe	$22,300	11%
John Cooper Works	$28,800	11%
John Cooper Works Convertible	$34,000	11%

Safety Checklist

Crash Tests:
  Frontal. . . . . Very Poor
  Side. . . . . Very Poor
Airbags:
  Head . . . . Std. Row 1 & 2 Curtain
  Chest/Torso . . . . Std. Row 1 Torso from Seat
  Roll-Sensing Side Airbag . . . . −
  Out-of-Position Test. . . . . . . Meets Requirements
Children:
  Built-in Child Safety Seat . . . . −
  Automatic Window Reversal . . . . −
Crash Avoidance:
  Frontal Collision Warning . . . . −
  Electronic Stability Control . . . . Standard
  Lane Departure Warning . . . . −
  Brake Assist . . . . Standard
General:
  Automatic Crash Notification . . . . −
  Daytime Running Lights . . . . Optional
  Automatic Door-Locking . . . . Optional
Safety Belt:
  Adjustable Front Belt . . . . −

Mini Coooper

Specifications

Drive . . . . FWD
Engine. 1.6-liter I4
Transmission . . . . 6-sp. Automatic
Tow Rating (lbs.). . . . . −
Head/Leg Room (in.) Cramped-38.8/41.4
Interior Space (cu. ft.) . . . . Very Cramped-76
Cargo Space (cu. ft.) . . . . Very Cramped-5.7
Wheelbase/Length (in.) 97.1/145.2

*Combines results of both front and side tests in relation to all tests for 2010 vehicles.

Mitsubishi Galant

Ratings—10 Best, 1 Worst

Combo Crash Tests	5
Safety Features	3
Rollover	8
Preventive Maintenance	8
Repair Costs	10
Warranty	9
Fuel Economy	7
Complaints	10
Insurance Costs	1
OVERALL RATING	**9**

Mitsubishi Galant

Mitsubishi Galant

At-a-Glance

Status. . . . . Unchanged
Year Series Started 2004
Twins . . . . —
Body Styles . . . . Sedan
Seating. 5
Anti-Theft Device . . . . . . Opt. Pass. Immobil. & Alarm
Parking Index Rating . . . . Hard
Where Made . . . . Normal, IL
Fuel Factor
  MPG Rating (city/hwy) Good-21/30
  Driving Range (mi.) . . . . Very Long-429.7
  Fuel Type. . . . . Regular
  Annual Fuel Cost . . . . Low-$1668
  Greenhouse Gas Emissions (tons/yr.) . . Average-7.7
  Barrels of Oil Used per year. Average-14.3

How the Competition Rates

Competitors	Rating	Pg.
Ford Fusion	9	139
Mazda 6	8	198
Nissan Maxima	7	222

Price Range	Retail	Markup
ES	$21,599	6%
SE	$23,999	6%

Safety Checklist

Crash Tests:
  Frontal. . . . . Poor
  Side . . . . Good
Airbags:
  Head . . . . Std. Row 1 & 2 Curtain
  Chest/Torso . . . . Std. Row 1 Torso from Seat
  Roll-Sensing Side Airbag . . . . —
  Out-of-Position Test. . . . . . . Meets Requirements
Children:
  Built-in Child Safety Seat . . . . —
  Automatic Window Reversal . . . . —
Crash Avoidance:
  Frontal Collision Warning . . . . —
  Electronic Stability Control . . . . Standard
  Lane Departure Warning . . . . —
  Brake Assist . . . . —
General:
  Automatic Crash Notification . . . . —
  Daytime Running Lights. . . . . Standard
  Automatic Door-Locking . . . . —
Safety Belt:
  Adjustable Front Belt . . . . Standard

Mitsubishi Galant

Specifications

Drive . . . . FWD
Engine. 2.4-liter I4
Transmission . . . . 4-sp. Automatic
Tow Rating (lbs.). . . . . —
Head/Leg Room (in.). Roomy-39.6/42.6
Interior Space (cu. ft.). Average-101
Cargo Space (cu. ft.) Cramped-13.3
Wheelbase/Length (in.) 108.3/191.1

*Combines results of both front and side tests in relation to all tests for 2010 vehicles.

213

Mitsubishi Lancer

Compact

Ratings—10 Best, 1 Worst

Combo Crash Tests	6
Safety Features	4
Rollover	6
Preventive Maintenance	6
Repair Costs	5
Warranty	9
Fuel Economy	4
Complaints	1
Insurance Costs	3
OVERALL RATING	**5**

Mitsubishi Lancer

Mitsubishi Lancer

At-a-Glance

Status. . . . . Unchanged
Year Series Started 2008
Twins . . . . –
Body Styles. . . . . Sedan, Hatchback
Seating 5
Anti-Theft Device . . . Opt. Pass. Immob. & Alarm, or both opt.
Parking Index Rating . . . . Very Easy
Where Made . . . . Mizushima, Japan / Okazaki, Japan
Fuel Factor
  MPG Rating (city/hwy) Poor-17/25
  Driving Range (mi.). . . . . Very Short-303.9
  Fuel Type. . . . . Premium
  Annual Fuel Cost. . . . . High-$2190
  Greenhouse Gas Emissions (tons/yr.) High-9.2
  Barrels of Oil Used per year. High-17.1

How the Competition Rates

Competitors	Rating	Pg.
Honda Civic	8	146
Mazda 3	6	196
Subaru Impreza	4	237

Price Range	Retail	Markup
DE Manual Transmission	$14,540	5%
ES Automatic Transmission	$17,640	5%
GTS Manual Transmission	$18,540	5%
Ralliart	$26,690	5%

Safety Checklist

Crash Tests:
  Frontal . . . . Good
  Side. . . . . Average
Airbags:
  Head . . . . Std. Row 1 & 2 Curtain
  Chest/Torso . . . . Std. Row 1 Torso from Seat
  Roll-Sensing Side Airbag . . . . –
  Out-of-Position Test. . . . . . . Meets Requirements
Children:
  Built-in Child Safety Seat . . . . –
  Automatic Window Reversal . . . . Std. Driver
Crash Avoidance:
  Frontal Collision Warning . . . . –
  Electronic Stability Control . . . . Standard
  Lane Departure Warning . . . . –
  Brake Assist . . . . Standard
General:
  Automatic Crash Notification . . . . –
  Daytime Running Lights. . . . . Standard
  Automatic Door-Locking . . . . –
Safety Belt:
  Adjustable Front Belt . . . . Standard

Mitsubishi Lancer

Specifications

Drive . . . . FWD
Engine. 2.0-liter I4
Transmission . . . . 6-sp. Automatic
Tow Rating (lbs.). . . . . –
Head/Leg Room (in.). Average-39.6/42.2
Interior Space (cu. ft.) Cramped-94.8
Cargo Space (cu. ft.) . . . . . Very Cramped-11.6
Wheelbase/Length (in.). 103.7/180

*Combines results of both front and side tests in relation to all tests for 2010 vehicles.

Ratings—10 Best, 1 Worst

Combo Crash Tests	6
Safety Features	7
Rollover	3
Preventive Maintenance	6
Repair Costs	5
Warranty	9
Fuel Economy	5
Complaints	3
Insurance Costs	5
OVERALL RATING	**6**

Mitsubishi Outlander

Mitsubishi Outlander

At-a-Glance

Status. . . . . Unchanged
Year Series Started 2007
Twins . . . . –
Body Styles. . . . . SUV
Seating 5
Anti-Theft Device. . . . . Std. Pass. Immob. & Pass. Alarm/Std. Active
Parking Index Rating . . . . Easy
Where Made . . . . Mizushima, Japan

Fuel Factor
MPG Rating (city/hwy) Average-19/25
Driving Range (mi.) Short-353.6
Fuel Type . . . . Premium
Annual Fuel Cost. . . . . Average-$2042
Greenhouse Gas Emissions (tons/yr.) High-8.7
Barrels of Oil Used per year. High-16.3

How the Competition Rates

Competitors	Rating	Pg.
Honda CR-V	10	148
Hyundai Tucson	–	161
Toyota RAV4	4	251

Price Range

	Retail	Markup
ES FWD	$20,840	5%
SE AWD	$22,240	6%
XLS FWD	$24,990	6%
GT AWD	$29,250	6%

Safety Checklist

Crash Tests:
Frontal . . . . Average
Side . . . . Good
Airbags:
Head . . . . Std. Row 1 & 2 Curtain
Chest/Torso . . . . Std. Row 1 Torso from Seat
Roll-Sensing Side Airbag . . . . Standard
Out-of-Position Test. . . . . . . Meets Requirements
Children:
Built-in Child Safety Seat . . . . –
Automatic Window Reversal . . . . Std. Driver
Crash Avoidance:
Frontal Collision Warning . . . . –
Electronic Stability Control . . . . Standard
Lane Departure Warning . . . . –
Brake Assist . . . . –
General:
Automatic Crash Notification . . . . –
Daytime Running Lights. . . . . Standard
Automatic Door-Locking . . . . –
Safety Belt:
Adjustable Front Belt . . . . Standard

Mitsubishi Outlander

Specifications

Drive . . . . FWD
Engine 3.0-liter V6
Transmission . . . . 6-sp. Automatic
Tow Rating (lbs.) Low-2000
Head/Leg Room (in.) Average-40.3/41.6
Interior Space (cu. ft.) Average-100.4
Cargo Space (cu. ft.) Cramped-14.9
Wheelbase/Length (in.) 105.1/182.7

*Combines results of both front and side tests in relation to all tests for 2010 vehicles.

Ratings—10 Best, 1 Worst

Combo Crash Tests	–
Safety Features	3
Rollover	10
Preventive Maintenance	10
Repair Costs	–
Warranty	2
Fuel Economy	5
Complaints	–
Insurance Costs	1
OVERALL RATING	**–**

Nissan 370Z

Nissan 370Z

At-a-Glance

Status	All New
Year Series Started	2010
Twins	–
Body Styles	Coupe, Convertible
Seating	2
Anti-Theft Device	Std. Pass. Immobil. & Pass. Alarm
Parking Index Rating	Very Easy
Where Made	Tochigi, Japan

Fuel Factor

MPG Rating (city/hwy)	Average-18/25
Driving Range (mi.)	Long-391.3
Fuel Type	Premium
Annual Fuel Cost	Average-$2112
Greenhouse Gas Emissions (tons/yr.)	High-8.7
Barrels of Oil Used per year	High-16.3

How the Competition Rates

Competitors	Rating	Pg.
Ford Mustang	7	140
Hyundai Genesis	9	158
Mazda MX-5 Miata	–	201

Price Range

	Retail	Markup
Base Manual Transmission	$36,970	8%
Base Automatic Transmission	$38,270	8%
Touring Manual Transmission	$40,520	8%
Touring Automatic Transmission	$41,820	8%

Safety Checklist

Crash Tests:
- Frontal . . . . –
- Side . . . . –

Airbags:
- Head . . . . Std. Row 1 Curtain
- Chest/Torso Std. Row 1 Torso & Pelvis from Seat
- Roll-Sensing Side Airbag . . . . –
- Out-of-Position Test . . . . . . Meets Requirements

Children:
- Built-in Child Safety Seat . . . . –
- Automatic Window Reversal . . . . Std. Front

Crash Avoidance:
- Frontal Collision Warning . . . . –
- Electronic Stability Control . . . . Standard
- Lane Departure Warning . . . . –
- Brake Assist . . . . Standard

General:
- Automatic Crash Notification . . . . –
- Daytime Running Lights . . . . –
- Automatic Door-Locking . . . . Standard

Safety Belt:
- Adjustable Front Belt . . . . –

Nissan 370Z

Specifications

Drive	RWD
Engine	3.7-liter V6
Transmission	7-sp. Automatic
Tow Rating (lbs.)	–
Head/Leg Room (in.)	Average-38.7/42.9
Interior Space (cu. ft.)	Very Cramped-52.3
Cargo Space (cu. ft.)	Very Cramped-4.2
Wheelbase/Length (in.)	100.4/167.2

*Combines results of both front and side tests in relation to all tests for 2010 vehicles.

Ratings—10 Best, 1 Worst

Combo Crash Tests	8
Safety Features	6
Rollover	8
Preventive Maintenance	7
Repair Costs	7
Warranty	2
Fuel Economy	8
Complaints	9
Insurance Costs	3
OVERALL RATING	**9**

Nissan Altima

Nissan Altima

At-a-Glance

Status . . . . Appearance Change
Year Series Started 2007
Twins . . . . −
Body Styles . . . . Sedan
Seating 5
Anti-Theft Device. . Std. Pass. Immobil. & Pass. Alarm
Parking Index Rating . . . . Easy
Where Made . . . . Decherd, TN / Canton, MS
Fuel Factor
  MPG Rating (city/hwy) Good-23/32
  Driving Range (mi.) . . . . Very Long-526.7
  Fuel Type. . . . . Regular
  Annual Fuel Cost . . . . Very Low-$1538
  Greenhouse Gas Emissions (tons/yr.) Low-6.8
  Barrels of Oil Used per year Low-12.7

How the Competition Rates

Competitors	Rating	Pg.
Chevrolet Malibu	9	114
Honda Accord	8	144
Toyota Camry	7	245

Price Range	Retail	Markup
2.5	$19,900	7%
2.5 S	$21,840	7%
3.5 SR	$24,520	8%

Safety Checklist

Crash Tests:
  Frontal . . . . Good
  Side . . . . Good
Airbags:
  Head . . . . Std. Row 1 & 2 Curtain
  Chest/Torso Std. Row 1 Torso & Pelvis from Seat
  Roll-Sensing Side Airbag . . . . −
  Out-of-Position Test. . . . . . . Meets Requirements
Children:
  Built-in Child Safety Seat . . . . −
  Auto. Window Reversal. Std. Driver & Opt. Fr. Pass.
Crash Avoidance:
  Frontal Collision Warning . . . . −
  Electronic Stability Control . . . . Standard
  Lane Departure Warning . . . . −
  Brake Assist . . . . −
General:
  Automatic Crash Notification . . . . −
  Daytime Running Lights . . . . −
  Automatic Door-Locking. . . . . Standard
Safety Belt:
  Adjustable Front Belt . . . . Standard

Nissan Altima

Specifications

Drive . . . . FWD
Engine. 2.5-liter I4
Transmission . . . . 6-sp. Automatic
Tow Rating (lbs.) . . . . −
Head/Leg Room (in.) . . . . . . Very Roomy-40.6/44.1
Interior Space (cu. ft.) Average-100.7
Cargo Space (cu. ft.) Cramped-15.3
Wheelbase/Length (in.) 109.3/190.7

*Combines results of both front and side tests in relation to all tests for 2010 vehicles.

Ratings—10 Best, 1 Worst

Combo Crash Tests	3
Safety Features	5
Rollover	9
Preventive Maintenance	7
Repair Costs	7
Warranty	2
Fuel Economy	8
Complaints	9
Insurance Costs	1
OVERALL RATING	**6**

Nissan Altima Coupe

Nissan Altima Coupe

At-a-Glance

Status . . . . Appearance Change
Year Series Started 2008
Twins . . . . —
Body Styles . . . . Coupe
Seating 5
Anti-Theft Device. . Std. Pass. Immobil. & Pass. Alarm
Parking Index Rating . . . . Very Easy
Where Made . . . . Decherd, TN / Smyrna, TN
Fuel Factor
  MPG Rating (city/hwy) Good-23/32
  Driving Range (mi.) . . . . Very Long-526.7
  Fuel Type. . . . . Regular
  Annual Fuel Cost . . . . Very Low-$1538
  Greenhouse Gas Emissions (tons/yr.) . . Average-7.1
  Barrels of Oil Used per year Low-13.2

How the Competition Rates

Competitors	Rating	Pg.
Mitsubishi Lancer	5	214
Scion tC	3	232
Subaru Impreza	4	237

Price Range

Price Range	Retail	Markup
2.5 S Manual Trans.	$22,440	7%
2.5 S CV Trans.	$22,940	7%
3.5 SR CV Trans.	$27,270	8%
3.5 SR Manual Trans.	$29,600	8%

Safety Checklist

Crash Tests:
  Frontal. . . . . Very Poor
  Side . . . . Good
Airbags:
  Head . . . . Std. Row 1 & 2 Curtain
  Chest/Torso Std. Row 1 Torso & Pelvis from Seat
  Roll-Sensing Side Airbag . . . . —
  Out-of-Position Test. . . . . . . Meets Requirements
Children:
  Built-in Child Safety Seat . . . . —
  Auto. Window Reversal. Std. Driver & Opt. Fr. Pass.
Crash Avoidance:
  Frontal Collision Warning . . . . —
  Electronic Stability Control . . . . Standard
  Lane Departure Warning . . . . —
  Brake Assist . . . . —
General:
  Automatic Crash Notification . . . . —
  Daytime Running Lights . . . . —
  Automatic Door-Locking. . . . . Standard
Safety Belt:
  Adjustable Front Belt . . . . —

Nissan Altima Coupe

Specifications

Drive . . . . FWD
Engine. 2.5-liter I4
Transmission . . . . 6-sp. Automatic
Tow Rating (lbs.) . . . . —
Head/Leg Room (in.) Roomy-39.7/42.5
Interior Space (cu. ft.) . . . . Very Cramped-89.3
Cargo Space (cu. ft.) . . . . Very Cramped-8.2
Wheelbase/Length (in.) 105.3/180.9

*Combines results of both front and side tests in relation to all tests for 2010 vehicles.

Ratings—10 Best, 1 Worst	Armada	QX56
Combo Crash Tests	–	–
Safety Features	8	9
Rollover	2	2
Preventive Maintenance	5	6
Repair Costs	4	3
Warranty	2	8
Fuel Economy	1	1
Complaints	3	6
Insurance Costs	5	8
OVERALL RATING	–	–

Nissan Armada

Infiniti QX56

At-a-Glance

Status	Unchanged
Year Series Started	2004
Twins	Infiniti QX56
Body Styles	SUV
Seating	7
Anti-Theft Device	Std. Pass. Immobil. & Pass. Alarm
Parking Index Rating	Very Hard
Where Made	Canton, MS

Fuel Factor

MPG Rating (city/hwy)	Very Poor-12/18
Driving Range (mi.)	Long-395.3
Fuel Type	Regular/E85
Annual Fuel Cost	Very High-$2869
Greenhouse Gas Emissions (tons/yr.)	Very High-13.1
Barrels of Oil Used per year	Very High-24.5

How the Competition Rates

Competitors	Rating	Pg.
Chevrolet Tahoe	8	117
Ford Expedition	6	134
Toyota Sequoia	–	252

Price Range	Retail	Markup
SE RWD	$37,210	10%
Titanium RWD	$42,140	10%
Titanium 4WD	$44,940	10%
Platinum 4WD	$52,190	10%

Safety Checklist

Crash Tests:
Frontal	Poor
Side	–

Airbags:
Head	Std. Curtain All Rows
Chest/Torso	Std. Row 1 Torso from Seat
Roll-Sensing Side Airbag	Standard
Out-of-Position Test	Meets Requirements

Children:
Built-in Child Safety Seat	–
Automatic Window Reversal	Opt. Front

Crash Avoidance:
Frontal Collision Warning	–
Electronic Stability Control	Standard
Lane Departure Warning	–
Brake Assist	Standard

General:
Automatic Crash Notification	–
Daytime Running Lights	–
Automatic Door-Locking	Standard

Safety Belt:
Adjustable Front Belt	Standard

Nissan Armada

Specifications

Drive	RWD
Engine	5.6-liter V8
Transmission	5-sp. Automatic
Tow Rating (lbs.)	Very High-9100
Head/Leg Room (in.)	Roomy-41/41.8
Interior Space (cu. ft.)	–
Cargo Space (cu. ft.)	Average-20
Wheelbase/Length (in.)	123.2/207.7

*Combines results of both front and side tests in relation to all tests for 2010 vehicles.

Ratings—10 Best, 1 Worst

Combo Crash Tests	3
Safety Features	7
Rollover	3
Preventive Maintenance	–
Repair Costs	–
Warranty	2
Fuel Economy	9
Complaints	–
Insurance Costs	10
OVERALL RATING	**5**

Nissan Cube

Nissan Cube

At-a-Glance

Status. . . . . Unchanged
Year Series Started 2009
Twins . . . .–
Body Styles 4-Door
Seating. 5
Anti-Theft Device . . . . . . Std. Active Immobil. & Alarm
Parking Index Rating . . . . Very Easy
Where Made. . . . . Oppama, Japan

Fuel Factor
MPG Rating (city/hwy) . . . . Very Good-28/30
Driving Range (mi.) Average-381.0
Fuel Type. . . . . Regular
Annual Fuel Cost . . . . Very Low-$1403
Greenhouse Gas Emissions (tons/yr.) Low-6.3
Barrels of Oil Used per year Low-11.8

How the Competition Rates

Competitors	Rating	Pg.
Kia Soul	6	181
Mini Cooper	6	212
Scion xD	4	234

Price Range

Price Range	Retail	Markup
Base Manual Trans.	$13,990	4%
S Manual Trans.	$14,690	4%
SL Auto. Trans.	$16,790	4%
Krom Auto. Trans.	$19,370	4%

Safety Checklist

Crash Tests:
Frontal. . . . . Very Poor
Side . . . . Good
Airbags:
Head . . . . Std. Row 1 & 2 Curtain
Chest/Torso . . Std. Row 1 Torso & Pelvis from Seat
Roll-Sensing Side Airbag . . . . –
Out-of-Position Test. . . . . . Meets Requirements
Children:
Built-in Child Safety Seat . . . . –
Automatic Window Reversal . . . . Standard
Crash Avoidance:
Frontal Collision Warning . . . . –
Electronic Stability Control . . . . Standard
Lane Departure Warning . . . . –
Brake Assist . . . . Standard
General:
Automatic Crash Notification . . . . –
Daytime Running Lights . . . . –
Automatic Door-Locking. . . . . Standard
Safety Belt:
Adjustable Front Belt . . . . Standard

Nissan Cube

Specifications

Drive . . . . FWD
Engine. 1.8-liter I4
Transmission . . . . CVT
Tow Rating (lbs.) . . . . –
Head/Leg Room (in.) . . . . . . Very Roomy-42.6/42.4
Interior Space (cu. ft.) Cramped-97.7
Cargo Space (cu. ft.) . . . . Very Cramped-11.4
Wheelbase/Length (in.) 99.6/156.7

*Combines results of both front and side tests in relation to all tests for 2010 vehicles.

Ratings—10 Best, 1 Worst

Combo Crash Tests	4
Safety Features	5
Rollover	2
Preventive Maintenance	7
Repair Costs	8
Warranty	2
Fuel Economy	2
Complaints	7
Insurance Costs	5
OVERALL RATING	**4**

Nissan Frontier

Nissan Frontier

At-a-Glance

Status. . . . . Unchanged
Year Series Started 2005
Twins . . . . –
Body Styles. . . . . Crew, Regular, Extended Cabs
Seating. 5
Anti-Theft Device . . . . . . Opt. Pass. Immobil. & Alarm
Parking Index Rating . . . . Very Hard
Where Made . . . . Smyrna, TN

Fuel Factor
MPG Rating (city/hwy) . . . . Very Poor-14/19
Driving Range (mi.) . . . . Very Short-335.1
Fuel Type. . . . . Regular
Annual Fuel Cost. . . . . Very High-$2550
Greenhouse Gas Emissions (tons/yr.) . Very High-11.4
Barrels of Oil Used per year . . . . Very High-21.4

How the Competition Rates

Competitors	Rating	Pg.
Chevrolet Colorado	3	109
Dodge Dakota	7	127
Toyota Tacoma	2	254

Price Range

Price Range	Retail	Markup
XE King Cab 2WD I4 Manual	$17,540	5%
SE Crew Cab 4WD LWB Auto.	$26,840	7%
PRO-4X Crew Cab 4WD Auto.	$29,060	8%
LE Crew Cab 4WD LWB Auto.	$29,820	8%

Safety Checklist

Crash Tests:
Frontal. . . . . Very Poor
Side . . . . Good
Airbags:
Head . . . . Std. Row 1 & 2 Curtain
Chest/Torso Std. Row 1 Torso fr. Seat & Dr. Pelvis fr. St.
Roll-Sensing Side Airbag . . . . Standard
Out-of-Position Test. . . . . . . Meets Requirements
Children:
Built-in Child Safety Seat . . . . –
Automatic Window Reversal . . . . –
Crash Avoidance:
Frontal Collision Warning . . . . –
Electronic Stability Control . . . . Optional
Lane Departure Warning . . . . –
Brake Assist . . . . –
General:
Automatic Crash Notification . . . . –
Daytime Running Lights . . . . –
Automatic Door-Locking. . . . . Standard
Safety Belt:
Adjustable Front Belt . . . . Standard

Nissan Frontier

Specifications

Drive 4WD
Engine 4.0-liter V6
Transmission . . . . 5-sp. Automatic
Tow Rating (lbs.) High-6100
Head/Leg Room (in.) Roomy-40/42.4
Interior Space (cu. ft.) Average-101.1
Cargo Space (cu. ft.) Roomy-27.1
Wheelbase/Length (in.) 125.9/205.5

*Combines results of both front and side tests in relation to all tests for 2010 vehicles.

Ratings—10 Best, 1 Worst

Combo Crash Tests	8
Safety Features	7
Rollover	8
Preventive Maintenance	7
Repair Costs	6
Warranty	2
Fuel Economy	5
Complaints	4
Insurance Costs	3
OVERALL RATING	**7**

Nissan Maxima

Nissan Maxima

At-a-Glance

Status. . . . . Unchanged
Year Series Started 2009
Twins . . . . –
Body Styles . . . . Sedan
Seating. 5
Anti-Theft Device. . Std. Pass. Immobil. & Pass. Alarm
Parking Index Rating . . . . Average
Where Made . . . . Decherd, TN / Smyrna, TN

Fuel Factor
MPG Rating (city/hwy) Average-19/26
Driving Range (mi.) . . . . Very Long-432.4
Fuel Type. . . . . Premium
Annual Fuel Cost. . . . . Average-$2012
Greenhouse Gas Emissions (tons/yr.) High-8.3
Barrels of Oil Used per year. Average-15.6

How the Competition Rates

Competitors	Rating	Pg.
Chevrolet Impala	9	113
Honda Accord	8	144
Toyota Camry	7	245

Price Range	Retail	Markup
S	$30,460	9%
SV	$33,180	9%

Safety Checklist

Crash Tests:
Frontal . . . . Good
Side . . . . Very Good
Airbags:
Head . . . . Std. Row 1 & 2 Curtain
Chest/Torso Std. Row 1 Torso & Pelvis from Seat
Roll-Sensing Side Airbag . . . . –
Out-of-Position Test. . . . . . . Meets Requirements
Children:
Built-in Child Safety Seat . . . . –
Automatic Window Reversal Std. Front, Opt. Rear
Crash Avoidance:
Frontal Collision Warning . . . . –
Electronic Stability Control . . . . Standard
Lane Departure Warning . . . . –
Brake Assist . . . . Standard
General:
Automatic Crash Notification . . . . –
Daytime Running Lights . . . . –
Automatic Door-Locking. . . . . Standard
Safety Belt:
Adjustable Front Belt . . . . Standard

Nissan Maxima

Specifications

Drive . . . . FWD
Engine 3.5-liter V6
Transmission . . . . CVT
Tow Rating (lbs.). . . . . Very Low-1000
Head/Leg Room (in.). Roomy-38.5/43.8
Interior Space (cu. ft.) Cramped-95.8
Cargo Space (cu. ft.) Cramped-14.2
Wheelbase/Length (in.) 109.3/190.6

*Combines results of both front and side tests in relation to all tests for 2010 vehicles.

Ratings—10 Best, 1 Worst

Combo Crash Tests	1
Safety Features	9
Rollover	3
Preventive Maintenance	6
Repair Costs	–
Warranty	2
Fuel Economy	4
Complaints	1
Insurance Costs	8
OVERALL RATING	**2**

Nissan Murano

Nissan Murano

At-a-Glance

Status. . . . . Unchanged
Year Series Started 2009
Twins . . . . –
Body Styles. . . . . SUV
Seating 5
Anti-Theft Device. . Std. Pass. Immobil. & Pass. Alarm
Parking Index Rating . . . . Hard
Where Made. . . . . Kyushu, Japan

Fuel Factor
 MPG Rating (city/hwy). Poor-18/23
 Driving Range (mi.) . . . . Very Long-433.0
 Fuel Type. . . . . Premium
 Annual Fuel Cost. . . . . High-$2180
 Greenhouse Gas Emissions (tons/yr.) High-9.2
 Barrels of Oil Used per year. High-17.1

How the Competition Rates

Competitors	Rating	Pg.
Acura MDX	–	81
Honda Pilot	7	153
Toyota Highlander	4	248

Price Range

Price Range	Retail	Markup
S FWD	$28,050	9%
SL FWD	$29,600	9%
SL AWD	$31,200	9%
LE AWD	$38,180	9%

Safety Checklist

Crash Tests:
 Frontal. . . . . Very Poor
 Side. . . . . Poor
Airbags:
 Head . . . . Std. Row 1 & 2 Curtain
 Chest/Torso Std. Row 1 Torso & Pelvis from Seat
 Roll-Sensing Side Airbag . . . . Standard
 Out-of-Position Test. . . . . . . Meets Requirements
Children:
 Built-in Child Safety Seat . . . . –
 Automatic Window Reversal. . . . . Std. Front
Crash Avoidance:
 Frontal Collision Warning . . . . –
 Electronic Stability Control . . . . Standard
 Lane Departure Warning . . . . –
 Brake Assist . . . . Standard
General:
 Automatic Crash Notification . . . . –
 Daytime Running Lights . . . . –
 Automatic Door-Locking. . . . . Standard
Safety Belt:
 Adjustable Front Belt . . . . Standard

Nissan Murano

Specifications

Drive. . . . . AWD
Engine 3.5-liter V6
Transmission . . . . CVT
Tow Rating (lbs.) Average-3500
Head/Leg Room (in.) . . . . . . Very Roomy-40.1/43.6
Interior Space (cu. ft.) Roomy-108.8
Cargo Space (cu. ft.) Roomy-30
Wheelbase/Length (in.) 111.2/188.5

*Combines results of both front and side tests in relation to all tests for 2010 vehicles.

Ratings—10 Best, 1 Worst

Combo Crash Tests	–
Safety Features	7
Rollover	1
Preventive Maintenance	7
Repair Costs	7
Warranty	2
Fuel Economy	2
Complaints	6
Insurance Costs	10
OVERALL RATING	–

Nissan Pathfinder

Nissan Pathfinder

At-a-Glance

Status	Unchanged
Year Series Started	2005
Twins	–
Body Styles	SUV
Seating	7/8
Anti-Theft Device	Std. Pass. Immobil. & Pass. Alarm
Parking Index Rating	Hard
Where Made	Smyrna, TN

Fuel Factor

MPG Rating (city/hwy)	Very Poor-15/22
Driving Range (mi.)	Short-369.4
Fuel Type	Premium
Annual Fuel Cost	Very High-$2485
Greenhouse Gas Emissions (tons/yr.)	Very High-10.8
Barrels of Oil Used per year	Very High-20.1

How the Competition Rates

Competitors	Rating	Pg.
Chevrolet Equinox	6	111
Toyota 4Runner	–	243
Volvo XC90	10	270

Price Range	Retail	Markup
S RWD	$27,440	7%
SE 4WD	$32,610	8%
LE 2WD	$36,910	8%
LE V8 4WD	$42,160	8%

Safety Checklist

Crash Tests:
- Frontal................................ Very Poor
- Side .... –

Airbags:
- Head .... Std. Curtain All Rows
- Chest/Torso . Std. Row 1 Torso/Pelvis fr. St. or Torso Fr. Pass. St.
- Roll-Sensing Side Airbag .... Standard
- Out-of-Position Test....... Meets Requirements

Children:
- Built-in Child Safety Seat .... –
- Automatic Window Reversal .... Opt. Front

Crash Avoidance:
- Frontal Collision Warning .... –
- Electronic Stability Control .... Standard
- Lane Departure Warning .... –
- Brake Assist .... –

General:
- Automatic Crash Notification .... –
- Daytime Running Lights .... –
- Automatic Door-Locking .... Standard

Safety Belt:
- Adjustable Front Belt .... Standard

Nissan Pathfinder

Specifications

Drive	RWD
Engine	4.0-liter V6
Transmission	5-sp. Automatic
Tow Rating (lbs.)	High-6000
Head/Leg Room (in.)	Roomy-40/42.4
Interior Space (cu. ft.)	Average-100.6
Cargo Space (cu. ft.)	Very Roomy-48.9
Wheelbase/Length (in.)	112.2/192.3

*Combines results of both front and side tests in relation to all tests for 2010 vehicles.

Ratings—10 Best, 1 Worst

Combo Crash Tests	3
Safety Features	8
Rollover	2
Preventive Maintenance	7
Repair Costs	6
Warranty	2
Fuel Economy	7
Complaints	6
Insurance Costs	8
OVERALL RATING	**5**

Nissan Rogue

Nissan Rogue

At-a-Glance

Status. . . . . Unchanged
Year Series Started 2008
Twins . . . . —
Body Styles. . . . . SUV
Seating. 5
Anti-Theft Device. . Std. Pass. Immobil. & Pass. Alarm
Parking Index Rating . . . . Average
Where Made. . . . . Kyushu, Japan

Fuel Factor
  MPG Rating (city/hwy) Good-22/27
  Driving Range (mi.) Average-381.6
  Fuel Type. . . . . Regular
  Annual Fuel Cost . . . . Low-$1688
  Greenhouse Gas Emissions (tons/yr.) . . Average-7.7
  Barrels of Oil Used per year. Average-14.3

How the Competition Rates

Competitors	Rating	Pg.
Dodge Journey	7	129
Kia Sorento	—	180
Volvo XC60	—	269

Price Range	Retail	Markup
S FWD	$20,340	5%
S AWD	$21,540	5%
SL FWD	$21,930	7%
SL AWD	$23,130	7%

Safety Checklist

Crash Tests:
  Frontal. . . . . Very Poor
  Side . . . . Average
Airbags:
  Head . . . . Std. Row 1 & 2 Curtain
  Chest/Torso . Std. Row 1 Torso/Pelvis fr. St. or Torso Fr. Pass. St.
  Roll-Sensing Side Airbag . . . . Standard
  Out-of-Position Test. . . . . . . Meets Requirements
Children:
  Built-in Child Safety Seat . . . . —
  Automatic Window Reversal. . . . . Opt. Driver
Crash Avoidance:
  Frontal Collision Warning . . . . —
  Electronic Stability Control . . . . Standard
  Lane Departure Warning . . . . —
  Brake Assist . . . . Standard
General:
  Automatic Crash Notification . . . . —
  Daytime Running Lights . . . . —
  Automatic Door-Locking. . . . . Standard
Safety Belt:
  Adjustable Front Belt . . . . Standard

Nissan Rogue

Specifications

Drive . . . . FWD
Engine. 2.5-liter I4
Transmission . . . . CVT
Tow Rating (lbs.). . . . . Very Low-1000
Head/Leg Room (in.). Roomy-40.4/42.5
Interior Space (cu. ft.) . . . . Very Roomy-126.4
Cargo Space (cu. ft.) Roomy-28.9
Wheelbase/Length (in.) 105.9/182.9

*Combines results of both front and side tests in relation to all tests for 2010 vehicles.

Ratings—10 Best, 1 Worst

Combo Crash Tests	5
Safety Features	4
Rollover	7
Preventive Maintenance	7
Repair Costs	8
Warranty	2
Fuel Economy	10
Complaints	7
Insurance Costs	1
OVERALL RATING	**7**

Nissan Sentra

Nissan Sentra

At-a-Glance

Status . . . . Appearance Change
Year Series Started 2007
Twins . . . . —
Body Styles . . . . Sedan
Seating. 5
Anti-Theft Device Std. Pass. Immobil./Opt. Pass. Immob. & Alarm
Parking Index Rating . . . . Easy
Where Made . . . . Tsuru, Mexico

Fuel Factor
MPG Rating (city/hwy) . . . . Very Good-26/34
Driving Range (mi.) Long-421.6
Fuel Type. . . . . Regular
Annual Fuel Cost . . . . Very Low-$1393
Greenhouse Gas Emissions (tons/yr.) Low-6.3
Barrels of Oil Used per year Low-11.8

How the Competition Rates

Competitors	Rating	Pg.
Chevrolet Cobalt	4	108
Honda Civic	8	146
Toyota Corolla	5	246

Price Range

Price Range	Retail	Markup
Base Manual Trans.	$15,420	4%
SR Auto. Trans.	$17,160	7%
SE-R Auto. Trans.	$19,580	7%
SE-R Spec V Manual	$20,080	7%

Safety Checklist

Crash Tests:
Frontal . . . . Good
Side. . . . . Poor
Airbags:
Head . . . . Std. Row 1 & 2 Curtain
Chest/Torso. . . Std. Row 1 Torso & Pelvis from Seat
Roll-Sensing Side Airbag . . . . —
Out-of-Position Test. . . . . . . Meets Requirements
Children:
Built-in Child Safety Seat . . . . —
Automatic Window Reversal . . . . Opt. Front
Crash Avoidance:
Frontal Collision Warning . . . . —
Electronic Stability Control . . . . Optional
Lane Departure Warning . . . . —
Brake Assist . . . . —
General:
Automatic Crash Notification . . . . —
Daytime Running Lights . . . . —
Automatic Door-Locking. . . . . Standard
Safety Belt:
Adjustable Front Belt . . . . Standard

Nissan Sentra

Specifications

Drive . . . . FWD
Engine. 2.0-liter I4
Transmission . . . . CVT
Tow Rating (lbs.). . . . . —
Head/Leg Room (in.). Roomy-40.6/42.4
Interior Space (cu. ft.) Cramped-97.4
Cargo Space (cu. ft.) Cramped-13.1
Wheelbase/Length (in.) 105.7/179.8

*Combines results of both front and side tests in relation to all tests for 2010 vehicles.

Ratings—10 Best, 1 Worst

Combo Crash Tests	–
Safety Features	7
Rollover	3
Preventive Maintenance	5
Repair Costs	5
Warranty	2
Fuel Economy	1
Complaints	1
Insurance Costs	3
OVERALL RATING	**–**

Nissan Titan

Nissan Titan

At-a-Glance

Status	Unchanged
Year Series Started	2004
Twins	–
Body Styles	King, Crew Cab
Seating	5
Anti-Theft Device	Std. Pass. Immobil. & Pass. Alarm
Parking Index Rating	Very Hard
Where Made	Canton, MS

Fuel Factor

MPG Rating (city/hwy)	Very Poor-13/18
Driving Range (mi.)	Long-416.0
Fuel Type	Regular/E85
Annual Fuel Cost	Very High-$2726
Greenhouse Gas Emissions (tons/yr.)	Very High-12.2
Barrels of Oil Used per year	Very High-22.8

How the Competition Rates

Competitors	Rating	Pg.
Chevrolet Silverado	8	115
Ford F-150	9	136
Honda Ridgeline	7	154

Price Range

	Retail	Markup
XE King Cab 79.1" RWD	$26,320	10%
SE King Cab 79.1" 4WD	$31,170	10%
SE Crew Cab 87" 4WD	$33,850	10%
LE Crew Cab 67.3" 4WD	$39,120	10%

Safety Checklist

Crash Tests:
Frontal . . . . Poor
Side . . . . –
Airbags:
Head . . . . Std. Row 1 & 2 Curtain
Chest/Torso . . . . Std. Row 1 Torso from Seat
Roll-Sensing Side Airbag . . . . Standard
Out-of-Position Test . . . . Meets Requirements
Children:
Built-in Child Safety Seat . . . . –
Automatic Window Reversal . . . . Opt. Front
Crash Avoidance:
Frontal Collision Warning . . . . –
Electronic Stability Control . . . . Standard
Lane Departure Warning . . . . –
Brake Assist . . . . Optional
General:
Automatic Crash Notification . . . . –
Daytime Running Lights . . . . –
Automatic Door-Locking . . . . Standard
Safety Belt:
Adjustable Front Belt . . . . Standard

Nissan Titan

Specifications

Drive	RWD
Engine	5.6-liter V8
Transmission	5-sp. Auto. w/Overdrive
Tow Rating (lbs.)	Very High-9500
Head/Leg Room (in.)	Roomy-41/41.8
Interior Space (cu. ft.)	–
Cargo Space (cu. ft.)	–
Wheelbase/Length (in.)	139.8/224.6

*Combines results of both front and side tests in relation to all tests for 2010 vehicles.

Ratings—10 Best, 1 Worst

Combo Crash Tests	1
Safety Features	4
Rollover	5
Preventive Maintenance	7
Repair Costs	8
Warranty	2
Fuel Economy	10
Complaints	7
Insurance Costs	3
OVERALL RATING	**5**

Nissan Versa

Nissan Versa

At-a-Glance

```
Status . . . . . . . . . . . . . . . . . . . Appearance Change
Year Series Started . . . . . . . . . . . . . . . . . . . 2006
Twins . . . . . . . . . . . . . . . . . . . . . . . . . . . . . . . . –
Body Styles. . . . . . . . . . . . . . . . Hatchback, Sedan
Seating. . . . . . . . . . . . . . . . . . . . . . . . . . . . . . . . 5
Anti-Theft Device Std. Pass. Immobi/Opt. Pass. Immobil. & Alarm
Parking Index Rating . . . . . . . . . . . . . . Very Easy
Where Made. . . . . . . . . . . . . . Aguascalientes, Mexico
```
Fuel Factor
```
  MPG Rating (city/hwy) . . . . . . . . . Very Good-28/34
  Driving Range (mi.) . . . . . . . . . . . . . Long-401.5
  Fuel Type. . . . . . . . . . . . . . . . . . . . . . . Regular
  Annual Fuel Cost . . . . . . . . . . . . Very Low-$1332
  Greenhouse Gas Emissions (tons/yr.) . . . . . Low-6.1
  Barrels of Oil Used per year . . . . . . . . . . Low-11.4
```

How the Competition Rates

Competitors	Rating	Pg.
Chevrolet Aveo	3	106
Honda Fit	8	150
Toyota Yaris	4	257

Price Range

Price Range	Retail	Markup
Base 1.6 Manual Trans.	$9,990	4%
1.6 Auto Trans.	$11,990	4%
1.8 S Auto. Trans.	$14,100	4%
1.8 SL CV Trans.	$16,530	4%

Safety Checklist

Crash Tests:
```
  Frontal. . . . . . . . . . . . . . . . . . . . . . . . Very Poor
  Side. . . . . . . . . . . . . . . . . . . . . . . . . . Very Poor
```
Airbags:
```
  Head . . . . . . . . . . . . . . Std. Row 1 & 2 Curtain
  Chest/Torso . . . . . . . Std. Row 1 Torso from Seat
  Roll-Sensing Side Airbag . . . . . . . . . . . . . . . . –
  Out-of-Position Test. . . . . . . Meets Requirements
```
Children:
```
  Built-in Child Safety Seat . . . . . . . . . . . . . . . . . –
  Automatic Window Reversal. . . . . . . . Opt. Driver
```
Crash Avoidance:
```
  Frontal Collision Warning . . . . . . . . . . . . . . . . . –
  Electronic Stability Control . . . . . . . . . . Standard
  Lane Departure Warning . . . . . . . . . . . . . . . . . –
  Brake Assist . . . . . . . . . . . . . . . . . . . . Optional
```
General:
```
  Automatic Crash Notification . . . . . . . . . . . . . . –
  Daytime Running Lights . . . . . . . . . . . . . . . . . –
  Automatic Door-Locking . . . . . . . . . . . Optional
```
Safety Belt:
```
  Adjustable Front Belt . . . . . . . . . . . . . . Standard
```

Nissan Versa

Specifications

```
Drive. . . . . . . . . . . . . . . . . . . . . . . . . . . . . . . . FWD
Engine. . . . . . . . . . . . . . . . . . . . . . . 1.8-liter I4
Transmission . . . . . . . . . . . . . . . . . . . . . . . . CVT
Tow Rating (lbs.) . . . . . . . . . . . . . . . . . . . . . . . . .
Head/Leg Room (in.) . . . . . . . . . . Average-40.6/41.4
Interior Space (cu. ft.) . . . . . . . . . . . . Cramped-95
Cargo Space (cu. ft.) . . . . . . . . . . . . Average-18
Wheelbase/Length (in.) . . . . . . . . . . . . 102.4/169.1
```

*Combines results of both front and side tests in relation to all tests for 2010 vehicles.

Ratings—10 Best, 1 Worst

Combo Crash Tests	5
Safety Features	5
Rollover	1
Preventive Maintenance	5
Repair Costs	8
Warranty	2
Fuel Economy	2
Complaints	3
Insurance Costs	10
OVERALL RATING	**3**

Nissan Xterra

Nissan Xterra

At-a-Glance

Status. . . . . Unchanged
Year Series Started 2005
Twins . . . . –
Body Styles. . . . . SUV
Seating. 5
Anti-Theft Device. . Std. Pass. Immobil. & Pass. Alarm
Parking Index Rating . . . . Easy
Where Made . . . . Smyrna, TN

Fuel Factor
MPG Rating (city/hwy). . . . . Very Poor-15/20
Driving Range (mi.). Short-356.6
Fuel Type. . . . . Regular
Annual Fuel Cost. . . . . High-$2396
Greenhouse Gas Emissions (tons/yr.) Very High-10.8
Barrels of Oil Used per year . . . . Very High-20.1

How the Competition Rates

Competitors	Rating	Pg.
Hyundai Santa Fe	–	159
Mazda CX-7	6	199
Volvo XC90	10	270

Price Range	Retail	Markup
X 2WD Manual Trans.	$22,450	5%
S 4WD Auto. Trans.	$27,470	6%
Off-Road 4WD Manual Trans.	$29,200	7%
SE 4WD Auto. Trans.	$30,400	7%

Safety Checklist

Crash Tests:
Frontal. . . . . Very Poor
Side . . . . Very Good
Airbags:
Head . . . . Std. Row 1 & 2 Curtain
Chest/Torso . Std. Row 1 Torso/Pelvis fr. St. or Torso Fr. Pass. St.
Roll-Sensing Side Airbag . . . . Standard
Out-of-Position Test. . . . . . . Meets Requirements
Children:
Built-in Child Safety Seat . . . . –
Automatic Window Reversal . . . . –
Crash Avoidance:
Frontal Collision Warning . . . . –
Electronic Stability Control . . . . Optional
Lane Departure Warning . . . . –
Brake Assist . . . . –
General:
Automatic Crash Notification . . . . –
Daytime Running Lights . . . . –
Automatic Door-Locking. . . . . Standard
Safety Belt:
Adjustable Front Belt . . . . Standard

Nissan Xterra

Specifications

Drive 4WD
Engine 4.0-liter V6
Transmission . . . . 5-sp. Automatic
Tow Rating (lbs.) Average-5000
Head/Leg Room (in.). Roomy-39.9/42.4
Interior Space (cu. ft.) Cramped-98.8
Cargo Space (cu. ft.). . . . . Very Roomy-36.3
Wheelbase/Length (in.) 106.3/178.7

*Combines results of both front and side tests in relation to all tests for 2010 vehicles.

Ratings—10 Best, 1 Worst

	Cayenne	Touareg
Combo Crash Tests	–	4
Safety Features	9	9
Rollover	4	4
Preventive Maintenance	6	9
Repair Costs	1	3
Warranty	3	9
Fuel Economy	2	2
Complaints	2	2
Insurance Costs	3	8
OVERALL RATING	–	5

Porsche Cayenne

Volkswagen Touareg

At-a-Glance

Status	Unchanged
Year Series Started	2007
Twins	Volkswagen Touareg
Body Styles	SUV
Seating	5
Anti-Theft Device	Std. Pass. Immobil. & Active Alarm
Parking Index Rating	Hard
Where Made	Leipzig, Germany

Fuel Factor

MPG Rating (city/hwy)	Very Poor-14/20
Driving Range (mi.)	Very Long-427.3
Fuel Type	Premium
Annual Fuel Cost	Very High-$2688
Greenhouse Gas Emissions (tons/yr.)	Very High-11.4
Barrels of Oil Used per year	Very High-21.4

How the Competition Rates

Competitors	Rating	Pg.
BMW X5	8	96
Mercedes-Benz M-Class	6	207
Volvo XC90	10	270

Price Range

Price Range	Retail	Markup
Base	$48,500	18%
S	$60,700	18%
GTS	$75,400	18%
Turbo S	$126,300	18%

Safety Checklist

Crash Tests:
Frontal	–
Side	–

Airbags:
Head	Std. Row 1 & 2 Curtain
Chest/Torso	Std. Row 1 Torso from Seat
Roll-Sensing Side Airbag	Standard
Out-of-Position Test	Meets Requirements

Children:
Built-in Child Safety Seat	–
Automatic Window Reversal	Std. Front and Rear

Crash Avoidance:
Frontal Collision Warning	–
Electronic Stability Control	Standard
Lane Departure Warning	–
Brake Assist	Standard

General:
Automatic Crash Notification	–
Daytime Running Lights	–
Automatic Door-Locking	Standard

Safety Belt:
Adjustable Front Belt	Standard

Porsche Cayenne

Specifications

Drive	4WD
Engine	3.6-liter V6
Transmission	6-sp. Automatic
Tow Rating (lbs.)	Average-3500
Head/Leg Room (in.)	Cramped-40/40.6
Interior Space (cu. ft.)	–
Cargo Space (cu. ft.)	Average-18.9
Wheelbase/Length (in.)	112.4/188.9

*Combines results of both front and side tests in relation to all tests for 2010 vehicles.

Ratings—10 Best, 1 Worst	
Combo Crash Tests	1
Safety Features	6
Rollover	6
Preventive Maintenance	10
Repair Costs	8
Warranty	8
Fuel Economy	6
Complaints	2
Insurance Costs	5
OVERALL RATING	**6**

Saab 9-3

Saab 9-3

At-a-Glance

Status	Unchanged
Year Series Started	2003
Twins	–
Body Styles	Sedan, Wagon, Coupe Convertible
Seating	5
Anti-Theft Device	Std. Pass. Immobil. & Pass. Alarm
Parking Index Rating	Hard
Where Made	Trollhättan, Sweden / Graz, Austria

Fuel Factor

MPG Rating (city/hwy)	Average-19/28
Driving Range (mi.)	Short-364.3
Fuel Type	Regular
Annual Fuel Cost	Low-$1823
Greenhouse Gas Emissions (tons/yr.)	High-8.3
Barrels of Oil Used per year	Average-15.6

How the Competition Rates

Competitors	Rating	Pg.
Audi A4	10	86
BMW 3 Series	7	92
Mercedes-Benz C-Class	–	203

Price Range	Retail	Markup
Touring	$30,360	5%
XWD	$36,395	5%
SportCombi Comfort	$35,315	5%
Convertible Aero	$51,330	5%

Safety Checklist

Crash Tests:

Frontal	Very Poor
Side	Very Poor

Airbags:

Head	Std. Row 1 & 2 Curtain
Chest/Torso	Std. Row 1 Torso from Seat
Roll-Sensing Side Airbag	–
Out-of-Position Test	Meets Requirements

Children:

Built-in Child Safety Seat	–
Automatic Window Reversal	Opt. Front

Crash Avoidance:

Frontal Collision Warning	–
Electronic Stability Control	Standard
Lane Departure Warning	–
Brake Assist	–

General:

Automatic Crash Notification	Standard
Daytime Running Lights	Standard
Automatic Door-Locking	Standard

Safety Belt:

Adjustable Front Belt	Standard

Saab 9-3

Specifications

Drive	FWD
Engine	2.0-liter I4
Transmission	5-sp. Automatic
Tow Rating (lbs.)	–
Head/Leg Room (in.)	Average-38.9/42.3
Interior Space (cu. ft.)	Very Cramped-90
Cargo Space (cu. ft.)	Cramped-15
Wheelbase/Length (in.)	105.3/182.5

*Combines results of both front and side tests in relation to all tests for 2010 vehicles.

Ratings—10 Best, 1 Worst

Combo Crash Tests	4
Safety Features	1
Rollover	7
Preventive Maintenance	2
Repair Costs	8
Warranty	2
Fuel Economy	7
Complaints	4
Insurance Costs	1
OVERALL RATING	**3**

Scion tC

Scion tC

At-a-Glance

Status	Unchanged
Year Series Started	2005
Twins	—
Body Styles	Sedan, Coupe
Seating	5
Anti-Theft Device	Std. Passive Immobil. Only
Parking Index Rating	Easy
Where Made	Toyota City, Japan
Fuel Factor	
MPG Rating (city/hwy)	Good-21/29
Driving Range (mi.)	Short-347.7
Fuel Type	Regular
Annual Fuel Cost	Low-$1689
Greenhouse Gas Emissions (tons/yr.)	Average-7.7
Barrels of Oil Used per year	Average-14.3

How the Competition Rates

Competitors	Rating	Pg.
Mazda 3	6	196
Mitsubishi Lancer	5	214
Subaru Impreza	4	237

Price Range	Retail	Markup
Base Manual Transmission	$17,000	5%
Base Automatic Transmission	$17,800	5%

Safety Checklist

Crash Tests:
Frontal . . . . Poor
Side . . . . Average
Airbags:
Head . . . . Std. Row 1 & 2 Curtain
Chest/Torso . . . . Std. Row 1 Torso from Seat
Roll-Sensing Side Airbag . . . . —
Out-of-Position Test . . . . Meets Requirements
Children:
Built-in Child Safety Seat . . . . —
Automatic Window Reversal . . . . Std. Front
Crash Avoidance:
Frontal Collision Warning . . . . —
Electronic Stability Control . . . . —
Lane Departure Warning . . . . —
Brake Assist . . . . —
General:
Automatic Crash Notification . . . . —
Daytime Running Lights . . . . —
Automatic Door-Locking . . . . —
Safety Belt:
Adjustable Front Belt . . . . —

Scion tC

Specifications

Drive	FWD
Engine	2.4-liter I4
Transmission	4-sp. Automatic
Tow Rating (lbs.)	—
Head/Leg Room (in.)	Very Cramped-37.6/41.6
Interior Space (cu. ft.)	Very Cramped-84.7
Cargo Space (cu. ft.)	Cramped-12.8
Wheelbase/Length (in.)	106.3/174

*Combines results of both front and side tests in relation to all tests for 2010 vehicles.

Ratings—10 Best, 1 Worst

Combo Crash Tests	2
Safety Features	4
Rollover	5
Preventive Maintenance	2
Repair Costs	7
Warranty	2
Fuel Economy	7
Complaints	1
Insurance Costs	5
OVERALL RATING	**1**

Scion xB

Scion xB

At-a-Glance

Status	Unchanged
Year Series Started	2008
Twins	–
Body Styles	4-Door
Seating	5
Anti-Theft Device	–
Parking Index Rating	Very Easy
Where Made	Iwata, Japan

Fuel Factor

MPG Rating (city/hwy)	Good-22/28
Driving Range (mi.)	Very Short-340.9
Fuel Type	Regular
Annual Fuel Cost	Low-$1663
Greenhouse Gas Emissions (tons/yr.)	Average-7.7
Barrels of Oil Used per year	Average-14.3

How the Competition Rates

Competitors	Rating	Pg.
Kia Soul	6	181
Nissan Cube	5	220
Toyota Yaris	4	257

Price Range

	Retail	Markup
Base Manual Transmission	$15,750	5%
Base Automatic Transmission	$16,700	5%

Safety Checklist

Crash Tests:
Frontal .... Very Poor
Side .... Poor

Airbags:
Head .... Std. Row 1 & 2 Curtain
Chest/Torso .... Std. Row 1 Torso from Seat
Roll-Sensing Side Airbag .... –
Out-of-Position Test ...... Meets Requirements

Children:
Built-in Child Safety Seat .... –
Automatic Window Reversal .... –

Crash Avoidance:
Frontal Collision Warning .... –
Electronic Stability Control .... Standard
Lane Departure Warning .... –
Brake Assist .... Standard

General:
Automatic Crash Notification .... –
Daytime Running Lights .... –
Automatic Door-Locking .... Standard

Safety Belt:
Adjustable Front Belt .... Standard

Scion xB

Specifications

Drive	FWD
Engine	2.4-liter I4
Transmission	4-sp. Automatic
Tow Rating (lbs.)	–
Head/Leg Room (in.)	Cramped-40/40.7
Interior Space (cu. ft.)	Average-100.8
Cargo Space (cu. ft.)	Average-21.7
Wheelbase/Length (in.)	102.4/167.3

*Combines results of both front and side tests in relation to all tests for 2010 vehicles.

Scion xD

Ratings—10 Best, 1 Worst

Combo Crash Tests	2
Safety Features	2
Rollover	4
Preventive Maintenance	3
Repair Costs	6
Warranty	2
Fuel Economy	10
Complaints	10
Insurance Costs	5
OVERALL RATING	**4**

Scion xD

Scion xD

At-a-Glance

Status. . . . . Unchanged
Year Series Started 2008
Twins . . . . −
Body Styles. . . . . Hatchback
Seating. 5
Anti-Theft Device . . . . −
Parking Index Rating . . . . Very Easy
Where Made . . . . Takaoka City, Japan
Fuel Factor
  MPG Rating (city/hwy) . . . . Very Good-27/33
  Driving Range (mi.). . . . . Very Short-326.4
  Fuel Type. . . . . Regular
  Annual Fuel Cost . . . . Very Low-$1377
  Greenhouse Gas Emissions (tons/yr.) Low-6.3
  Barrels of Oil Used per year Low-11.8

How the Competition Rates

Competitors	Rating	Pg.
Chevrolet Aveo	3	106
Kia Rio	5	177
Suzuki SX4	2	242

Price Range

Price Range	Retail	Markup
Base Manual Transmission	$14,800	5%
Base Automatic Transmission	$15,600	5%

Safety Checklist

Crash Tests:
  Frontal. . . . . Very Poor
  Side. . . . . Average
Airbags:
  Head . . . . Std. Row 1 & 2 Curtain
  Chest/Torso . . . . Std. Row 1 Torso from Seat
  Roll-Sensing Side Airbag . . . . −
  Out-of-Position Test. . . . . . . Meets Requirements
Children:
  Built-in Child Safety Seat . . . . −
  Automatic Window Reversal . . . . −
Crash Avoidance:
  Frontal Collision Warning . . . . −
  Electronic Stability Control . . . . Optional
  Lane Departure Warning . . . . −
  Brake Assist . . . . Standard
General:
  Automatic Crash Notification . . . . −
  Daytime Running Lights . . . . −
  Automatic Door-Locking . . . . −
Safety Belt:
  Adjustable Front Belt . . . . Standard

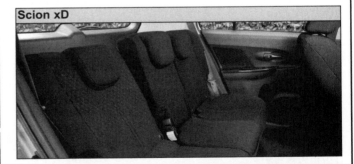

Scion xD

Specifications

Drive . . . . FWD
Engine. 1.8-liter I4
Transmission . . . . 4-sp. Automatic
Tow Rating (lbs.). . . . . −
Head/Leg Room (in.). . . . . Very Cramped-38.9/40.3
Interior Space (cu. ft.) . . . . Very Cramped-84.5
Cargo Space (cu. ft.) . . . . Very Cramped-10.5
Wheelbase/Length (in.) 96.9/154.7

*Combines results of both front and side tests in relation to all tests for 2010 vehicles.

Ratings—10 Best, 1 Worst

Combo Crash Tests	1
Safety Features	2
Rollover	2
Preventive Maintenance	–
Repair Costs	–
Warranty	1
Fuel Economy	10
Complaints	2
Insurance Costs	10
OVERALL RATING	**1**

Smart ForTwo

Smart ForTwo

At-a-Glance

Status . . . . Unchanged
Year Series Started 2008
Twins . . . . –
Body Styles . . . . Two Seater
Seating 2
Anti-Theft Device . Std. Pass. Immobil. & Active Alarm
Parking Index Rating . . . . Very Easy
Where Made . . . . Hambach, France

Fuel Factor
  MPG Rating (city/hwy) . . . . Very Good-33/41
  Driving Range (mi.) . . . . Very Short-314.7
  Fuel Type . . . . Regular
  Annual Fuel Cost . . . . Very Low-$1120
  Greenhouse Gas Emissions (tons/yr.) . Very Low-5.1
  Barrels of Oil Used per year . . . . Very Low-9.5

How the Competition Rates

Competitors	Rating	Pg.
Chevrolet Aveo	3	106
Honda Fit	8	150
Suzuki SX4	2	242

Price Range

Price Range	Retail	Markup
Pure Coupe	$11,990	8%
Passion Coupe	$13,990	8%
Passion Cabriolet	$16,990	8%

Safety Checklist

Crash Tests:
  Frontal . . . . Very Poor
  Side . . . . Poor
Airbags:
  Head . . . . Std. Row 1 Combo
  Chest/Torso . . . . . . Std. Row 1 Combo from Seat
  Roll-Sensing Side Airbag . . . . –
  Out-of-Position Test . . . . Meets Requirements
Children:
  Built-in Child Safety Seat . . . . –
  Automatic Window Reversal . . . . Std. Front
Crash Avoidance:
  Frontal Collision Warning . . . . –
  Electronic Stability Control . . . . Standard
  Lane Departure Warning . . . . –
  Brake Assist . . . . Standard
General:
  Automatic Crash Notification . . . . –
  Daytime Running Lights . . . . –
  Automatic Door-Locking . . . . Standard
Safety Belt:
  Adjustable Front Belt . . . . –

Smart ForTwo

Specifications

Drive . . . . FWD
Engine 1.0-liter I3
Transmission . . . . 5-sp. Manual
Tow Rating (lbs.) . . . . –
Head/Leg Room (in.) Cramped-39.7/41.2
Interior Space (cu. ft.) . . . . Very Cramped-45.4
Cargo Space (cu. ft.) . . . . Very Cramped-7.8
Wheelbase/Length (in.) 73.5/106.1

*Combines results of both front and side tests in relation to all tests for 2010 vehicles.

Ratings—10 Best, 1 Worst

Combo Crash Tests	8
Safety Features	7
Rollover	3
Preventive Maintenance	4
Repair Costs	8
Warranty	3
Fuel Economy	6
Complaints	2
Insurance Costs	5
OVERALL RATING	**6**

Subaru Forester

Subaru Forester

At-a-Glance

Status. . . . . Unchanged
Year Series Started 2009
Twins . . . . –
Body Styles. . . . . .SUV
Seating 5
Anti-Theft Device . Std. Pass. Immobil. & Active Alarm
Parking Index Rating . . . . Very Easy
Where Made . . . . Tokyo, Japan

Fuel Factor
MPG Rating (city/hwy) Average-20/26
Driving Range (mi.) Average-377.2
Fuel Type. . . . . Regular
Annual Fuel Cost . . . . Low-$1815
Greenhouse Gas Emissions (tons/yr.) High-8.3
Barrels of Oil Used per year. Average-15.6

How the Competition Rates

Competitors	Rating	Pg.
Honda CR-V	10	148
Hyundai Tucson	–	161
Toyota RAV4	4	251

Price Range

Price Range	Retail	Markup
X Manual Transmission	$20,295	6%
X Premium Auto. Transmission	$23,795	6%
XT Premium Auto. Transmission	$26,495	7%
XT Limited Auto. Transmission	$28,495	7%

Safety Checklist

Crash Tests:
 Frontal . . . . Very Good
 Side . . . . Average
Airbags:
 Head . . . . Std. Row 1 & 2 Curtain
 Chest/Torso . . . . Std. Row 1 Torso from Seat
 Roll-Sensing Side Airbag . . . . Standard
 Out-of-Position Test. . . . . . . Meets Requirements
Children:
 Built-in Child Safety Seat . . . . –
 Automatic Window Reversal . . . . –
Crash Avoidance:
 Frontal Collision Warning . . . . –
 Electronic Stability Control . . . . Standard
 Lane Departure Warning . . . . –
 Brake Assist . . . . –
General:
 Automatic Crash Notification . . . . –
 Daytime Running Lights. . . . . Standard
 Automatic Door-Locking . . . . –
Safety Belt:
 Adjustable Front Belt . . . . Standard

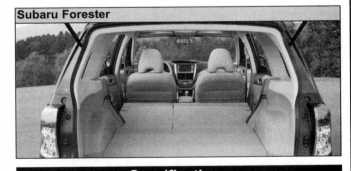

Subaru Forester

Specifications

Drive . . . . AWD
Engine. 2.5-liter I4
Transmission . . . . 4-sp. Automatic
Tow Rating (lbs.) Low-2400
Head/Leg Room (in.) . . . . . . Very Roomy-41.6/43.1
Interior Space (cu. ft.) Roomy-107.6
Cargo Space (cu. ft.). Roomy-33.5
Wheelbase/Length (in.). 103/179.5

*Combines results of both front and side tests in relation to all tests for 2010 vehicles.

Ratings—10 Best, 1 Worst

Combo Crash Tests	4
Safety Features	3
Rollover	8
Preventive Maintenance	5
Repair Costs	6
Warranty	3
Fuel Economy	6
Complaints	2
Insurance Costs	5
OVERALL RATING	**4**

Subaru Impreza

Subaru Impreza

At-a-Glance

Status. . . . . Unchanged
Year Series Started 2008
Twins . . . . –
Body Styles. . . . . Sedan, Wagon
Seating. 5
Anti-Theft Device . Std. Pass. Immobil. & Active Alarm
Parking Index Rating . . . . Easy
Where Made . . . . Tokyo, Japan
Fuel Factor
  MPG Rating (city/hwy) Average-20/26
  Driving Range (mi.) Average-377.2
  Fuel Type. . . . . Regular
  Annual Fuel Cost . . . . Low-$1815
  Greenhouse Gas Emissions (tons/yr.) High-8.3
  Barrels of Oil Used per year. Average-15.6

How the Competition Rates

Competitors	Rating	Pg.
Honda Civic	8	146
Mazda 3	6	196
Mitsubishi Lancer	5	214

Price Range	Retail	Markup
2.5i Manual Transmission	$17,495	5%
Outback Sport Wagon	$20,995	5%
2.5i Premium Sedan w/ Nav	$22,495	6%
WRX Sti Wagon w/Nav 6-sp. Trans.	$38,795	7%

Safety Checklist

Crash Tests:
  Frontal . . . . Average
  Side. . . . . Very Poor
Airbags:
  Head . . . . Std. Row 1 & 2 Curtain
  Chest/Torso . . . . Std. Row 1 Torso from Seat
  Roll-Sensing Side Airbag . . . . –
  Out-of-Position Test. . . . . . . Meets Requirements
Children:
  Built-in Child Safety Seat . . . . –
  Automatic Window Reversal . . . . –
Crash Avoidance:
  Frontal Collision Warning . . . . –
  Electronic Stability Control . . . . Standard
  Lane Departure Warning . . . . –
  Brake Assist . . . . –
General:
  Automatic Crash Notification . . . . –
  Daytime Running Lights . . . . Standard
  Automatic Door-Locking . . . . –
Safety Belt:
  Adjustable Front Belt . . . . Standard

Subaru Impreza

Specifications

Drive . . . . AWD
Engine. 2.5-liter I4
Transmission . . . . 4-sp. Automatic
Tow Rating (lbs.). . . . . –
Head/Leg Room (in.) . . . . . . Very Roomy-40.3/43.5
Interior Space (cu. ft.) Cramped-94.6
Cargo Space (cu. ft.) . . . . . . Very Cramped-11.3
Wheelbase/Length (in.) 103.1/180.3

*Combines results of both front and side tests in relation to all tests for 2010 vehicles.

Ratings—10 Best, 1 Worst

Combo Crash Tests	10
Safety Features	7
Rollover	3
Preventive Maintenance	2
Repair Costs	–
Warranty	3
Fuel Economy	8
Complaints	–
Insurance Costs	5
OVERALL RATING	**7**

Subaru Outback

Subaru Legacy

At-a-Glance

Status	All New
Year Series Started	2010
Twins	–
Body Styles	Wagon, Sedan
Seating	5
Anti-Theft Device	Std. Pass. Immobil. & Active Alarm
Parking Index Rating	Average
Where Made	Lafayette, IN

Fuel Factor

MPG Rating (city/hwy)	Good-22/29
Driving Range (mi.)	Very Long-456.6
Fuel Type	Regular
Annual Fuel Cost	Low-$1641
Greenhouse Gas Emissions (tons/yr.)	Average-7.7
Barrels of Oil Used per year	Average-14.3

How the Competition Rates

Competitors	Rating	Pg.
Toyota Camry	7	245
Volkswagen Passat	6	263
Volvo V70	–	268

Price Range

	Retail	Markup
Base Manual Transmission	$22,995	6%
Premium Automatic Transmission	$25,295	6%
3.6R Automatic Transmission	$27,995	7%
3.6R Limited Auto. Transmission	$30,995	7%

Safety Checklist

Crash Tests:
Frontal . . . . Very Good
Side . . . . Very Good

Airbags:
Head . . . . Std. Row 1 & 2 Curtain
Chest/Torso . . . . Std. Row 1 Torso from Seat
Roll-Sensing Side Airbag . . . . Standard
Out-of-Position Test . . . . Meets Requirements

Children:
Built-in Child Safety Seat . . . . –
Automatic Window Reversal . . . . Std. Driver

Crash Avoidance:
Frontal Collision Warning . . . . –
Electronic Stability Control . . . . Standard
Lane Departure Warning . . . . –
Brake Assist . . . . –

General:
Automatic Crash Notification . . . . –
Daytime Running Lights . . . . Standard
Automatic Door-Locking . . . . –

Safety Belt:
Adjustable Front Belt . . . . Standard

Subaru Outback

Specifications

Drive	AWD
Engine	2.5-liter I4
Transmission	CVT
Tow Rating (lbs.)	–
Head/Leg Room (in.)	Very Roomy-40.8/43
Interior Space (cu. ft.)	Roomy-105.4
Cargo Space (cu. ft.)	Very Roomy-34.3
Wheelbase/Length (in.)	107.9/188.2

*Combines results of both front and side tests in relation to all tests for 2010 vehicles.

Ratings—10 Best, 1 Worst

Combo Crash Tests	6
Safety Features	7
Rollover	4
Preventive Maintenance	3
Repair Costs	7
Warranty	3
Fuel Economy	3
Complaints	4
Insurance Costs	8
OVERALL RATING	**5**

Subaru Tribeca

Subaru Tribeca

At-a-Glance

Status . . . . Unchanged
Year Series Started 2006
Twins . . . . –
Body Styles . . . . SUV
Seating 5/7
Anti-Theft Device . Std. Pass. Immobil. & Active Alarm
Parking Index Rating . . . . Average
Where Made . . . . Lafayette, IN

Fuel Factor
MPG Rating (city/hwy) Poor-16/21
Driving Range (mi.) . . . . Very Short-302.8
Fuel Type . . . . Regular
Annual Fuel Cost . . . . High-$2260
Greenhouse Gas Emissions (tons/yr.) High-10.2
Barrels of Oil Used per year High-19.0

How the Competition Rates

Competitors	Rating	Pg.
Acura MDX	–	81
Honda Pilot	7	153
Toyota Highlander	4	248

Price Range

	Retail	Markup
3.6R Premium	$30,495	7%
3.6R Limited	$32,495	7%
3.6R Touring	$35,795	7%

Safety Checklist

Crash Tests:
Frontal . . . . Good
Side . . . . Average
Airbags:
Head . . . . Std. Row 1 & 2 Curtain
Chest/Torso . . . . Std. Row 1 Torso from Seat
Roll-Sensing Side Airbag . . . . Standard
Out-of-Position Test . . . . . . Meets Requirements
Children:
Built-in Child Safety Seat . . . . –
Automatic Window Reversal . . . . –
Crash Avoidance:
Frontal Collision Warning . . . . –
Electronic Stability Control . . . . Standard
Lane Departure Warning . . . . –
Brake Assist . . . . –
General:
Automatic Crash Notification . . . . –
Daytime Running Lights . . . . Standard
Automatic Door-Locking . . . . –
Safety Belt:
Adjustable Front Belt . . . . Standard

Subaru Tribeca

Specifications

Drive . . . . AWD
Engine . . . . 3.6-liter -
Transmission . . . . 5-sp. Automatic
Tow Rating (lbs.) Low-2000
Head/Leg Room (in.) Average-38.9/42.3
Interior Space (cu. ft.) . . . . –
Cargo Space (cu. ft.) . . . . Very Roomy-37.6
Wheelbase/Length (in.) 108.2/191.2

*Combines results of both front and side tests in relation to all tests for 2010 vehicles.

Ratings—10 Best, 1 Worst

Combo Crash Tests	2
Safety Features	7
Rollover	3
Preventive Maintenance	3
Repair Costs	2
Warranty	5
Fuel Economy	5
Complaints	4
Insurance Costs	3
OVERALL RATING	**1**

Suzuki Grand Vitara

Suzuki Grand Vitara

Suzuki Grand Vitara

At-a-Glance

Status. . . . . Unchanged
Year Series Started 2006
Twins . . . . –
Body Styles. . . . . SUV
Seating 5
Anti-Theft Device . . . . –
Parking Index Rating . . . . Easy
Where Made . . . . Iwata, Japan
Fuel Factor
MPG Rating (city/hwy) Average-19/25
Driving Range (mi.) Short-370.6
Fuel Type. . . . . Regular
Annual Fuel Cost. . . . . Average-$1901
Greenhouse Gas Emissions (tons/yr.) High-8.7
Barrels of Oil Used per year. High-16.3

How the Competition Rates

Competitors	Rating	Pg.
Honda CR-V	10	148
Kia Sportage	5	182
Toyota RAV4	4	251

Price Range	Retail	Markup
Base	$18,999	4%
Premium 4WD	$21,999	4%
Xsport 4WD	$25,499	4%
Limited 4WD V6	$26,999	4%

Safety Checklist

Crash Tests:
Frontal. . . . . Very Poor
Side. . . . . Poor
Airbags:
Head . . . . Std. Row 1 & 2 Curtain
Chest/Torso . . . . Std. Row 1 Torso from Seat
Roll-Sensing Side Airbag . . . . Standard
Out-of-Position Test. . . . . . Meets Requirements
Children:
Built-in Child Safety Seat . . . . –
Automatic Window Reversal . . . . –
Crash Avoidance:
Frontal Collision Warning . . . . –
Electronic Stability Control . . . . Standard
Lane Departure Warning . . . . –
Brake Assist . . . . Standard
General:
Automatic Crash Notification . . . . –
Daytime Running Lights. . . . . Standard
Automatic Door-Locking . . . . –
Safety Belt:
Adjustable Front Belt . . . . Standard

Suzuki Grand Vitara

Specifications

Drive. . . . . RWD
Engine. 2.4-liter I4
Transmission . . . . 4-sp. Automatic
Tow Rating (lbs.) Low-3000
Head/Leg Room (in.) Average-40/41.3
Interior Space (cu. ft.) . . . . Very Roomy-125.4
Cargo Space (cu. ft.). Roomy-24.4
Wheelbase/Length (in.) 103.9/177.1

*Combines results of both front and side tests in relation to all tests for 2010 vehicles.

Ratings—10 Best, 1 Worst

Combo Crash Tests	–
Safety Features	3
Rollover	7
Preventive Maintenance	–
Repair Costs	–
Warranty	5
Fuel Economy	8
Complaints	–
Insurance Costs	–
OVERALL RATING	–

Suzuki Kizashi

Suzuki Kizashi

At-a-Glance

Status	All New
Year Series Started	2010
Twins	–
Body Styles	Sedan
Seating	5
Anti-Theft Device	Std. Pass. Immobil. & Pass. Alarm
Parking Index Rating	Very Easy
Where Made	Sagara, Japan

Fuel Factor

MPG Rating (city/hwy)	Good-23/31
Driving Range (mi.)	Very Long-432.0
Fuel Type	–
Annual Fuel Cost	Very Low-$1576
Greenhouse Gas Emissions (tons/yr.)	–
Barrels of Oil Used per year	–

How the Competition Rates

Competitors	Rating	Pg.
Mazda 3	6	196
Mitsubishi Lancer	5	214
Subaru Impreza	4	237

Price Range	Retail	Markup
S FWD Manual Trans.	$18,999	4%
SE FWD	$21,499	4%
S AWD	$21,749	4%
GTS CV Trans. AWD	$24,849	4%

Safety Checklist

Crash Tests:
Frontal . . . . –
Side . . . . –

Airbags:
Head . . . . Std. Row 1 & 2 Curtain
Chest/Torso . . . . Std. Row 1 Torso from Seat
Roll-Sensing Side Airbag . . . . –
Out-of-Position Test . . . . –

Children:
Built-in Child Safety Seat . . . . –
Automatic Window Reversal . . . . Std. Front

Crash Avoidance:
Frontal Collision Warning . . . . –
Electronic Stability Control . . . . Standard
Lane Departure Warning . . . . –
Brake Assist . . . . Standard

General:
Automatic Crash Notification . . . . –
Daytime Running Lights . . . . Standard
Automatic Door-Locking . . . . –

Safety Belt:
Adjustable Front Belt . . . . Standard

Suzuki Kizashi

Specifications

Drive	FWD
Engine	2.4-liter I4
Transmission	CVT
Tow Rating (lbs.)	–
Head/Leg Room (in.)	Cramped-39.3/41.7
Interior Space (cu. ft.)	Cramped-92.1
Cargo Space (cu. ft.)	Cramped-13.3
Wheelbase/Length (in.)	106.3/183.1

*Combines results of both front and side tests in relation to all tests for 2010 vehicles.

Ratings—10 Best, 1 Worst

Combo Crash Tests	2
Safety Features	3
Rollover	6
Preventive Maintenance	1
Repair Costs	3
Warranty	5
Fuel Economy	8
Complaints	6
Insurance Costs	3
OVERALL RATING	**2**

Suzuki SX4

Suzuki SX4

Suzuki SX4

At-a-Glance

Status	Unchanged
Year Series Started	2007
Twins	—
Body Styles	Hatchback, Sedan
Seating	5
Anti-Theft Device	—
Parking Index Rating	Very Easy
Where Made	Sagara, Japan

Fuel Factor

MPG Rating (city/hwy)	Good-23/30
Driving Range (mi.)	Very Short-339.2
Fuel Type	Regular
Annual Fuel Cost	Very Low-$1576
Greenhouse Gas Emissions (tons/yr.)	Average-7.1
Barrels of Oil Used per year	Low-13.2

How the Competition Rates

Competitors	Rating	Pg.
Honda Fit	8	150
Kia Rio	5	177
Nissan Versa	5	228

Price Range	Retail	Markup
Base Sedan	$13,359	4%
S Sport Manual Trans.	$16,149	4%
GTS Sedan	$18,849	4%
GTS SportBack Auto. Trans.	$19,099	4%

Safety Checklist

Crash Tests:

Frontal	Very Poor
Side	Average

Airbags:

Head	Std. Row 1 & 2 Curtain
Chest/Torso	Std. Row 1 Torso from Seat
Roll-Sensing Side Airbag	—
Out-of-Position Test	Meets Requirements

Children:

Built-in Child Safety Seat	—
Automatic Window Reversal	—

Crash Avoidance:

Frontal Collision Warning	—
Electronic Stability Control	Optional
Lane Departure Warning	—
Brake Assist	Standard

General:

Automatic Crash Notification	—
Daytime Running Lights	Standard
Automatic Door-Locking	—

Safety Belt:

Adjustable Front Belt	Standard

Suzuki SX4

Specifications

Drive	FWD
Engine	2.0-liter I4
Transmission	4-sp. Automatic
Tow Rating (lbs.)	Very Low-1000
Head/Leg Room (in.)	Cramped-39.6/41.4
Interior Space (cu. ft.)	—
Cargo Space (cu. ft.)	Cramped-15.5
Wheelbase/Length (in.)	98.4/177.6

*Combines results of both front and side tests in relation to all tests for 2010 vehicles.

Ratings—10 Best, 1 Worst	
Combo Crash Tests	–
Safety Features	8
Rollover	2
Preventive Maintenance	2
Repair Costs	5
Warranty	2
Fuel Economy	3
Complaints	9
Insurance Costs	10
OVERALL RATING	–

Toyota 4Runner

Toyota 4Runner

At-a-Glance

Status	Appearance Change
Year Series Started	2006
Twins	–
Body Styles	SUV
Seating	5/7
Anti-Theft Device	Std. Passive Immobil. Only
Parking Index Rating	Average
Where Made	Tahara, Japan

Fuel Factor

MPG Rating (city/hwy)	Poor-17/22
Driving Range (mi.)	Very Long-454.5
Fuel Type	Regular
Annual Fuel Cost	High-$2139
Greenhouse Gas Emissions (tons/yr.)	High-9.6
Barrels of Oil Used per year	High-18.0

How the Competition Rates

Competitors	Rating	Pg.
Ford Explorer	5	135
Honda Pilot	7	153
Nissan Pathfinder	–	224

Price Range	Retail	Markup
SR5 L4 2WD	$27,500	11%
SR5 V6 4WD	$30,915	11%
Trail V6 4WD	$35,700	11%
Limited V6 4WD	$39,800	11%

Safety Checklist

Crash Tests:
Frontal . . . . –
Side . . . . –
Airbags:
Head . . . . Std. Curtain All Rows
Chest/Torso . . . . Std. Row 1 Torso from Seat
Roll-Sensing Side Airbag . . . . Standard
Out-of-Position Test . . . . –
Children:
Built-in Child Safety Seat . . . . –
Automatic Window Reversal . . Std. Front and Rear
Crash Avoidance:
Frontal Collision Warning . . . . –
Electronic Stability Control . . . . Standard
Lane Departure Warning . . . . –
Brake Assist . . . . Standard
General:
Automatic Crash Notification . . . . Optional
Daytime Running Lights . . . . Standard
Automatic Door-Locking . . . . Standard
Safety Belt:
Adjustable Front Belt . . . . Standard

Toyota 4Runner

Specifications

Drive	4WD
Engine	4.0-liter V6
Transmission	5-sp. Automatic
Tow Rating (lbs.)	Average-5000
Head/Leg Room (in.)	Cramped-39.3/41.7
Interior Space (cu. ft.)	Cramped-97.3
Cargo Space (cu. ft.)	Very Roomy-47.2
Wheelbase/Length (in.)	109.8/189.9

*Combines results of both front and side tests in relation to all tests for 2010 vehicles.

Toyota Avalon

Ratings—10 Best, 1 Worst

Combo Crash Tests	9
Safety Features	7
Rollover	7
Preventive Maintenance	3
Repair Costs	4
Warranty	2
Fuel Economy	6
Complaints	4
Insurance Costs	5
OVERALL RATING	**6**

Toyota Avalon

Toyota Avalon

At-a-Glance

Status. . . . . Unchanged
Year Series Started 2006
Twins . . . . −
Body Styles . . . . Sedan
Seating. 5
Anti-Theft Device Std. Pass. Immob./Opt. Pass. Immob. & Alarm
Parking Index Rating . . . . Average
Where Made . . . . Georgetown, KY
Fuel Factor
  MPG Rating (city/hwy) Average-19/28
  Driving Range (mi.) Long-410.9
  Fuel Type. . . . . Regular
  Annual Fuel Cost . . . . Low-$1823
  Greenhouse Gas Emissions (tons/yr.) . . Average-8.0
  Barrels of Oil Used per year. Average-14.9

How the Competition Rates

Competitors	Rating	Pg.
Ford Fusion	9	139
Nissan Altima	9	217
Subaru Impreza	4	237

Price Range	Retail	Markup
XL	$27,945	11%
XLS	$32,245	12%
Limited	$35,285	12%

Safety Checklist

Crash Tests:
  Frontal . . . . Very Good
  Side . . . . Good
Airbags:
  Head . . . . Std. Row 1 & 2 Curtain
  Chest/Torso . . . . Std. Row 1 Torso from Seat
  Roll-Sensing Side Airbag . . . . −
  Out-of-Position Test. . . . . . . Meets Requirements
Children:
  Built-in Child Safety Seat . . . . −
  Automatic Window Reversal. Std. Front and Rear
Crash Avoidance:
  Frontal Collision Warning . . . . −
  Electronic Stability Control . . . . Standard
  Lane Departure Warning . . . . −
  Brake Assist . . . . Standard
General:
  Automatic Crash Notification . . . . −
  Daytime Running Lights. . . . . Standard
  Automatic Door-Locking. . . . . Standard
Safety Belt:
  Adjustable Front Belt . . . . Standard

Toyota Avalon

Specifications

Drive . . . . FWD
Engine 3.5-liter V6
Transmission . . . . 6-sp. Automatic
Tow Rating (lbs.). . . . . Very Low-1000
Head/Leg Room (in.) Cramped-38.8/41.3
Interior Space (cu. ft.) Roomy-106.9
Cargo Space (cu. ft.) Cramped-14.4
Wheelbase/Length (in.) 111/197.6

*Combines results of both front and side tests in relation to all tests for 2010 vehicles.

Toyota Camry Intermediate

Ratings—10 Best, 1 Worst

Combo Crash Tests	6
Safety Features	7
Rollover	8
Preventive Maintenance	2
Repair Costs	7
Warranty	2
Fuel Economy	8
Complaints	6
Insurance Costs	8
OVERALL RATING	**7**

Toyota Camry

Toyota Camry

Safety Checklist

Crash Tests:
Frontal . . . . Average
Side . . . . Good
Airbags:
Head . . . . Std. Row 1 & 2 Curtain
Chest/Torso . . . . Std. Row 1 Torso from Seat
Roll-Sensing Side Airbag . . . . –
Out-of-Position Test . . . . . . Meets Requirements
Children:
Built-in Child Safety Seat . . . . –
Automatic Window Reversal . Std. Front and Rear
Crash Avoidance:
Frontal Collision Warning . . . . –
Electronic Stability Control . . . . Standard
Lane Departure Warning . . . . –
Brake Assist . . . . Standard
General:
Automatic Crash Notification . . . . –
Daytime Running Lights . . . . Standard
Automatic Door-Locking . . . . Standard
Safety Belt:
Adjustable Front Belt . . . . Standard

At-a-Glance

Status . . . . Appearance Change
Year Series Started 2007
Twins . . . . Lexus ES
Body Styles . . . . Sedan
Seating 5
Anti-Theft Device . . Std. Pass. Immob./Opt. Pass. Immob. & Alarm
Parking Index Rating . . . . Easy
Where Made . . . . Georgetown, KY
Fuel Factor
MPG Rating (city/hwy) Good-22/32
Driving Range (mi.) . . . . Very Long-473.6
Fuel Type . . . . Regular
Annual Fuel Cost . . . . Very Low-$1582
Greenhouse Gas Emissions (tons/yr.) . . Average-7.1
Barrels of Oil Used per year Low-13.2

How the Competition Rates

Competitors	Rating	Pg.
Chevrolet Malibu	9	114
Ford Fusion	9	139
Mazda 6	8	198

Price Range

Price Range	Retail	Markup
Base Manual Transmission	$19,395	8%
LE V6 Automatic Transmission	$24,565	11%
Hybrid	$26,150	10%
XLE V6 Automatic Transmission	$29,045	11%

Toyota Camry

Specifications

Drive . . . . FWD
Engine 2.5-liter I4
Transmission . . . . 6-sp. Automatic
Tow Rating (lbs.) . . . . Very Low-1000
Head/Leg Room (in.) Cramped-38.8/41.7
Interior Space (cu. ft.) Average-101.4
Cargo Space (cu. ft.) Cramped-15
Wheelbase/Length (in.) 109.3/189.2

*Combines results of both front and side tests in relation to all tests for 2010 vehicles.

Ratings—10 Best, 1 Worst

Combo Crash Tests	3
Safety Features	5
Rollover	6
Preventive Maintenance	2
Repair Costs	9
Warranty	2
Fuel Economy	10
Complaints	7
Insurance Costs	3
OVERALL RATING	**5**

Toyota Corolla

Toyota Corolla

At-a-Glance

Status. . . . . Unchanged
Year Series Started 2003
Twins . . . . –
Body Styles . . . . Sedan
Seating. 5
Anti-Theft Device. . . . . Std. Passive Immobil. Only
Parking Index Rating . . . . Easy
Where Made. . . . . Fremont, CA / Ontaria, Canada
Fuel Factor
  MPG Rating (city/hwy) . . . . Very Good-26/34
  Driving Range (mi.) Average-383.8
  Fuel Type. . . . . Regular
  Annual Fuel Cost . . . . Very Low-$1393
  Greenhouse Gas Emissions (tons/yr.) Low-6.3
  Barrels of Oil Used per year Low-11.8

How the Competition Rates

Competitors	Rating	Pg.
Honda Civic	8	146
Mazda 3	6	196
Volkswagen Jetta	7	262

Price Range	Retail	Markup
Base Manual Transmission	$15,350	7%
LE Automatic Transmission	$16,750	9%
S Automatic Transmission	$17,250	9%
XRS Automatic Transmission	$20,050	9%

Safety Checklist

Crash Tests:
  Frontal. . . . . Poor
  Side. . . . . Poor
Airbags:
  Head . . . . Std. Row 1 & 2 Curtain
  Chest/Torso . . . . Std. Row 1 Torso from Seat
  Roll-Sensing Side Airbag . . . . –
  Out-of-Position Test. . . . . . . Meets Requirements
Children:
  Built-in Child Safety Seat . . . . –
  Automatic Window Reversal . . . . –
Crash Avoidance:
  Frontal Collision Warning . . . . –
  Electronic Stability Control . . . . Standard
  Lane Departure Warning . . . . –
  Brake Assist . . . . Standard
General:
  Automatic Crash Notification . . . . –
  Daytime Running Lights. . . . . Standard
  Automatic Door-Locking . . . . Optional
Safety Belt:
  Adjustable Front Belt . . . . Standard

Toyota Corolla

Specifications

Drive. . . . . FWD
Engine. 1.8-liter I4
Transmission . . . . 4-sp. Automatic
Tow Rating (lbs.). . . . . Very Low-1500
Head/Leg Room (in.) Cramped-38.8/41.7
Interior Space (cu. ft.). . . . . Very Cramped-92
Cargo Space (cu. ft.). Average-16.6
Wheelbase/Length (in.) 102.4/178.7

*Combines results of both front and side tests in relation to all tests for 2010 vehicles.

Ratings—10 Best, 1 Worst

Combo Crash Tests	5
Safety Features	4
Rollover	1
Preventive Maintenance	1
Repair Costs	3
Warranty	2
Fuel Economy	3
Complaints	1
Insurance Costs	3
OVERALL RATING	**1**

Toyota FJ Cruiser

Toyota FJ Cruiser

At-a-Glance

Status	Unchanged
Year Series Started	2007
Twins	–
Body Styles	SUV
Seating	5
Anti-Theft Device	Std. Passive Immobil. Only
Parking Index Rating	Hard
Where Made	Hamura, Japan

Fuel Factor

MPG Rating (city/hwy)	Poor-17/21
Driving Range (mi.)	Short-353.3
Fuel Type	Premium
Annual Fuel Cost	High-$2313
Greenhouse Gas Emissions (tons/yr.)	High-10.2
Barrels of Oil Used per year	High-19.0

How the Competition Rates

Competitors	Rating	Pg.
Chevrolet Tahoe	8	117
GMC Acadia	8	143
Jeep Commander	–	168

Price Range

Price Range	Retail	Markup
2WD	$23,680	9%
4WD Manul Trans.	$24,860	9%
4WD Auto. Trans.	$25,270	9%

Safety Checklist

Crash Tests:
Frontal . . . . Poor
Side . . . . Good

Airbags:
Head . . . . Std. Row 1 & 2 Curtain
Chest/Torso . . . . Std. Row 1 Torso from Seat
Roll-Sensing Side Airbag . . . . –
Out-of-Position Test . . . . . . Meets Requirements

Children:
Built-in Child Safety Seat . . . . –
Automatic Window Reversal . . . . –

Crash Avoidance:
Frontal Collision Warning . . . . –
Electronic Stability Control . . . . Standard
Lane Departure Warning . . . . –
Brake Assist . . . . Standard

General:
Automatic Crash Notification . . . . –
Daytime Running Lights . . . . Optional
Automatic Door-Locking . . . . –

Safety Belt:
Adjustable Front Belt . . . . Standard

Specifications

Drive	4WD
Engine	4.0-liter V6
Transmission	5-sp. Automatic
Tow Rating (lbs.)	Average-5000
Head/Leg Room (in.)	Roomy-41.3/41.9
Interior Space (cu. ft.)	–
Cargo Space (cu. ft.)	Roomy-27.9
Wheelbase/Length (in.)	105.9/183.9

*Combines results of both front and side tests in relation to all tests for 2010 vehicles.

Ratings—10 Best, 1 Worst

Combo Crash Tests	5
Safety Features	8
Rollover	2
Preventive Maintenance	2
Repair Costs	1
Warranty	2
Fuel Economy	4
Complaints	9
Insurance Costs	10
OVERALL RATING	**4**

Toyota Highlander

At-a-Glance

Status. . . . . Unchanged
Year Series Started 2008
Twins . . . . –
Body Styles. . . . . SUV
Seating. 7
Anti-Theft Device . . Std. Pass. Immob/Opt. Pass. Immob. & Alarm
Parking Index Rating . . . . Hard
Where Made. . . . . Princeton, IN / Kyushu, Japan
Fuel Factor
MPG Rating (city/hwy). Poor-17/23
Driving Range (mi.). Short-369.8
Fuel Type. . . . . Regular
Annual Fuel Cost. . . . . Average-$2103
Greenhouse Gas Emissions (tons/yr.) High-9.6
Barrels of Oil Used per year. High-18.0

How the Competition Rates

Competitors	Rating	Pg.
Audi A5	–	87
Honda Pilot	7	153
Nissan Murano	2	223

Price Range	Retail	Markup
Base I4 FWD	$25,705	11%
Base AWD	$29,050	11%
Limited AWD	$34,520	11%
Hybrid Limited 4WD	$41,020	10%

Toyota Highlander

Safety Checklist

Crash Tests:
Frontal . . . . Average
Side . . . . Average
Airbags:
Head . . . . Std. Curtain All Rows
Chest/Torso . . . . Std. Row 1 Torso from Seat
Roll-Sensing Side Airbag . . . . Standard
Out-of-Position Test. . . . . . . Meets Requirements
Children:
Built-in Child Safety Seat . . . . –
Automatic Window Reversal . . . . Std. Driver
Crash Avoidance:
Frontal Collision Warning . . . . –
Electronic Stability Control . . . . Standard
Lane Departure Warning . . . . –
Brake Assist . . . . Standard
General:
Automatic Crash Notification . . . . –
Daytime Running Lights . . . . Optional
Automatic Door-Locking. . . . . Standard
Safety Belt:
Adjustable Front Belt . . . . Standard

Toyota Highlander

Specifications

Drive 4WD
Engine 3.5-liter V6
Transmission . . . . 5-sp. Automatic
Tow Rating (lbs.). Low-2000
Head/Leg Room (in.). Roomy-39.7/43.2
Interior Space (cu. ft.) . . . . Very Roomy-145.7
Cargo Space (cu. ft.) . . . . Very Cramped-10.3
Wheelbase/Length (in.) 109.8/188.4

*Combines results of both front and side tests in relation to all tests for 2010 vehicles.

Toyota Matrix | Compact

Ratings—10 Best, 1 Worst

Combo Crash Tests	5
Safety Features	5
Rollover	5
Preventive Maintenance	3
Repair Costs	8
Warranty	2
Fuel Economy	9
Complaints	6
Insurance Costs	3
OVERALL RATING	**5**

Toyota Matrix

Toyota Matrix

At-a-Glance

Status.	Unchanged
Year Series Started	2003
Twins	Pontiac Vibe
Body Styles	Hatchback
Seating	5
Anti-Theft Device	Opt. Passive Immobil. Only
Parking Index Rating	Easy
Where Made	Cambridge, Ontario

Fuel Factor

MPG Rating (city/hwy)	Very Good-25/31
Driving Range (mi.)	Short-361.5
Fuel Type.	Regular
Annual Fuel Cost	Very Low-$1479
Greenhouse Gas Emissions (tons/yr.)	Low-6.6
Barrels of Oil Used per year	Low-12.2

How the Competition Rates

Competitors	Rating	Pg.
Mazda 3	6	196
Subaru Impreza	4	237
Volkswagen Golf	6	261

Price Range

Price Range	Retail	Markup
Base Manual Transmission	$16,550	7%
S Automatic Transmission	$19,650	9%
XRS Manual Transmission	$20,770	9%
XRS Automatic Transmission	$21,960	9%

Safety Checklist

Crash Tests:
Frontal. . . . . Poor
Side . . . . Good

Airbags:
Head . . . . Std. Row 1 & 2 Curtain
Chest/Torso . . . . Std. Row 1 Torso from Seat
Roll-Sensing Side Airbag . . . . —
Out-of-Position Test. . . . . . . Meets Requirements

Children:
Built-in Child Safety Seat . . . . —
Automatic Window Reversal . . . . —

Crash Avoidance:
Frontal Collision Warning . . . . —
Electronic Stability Control . . . . Standard
Lane Departure Warning . . . . —
Brake Assist . . . . Standard

General:
Automatic Crash Notification . . . . —
Daytime Running Lights . . . . Standard
Automatic Door-Locking . . . . Optional

Safety Belt:
Adjustable Front Belt . . . . Standard

Toyota Matrix

Specifications

Drive .	FWD
Engine.	1.8-liter I4
Transmission	4-sp. Automatic
Tow Rating (lbs.).	Very Low-1500
Head/Leg Room (in.)	Cramped-40.5/40.5
Interior Space (cu. ft.)	Cramped-94
Cargo Space (cu. ft.)	Average-19.8
Wheelbase/Length (in.)	102.4/171.9

*Combines results of both front and side tests in relation to all tests for 2010 vehicles.

Toyota Prius

Ratings—10 Best, 1 Worst

Combo Crash Tests	4
Safety Features	7
Rollover	6
Preventive Maintenance	3
Repair Costs	–
Warranty	2
Fuel Economy	10
Complaints	–
Insurance Costs	5
OVERALL RATING	**5**

Toyota Prius

Toyota Prius

Toyota Prius

At-a-Glance

Status	All New
Year Series Started	2010
Twins	–
Body Styles	Hatchback, Sedan
Seating	5
Anti-Theft Device	Std. Passive Immobil. Only
Parking Index Rating	Very Easy
Where Made	Toyota City, Japan

Fuel Factor

MPG Rating (city/hwy)	Very Good-51/48
Driving Range (mi.)	Very Long-590.3
Fuel Type	Regular
Annual Fuel Cost	Very Low-$816
Greenhouse Gas Emissions (tons/yr.)	Very Low-3.7
Barrels of Oil Used per year	Very Low-6.9

How the Competition Rates

Competitors	Rating	Pg.
Scion xD	4	234
Toyota Matrix	5	249
Volkswagen Golf	6	261

Price Range

Price Range	Retail	Markup
II	$22,000	5%
III	$23,000	7%
IV	$25,800	7%
V	$27,270	7%

Safety Checklist

Crash Tests:
Frontal . . . Poor
Side . . . Average
Airbags:
Head . . . Std. Row 1 & 2 Curtain
Chest/Torso . . . Std. Row 1 Torso from Seat
Roll-Sensing Side Airbag . . . –
Out-of-Position Test . . . Meets Requirements
Children:
Built-in Child Safety Seat . . . –
Automatic Window Reversal . . . Std. Front and Rear
Crash Avoidance:
Frontal Collision Warning . . . Optional
Electronic Stability Control . . . Standard
Lane Departure Warning . . . –
Brake Assist . . . Standard
General:
Automatic Crash Notification . . . Optional
Daytime Running Lights . . . –
Automatic Door-Locking . . . –
Safety Belt:
Adjustable Front Belt . . . Standard

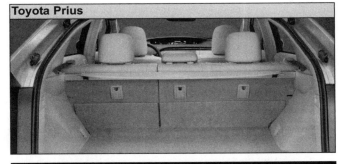

Specifications

Drive	FWD
Engine	1.8-liter I4
Transmission	ECVT
Tow Rating (lbs.)	–
Head/Leg Room (in.)	Average-38.6/42.5
Interior Space (cu. ft.)	Cramped-93.7
Cargo Space (cu. ft.)	Average-21.6
Wheelbase/Length (in.)	106.3/175.6

*Combines results of both front and side tests in relation to all tests for 2010 vehicles.

Ratings—10 Best, 1 Worst

Combo Crash Tests	1
Safety Features	7
Rollover	3
Preventive Maintenance	3
Repair Costs	8
Warranty	2
Fuel Economy	7
Complaints	8
Insurance Costs	8
OVERALL RATING	**4**

Toyota RAV4

Toyota RAV4

At-a-Glance

Status . . . . Unchanged
Year Series Started 2006
Twins . . . . –
Body Styles . . . . SUV
Seating 5/7
Anti-Theft Device . . . . Std. Passive Immobil. Only
Parking Index Rating . . . . Very Easy
Where Made . . . . Tahara, Japan

Fuel Factor
MPG Rating (city/hwy) Good-21/27
Driving Range (mi.) Short-371.0
Fuel Type . . . . Regular
Annual Fuel Cost . . . . Low-$1736
Greenhouse Gas Emissions (tons/yr.) . . Average-7.7
Barrels of Oil Used per year Average-14.3

How the Competition Rates

Competitors	Rating	Pg.
Ford Escape	6	133
Honda CR-V	10	148
Hyundai Tucson	–	161

Price Range

Price Range	Retail	Markup
Base FWD 4-cyl.	$21,500	7%
Base V6 4WD	$24,935	9%
Sport V6 FWD	$25,130	7%
Limited 4WD V6	$27,810	9%

Safety Checklist

Crash Tests:
Frontal . . . . Poor
Side . . . . Very Poor

Airbags:
Head . . . . Std. Row 1 & 2 Curtain
Chest/Torso . . . . Std. Row 1 Torso from Seat
Roll-Sensing Side Airbag . . . . Standard
Out-of-Position Test . . . . . . Meets Requirements

Children:
Built-in Child Safety Seat . . . . –
Automatic Window Reversal . . . . Std. Driver

Crash Avoidance:
Frontal Collision Warning . . . . –
Electronic Stability Control . . . . Standard
Lane Departure Warning . . . . –
Brake Assist . . . . Standard

General:
Automatic Crash Notification . . . . –
Daytime Running Lights . . . . Optional
Automatic Door-Locking . . . . –

Safety Belt:
Adjustable Front Belt . . . . Standard

Toyota RAV4

Specifications

Drive 4WD
Engine 2.5-liter I4
Transmission . . . . 4-sp. Automatic
Tow Rating (lbs.) . . . . Very Low-1500
Head/Leg Room (in.) Roomy-40.8/41.8
Interior Space (cu. ft.) . . . . Very Roomy-139.2
Cargo Space (cu. ft.) . . . . Very Cramped-12.3
Wheelbase/Length (in.) 104.7/181.9

*Combines results of both front and side tests in relation to all tests for 2010 vehicles.

Ratings—10 Best, 1 Worst

Combo Crash Tests	–
Safety Features	8
Rollover	3
Preventive Maintenance	2
Repair Costs	5
Warranty	2
Fuel Economy	2
Complaints	7
Insurance Costs	8
OVERALL RATING	**–**

Toyota Sequoia

At-a-Glance

Status	Unchanged
Year Series Started	2008
Twins	–
Body Styles	SUV
Seating	8
Anti-Theft Device	Std. Pass. Immobil. & Pass. Alarm
Parking Index Rating	Very Hard
Where Made	Princeton, IN

Fuel Factor

MPG Rating (city/hwy)	Very Poor-14/19
Driving Range (mi.)	Long-419.2
Fuel Type	Regular
Annual Fuel Cost	Very High-$2550
Greenhouse Gas Emissions (tons/yr.)	Very High-11.4
Barrels of Oil Used per year	Very High-21.4

How the Competition Rates

Competitors	Rating	Pg.
Cadillac Escalade	6	102
Chevrolet Tahoe	8	117
Nissan Armada	–	219

Price Range	Retail	Markup
SR5 4.6L 2WD	$38,530	11%
SR5 5.7L 4WD FFV	$42,380	11%
Limited 4WD	$51,865	11%
Platinum 4WD FFV	$58,905	11%

Toyota Sequoia

Safety Checklist

Crash Tests:
- Frontal . . . . –
- Side . . . . –

Airbags:
- Head . . . . Std. Curtain All Rows
- Chest/Torso . . . . Std. Row 1 Torso from Seat
- Roll-Sensing Side Airbag . . . . Standard
- Out-of-Position Test . . . . . . Meets Requirements

Children:
- Built-in Child Safety Seat . . . . –
- Automatic Window Reversal . . . . Std. Front

Crash Avoidance:
- Frontal Collision Warning . . . . –
- Electronic Stability Control . . . . Standard
- Lane Departure Warning . . . . –
- Brake Assist . . . . Standard

General:
- Automatic Crash Notification . . . . –
- Daytime Running Lights . . . . –
- Automatic Door-Locking . . . . Standard

Safety Belt:
- Adjustable Front Belt . . . . Standard

Toyota Sequoia

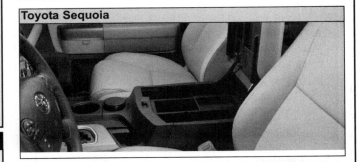

Specifications

Drive	RWD
Engine	4.6-liter V8
Transmission	6-sp. Automatic
Tow Rating (lbs.)	High-7300
Head/Leg Room (in.)	Roomy-39.7/42.5
Interior Space (cu. ft.)	–
Cargo Space (cu. ft.)	Average-18.9
Wheelbase/Length (in.)	122/205.1

*Combines results of both front and side tests in relation to all tests for 2010 vehicles.

Toyota Sienna | Minivan

Toyota Sienna

Ratings—10 Best, 1 Worst

Combo Crash Tests	4
Safety Features	6
Rollover	4
Preventive Maintenance	2
Repair Costs	2
Warranty	2
Fuel Economy	4
Complaints	3
Insurance Costs	8
OVERALL RATING	**1**

Toyota Sienna

At-a-Glance

```
Status. . . . . . . . . . . . . . . . . . . . . . . . . . . Unchanged
Year Series Started . . . . . . . . . . . . . . . . 2004
Twins . . . . . . . . . . . . . . . . . . . . . . . . . . . . . –
Body Styles. . . . . . . . . . . . . . . . . . . . . . . . SUV
Seating . . . . . . . . . . . . . . . . . . . . . . . . . 7/8
Anti-Theft Device . . Std. Pass. Immob./Opt. Pass. Immob. & Alarm
Parking Index Rating . . . . . . . . . . . . . . . . . Hard
Where Made . . . . . . . . . . . . . . . . . . . Princeton, IN
```

Fuel Factor
```
MPG Rating (city/hwy). . . . . . . . . . . . . . Poor-17/23
Driving Range (mi.) . . . . . . . . . . . . Average-385.2
Fuel Type. . . . . . . . . . . . . . . . . . . . . . . . Regular
Annual Fuel Cost. . . . . . . . . . . . . . Average-$2103
Greenhouse Gas Emissions (tons/yr.) . . . . . High-9.6
Barrels of Oil Used per year. . . . . . . . . . High-18.0
```

How the Competition Rates

Competitors	Rating	Pg.
Dodge Grand Caravan	7	128
Honda Odyssey	6	152
Kia Sedona	5	179

Price Range	Retail	Markup
CE 7-pass. FWD	$24,540	10%
LE 8-pass. FWD	$26,215	10%
XLE 7-pass. AWD	$32,485	11%
Limited 7-pass. AWD	$37,865	11%

Safety Checklist

Crash Tests:
```
Frontal . . . . . . . . . . . . . . . . . . . . . . . . . Average
Side . . . . . . . . . . . . . . . . . . . . . . . . Very Good
```
Airbags:
```
Head . . . . . . . . . . . . . . . Std. Curtain All Rows
Chest/Torso . . . . . . . Std. Row 1 Torso from Seat
Roll-Sensing Side Airbag . . . . . . . . . . . . . . . . . –
Out-of-Position Test. . . . . . Meets Requirements
```
Children:
```
Built-in Child Safety Seat . . . . . . . . . . . . . . . . . –
Automatic Window Reversal . . . . . . . . Std. Driver
```
Crash Avoidance:
```
Frontal Collision Warning . . . . . . . . . . Optional
Electronic Stability Control . . . . . . . . . . Standard
Lane Departure Warning . . . . . . . . . . . . . . . . . –
Brake Assist . . . . . . . . . . . . . . . . . . . Standard
```
General:
```
Automatic Crash Notification . . . . . . . . . . . . . . –
Daytime Running Lights . . . . . . . . . . . Optional
Automatic Door-Locking. . . . . . . . . . . . Standard
```
Safety Belt:
```
Adjustable Front Belt . . . . . . . . . . . . . . Standard
```

Toyota Sienna

Specifications

```
Drive . . . . . . . . . . . . . . . . . . . . . . . . . . . . . FWD
Engine . . . . . . . . . . . . . . . . . . . . . . . 3.5-liter V6
Transmission . . . . . . . . . . . . . . . 5-sp. Automatic
Tow Rating (lbs.) . . . . . . . . . . . . . . Average-3500
Head/Leg Room (in.) . . . . . . . . Very Roomy-42/42.9
Interior Space (cu. ft.) . . . . . . . . Very Roomy-176.5
Cargo Space (cu. ft.). . . . . . . . Very Roomy-43.6
Wheelbase/Length (in.). . . . . . . . . . . . 119.3/201
```

*Combines results of both front and side tests in relation to all tests for 2010 vehicles.

Ratings—10 Best, 1 Worst

Combo Crash Tests	7
Safety Features	7
Rollover	5
Preventive Maintenance	1
Repair Costs	3
Warranty	2
Fuel Economy	3
Complaints	1
Insurance Costs	5
OVERALL RATING	**2**

Toyota Tacoma Access Cab

Toyota Tacoma Double Cab

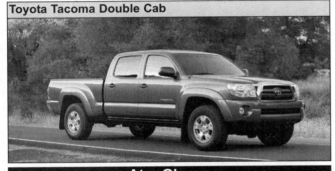

At-a-Glance

Status	Unchanged
Year Series Started	2009
Twins	–
Body Styles	Access, Regular, Double Cabs
Seating	4
Anti-Theft Device	Std. Passive Immobil. Only
Parking Index Rating	Very Hard
Where Made	Fremont, CA

Fuel Factor

MPG Rating (city/hwy)	Poor-17/21
Driving Range (mi.)	Average-390.5
Fuel Type	Regular
Annual Fuel Cost	High-$2178
Greenhouse Gas Emissions (tons/yr.)	High-10.2
Barrels of Oil Used per year	High-19.0

How the Competition Rates

Competitors	Rating	Pg.
Chevrolet Colorado	3	109
Dodge Dakota	7	127
Nissan Frontier	4	221

Price Range

Price Range	Retail	Markup
Base Reg. Cab 2WD Man. Trans.	$15,170	7%
Prerunner DblCab 2WD V6 Auto.	$23,500	9%
X Runner Access Cab 2WD 6-sp.	$25,285	8%
Base Access Cab 4WD V6 Auto.	$25,475	8%

Safety Checklist

Crash Tests:
Frontal . . . . Good
Side . . . . Average

Airbags:
Head . . . . Std. Row 1 & 2 Curtain
Chest/Torso . . . . Std. Row 1 Torso from Seat
Roll-Sensing Side Airbag . . . . Standard
Out-of-Position Test . . . . . . Meets Requirements

Children:
Built-in Child Safety Seat . . . . –
Automatic Window Reversal . . . . –

Crash Avoidance:
Frontal Collision Warning . . . . –
Electronic Stability Control . . . . Standard
Lane Departure Warning . . . . –
Brake Assist . . . . Standard

General:
Automatic Crash Notification . . . . –
Daytime Running Lights . . . . Optional
Automatic Door-Locking . . . . –

Safety Belt:
Adjustable Front Belt . . . . Standard

Toyota Tacoma

Specifications

Drive	RWD
Engine	4.0-liter V6
Transmission	5-sp. Automatic
Tow Rating (lbs.)	Average-3500
Head/Leg Room (in.)	Average-40/41.3
Interior Space (cu. ft.)	–
Cargo Space (cu. ft.)	Very Roomy-35
Wheelbase/Length (in.)	127.4/208.1

*Combines results of both front and side tests in relation to all tests for 2010 vehicles.

Ratings—10 Best, 1 Worst

Combo Crash Tests	–
Safety Features	8
Rollover	2
Preventive Maintenance	1
Repair Costs	4
Warranty	2
Fuel Economy	2
Complaints	8
Insurance Costs	5
OVERALL RATING	**–**

Toyota Tundra Regular Cab

Safety Checklist

Crash Tests:
Frontal . . . . Poor
Side . . . . –

Airbags:
Head . . . . Std. Row 1 & 2 Curtain
Chest/Torso . . . . Std. Row 1 Torso from Seat
Roll-Sensing Side Airbag . . . . Standard
Out-of-Position Test . . . . Meets Requirements

Children:
Built-in Child Safety Seat . . . . –
Automatic Window Reversal . . . . –

Crash Avoidance:
Frontal Collision Warning . . . . –
Electronic Stability Control . . . . Standard
Lane Departure Warning . . . . –
Brake Assist . . . . Standard

General:
Automatic Crash Notification . . . . –
Daytime Running Lights . . . . Optional
Automatic Door-Locking . . . . Standard

Safety Belt:
Adjustable Front Belt . . . . Standard

Toyota Tundra Double Cab

At-a-Glance

Status . . . . Appearance Change
Year Series Started 2007
Twins . . . . –
Body Styles . . . . Double, Regular, CrewMax Cabs
Seating 5/6
Anti-Theft Device . . Std. Pass. Immob./Opt. Pass. Immobi & Alarm
Parking Index Rating . . . . Very Hard
Where Made . . . . San Antonio, TX

Fuel Factor
MPG Rating (city/hwy). . . . . Very Poor-15/20
Driving Range (mi.) . . . . Very Long-446.2
Fuel Type. . . . . Regular
Annual Fuel Cost. . . . . High-$2396
Greenhouse Gas Emissions (tons/yr.) Very High-10.8
Barrels of Oil Used per year . . . . . . Very High-20.1

How the Competition Rates

Competitors	Rating	Pg.
Chevrolet Silverado	8	115
Ford F-150	9	136
Nissan Titan	–	227

Price Range

Price Range	Retail	Markup
Base Regular Cab 2WD V6	$23,155	9%
Base Crew Max 4WD 5.7LV8	$32,815	9%
Limited DblCab 4WD 5.7L V8	$39,620	9%
Limited Crew Max 4WD 5.7L FFV	$42,155	9%

Toyota Tundra CrewMax

Specifications

Drive. . . . . RWD
Engine 4.6-liter V8
Transmission . . . . 6-sp. Auto. w/Overdrive
Tow Rating (lbs.) . . . . Very High-10400
Head/Leg Room (in.) Roomy-40.2/42.5
Interior Space (cu. ft.) . . . . –
Cargo Space (cu. ft.). . . . . Very Roomy-51.3
Wheelbase/Length (in.) 145.7/228.7

*Combines results of both front and side tests in relation to all tests for 2010 vehicles.

Ratings—10 Best, 1 Worst	
Combo Crash Tests	6
Safety Features	7
Rollover	4
Preventive Maintenance	–
Repair Costs	–
Warranty	2
Fuel Economy	7
Complaints	8
Insurance Costs	8
OVERALL RATING	**6**

Toyota Venza

Toyota Venza

At-a-Glance

Status	Unchanged
Year Series Started	2009
Twins	–
Body Styles	SUV
Seating	5
Anti-Theft Device	Std. Pass. Immob./Opt. Pass. Immob. & Alarm
Parking Index Rating	Hard
Where Made	Georgetown, KY
Fuel Factor	
MPG Rating (city/hwy)	Good-21/29
Driving Range (mi.)	Very Long-424.4
Fuel Type	Regular
Annual Fuel Cost	Low-$1689
Greenhouse Gas Emissions (tons/yr.)	Average-7.7
Barrels of Oil Used per year	Average-14.3

How the Competition Rates

Competitors	Rating	Pg.
Honda Pilot	7	153
Kia Borrego	8	174
Mazda CX-7	6	199

Price Range	Retail	Markup
L4 FWD	$26,275	11%
L4 4WD	$27,725	11%
V6 FWD	$28,100	11%
V6 4WD	$29,550	11%

Safety Checklist

Crash Tests:
Frontal . . . . Very Good
Side . . . . Very Poor

Airbags:
Head . . . . Std. Row 1 & 2 Curtain
Chest/Torso . . . . Std. Row 1 Torso from Seat
Roll-Sensing Side Airbag . . . . –
Out-of-Position Test . . . . Meets Requirements

Children:
Built-in Child Safety Seat . . . . –
Automatic Window Reversal . Std. Front and Rear

Crash Avoidance:
Frontal Collision Warning . . . . –
Electronic Stability Control . . . . Standard
Lane Departure Warning . . . . –
Brake Assist . . . . Standard

General:
Automatic Crash Notification . . . . –
Daytime Running Lights . . . . Standard
Automatic Door-Locking . . . . Standard

Safety Belt:
Adjustable Front Belt . . . . Standard

Toyota Venza

Specifications

Drive	FWD
Engine	2.7-liter I4
Transmission	6-sp. Automatic
Tow Rating (lbs.)	Low-2500
Head/Leg Room (in.)	Very Cramped-39.6/40.2
Interior Space (cu. ft.)	Roomy-108
Cargo Space (cu. ft.)	Very Roomy-34.4
Wheelbase/Length (in.)	109.3/189

*Combines results of both front and side tests in relation to all tests for 2010 vehicles.

Ratings—10 Best, 1 Worst	
Combo Crash Tests	1
Safety Features	3
Rollover	6
Preventive Maintenance	3
Repair Costs	9
Warranty	2
Fuel Economy	10
Complaints	9
Insurance Costs	3
OVERALL RATING	**4**

Toyota Yaris

Toyota Yaris

At-a-Glance

```
Status. . . . . . . . . . . . . . . . . . . . . . . . . Unchanged
Year Series Started . . . . . . . . . . . . . . . . 2007
Twins . . . . . . . . . . . . . . . . . . . . . . . . . . . . . . . –
Body Styles. . . . . . . . . . . . . Sedan, Hatchback
Seating. . . . . . . . . . . . . . . . . . . . . . . . . . . . . . 5
Anti-Theft Device . . . . . . . Opt. Passive Immobil. Only
Parking Index Rating . . . . . . . . . . . . . . . Very Easy
Where Made . . . . . . . . . . . . . . Kanto Jidosha, Japan
```

Fuel Factor

```
MPG Rating (city/hwy) . . . . . . . . . Very Good-29/35
Driving Range (mi.). . . . . . . . . . . . . . Short-348.8
Fuel Type. . . . . . . . . . . . . . . . . . . . . . . . Regular
Annual Fuel Cost . . . . . . . . . . . . Very Low-$1289
Greenhouse Gas Emissions (tons/yr.) . Very Low-5.9
Barrels of Oil Used per year . . . . . . . Very Low-11.0
```

How the Competition Rates

Competitors	Rating	Pg.
Chevrolet Aveo	3	106
Honda Fit	8	150
Nissan Versa	5	228

Price Range	Retail	Markup
2dr. Hatchback Manual	$12,355	5%
Sedan Manual Trans.	$13,115	5%
4dr. Hatchback Auto. Trans.	$13,455	5%
Sedan Auto. Trans.	$13,915	5%

Safety Checklist

Crash Tests:
```
Frontal. . . . . . . . . . . . . . . . . . . . . . . . . . . Poor
Side. . . . . . . . . . . . . . . . . . . . . . . . . Very Poor
```
Airbags:
```
Head . . . . . . . . . . . . . . Std. Row 1 & 2 Curtain
Chest/Torso . . . . . . . Std. Row 1 Torso from Seat
Roll-Sensing Side Airbag . . . . . . . . . . . . . . . . –
Out-of-Position Test. . . . . . Meets Requirements
```
Children:
```
Built-in Child Safety Seat . . . . . . . . . . . . . . . . –
Automatic Window Reversal . . . . . . . . . . . . . . –
```
Crash Avoidance:
```
Frontal Collision Warning . . . . . . . . . . . . . . . . –
Electronic Stability Control . . . . . . . . . . Standard
Lane Departure Warning . . . . . . . . . . . . . . . . –
Brake Assist . . . . . . . . . . . . . . . . . . . . Standard
```
General:
```
Automatic Crash Notification . . . . . . . . . . . . . . –
Daytime Running Lights . . . . . . . . . . . . . . . . . –
Automatic Door-Locking . . . . . . . . . . . . . . . . . –
```
Safety Belt:
```
Adjustable Front Belt . . . . . . . . . . . . . . Standard
```

Toyota Yaris

Specifications

```
Drive. . . . . . . . . . . . . . . . . . . . . . . . . . . . . . FWD
Engine. . . . . . . . . . . . . . . . . . . . . . . . 1.5-liter I4
Transmission . . . . . . . . . . . . . . . 4-sp. Automatic
Tow Rating (lbs.). . . . . . . . . . . . . . . . . . . . . . . –
Head/Leg Room (in.) . . . . . . . . . Cramped-38.8/42.2
Interior Space (cu. ft.) . . . . . . . . Very Cramped-87.1
Cargo Space (cu. ft.) . . . . . . . . . . . . Cramped-12.9
Wheelbase/Length (in.) . . . . . . . . . . . 100.4/169.3
```

*Combines results of both front and side tests in relation to all tests for 2010 vehicles.

Ratings—10 Best, 1 Worst

Combo Crash Tests	1
Safety Features	3
Rollover	7
Preventive Maintenance	9
Repair Costs	6
Warranty	9
Fuel Economy	6
Complaints	3
Insurance Costs	5
OVERALL RATING	**5**

Volkswagen Beetle

Volkswagen Beetle

At-a-Glance

Status. . . . . Unchanged
Year Series Started 1998
Twins . . . . —
Body Styles . . . . Coupe, Convertible
Seating. 4
Anti-Theft Device. . Std. Pass. Immobil. & Pass. Alarm
Parking Index Rating . . . . Very Easy
Where Made . . . . Puebla, Mexico

Fuel Factor
MPG Rating (city/hwy) Average-20/29
Driving Range (mi.). . . . . Very Short-337.1
Fuel Type. . . . . Regular
Annual Fuel Cost . . . . Low-$1742
Greenhouse Gas Emissions (tons/yr.) . . Average-8.0
Barrels of Oil Used per year. Average-14.9

How the Competition Rates

Competitors	Rating	Pg.
Chevrolet Aveo	3	106
Smart ForTwo	1	235
Suzuki SX4	2	242

Price Range	Retail	Markup
2.5L	$18,540	5%
2.5L PZEV	$19,640	5%
2.5L Convertible	$26,170	5%

Safety Checklist

Crash Tests:
Frontal. . . . . Poor
Side. . . . . Very Poor

Airbags:
Head . . . . Std. Row 1 Combo
Chest/Torso . . . . . . Std. Row 1 Combo from Seat
Roll-Sensing Side Airbag . . . . —
Out-of-Position Test. . . . . . . Meets Requirements

Children:
Built-in Child Safety Seat . . . . —
Automatic Window Reversal. . . . . Std. Front

Crash Avoidance:
Frontal Collision Warning . . . . —
Electronic Stability Control . . . . Standard
Lane Departure Warning . . . . —
Brake Assist . . . . Standard

General:
Automatic Crash Notification . . . . —
Daytime Running Lights. . . . . Standard
Automatic Door-Locking. . . . . Standard

Safety Belt:
Adjustable Front Belt . . . . Standard

Volkswagen Beetle

Specifications

Drive . . . . FWD
Engine. 2.5-liter I5
Transmission . . . . 5-sp. Manual
Tow Rating (lbs.). . . . . —
Head/Leg Room (in.) Cramped-40.7/39.4
Interior Space (cu. ft.). . . . . Very Cramped-78
Cargo Space (cu. ft.) . . . . Very Cramped-5
Wheelbase/Length (in.) 98.8/161.1

*Combines results of both front and side tests in relation to all tests for 2010 vehicles.

Ratings—10 Best, 1 Worst

Combo Crash Tests	2
Safety Features	7
Rollover	6
Preventive Maintenance	6
Repair Costs	4
Warranty	9
Fuel Economy	8
Complaints	8
Insurance Costs	3
OVERALL RATING	**6**

Volkswagen CC

Volkswagen CC

At-a-Glance

Status. . . . . Unchanged
Year Series Started 2009
Twins . . . . –
Body Styles . . . . Sedan
Seating. 4
Anti-Theft Device. . Std. Pass. Immobil. & Pass. Alarm
Parking Index Rating . . . . Easy
Where Made. . . . . Ewden, Germany
Fuel Factor
  MPG Rating (city/hwy) Good-22/31
  Driving Range (mi.) . . . . Very Long-468.2
  Fuel Type. . . . . Premium
  Annual Fuel Cost . . . . Low-$1719
  Greenhouse Gas Emissions (tons/yr.) . . Average-7.3
  Barrels of Oil Used per year. Average-13.7

How the Competition Rates

Competitors	Rating	Pg.
Acura TSX	10	84
Hyundai Genesis	9	158
Toyota Camry	7	245

Price Range	Retail	Markup
Sport Manual Trans.	$27,550	7%
Luxury Manual Trans.	$32,830	7%
VR6 Sport Auto. Trans.	$39,015	7%
VR5 4Motion Auto Trans.	$40,115	7%

Safety Checklist

Crash Tests:
  Frontal. . . . . Very Poor
  Side. . . . . Poor
Airbags:
  Head . . . . Std. Row 1 & 2 Curtain
  Chest/Torso . Std. Row 1 & Opt. Row 2 Torso fr. Seat
  Roll-Sensing Side Airbag . . . . –
  Out-of-Position Test. . . . . . Meets Requirements
Children:
  Built-in Child Safety Seat . . . . –
  Automatic Window Reversal. Std. Front and Rear
Crash Avoidance:
  Frontal Collision Warning . . . . –
  Electronic Stability Control . . . . Standard
  Lane Departure Warning . . . . –
  Brake Assist . . . . Standard
General:
  Automatic Crash Notification . . . . –
  Daytime Running Lights. . . . . Standard
  Automatic Door-Locking. . . . . Standard
Safety Belt:
  Adjustable Front Belt . . . . Standard

Volkswagen CC

Specifications

Drive . . . . FWD
Engine. 2.0-liter I4
Transmission . . . . 6-sp. Automatic
Tow Rating (lbs.). . . . . –
Head/Leg Room (in.) . . . . . Very Cramped-37.4/41.6
Interior Space (cu. ft.) Cramped-96.3
Cargo Space (cu. ft.). Cramped-13
Wheelbase/Length (in.) 106.7/188.9

*Combines results of both front and side tests in relation to all tests for 2010 vehicles.

Ratings—10 Best, 1 Worst	
Combo Crash Tests	–
Safety Features	3
Rollover	8
Preventive Maintenance	9
Repair Costs	6
Warranty	9
Fuel Economy	8
Complaints	1
Insurance Costs	3
OVERALL RATING	**–**

Volkswagen Eos

Volkswagen Eos

At-a-Glance

Status	Unchanged
Year Series Started	2007
Twins	–
Body Styles	Hardtop Convertible
Seating	4
Anti-Theft Device	Std. Pass. Immobil. & Pass. Alarm
Parking Index Rating	Very Easy
Where Made	Pamela, Portugal
Fuel Factor	
MPG Rating (city/hwy)	Good-22/29
Driving Range (mi.)	Short-357.9
Fuel Type	Premium
Annual Fuel Cost	Low-$1763
Greenhouse Gas Emissions (tons/yr.)	Average-7.3
Barrels of Oil Used per year	Average-13.7

How the Competition Rates

Competitors	Rating	Pg.
Honda Accord Coupe	8	145
Nissan Altima Coupe	6	218
Volvo S40	9	266

Price Range	Retail	Markup
Komfort	$31,990	7%
Komfort SULEV	$33,090	7%
Lux SULEV	$35,490	7%

Safety Checklist

Crash Tests:
 Frontal . . . . –
 Side . . . . –
Airbags:
 Head . . . . Std. Row 1 Combo
 Chest/Torso . . . . . . Std. Row 1 Combo from Seat
 Roll-Sensing Side Airbag . . . . –
 Out-of-Position Test . . . . . . Meets Requirements
Children:
 Built-in Child Safety Seat . . . . –
 Automatic Window Reversal . Std. Front and Rear
Crash Avoidance:
 Frontal Collision Warning . . . . –
 Electronic Stability Control . . . . Standard
 Lane Departure Warning . . . . –
 Brake Assist . . . . Standard
General:
 Automatic Crash Notification . . . . –
 Daytime Running Lights . . . . Standard
 Automatic Door-Locking . . . . Standard
Safety Belt:
 Adjustable Front Belt . . . . –

Volkswagen Eos

Specifications

Drive	FWD
Engine	2.0-liter I4
Transmission	6-sp. Automatic
Tow Rating (lbs.)	–
Head/Leg Room (in.)	Very Cramped-37.5/41.7
Interior Space (cu. ft.)	Very Cramped-77.4
Cargo Space (cu. ft.)	Very Cramped-10.5
Wheelbase/Length (in.)	101.5/173.5

*Combines results of both front and side tests in relation to all tests for 2010 vehicles.

Ratings—10 Best, 1 Worst

Combo Crash Tests	3
Safety Features	7
Rollover	6
Preventive Maintenance	–
Repair Costs	–
Warranty	9
Fuel Economy	8
Complaints	–
Insurance Costs	5
OVERALL RATING	**6**

Volkswagen Golf

Volkswagen Golf

At-a-Glance

Status	All New
Year Series Started	2010
Twins	–
Body Styles	Hatchback
Seating	5
Anti-Theft Device	Std. Pass. Immobil. & Pass. Alarm
Parking Index Rating	Very Easy
Where Made	Wolfgang, Germany

Fuel Factor

MPG Rating (city/hwy)	Good-23/30
Driving Range (mi.)	Average-372.6
Fuel Type	Regular
Annual Fuel Cost	Very Low-$1576
Greenhouse Gas Emissions (tons/yr.)	Average-7.1
Barrels of Oil Used per year	Low-13.2

How the Competition Rates

Competitors	Rating	Pg.
Mazda 3	6	196
Subaru Impreza	3	237
Toyota Matrix	5	249

Price Range	Retail	Markup
Coupe 2.5L	$17,490	6%
Coupe TDI	$18,590	7%
Sedan 2.5L	$19,190	6%
Sedan TDI	$23,690	7%

Safety Checklist

Crash Tests:
Frontal . . . . Very Poor
Side . . . . Good

Airbags:
Head . . . . Std. Row 1 & 2 Curtain
Chest/Torso . Std. Row 1 & Opt. Row 2 Torso fr. Seat
Roll-Sensing Side Airbag . . . . –
Out-of-Position Test . . . . Meets Requirements

Children:
Built-in Child Safety Seat . . . . –
Automatic Window Reversal. Std. Front and Rear

Crash Avoidance:
Frontal Collision Warning . . . . –
Electronic Stability Control . . . . Standard
Lane Departure Warning . . . . –
Brake Assist . . . . Standard

General:
Automatic Crash Notification . . . . –
Daytime Running Lights . . . . Standard
Automatic Door-Locking . . . . Standard

Safety Belt:
Adjustable Front Belt . . . . Standard

Volkswagen Golf

Specifications

Drive	FWD
Engine	2.5-liter I5
Transmission	6-sp. Automatic
Tow Rating (lbs.)	–
Head/Leg Room (in.)	Cramped-39.3/41.2
Interior Space (cu. ft.)	Cramped-93
Cargo Space (cu. ft.)	Cramped-15
Wheelbase/Length (in.)	101.5/165.4

*Combines results of both front and side tests in relation to all tests for 2010 vehicles.

Ratings—10 Best, 1 Worst

Combo Crash Tests	3
Safety Features	7
Rollover	6
Preventive Maintenance	10
Repair Costs	6
Warranty	9
Fuel Economy	8
Complaints	2
Insurance Costs	5
OVERALL RATING	**7**

Volkswagen Jetta

Volkswagen Jetta

At-a-Glance

Status. . . . . Unchanged
Year Series Started 2006
Twins . . . . −
Body Styles. Sedan, Wagon
Seating. 5
Anti-Theft Device. . Std. Pass. Immobil. & Pass. Alarm
Parking Index Rating . . . . Easy
Where Made. . . . . Wolfgang, Germany

Fuel Factor
MPG Rating (city/hwy) Good-23/30
Driving Range (mi.) Average-372.6
Fuel Type. . . . . Regular
Annual Fuel Cost . . . . Very Low-$1576
Greenhouse Gas Emissions (tons/yr.) . . Average-7.3
Barrels of Oil Used per year. Average-13.7

How the Competition Rates

Competitors	Rating	Pg.
Ford Focus	6	138
Honda Civic	8	146
Toyota Corolla	5	246

Price Range	Retail	Markup
S Manual Trans.	$17,605	4%
SE PZEV Auto Trans.	$21,495	6%
SEL Auto Trans.	$23,280	6%
SportWagen TDI	$25,410	7%

Safety Checklist

Crash Tests:
  Frontal. . . . . Very Poor
  Side . . . . Good
Airbags:
  Head . . . . Std. Row 1 & 2 Curtain
  Chest/Torso . Std. Row 1 & Opt. Row 2 Torso fr. Seat
  Roll-Sensing Side Airbag . . . . −
  Out-of-Position Test. . . . . . Meets Requirements
Children:
  Built-in Child Safety Seat . . . . −
  Automatic Window Reversal. Std. Front and Rear
Crash Avoidance:
  Frontal Collision Warning . . . . −
  Electronic Stability Control . . . . Standard
  Lane Departure Warning . . . . −
  Brake Assist . . . . Standard
General:
  Automatic Crash Notification . . . . −
  Daytime Running Lights . . . . Standard
  Automatic Door-Locking . . . . Standard
Safety Belt:
  Adjustable Front Belt . . . . Standard

Volkswagen Jetta

Specifications

Drive . . . . FWD
Engine. 2.5-liter I5
Transmission . . . . 6-sp. Automatic
Tow Rating (lbs.). . . . . −
Head/Leg Room (in.) . . . . . Very Cramped-38.5/41.2
Interior Space (cu. ft.). . . . . Very Cramped-91
Cargo Space (cu. ft.). Cramped-16
Wheelbase/Length (in.) 101.5/179.3

*Combines results of both front and side tests in relation to all tests for 2010 vehicles.

Ratings—10 Best, 1 Worst

Combo Crash Tests	2
Safety Features	7
Rollover	6
Preventive Maintenance	9
Repair Costs	5
Warranty	9
Fuel Economy	8
Complaints	2
Insurance Costs	5
OVERALL RATING	**6**

Volkswagen Passat

Volkswagen Passat

Volkswagen Passat

At-a-Glance

Status. . . . . Unchanged
Year Series Started 2006
Twins . . . . –
Body Styles. . . . . Sedan, Wagon
Seating. 5
Anti-Theft Device. . Std. Pass. Immobil. & Pass. Alarm
Parking Index Rating . . . . Easy
Where Made. . . . . Ewden, Germany

Fuel Factor
MPG Rating (city/hwy) Good-22/31
Driving Range (mi.) . . . . Very Long-468.2
Fuel Type. . . . . Premium
Annual Fuel Cost . . . . Low-$1719
Greenhouse Gas Emissions (tons/yr.) . . Average-7.3
Barrels of Oil Used per year. Average-13.7

How the Competition Rates

Competitors	Rating	Pg.
Chevrolet Malibu	9	114
Honda Accord	8	144
Toyota Camry	7	245

Price Range	Retail	Markup
Komfort	$26,995	7%
Komfort Wagon	$28,395	7%
Komfort w/ Nav.	$28,985	7%

Safety Checklist

Crash Tests:
Frontal. . . . . Very Poor
Side. . . . . Poor
Airbags:
Head . . . . Std. Row 1 & 2 Curtain
Chest/Torso . Std. Row 1 & Opt. Row 2 Torso fr. Seat
Roll-Sensing Side Airbag . . . . –
Out-of-Position Test. . . . . . . Meets Requirements
Children:
Built-in Child Safety Seat . . . . –
Automatic Window Reversal . Std. Front and Rear
Crash Avoidance:
Frontal Collision Warning . . . . –
Electronic Stability Control . . . . Standard
Lane Departure Warning . . . . –
Brake Assist . . . . Standard
General:
Automatic Crash Notification . . . . –
Daytime Running Lights. . . . . Standard
Automatic Door-Locking. . . . . Standard
Safety Belt:
Adjustable Front Belt . . . . Standard

Volkswagen Passat

Specifications

Drive . . . . FWD
Engine. 2.0-liter I4
Transmission . . . . 6-sp. Automatic
Tow Rating (lbs.). . . . . –
Head/Leg Room (in.). . . . . Very Cramped-38.4/41.4
Interior Space (cu. ft.) Cramped-96.3
Cargo Space (cu. ft.) Cramped-14.2
Wheelbase/Length (in.) 106.7/188.2

*Combines results of both front and side tests in relation to all tests for 2010 vehicles.

Volkswagen Routan

Minivan

Volkswagen Routan

Ratings—10 Best, 1 Worst

Combo Crash Tests	7
Safety Features	5
Rollover	4
Preventive Maintenance	–
Repair Costs	–
Warranty	9
Fuel Economy	3
Complaints	1
Insurance Costs	8
OVERALL RATING	**5**

Volkswagen Routan

At-a-Glance

Status. . . . . Unchanged
Year Series Started 2009
Twins . . . . –
Body Styles . . . . Minivan
Seating. 7
Anti-Theft Device. . Std. Pass. Immobil. & Pass. Alarm
Parking Index Rating . . . . Hard
Where Made . . . . Ontaria, Canada
Fuel Factor
  MPG Rating (city/hwy). Poor-16/23
  Driving Range (mi.) Average-380.1
  Fuel Type. . . . . Regular
  Annual Fuel Cost. . . . . High-$2185
  Greenhouse Gas Emissions (tons/yr.) High-10.2
  Barrels of Oil Used per year. High-19.0

How the Competition Rates

Competitors	Rating	Pg.
Kia Rondo	5	178
Kia Sedona	5	179
Mazda 5	4	197

Price Range

	Retail	Markup
S	$25,900	6%
SE w/Rear Ent. & Nav.	$33,500	7%
SEL w/Rear Ent. & Nav.	$38,500	7%
SEL Premium	$42,400	7%

Safety Checklist

Crash Tests:
  Frontal . . . . Good
  Side . . . . Very Good
Airbags:
  Head . . . . Std. Curtain All Rows
  Chest/Torso . . . . –
  Roll-Sensing Side Airbag . . . . Standard
  Out-of-Position Test. . . . . . Meets Requirements
Children:
  Built-in Child Safety Seat . . . . –
  Automatic Window Reversal . . . . Std. Driver
Crash Avoidance:
  Frontal Collision Warning . . . . –
  Electronic Stability Control . . . . Standard
  Lane Departure Warning . . . . –
  Brake Assist . . . . Standard
General:
  Automatic Crash Notification . . . . –
  Daytime Running Lights . . . . Optional
  Automatic Door-Locking. . . . . Standard
Safety Belt:
  Adjustable Front Belt . . . . Standard

Volkswagen Routan

Specifications

Drive . . . . FWD
Engine 3.8-liter V6
Transmission . . . . 6-sp. Automatic
Tow Rating (lbs.). Low-2000
Head/Leg Room (in.) . . . . . Very Cramped-37.2/40.6
Interior Space (cu. ft.) . . . . Very Roomy-163.5
Cargo Space (cu. ft.). –
Wheelbase/Length (in.) 121.4/202.5

*Combines results of both front and side tests in relation to all tests for 2010 vehicles.

Ratings—10 Best, 1 Worst

Combo Crash Tests	5
Safety Features	10
Rollover	3
Preventive Maintenance	–
Repair Costs	–
Warranty	9
Fuel Economy	4
Complaints	1
Insurance Costs	8
OVERALL RATING	**6**

Volkswagen Tiguan

Volkswagen Tiguan

At-a-Glance

Status	Unchanged
Year Series Started	2009
Twins	–
Body Styles	SUV
Seating	5
Anti-Theft Device	Std. Pass. Immobil. & Pass. Alarm
Parking Index Rating	Average
Where Made	Wolfgang, Germany / Kaluga, Russia

Fuel Factor

MPG Rating (city/hwy)	Poor-18/24
Driving Range (mi.)	Very Short-340.7
Fuel Type	Premium
Annual Fuel Cost	High-$2145
Greenhouse Gas Emissions (tons/yr.)	High-8.7
Barrels of Oil Used per year	High-16.3

How the Competition Rates

Competitors	Rating	Pg.
Hyundai Tucson	–	161
Subaru Forester	6	236
Toyota RAV4	4	251

Price Range

	Retail	Markup
S Manual Trans.	$23,200	7%
S 4Motion Auto Trans.	$26,250	7%
SE 4Motion w/Leather	$30,500	7%
SEL 4Motion	$33,215	7%

Safety Checklist

Crash Tests:
Frontal . . . . Poor
Side . . . . Good

Airbags:
Head . . . . Std. Row 1 & 2 Curtain
Chest/Torso . Std. Row 1 & Opt. Row 2 Torso fr. Seat
Roll-Sensing Side Airbag . . . . Standard
Out-of-Position Test . . . . Meets Requirements

Children:
Built-in Child Safety Seat . . . . –
Automatic Window Reversal . Std. Front and Rear

Crash Avoidance:
Frontal Collision Warning . . . . –
Electronic Stability Control . . . . Standard
Lane Departure Warning . . . . –
Brake Assist . . . . Standard

General:
Automatic Crash Notification . . . . –
Daytime Running Lights . . . . Standard
Automatic Door-Locking . . . . Standard

Safety Belt:
Adjustable Front Belt . . . . Standard

Volkswagen Tiguan

Specifications

Drive	FWD
Engine	2.0-liter I4
Transmission	6-sp. Automatic
Tow Rating (lbs.)	Low-2200
Head/Leg Room (in.)	Very Cramped-39.1/40.1
Interior Space (cu. ft.)	Cramped-95.3
Cargo Space (cu. ft.)	Roomy-23.8
Wheelbase/Length (in.)	102.5/174.3

*Combines results of both front and side tests in relation to all tests for 2010 vehicles.

Ratings—10 Best, 1 Worst

Combo Crash Tests	3
Safety Features	8
Rollover	7
Preventive Maintenance	10
Repair Costs	6
Warranty	10
Fuel Economy	7
Complaints	8
Insurance Costs	3
OVERALL RATING	**9**

Volvo S40

Volvo S40

At-a-Glance

Status . . . . Unchanged
Year Series Started 2005
Twins . . . . –
Body Styles . . . . Sedan
Seating 5
Anti-Theft Device . Std. Pass. Immobil. & Active Alarm
Parking Index Rating . . . . Very Easy
Where Made . . . . Ghent, Belgium
Fuel Factor
MPG Rating (city/hwy) Good-20/31
Driving Range (mi.) Average-378.4
Fuel Type . . . . Regular
Annual Fuel Cost . . . . Low-$1702
Greenhouse Gas Emissions (tons/yr.) . . Average-7.7
Barrels of Oil Used per year Average-14.3

How the Competition Rates

Competitors	Rating	Pg.
Audi A4	10	86
BMW 1 Series	–	91
Mercedes-Benz C-Class	–	203

Price Range	Retail	Markup
2.4i	$26,200	6%
T5 R FWD	$31,150	6%
T5 R AWD	$31,350	6%

Safety Checklist

Crash Tests:
Frontal . . . . Poor
Side . . . . Poor
Airbags:
Head . . . . Std. Row 1 & 2 Curtain
Chest/Torso . . . . Std. Row 1 Torso from Seat
Roll-Sensing Side Airbag . . . . –
Out-of-Position Test . . . . Meets Requirements
Children:
Built-in Child Safety Seat . . . . Optional
Automatic Window Reversal . Std. Front and Rear
Crash Avoidance:
Frontal Collision Warning . . . . –
Electronic Stability Control . . . . Standard
Lane Departure Warning . . . . –
Brake Assist . . . . Standard
General:
Automatic Crash Notification . . . . –
Daytime Running Lights . . . . Standard
Automatic Door-Locking . . . . Standard
Safety Belt:
Adjustable Front Belt . . . . Standard

Volvo S40

Specifications

Drive . . . . FWD
Engine 2.4-liter I5
Transmission . . . . 5-sp. Automatic
Tow Rating (lbs.) Low-2000
Head/Leg Room (in.) . . . . . Very Cramped-38.1/41.6
Interior Space (cu. ft.) . . . . Very Cramped-92
Cargo Space (cu. ft.) Cramped-12.6
Wheelbase/Length (in.) 103.9/176.2

*Combines results of both front and side tests in relation to all tests for 2010 vehicles.

Ratings—10 Best, 1 Worst

Combo Crash Tests	–
Safety Features	9
Rollover	7
Preventive Maintenance	10
Repair Costs	4
Warranty	10
Fuel Economy	5
Complaints	9
Insurance Costs	5
OVERALL RATING	**–**

Volvo S80

At-a-Glance

Status. . . . . Unchanged
Year Series Started 2008
Twins . . . . –
Body Styles . . . . Sedan
Seating. 5
Anti-Theft Device . Std. Pass. Immobil. & Active Alarm
Parking Index Rating . . . . Average
Where Made . . . . Torslanda, Sweden
Fuel Factor
  MPG Rating (city/hwy) Average-18/27
  Driving Range (mi.) Long-391.8
  Fuel Type. . . . . Regular
  Annual Fuel Cost. . . . . Average-$1913
  Greenhouse Gas Emissions (tons/yr.) High-8.7
  Barrels of Oil Used per year. High-16.3

How the Competition Rates

Competitors	Rating	Pg.
BMW 7 Series	–	94
Infiniti M	–	166
Lexus LS	–	189

Price Range	Retail	Markup
3.2	$39,200	6%
T6	$42,950	6%
V8 AWD	$50,950	6%

Volvo S80

Safety Checklist

Crash Tests:
  Frontal. . . . . –
  Side . . . . –
Airbags:
  Head . . . . Std. Row 1 & 2 Curtain
  Chest/Torso . . . . Std. Row 1 Torso from Seat
  Roll-Sensing Side Airbag . . . . –
  Out-of-Position Test. . . . . . . Meets Requirements
Children:
  Built-in Child Safety Seat . . . . –
  Automatic Window Reversal. Std. Front and Rear
Crash Avoidance:
  Frontal Collision Warning . . . . Optional
  Electronic Stability Control . . . . Standard
  Lane Departure Warning. . . . . Optional
  Brake Assist . . . . Standard
General:
  Automatic Crash Notification . . . . –
  Daytime Running Lights. . . . . Standard
  Automatic Door-Locking. . . . . Standard
Safety Belt:
  Adjustable Front Belt . . . . Standard

Volvo S80

Specifications

Drive. . . . . FWD
Engine. 3.2-liter I6
Transmission . . . . 6-sp. Automatic
Tow Rating (lbs.). Low-3300
Head/Leg Room (in.). . . . . Very Cramped-37.8/41.9
Interior Space (cu. ft.) Cramped-98
Cargo Space (cu. ft.) Cramped-14.9
Wheelbase/Length (in.). 111.6/191

*Combines results of both front and side tests in relation to all tests for 2010 vehicles.

Ratings—10 Best, 1 Worst

Combo Crash Tests	–
Safety Features	10
Rollover	6
Preventive Maintenance	10
Repair Costs	5
Warranty	10
Fuel Economy	5
Complaints	9
Insurance Costs	5
OVERALL RATING	**–**

Volvo V70

Volvo V70

At-a-Glance

Status . . . . Unchanged
Year Series Started 2008
Twins . . . . –
Body Styles . . . . Wagon
Seating 5
Anti-Theft Device . Std. Pass. Immobil. & Active Alarm
Parking Index Rating . . . . Average
Where Made . . . . Torslanda, Sweden
Fuel Factor
  MPG Rating (city/hwy) Average-18/27
  Driving Range (mi.) Long-391.8
  Fuel Type. . . . . Regular
  Annual Fuel Cost. . . . . Average-$1913
  Greenhouse Gas Emissions (tons/yr.) High-8.7
  Barrels of Oil Used per year. High-16.3

How the Competition Rates

Competitors	Rating	Pg.
Chevrolet Malibu	9	114
Subaru Outback	7	238
Volkswagen Passat	6	263

Price Range	Retail	Markup
Base	$33,550	6%
3.2R	$38,000	6%

Safety Checklist

Crash Tests:
  Frontal. . . . . –
  Side . . . . –
Airbags:
  Head . . . . Std. Row 1 & 2 Curtain
  Chest/Torso . . . . Std. Row 1 Torso from Seat
  Roll-Sensing Side Airbag . . . . –
  Out-of-Position Test. . . . . . . Meets Requirements
Children:
  Built-in Child Safety Seat . . . . Optional
  Automatic Window Reversal. Std. Front and Rear
Crash Avoidance:
  Frontal Collision Warning . . . . Optional
  Electronic Stability Control . . . . Standard
  Lane Departure Warning. . . . . Optional
  Brake Assist . . . . Standard
General:
  Automatic Crash Notification . . . . –
  Daytime Running Lights. . . . . Standard
  Automatic Door-Locking. . . . . Standard
Safety Belt:
  Adjustable Front Belt . . . . Standard

Volvo V70

Specifications

Drive . . . . FWD
Engine. 3.2-liter I6
Transmission . . . . 6-sp. Automatic
Tow Rating (lbs.) Low-3300
Head/Leg Room (in.) Cramped-38.8/41.9
Interior Space (cu. ft.) Cramped-98
Cargo Space (cu. ft.) Roomy-33.3
Wheelbase/Length (in.) 110.8/189.9

*Combines results of both front and side tests in relation to all tests for 2010 vehicles.

Volvo XC60 — Mid-Size SUV

Ratings—10 Best, 1 Worst

Combo Crash Tests	–
Safety Features	10
Rollover	3
Preventive Maintenance	10
Repair Costs	–
Warranty	10
Fuel Economy	3
Complaints	–
Insurance Costs	5
OVERALL RATING	–

Volvo XC60

Volvo XC60

At-a-Glance

Status	Unchanged
Year Series Started	2009
Twins	–
Body Styles	SUV
Seating	5
Anti-Theft Device	Std. Pass. Immobil. & Active Alarm
Parking Index Rating	Average
Where Made	Ghent, Belgium

Fuel Factor

MPG Rating (city/hwy)	Poor-16/21
Driving Range (mi.)	Very Short-331.5
Fuel Type	Regular
Annual Fuel Cost	High-$2260
Greenhouse Gas Emissions (tons/yr.)	High-10.2
Barrels of Oil Used per year	High-19.0

How the Competition Rates

Competitors	Rating	Pg.
Acura MDX	–	81
Honda Pilot	7	153
Toyota 4Runner	–	243

Price Range	Retail	Markup
3.2 FWD	$32,395	6%
T6 AWD	$37,200	6%

Safety Checklist

Crash Tests:
Frontal . . . . –
Side . . . . –

Airbags:
Head . . . . Std. Row 1 & 2 Curtain
Chest/Torso . . . . Std. Row 1 Torso from Seat
Roll-Sensing Side Airbag . . . . Standard
Out-of-Position Test . . . . Meets Requirements

Children:
Built-in Child Safety Seat . . . . Optional
Automatic Window Reversal . Std. Front and Rear

Crash Avoidance:
Frontal Collision Warning . . . . Optional
Electronic Stability Control . . . . Standard
Lane Departure Warning . . . . Optional
Brake Assist . . . . Standard

General:
Automatic Crash Notification . . . . –
Daytime Running Lights . . . . Standard
Automatic Door-Locking . . . . Standard

Safety Belt:
Adjustable Front Belt . . . . Standard

Volvo XC60

Specifications

Drive	AWD
Engine	3.0-liter I6
Transmission	6-sp. Automatic
Tow Rating (lbs.)	Low-3300
Head/Leg Room (in.)	Cramped-39/41.2
Interior Space (cu. ft.)	Average-99
Cargo Space (cu. ft.)	Roomy-30.8
Wheelbase/Length (in.)	109.2/182.2

*Combines results of both front and side tests in relation to all tests for 2010 vehicles.

Ratings—10 Best, 1 Worst

Combo Crash Tests	10
Safety Features	10
Rollover	3
Preventive Maintenance	10
Repair Costs	3
Warranty	10
Fuel Economy	2
Complaints	4
Insurance Costs	10
OVERALL RATING	**10**

Volvo XC90

Volvo XC90

At-a-Glance

```
Status. . . . . . . . . . . . . . . . . . . . . . Unchanged
Year Series Started . . . . . . . . . . . . . . 2003
Twins . . . . . . . . . . . . . . . . . . . . . . . . . . . . . —
Body Styles. . . . . . . . . . . . . . . . . . . . . . SUV
Seating. . . . . . . . . . . . . . . . . . . . . . . . . . 7
Anti-Theft Device . Std. Pass. Immobil. & Active Alarm
Parking Index Rating . . . . . . . . . . . . . . . . Hard
Where Made . . . . . . . . . . . . . . Torslanda, Sweden
```

Fuel Factor
```
  MPG Rating (city/hwy). . . . . . . . . Very Poor-15/22
  Driving Range (mi.). . . . . . . . . . Short-369.4
  Fuel Type. . . . . . . . . . . . . . . . . . . . . Regular
  Annual Fuel Cost. . . . . . . . . . . . . . High-$2311
  Greenhouse Gas Emissions (tons/yr.) . . . . High-10.2
  Barrels of Oil Used per year. . . . . . . . . High-19.0
```

How the Competition Rates

Competitors	Rating	Pg.
BMW X5	8	96
Mercedes-Benz M-Class	6	207
Volkswagen Touareg	5	230

Price Range	Retail	Markup
3.2 FWD	$37,700	6%
3.2 R FWD	$39,500	6%
V8 AWD	$47,500	6%

Safety Checklist

Crash Tests:
```
  Frontal . . . . . . . . . . . . . . . . . . . . . . . Very Good
  Side . . . . . . . . . . . . . . . . . . . . . . . . . Very Good
```
Airbags:
```
  Head . . . . . . . . . . . . . . . Std. Curtain All Rows
  Chest/Torso . . . . . . Std. Row 1 Torso from Seat
  Roll-Sensing Side Airbag . . . . . . . . . . . Standard
  Out-of-Position Test. . . . . . Meets Requirements
```
Children:
```
  Built-in Child Safety Seat . . . . . . . . . . . Optional
  Automatic Window Reversal. Std. Front and Rear
```
Crash Avoidance:
```
  Frontal Collision Warning . . . . . . . . . . . . . . . . —
  Electronic Stability Control . . . . . . . . . . Standard
  Lane Departure Warning . . . . . . . . . . . . . . . . . —
  Brake Assist . . . . . . . . . . . . . . . . . . . . Standard
```
General:
```
  Automatic Crash Notification . . . . . . . . . . . . . —
  Daytime Running Lights . . . . . . . . . . . . Standard
  Automatic Door-Locking. . . . . . . . . . . . Standard
```
Safety Belt:
```
  Adjustable Front Belt . . . . . . . . . . . . . . Standard
```

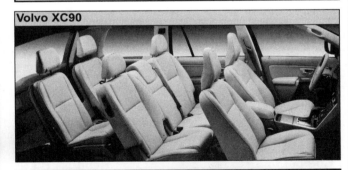
Volvo XC90

Specifications

```
Drive . . . . . . . . . . . . . . . . . . . . . . . . . . . . . . FWD
Engine. . . . . . . . . . . . . . . . . . . . . 3.2-liter I6
Transmission . . . . . . . . . . . . . 6-sp. Automatic
Tow Rating (lbs.) . . . . . . . . . . . . . . . Average-3970
Head/Leg Room (in.) . . . . . . . . . Cramped-39.7/41
Interior Space (cu. ft.) . . . . . . . . . . . . . . . . . . —
Cargo Space (cu. ft.) . . . . . . . . . Very Cramped-8.8
Wheelbase/Length (in.) . . . . . . . . . . . . 112.6/189.3
```

*Combines results of both front and side tests in relation to all tests for 2010 vehicles.

Use this page to keep some notes on the choices you are considering. Include any comments your friends make, statements made by the dealer that may be important later, and your own personal reactions to the car and the test drive. After you've looked at 4 or 5 cars, it's easy to mix up the details.

MAKE/MODEL:_____ **PRICE RANGE:**_____ **PAGE:** _____

PROS: | CONS:

NOTES:

MAKE/MODEL:_____ **PRICE RANGE:**_____ **PAGE:** _____

PROS: | CONS:

NOTES:

MAKE/MODEL:_____ **PRICE RANGE:**_____ **PAGE:** _____

PROS: | CONS:

NOTES: